ANNALS OF COMMUNISM

Each volume in the series Annals of Communism will publish selected and previously inaccessible documents from former Soviet state and party archives in a narrative that develops a particular topic in the history of Soviet and international communism. Separate English and Russian editions will be prepared. Russian and Western scholars work together to prepare the documents for each volume. Documents are chosen not for their support of any single interpretation but for their particular historical importance or their general value in deepening understanding and facilitating discussion. The volumes are designed to be useful to students, scholars, and interested general readers.

The History of the Gulag

From Collectivization to the
Great Terror

Oleg V. Khlevniuk

Translated by Vadim A. Staklo
With editorial assistance and commentary by David J. Nordlander
Foreword by Robert Conquest

Yale University Press
New Haven & London

This volume has been prepared with the cooperation of the State Archive of the Russian Federation (GARF) of the State Archival Service of Russia in the framework of an agreement concluded between GARF and Yale University Press.

Published with assistance from the Louis Stern Memorial Fund.

The photographs from the two photo albums, on constructing the Soroka–Obozerskaya railway and on Kolyma, are reproduced courtesy of GARF. The other photographs are reproduced courtesy of the Memorial Society. The documents held by GARF and the Memorial Society, like the photographs, are used by permission.

Designed by James J. Johnson and set in Sabon Roman types by The Composing Room of Michigan, Inc. Printed in the United States of America by Vail-Ballou Press, Binghamton, New York.

Library of Congress Cataloging-in-Publication Data

Khlevniuk, O. V. (Oleg Vital'evich)
   The history of the Gulag : from collectivization to the great terror / Oleg V. Khlevniuk ; foreword by Robert Conquest ; translated by Vadim A. Staklo.
      p. cm. — (Annals of Communism)
   Includes bibliographical references and index.
   ISBN 0-300-09284-9 (hardcover)
   1. Concentration camps—Soviet Union—History.   2. Forced labor—Soviet Union—History.   3. Political prisoners—Soviet Union.   4. Prisons—Soviet Union—History.
5. Soviet Union—Politics and government.   I. Title.   II. Series.
HV8964.S65K48 2004
365′.45′094709043—dc22

                                                          2004010969

A catalogue record for this book is available from the British Library.

The paper in this book meets the guidelines for permanence and durability of the Committee on Production Guidelines for Book Longevity of the Council on Library Resources.

Yale University Press gratefully acknowledges the financial support given for this publication by the Daphne Seybolt Culpeper Foundation, the David Woods Kemper Memorial Foundation, Joseph W. Donner, the Edward H. Andrews Foundation, the Historical Research Foundation, the John M. Olin Foundation, the Lynde and Harry Bradley Foundation, Jeremiah Milbank, Roger Milliken, the Milton V. Brown Foundation, Lloyd H. Smith, the William H. Donner Foundation, and Keith Young.

Contents

Illustrations follow page 286

Foreword

Robert Conquest

What a long, extraordinary process digging into the deepest secrets of the Gulag has been. Now, here is its history, fully, factually, and humanly effected for the present day by Oleg Khlevniuk.

Dozens of firsthand accounts were available by the late 1940s from such clear and meticulous witnesses as Eleanor Lipper, Vladimir Petrov, and the anonymous Poles in the *Dark Side of the Moon,* edited by T. S. Eliot. In 1946, David Dallin and Boris Nikolaevsky produced their wide-ranging and broadly documented *Forced Labor in the Soviet Union,* covering 125 camps and camp clusters. But this *History of the Gulag,* built on many documents in the Soviet archives, brings the story to a contemporary audience.

Although it is sometimes suggested that the Gulag was in some way derived from an older Russia, one has only to read about Dostoevsky's experiences as a political prisoner in *The House of the Dead* to find many differences. By the early twentieth century a number of Russian people—far fewer of them in any case than in Soviet times—were either in prison or in "exile." The latter penalty, whose victims included Lenin and Stalin, simply meant forced residence at some distant village, with a monetary allowance, sometimes with wives, but with no barbed wire or penal labor. The Gulag is only one example of how the Soviet regime represented a huge decline in civilization in Russia. But it is a revealing one.

Areas of the Stalinist experience still remain obscure. But with the

Gulag, extreme secrecy was not possible. The existence of the Gulag was either denied or misrepresented, of course. Corrective labor existed, said apologists, but as part of a deeply humanist attitude toward crime: to reclaim the sinners for society. "Labor" in the camps was as humanely and progressively carried out as possible, apart from the necessary restraints—far more kindly and constructively than in prison systems in the West.

Some in the West were taken in. They might be called Gulag-deniers. Not that they denied its *existence;* rather, they contradicted its nature. Jean Lafitte, a witness at the David Rousset libel trial in 1950, was asked, "If labor camps like those which have been described to us do exist at Kolyma, would you agree to condemn them?" He answered, "If I am asked, 'If your mother is a murderer, would you condemn her?' I would reply, 'Sir, my mother is my mother, and will not be a murderer.'"

Still, Soviet denials and misrepresentations of realities, along with Soviet suppressions of the documents concerning them, were not quite successful, even with the Gulag-deniers. The U.K. delegation to the United Nations was able to bring up the Soviet Forced Labor Codex in 1950, for example, and many of the Poles released to the West in 1941 carried their penal identity cards (with location).

Eventually the truth about the realities emerged in Moscow itself, and in 1962 came the publication of Aleksandr Solzhenitsyn's *One Day in the Life of Ivan Denisovich.* As Galina Vishnevskaya put it, the genie was out of its bottle, and no one could put it back. Soon Aleksandr Tvardovsky published in *Izvestia* a powerful and revealing verse on the Gulag, in his *Tyorkin in the Other World.*

Articles and books followed. Some, like Evgenia Ginzburg's, were printed only in the West, though without penalty to her. Solzhenitsyn's *Gulag Archipelago, 1918–1956*—another one not published in the USSR itself—effectively destroyed doubts and delusions in the West (it is reported to have effected a radical change in the French intelligentsia in particular). But not until the late 1980s, with glasnost, did a flood of firsthand accounts of the system come out in Russia.

These did not at once give us a complete picture. We came to know in greater detail what we already knew in general: the inhuman conditions of Soviet slave labor. But the whole interior mechanism, the motivations behind the system, the official decisions and correspondence, were hard to get at.

Just a few years ago, the Memorial Society, established to remember the victims of the 1930s, published an almost complete order of battle of the whole Gulag—*The System of Corrective Labor Camps in the USSR* (Moscow, 1998)—with locations, the names of many commandants, and many reports on the number of people in most camps at given dates. Since then it has been possible to cover human and local details more comprehensively, as with Anne Applebaum's *Gulag* (2003). To access the key archival materials, to engage in complex, long-drawn-out research into documentation at the highest level, has remained hard, however.

We are fortunate that Oleg Khlevniuk, one of Russia's most reliable researchers and historians, has undertaken the task. He presents the story of the first phase of the Gulag, to 1941, disclosing all its profounder secrets but also offering a finely projected perspective of the whole terror regime. This book is in fact, as with much else he has written, truly groundbreaking: he discovered and presents crucial documents in the full context of the Stalinist order, that extraordinary meld of fantasy, falsification, torture, and terror that was a key phenomenon of the twentieth century.

If a historian's problem in Soviet history used to be a shortage of material, the current challenge is the opposite: the enormous number of documents available. Some of these give us a greatly improved picture of the times, as with the documents on the mass terror of 1937–38. These days a historian needs, besides devoted research, the equally uncommon ability to discriminate among and interpret masses of material (and to be aware of material still missing). Khlevniuk demonstrates both attributes in this book.

A true historian is a rarity, and his qualifications are not easily defined. As Jacques Barzun and Henry F. Graff tell us in *The Modern Researcher,* historical verification is "conducted on many planes, and its technique is not fixed. It relies on attention to detail, on common-sense reasoning, on a developed 'feel' for history and chronology, on familiarity with human behaviour, and on ever enlarging stores of information." They conclude, "No interesting or important question . . . can be settled without detailed knowledge, solid judgement, lively imagination and ability to think straight. What to do and how to go about it come with practice; to enumerate rules would be endless and of little use." This is the crux: "judgement" is needed. Judgment is a delicate matter; mechanical criteria do not exist.

Khlevniuk points out that many documents are still unavailable. Although he does manage to quote an important personal intervention of

Stalin's in 1938, plus a useful array of top secret documents only slightly less confidential, documents at the top political level are still largely inaccessible. As Khlevniuk notes, even Politburo discussions are mostly available only in the form of final agreed-on resolutions—which has led some less sophisticated writers to conclude that unanimity prevailed in the early 1930s, an easily disprovable notion. For the most secret information the rule was "word of mouth only." The deepest secrets thus remain untraceable, except by deduction, as Khlevniuk says elsewhere. He himself has been traduced for asserting Stalin's innocence in the Kirov assassination, when what he sensibly wrote was that "political murders are planned in the strictest secrecy, and not formally registered." As Macaulay says of similar absences of "hard" evidence, "An acquittal so obtained cannot be pleaded in the bar of the judgment of history." (We find that the MGB murderers of Solomon Mikhoels were specifically ordered to avoid putting anything in writing.).

On the Gulag, and on much of the general background of the terror, which Khlevniuk explicates here, little is now highly obscure; and even the remotest details are likely to be confirmed by almost identical material in parallel cases. But Khlevniuk does not just cite records. Besides using as documents much that is recorded, he also represents (however unprovocatively) the revulsions felt, even at the time, that were registered in the official files. And because he has elsewhere examined evidence of suppressed, falsified, and even more intractable matters of Stalinist high politics, he brings to the presentation of the Gulag a truly broad and informed perspective. In *The History of the Gulag,* then, Khlevniuk has succeeded in doing what the best historians have always attempted: combining investigation of often evasive facts, or clear evidence of them, with their presentation to the world public.

Acknowledgments

Seven years ago Jonathan Brent of Yale University Press proposed that the State Archive of the Russian Federation (GARF) prepare a history of the Gulag for the renowned Annals of Communism series. This looked like a formidable and complex task, and it turned out to be so in reality.

To assess and analyze the huge number of publications on Stalin's Terror and the thousands of archival documents declassified in the 1990s would have been virtually impossible without the help of my colleagues, historians and archivists alike. I would like to express my deepest gratitude to R. W. Davies, who has been my partner and mentor in investigating various aspects of Soviet history in the 1930s. Participation in the Documents of Soviet History project, initiated twelve years ago by Andrea Graziosi and Moshe Lewin, has been an invaluable experience in understanding and publishing the newly available archival materials.

Among my colleagues, friends, and partners in researching the Stalinist Terror are Yves Cohen, Marta Craveri, Sheila Fitzpatrick, Arch Getty, Melanie Ilič, Aleksandr Kokurin, V. A. Kozlov, Hiroaki Kuromiya, Terry Martin, Nikita Okhotin, Nikita Petrov, Afron Rees, Gabor Rittersporn, Arseny Roginsky, Yuri Shapoval, David Shearer, Ronald Suny, Takeshi Tomita, Valery Vasiliev, Lynn Viola, Haruki Wada, Nicolas Werth, and Stephen Wheatcroft. It was extremely beneficial to discuss professional issues with them, and we often engaged in heated, but always friendly, arguments. My special thanks go to Peter Solomon, Jr., who has unfailingly provided pertinent advice and observations.

GARF, in cooperation with the Hoover Institution on War, Revolution and Peace, and the ROSSPEN publishing house have prepared a six-volume collection of Gulag documents, *Stalinskii Gulag [Stalinist Gulag]*. I would like to extend my gratitude to the Hoover Institution and, in particular, to Paul Gregory, with whom I have been working on the problems of forced labor for the past several years.

This book owes its existence to the active support provided by my longtime partners and friends the archivists L. P. Kosheleva, G. A. Kuznetsova, D. N. Nokhotovich, L. A. Rogovaya, S. V. Somonova, and T. Yu. Zhukova. I am extremely grateful to Vadim Staklo, who did the enormous job of translating the manuscript into English. My special thanks go to David Nordlander for his editorial assistance and to Mary Pasti, my editor at Yale University Press, and Judy Hunt, my indexer, for their special contribution toward converting the manuscript into a book.

The final stage of preparation of the manuscript was blessed by the everyday assistance and involvement of my colleagues at the University of Tübingen in Germany: Jorg Baberowski, D. Beyrau, Marc Elie, Benno Ennker, Klaus Gestwa, Anna Krylova, Jan Plamper, and Ingrid Schierle. I am happy that Robert Conquest, whose famous book on the Great Terror profoundly influenced my work on Soviet history, endorsed this book and kindly agreed to write an introduction to it.

I also want to thank my wife and my daughter for support and patience, the meaning and importance of which goes without saying.

Abbreviations

BAM	Baikal–Amur railway
BBK	White Sea–Baltic Sea complex
Belomorkanal	White Sea–Baltic Sea canal
Belomorstroi	construction of the White Sea–Baltic Sea canal
CC VKP(b)	Central Committee of the VKP(b)
Com.	Comrade
CP(b)	Communist Party (Bolshevik)
CPC	Party Control Commission of the Central Committee
CPSU	Communist Party of the Soviet Union
CSC	Soviet Control Commission of the SNK
ECO	Economic Department
GARF	State Archive of the Russian Federation
GEU	Chief Economic Administration of the NKVD
GIM	Chief Police Inspection
GUGB	Main Administration for State Security
GUITU	Chief Administration for Corrective Labor Facilities of the People's Commissariat of Justice of the RSFSR
GULAG	Chief Administration of Camps of the OGPU-NKVD
GULZhS	Chief Administration of Camps for Railroad Construction of the NKVD

GURKM	Chief Administration for the Workers' and Peasants' Police of the NKVD
ITK	corrective labor colony
ITL	corrective labor camp
KGB	Committee for State Security of the Council of Ministers of the USSR
Komsevmorput	Committee for the Northern Sea Route
Komsomol	All-Union Leninist Youth League
KRO	Counterintelligence Department of the NKVD
Kuznetskstroi	construction of the Kuznetsk steel complex
KVCh	Culture and Education Division
KVO	Culture and Education Department
Lenzoloto	Lena State Gold Production Conglomerate
LPKh	timber industry enterprise
LVO	Leningrad Military District
MGB	Ministry of State Security
MVD	Ministry of Internal Affairs
Narkompros	People's Commissariat of Education
Narkomvnutorg	People's Commissariat of Domestic Trade
Narkomzem	People's Commissariat of Agriculture
NK (narkomat)	people's commissariat (ministry)
NKF	People's Commissariat of Finance
NKGB	People's Commissariat of State Security
NKIu	People's Commissariat of Justice
NKO	People's Commissariat of Defense
NKPS	People's Commissariat of Communications
NKVD, Narkomvnudel	People's Commissariat of Internal Affairs
NKVM	People's Commissariat of Military and Naval Affairs
NKVMF	People's Commissariat of the Navy
Norilskstroi	construction of the Norilsk nickel complex
OGPU	Unified State Political Administration (state security)
OITK	Department of Corrective Labor Colonies
OLP	separate camp section, division
OMZ	Department of Corrective Facilities
OTP	Department of Labor Settlements
OVIR	Visas and Permissions Department
PP	plenipotentiary representative of the OGPU

RGASPI	Russian State Archive of Social and Political History
RIK	district executive committee
RKI	Workers' and Peasants' Inspection
RKKA	Workers' and Peasants' Red Army
RKM	Workers' and Peasants' Police
RO NKVD	district department of the NKVD
RSFSR	Russian Soviet Federated Socialist Republic
RVS	Revolutionary Military Council
Segezhstroi	construction of the Segezh pulp and paper chemical complex
Sibkombainstroi	construction of the Novosibirsk agricultural machine plant
SNK, Sovnarkom	Council of People's Commissars
SOE	socially dangerous element
Solikambumstroi	construction of the Solikamsk pulp and paper mill
Sovnarkom	SNK
STO	Labor and Defense Council
SVE	socially harmful element
TOF	Pacific Fleet
TsA FSB	Central Archive of the Federal Security Service
TsAGI	Central Institute for Aerodynamics and Hydrodynamics
TsChO	Central Black Soil region
TsIK	Central Executive Committee
TsKK	Central Control Commission of the VKP(b)
UGB	Administration of State Security of the NKVD
UITK	Administration of Corrective Labor Colonies
ULAG	Camp Administration
UNKVD	local NKVD administration or directorate
UPK	Criminal Law Procedure Code
UPVO	Administration of Border and Internal Troops
URO	Accounting and Distribution Department
UVS	Military Supplies Administration
VAO	All-Union Association of the Aviation Industry
VChK (ChK, Cheka)	All-Russian Extraordinary Commission for Combating Counterrevolution and Sabotage
VKP(b)	All-Union Communist Party (Bolshevik)

VLKSM	Komsomol, All-Union Leninist Youth League
VMN	ultimate penalty
VOKhR	militarized (armed) guards
Volgostroi	construction of hydrotechnical projects in Uglich and Rybinsk
VSNKh	Supreme Economic Council
VTsIK	All-Russian Central Executive Committee
ZhDSU	Administration of Camps for Railroad Construction

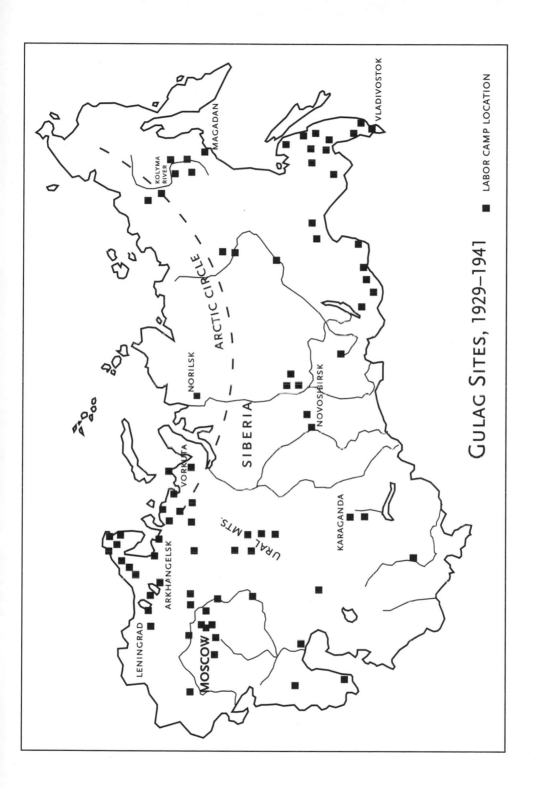

GULAG SITES, 1929–1941

■ LABOR CAMP LOCATION

VLADIVOSTOK

MAGADAN

KOLYMA RIVER

ARCTIC CIRCLE

NORILSK

SIBERIA

NOVOSIBIRSK

VORKUTA

KARAGANDA

URAL MTS.

ARKHANGELSK

LENINGRAD

MOSCOW

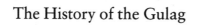

The History of the Gulag

Introduction

The Stalinist penal system was formed and entrenched during the 1930s—more precisely, between 1929 and 1941. Although its foundations had been laid earlier, the years 1929–30 were an important turning point, when the accelerated and intensive formation of Stalinist state structures, including the Gulag, began. The opening of war with Germany in 1941 logically ends this period.

Despite the apparent homogeneity of the prewar decade, historians have identified several distinct stages within it. For the most part, the history of the Gulag, and of repressive policy in general, follows that periodization. Key events of the late 1920s–early 1930s set the stage: mass dekulakization, the creation of a broad network of corrective labor camps and special "kulak" settlements, and the organization of the first major sites of the forced-labor economy. All of this shaped Gulag development over the next several decades.

A new impulse for the expansion of repression and the Gulag came with the systemic crisis of 1932–33, brought on by the Stalinist policy of collectivization and industrialization. The crisis was most vividly and tragically characterized by mass starvation, which, together with the crisis itself, had a strong impact on the Gulag and penal policy. Temporary stabilization of the system brought a better time in the history of the Gulag: terror and violence were curbed to some extent, convicts had improved chances of survival, and former kulaks harbored hopes for possible release from prison. The short-lived liberalism was replaced by the Great Terror in 1937–38, when acts of state-sponsored mass terror became one of the symbols of the Stalinist system. Not surprisingly, those acts had a profound impact on the camp system.

When the Great Terror came to an end, the new people's commissar of internal affairs, Lavrenty Beria, strengthened the crisis-stricken Gulag. A ruthless and energetic administrator, he established order with an iron fist. In the last years before the war, use of convict labor expanded dramatically, and the NKVD took over control of the most important sites of strategic and military importance. Once World War II started, the Gulag expanded further by absorbing the war's victims. Select data about the number of those arrested, convicted, and executed, as well as the number of inmates in prisons, colonies, and special settlements, round out the picture and establish the scope of Stalinist repression in the prewar period.

The available sources determined to a great degree the character and shape of this history. Among them are documents produced by the main Soviet ministries involved in the planning and implementation of the policy of terror: the Politburo, the Council of People's Commissars (Sovnarkom), the Procuracy, the OGPU-NKVD (state security), the Chief Administration of Corrective Labor Camps (GULAG), and the Department of Labor Settlements. Most of the official paperwork is one-sided and incomplete as a historical source.[1] All such documents tend to concentrate on the apparent functioning of the apparatus and its subordinate structures and cadres rather than the realities of the situation. This points to an important distinction. For us the Gulag is a phenomenon, but at the time it was just an acronym for an organization. Contemporaries did not attach any more significance to the name than to "USSR." The Gulag did not exist then. The GULAG did.

The prewar archives of the repressive organs provide a good opportunity to re-create the bureaucratic history of the Gulag, its penal departments, and its substructures. For the most part, these are dry orders and instructions from the OGPU-NKVD, including memorandums and reports. To extract from these documents information about the real situation in the camps, "kulak settlements," colonies, and prisons and to fill in the history of the Gulag with events, individuals, and problems, a patient search for essential sources is necessary. Meticulous comparison of voluminous data is also required, as well as careful (often between-the-lines) reading of tedious records overburdened with tabulations.

No matter how detailed the research, a camp subculture, however real, cannot be effectively studied on the basis of available archives.

The Gulag administration did not collect folklore, nor did it organize ethnographic expeditions. The political and cultural education departments in contact with camp culture limited their work to producing reports on the number of lectures delivered and statistics for plan fulfillment, statistics purportedly affected in a positive fashion by agitation and propaganda.

In the final analysis, such disregard for social information found reflection in the very compilation of penal archives and in the storage periods for administrative papers. The following document provides a glimpse of the priorities.

· 1 ·

Excerpt from the Nomenclature of Documents, Department of
Labor Settlements of the GULAG of the NKVD USSR
[22 May 1940][2]

Folder	To Be Stored
Resolutions and decrees of government organs on labor settlements	Permanently
NKVD orders and instructions	Permanently
GULAG instructions and resolutions on labor settlements	Permanently
Reports and memorandums on labor settlements sent to the people's commissar of internal affairs and his deputies [. . .]	Permanently
[Information on] the structure, staff, and personnel of the department of labor settlements and internal correspondence	5 years
Correspondence with NKVD boards and departments regarding labor settlements	5 years
Correspondence with people's commissariats and central offices regarding labor settlements	5 years
Reports from republican, territorial, and provincial departments for labor settlements of the NKVD-UNKVD [local NKVD]; information on the location and personnel of labor settlements (individually for each province)	10 years
Correspondence with UNKVD departments of labor settlements regarding special settlers (by province) [. . .]	5 years

continued

continued

Folder	To Be Stored
Correspondence regarding complaints from special settlers (by province) [. . .]	3 years
Contracts with economic management organs (central and local) on employing special settlers	5 years

Head of OTP [Department of Labor Settlements] of the GULAG of the NKVD USSR

Captain of State Security Konradov*

This list reveals the divergence of interests between the bureaucrats and the historians. For bureaucrats concerned with the smooth operation of the system it was important to preserve both government resolutions and NKVD directives. Historians wanted reports and accounts from local NKVD boards, correspondence related to convicts' complaints, and other nonprocedural materials.

Gulag materials, including the prewar collection from the Department of Labor Settlements, unfortunately reveal that the rules outlined in the Nomenclature of Documents were observed. Archival collections primarily contain regulatory papers (orders, circular letters, NKVD and Gulag instructions), statistical reports, memorandums on the camp economy, and so forth. Missing are such important materials as written complaints from Gulag prisoners, even though a large number of such complaints were sent to the government (and usually forwarded to the Gulag for investigation), as well as sent to the administration of the OGPU, the NKVD, and the Gulag itself.

· 2 ·

Excerpt from Order no. 208 by the GULAG of the NKVD USSR
25 December 1938[3]

Secret.

The bureau of complaints of the GULAG conducted an investigation, and an inspection team has found an inadmissible level of red tape in reviewing complaints by citizens and convicts addressed to the GULAG.

* Handwritten on the document: "Approved 22 May [19]40."

At the time of the investigation, 4,000 new complaints were registered, including 125 complaints sent for review by the central party and government organs. The majority of these complaints arrived during the past twenty days. However, the inspection team noticed the entirely unacceptable failure to process complaints received in July, August, and September 1938. Though facing such a high volume of complaints and statements (more than 20,000 each month), the GULAG apparatus still lacks procedures regulating the review of, and response to, these complaints. As a result, incoming complaints are often left unanswered, which leads to a large number of duplicate complaints. [. . .]

Many documents were lost during the war, exacerbating problems related to the organization of the archives. On the eve of war, the central Gulag archive contained materials of the Gulag central apparatus and two Gulag departments of Moscow province: the Moscow–Volga Canal Construction Board (MVS) and the Dmitrovsky camp (Dmitlag), as well as materials of the construction office for the Moscow water supply station. The files contained convict registration cards and information about the activities of these camp subdivisions. A small number of documents from the Kharkov school, which prepared cadres for the Gulag, were also sent to the central archive for preservation. These collections were extensively winnowed during the wartime evacuation. The following memorandum reflects the scope of the winnowing.

· 3 ·

Memorandum on the removal of materials unsuitable for further preservation from the GULAG archive in connection with the evacuation of the GULAG of the NKVD USSR from Moscow to Chkalov
18 October 1941[4]

Office	Number of Materials Before the Transfer	[Number of Materials] Recycled	[Number of Materials] Transferred to Chkalov
GULAG of the NKVD MVS and NKVD Dmitlag Board:	55,296	47,747	7,549

continued

continued Office	Number of Materials Before the Transfer	[Number of Materials] Recycled	[Number of Materials] Transferred to Chkalov
a) files	438,237	392,529	45,708
b) cards	668,625	631,625	37,000
Construction of the Stalin water supply station:			
a) files	16,186	14,470	1,716
b) cards	89,738	86,000	3,738
Kharkov GULAG School			
Total:	20	17	3
a) files	509,739	454,763	54,976
b) cards	758,363	717,625	40,738

Head of the Archival Department of the GULAG
Levin
18 October 1941

Other archives suffered similar losses. There are indications that the elimination of documents was often not a mere formality but a political act. According to a December 1954 review of the Vyshinsky files, "The Procuracy of the USSR contains sixteen files of special correspondence between the Procurator of the USSR, A. Ya. Vyshinsky, and the Central Committee, the Council of People's Commissars, the Party Control Commission, the NKVD, the People's Commissariat of Justice of the Russian Federation, and other organizations for 1935, 1936, and 1938. [. . .] Special correspondence of the Procurator of the USSR, A. Ya. Vyshinsky, for 1937 has been destroyed, a fact that has been officially confirmed by a record."[5] The destruction of the 1937 documents was not accidental.

Historians often manage to compensate for gaps in certain collections by using other materials. Several groups of documents are helpful for studying both the Stalinist terror of the 1930s and the penitentiary system. First, there are the materials of the Gulag and its subdivisions, as well as orders and directives from the OGPU-NKVD. Despite noticeable lacunae, this large corpus of documents contains very important information. Mechanisms of terror are evident in the correspondence between the OGPU-NKVD, the Politburo, and the government and in reports sent to Stalin, together with his subsequent instructions. Although obtaining these documents from the former KGB archive is problematic, they can be found in the party and state archives. Personal memoirs and testimonials by the victims of terror—the Gulag prisoners—that were published in recent years have been supplemented by materials from the Memorial Society, which has been scrupulously collecting personal documents and memoirs. Careful examination of these collections should satisfy even the most voracious historians of the Gulag and the Soviet totalitarian system if they make an effort to embark on this uneasy search.[6]

A historian working with internal documents requires good organization and a large grain of salt. Soviet bureaucrats writing official documents and letters almost always had their own agendas. In the documents of the Stalinist repressive apparatus one can find not only inaccuracies but outright falsifications made with criminal intent. A case in point is falsification of materials used at the show trials of "terrorists" and "saboteurs" and in the millions of trials of ordinary victims of terror.[7]

In general, historians have learned to detect archival bias by using, in addition to common sense and professional intuition, comparative analysis of materials and facts, that is, by studying the origins of documents and the possibilities of alteration. Experience working in the Soviet archives shows that reports of various independent inspections and reviews conducted by competing organs or by new managers trying to defame their predecessors are relatively complete and reliable. In the 1930s an organ competing with the OGPU and the NKVD was the Procuracy; therefore, materials on procuratorial inspections of camps and other Gulag departments, though scarce, are extremely useful.

Other helpful materials are reviews conducted after 1938, when a decision was made to curb the mass repression, and the security forces were once again purged. As was usual in times of policy shift, central party and state organs received a large number of materials exposing problems: complaints written by convicts, reports from local leaders, reports by the procurators who investigated NKVD practices, confessions by chekists (secret police). Khrushchev's rehabilitation of victims in the late 1950s and perestroika in the 1980s notably contributed to these collections; they are the only complete and reliable documentary collections of the prewar period.

Memoirs had already appeared under Stalin, and their number grew dramatically during Khrushchev's thaw. They formed the basis for such classic works as *The Gulag Archipelago* by Solzhenitsyn, *The*

Great Terror by Robert Conquest, *Let History Judge* by Roy Medvedev, and *The Gulag Handbook* by Jacques Rossi.

The late 1980s and 1990s saw an explosion of publications about Stalin's terror.[8] Most of these publications dealt with the already known facts and materials and, although they played an important social and political role, were of little scholarly value. The collections of documents related to terror and the books commemorating the victims of political repression and listing the names of those executed are more than just means of overcoming Stalinism, however, and represent important historical sources.

Historians who used new archival documents produced four main groups of works: (1) encyclopedias and general studies of the history of repression, camps, and repressive organs;[9] (2) documentary publications and studies of "dekulakization"—the mass repression of peasantry and forced collectivization;[10] (3) analyses of internal OGPU-NKVD statistics providing the numbers of those repressed, imprisoned, and exiled; and (4) the histories of various departments and camps of the Gulag.[11]

This book is an attempt to reconstruct the history of the Gulag on the basis of new archival documents in combination with the already known and researched facts and sources. Any kind of generalization has limitations. Let me say, however, that the Gulag is more than just an episode in the history of the Soviet Union: it is its almost direct reflection. The history of the Gulag is the history of establishing a dictatorship; of forming the most important segment of the Soviet economy—forced labor; of creating a distinct social milieu of convicts and their guards and prosecutors. It is the history of a specific camp culture and mentality, which strongly affected the culture, traditions, and worldview of Soviet society at large. As the list of comparisons goes on, it becomes clear that the history of the Gulag is just as important to our understanding of the past as the history of the USSR or the United States—and just as applicable to new sets of problems.

CHAPTER 1

Origins of the Stalinist Gulag

On 27 June 1929 the Politburo, aiming to conserve state resources, decided to create a network of self-supporting camps to replace the existing system of prisons. The OGPU concentration camps, renamed corrective labor camps by this resolution, were to receive all inmates sentenced to three or more years. The result was the creation of new camps—in addition to the Solovetsky Camp of Special Designation (SLON)—capable of holding altogether 50,000 inmates. The task of the camps was to colonize remote regions of the country and to "develop mineral deposits using convict labor." People sentenced to less than three years remained under the supervision of the NKVDs of the union republics and had to work in special agricultural or industrial colonies.[1]

This decision could have remained just another attempt to reorganize the penitentiary system had it not coincided with events that changed the course of Soviet history. In 1929 the Stalinist leadership adopted a policy of forced collectivization in the countryside and rapid industrial development. The resultant purge was aimed at the isolation or extermination of the segment of the population that resisted or could potentially oppose the government's plans. The collectivization of the countryside was accompanied by mass arrests, executions, and the deportation of peasants, primarily wealthy farmers (the so-called kulaks), and the village intelligentsia, including priests. In the cities the

OGPU fabricated cases of numerous "counterrevolutionary organizations" and targeted the old intelligentsia, the so-called bourgeois specialists. The famed Shakhty trial (1928) and the trials of the Union Menshevik Bureau, the Union for the Liberation of the Ukraine, and the Industrial Party (1929–30) are only a few of the many trials that decimated the urban intelligentsia.[2] Related to these developments was a purge in the All-Union Communist Party (Bolshevik) itself—the VKP(b)—aimed at the more moderate "right deviationists."

Adoption of a policy of mass repression altered the original plans for the penitentiary system. Not only did the camps grow faster than projected, but the OGPU was now in charge of the special settlements for hundreds of thousands of exiled peasants. Gradually, through suffering and death, this welter of camps and special settlements was turned into an organized system of terror and exploitation of forced labor.

The Peasant Zone

Stepped-up repression and the activation of security organs in the late 1920s were related, foremost, to the sharp deterioration in relations between the government and the peasants, who were the majority of the country's population. At the height of the grain-procurement crisis in the fall and winter of 1927–28, the leadership decided to extract grain forcefully from the countryside, through arrests and confiscation. These temporary measures soon turned into permanent policy. Naturally, many peasants resisted.[3]

The Stalinist leadership did not hesitate to use draconian measures to subdue the countryside and make millions of peasants work for nothing. One of the main instruments of mass collectivization, which started in late 1929, was dekulakization—the arrest and exile of the most dangerous sector (to the regime) of the rural population. Mass terror was the key method used in creating the kolkhozes: Peasants fearful of the fate of fellow villagers who had been repressed joined the hated kolkhozes, gritting their teeth as they did so. At the same time, the confiscated property of those repressed constituted a base for the productive resources of the kolkhozes. Rivalries between peasants and abuses of power by local administrators—many of whom, acting like gangsters, took the property of those dekulakized—contributed to the escalation of the repression.

With Moscow demanding "liquidation of the kulaks as a class" and local leaders and activists taking the initiative, the terror spread. It reached its apogee in the countryside when the Politburo and OGPU were drawing up plans for a centralized operation against the kulaks.[4] This nationwide action was fully described in the Politburo resolution of 30 January 1930, "On measures to liquidate kulak farms in the areas of total collectivization."[5] All "kulaks" (including peasants disgruntled with the authorities or even suspected of opposition) were divided into three categories: "counterrevolutionary kulak activists," to be imprisoned or executed; "other kulak activists," to be exiled to remote areas; and "kulaks," who were permitted to stay in their villages but ordered to live and work on neglected or abandoned land. The Politburo mandated the completion of repressive measures against the first two groups within four months, in February–May 1930, and established a quota of 49,000–60,000 people to be sent to the camps and 129,000–154,000 to be exiled. Since the families of these 200,000 "kulaks" also had to be exiled, a total of 1,000,000 people were destined for repression. Nor did these figures constitute a final total. A number of regions and republics were assigned supplementary quotas.

Following the Politburo resolution, on 2 February 1930 the OGPU issued Order no. 44/21, which outlined procedures. The local OGPU offices set up troikas (consisting of representatives of the OGPU, the territorial Bolshevik party [VKP(b)] committee, and the Procuracy) plus "operative troikas" to conduct the relocation of exiles. A detailed addendum to this order explained the procedure for deportations.[6]

Documents outlining this first mass punitive action of the Stalinist period provided a model for future acts of state terror, including operations against "anti-Soviet elements," which formed the backbone of the Great Terror in 1937–38. The arrests and deportations of the kulaks revealed the characteristic features of Stalinist repressive actions: extreme cruelty stemming from orders by Moscow, excesses by the participants, and a lack of resources to supply even starvation rations to the "special settlers."

The OGPU found the directives regarding the first category of kulaks the easiest to fulfill. According to internal statistics, the OGPU arrested over 330,000 people in 1930. It then convicted 208,000, including 180,000 sentenced by the troikas (see Document 90). Of those convicted, 114,000 were sent to the camps, and more than 20,000 were executed. The numbers convicted and executed by the VChK-OGPU over the previous nine years (1921–29) are comparable.[7] (The Soviet secret police changed names and acronyms several times over the years, with the main incarnations being VChK [Cheka], GPU,

OGPU, NKVD, MVD, MGB, and then KGB.) A significant portion of those arrested by the OGPU in 1930 were victims of the dekulakization campaign. Between 1 January and 1 October 1930 the number of "kulaks" arrested as belonging to the first category was 283,700.[8] This overfulfilled the original plan for the first category several times over.

The situation was different with kulaks convicted under the second category. From the very beginning, it was clear that there were insufficient resources to relocate hundreds of thousands of people. That was not a reason to ditch the idea of deportations, however. Dozens of trains filled with peasant families moved to the Urals, Siberia, and the northern regions of the Soviet Union. The journeys took many days and were an ordeal. Exhausted people were often made to walk for many kilometers from the railway station to their final destination. They were accommodated in unsuitable barracks and former churches. As a rule, men were separated from their families and sent to do hard labor. Women, children, and the elderly were left without means for survival. Terrible conditions, hunger, and hard labor caused high mortality, particularly among children.

Complaints and petitions by these initial special settlers exhibit the difficulties of their life. I reproduce two such letters by colonists who were exiled from the Crimea to the Urals. The letters were sent to the Political Red Cross, then forwarded to the OGPU. Written by different people deported to different areas of the Urals, the letters reveal strikingly similar problems. The authors' names remain unknown. The letters may have been anonymous, or perhaps the Political Red Cross made anonymous copies for the OGPU.

· 4 ·

Complaint from a special settler to the Political Red Cross
25 April 1930[9]

The truth about exiles.

We want to make sure that the center knows how the measures of the party and the Soviet regime are being distorted. Considering that we live in the freest country, with neither oppressors nor oppressed, it is impossible to keep silent about the flagrant abuses that we have witnessed during the time of our exile.

To start with our departure from the Crimea: many were taken from their houses and given only twenty minutes to prepare for exile. They were not given any indictment or legal explanation; their property was confiscated without leaving a bare minimum for survival, with no consideration for age, pregnancy, or disability. They were locked up, forty people to a carriage, and handed three buckets, one to be used as a toilet and two others for water. Here the unfortunate passengers felt, for the first time in many years, that they were not in a free country and that those who treated them like that should not be called authorities. Eighteen hundred people, among them women, the elderly, and infants, felt mocked by someone.

Water was not provided upon departure, and the empty buckets were an omen of the coming sorrowful and mysterious journey. What came next? Next came the unspeakable, for it was a shame to pass by cultural centers where no one knew that 1,800 people were being transported somewhere in manifestly unsanitary conditions, without food or water. The bucket, used by everyone without regard to sex, age, or time of day, was full. The rocking of the car caused it to spill its stinking contents over those sleeping on the floor. Water was provided at will by the train warden and was absolutely insufficient. Baby diapers rotted without enough water to launder them and poisoned the already stifling air of the locked car. This lasted for ten days, during which time food was provided only four times, and hot water once a day. People contracted infectious diseases. There were cases of infant deaths. In Nadezhdinsk, during the change of cars, there were cases of direct public badgering. Police and some party workers openly beat up the young and the old who moved slowly or who were suspected of an unwillingness to change cars. During the transfer to other cars, they were constantly yelling, "Go, parasite." The arrival at our destination, Bogoslovsky plant, fully demonstrated the degradation and misery of our situation. They call us settlers, but we do not know who we are, of which country we are citizens, or what rights and responsibilities we have. We are ordered to forestry work, accompanied by our families. They took men to the forest for logging while their families remained in the village, starving and waiting to be sent to their husbands. Some families live in the forest. If the rest come to live there, however, there will be massive infant mortality in the summer because everybody lives in common barracks without sanitation or medical assistance. Those who work receive meager food rations, with no chance to share it with their families. Families receive absolutely nothing. Those who brought some food with them can eat, while others starve. It is impossible to buy anything, for they sell nothing to the settlers, who at any rate have no money. They survive by exchanging personal belongings and bedsheets for food. The food situation is getting hopeless, and our relations with the administration have become hostile. The authorities have warned the local population not to supply us with newspapers. There is a sign in the movie theater saying that settlers are not allowed to go to the cinema, under fear of reprisal, with punishment for those caught purchasing tickets. Packages received by mail are opened and torn before being given to the addressees.

There are still more facts. They order people to work on *subbotniks,** which means that, when necessary (i.e., every day), they take settlers from the streets, regardless of age or sex, and send them under guard to load timber or coal. They do not announce where they take people. People go hungry for eight to ten hours and get no food after the work is done, suffering tremendously.

Some settlers live in a church, which is overcrowded and has no ovens or fuel for cooking. This has caused widespread disease, high infant mortality, and deep depression. People are not born here, but they die here. Medical care is available only for money. If someone has no money, he is on his own. A pregnant woman who refused to go to work because of her pregnancy was arrested by the authorities and locked up in a cell, where she gave birth to a stillborn child. Workers in the forest are subject to the most cruel, inhuman treatment. Besides all these misfortunes that have nothing to do with the settlers themselves, an important factor is that all of them are from the southern Crimea: gardeners, horticulturists, and tobacco growers, unable to survive both timber harvesting and the harsh climate. The question arises, Who needs this senseless system of isolation and badgering of people, whose hostility toward the Soviet regime has not been established at all or was fabricated from the statements of their personal enemies? Being in full agreement with the Soviet regime, we trust that the center will demonstrate at least a minimum of concern and alleviate our present situation.

· 5 ·

Complaint from a special settler to the Political Red Cross
[Before 8 August 1930][10]

———————————

Trip in a cargo train: Sevastopol–Moscow–Sverdlovsk–Nadezhdinsk
(26 March–4 April 1930)
They loaded only part of the luggage; the rest was left behind in Sevastopol and lost. There were forty to forty-two people in each car. [We] were let out to go to the toilet no more than four or five times, irregularly and without regard to sex. At other times, people had to use buckets. They

———————————

* *Subbotnik*—traditionally a weekend day of voluntary work at one's enterprise or in a public area (Trans.).

gave free bread in Sevastopol upon departure. Later it was possible to buy some more at the stations. As a rule, potable water was scarce. We often spent a whole day without water. Children suffered from thirst the most. We received hot food three times in ten days, twice at night and once during the day, when they filmed us.

In Nadezhdinsk the receiving officers were particularly rude. The air was filled with profanity; they pushed and hit people, men and women alike. This was in sharp contrast with the polite behavior in Massandra and during the train journey to Nadezhdinsk.

We were then put on a narrow-gauge train, Nadezhdinsk to Sosva. Two cars, loaded mostly with flour, as well as fats, dry fruit, etc., were not reloaded onto the narrow-gauge train. It is unclear who disposed of them or how they did it. The cargo consisted of the confiscated property of the settlers. We traveled thirty-two kilometers on a narrow-gauge track to Pospelkovo, where we immediately stepped off into the snow but were forbidden to enter the station to warm up. People spent three days and nights in the snow, in the −12° C cold, including the children, many of whom were barefoot. Children formed at least 40 percent of the entire mass of people. For three days officials did not show up, except for one warden. We received neither hot water nor bread for three days.

It took three days to transport the luggage to the villages, and only the old women were allowed to ride. Often children under seven walked in the snow up to their knees and in the −15° C cold through the night.

The next week they again gave us no food and refused to distribute what arrived in the aforementioned cars. One week later, in the −18° C cold, they started to assign people to the barracks of the Morozkovsk forestry camp. With rare exceptions, people had to walk on their own. There were cases of children dying of cold in the arms of their poorly dressed mothers. It was probably then that an old Tatar man was lost. His body was found on the road from Semionovo to the Pinkino station after the snow had melted. In the Pinkino station barracks, measles broke out among the workers' children. Despite the parents' protests, [healthy] children were also put into these barracks, and they immediately contracted measles, resulting in two deaths. Pleas for help by the forestry camp's medical attendant went unheeded (although the Morozkovo station was only eight versts* away).

Soon they started to force people to work in the forest, with no exceptions for mothers of sick children. There was no medical care for seriously ill adults, either. A week later, we started collecting twigs while knee-deep in water. Everybody had to work, including ten- and twelve-year-old chil-

---

* *Versta*—old Russian measure of distance, approximately 1.06 kilometers (Trans.).

dren. Our four-day pay was 2.5 pounds of bread. No other food was provided, including that brought by the settlers themselves.

Starting in June, working settlers were allowed to purchase rations for nonworking family members (limited to 5.5 kilograms of flour and several grams of other foodstuffs). Some of the disabled settlers started receiving such rations, for which they had to pay. After June more people were allowed to purchase rations.

After 30 March children were also sent to load lumber [. . .]. Loading lumber proved disastrous: bleeding, spitting of blood, prolapse, etc. So many people fell ill. For a short time, they stopped forcing people to work, but also stopped providing food [. . .]. People continued to die and give birth in the barracks, because going to the Nadezhdinsk hospital was forbidden, with rare exceptions, even in the case of fractures and surgery.

Forced labor returned in early July, when children under the age of sixteen were ordered to collect resin ten to fifteen versts away, without parental accompaniment. The was a mass recruitment to load timber, despite medical certificates of tuberculosis, female diseases, etc. Treatment was very rude, because foremen were almost always drunk. They even made sixty-four-year-old men work. One old Jew was particularly harassed for being a Jew. In addition to the typical rudeness and curses by the administrators, there were instances when special police beat up two children, aged ten and thirteen, and foremen assaulted two young people who had passes. They talk a lot about similar cases in other sectors of the camp. They say there were cases of rape at the Sotkno station by a foreman and by a special policeman, Bykov. The higher administration promised to punish them all but always spared the head of the station, Efim, who participated in the assaults.

According to OGPU data, only 113,013 families (551,330 people) were exiled in 1930, half the number set by the Politburo in January–February 1930.[11] One of the main reasons for this underfulfillment of the plan was the dismal situation with regard to placing and employing kulaks in exile. A snapshot of this problem can be seen in the Urals (one of the main exile centers) in February 1931, one year after the deportations began. Only 74,500 out of the 134,000 special settlers in the Urals were housed there in buildings erected for them, with 0.9 square meters per person. Other special settlers took shelter in the villages with local residents. Terrible overcrowding, as well as a lack of food and clothing, led to exhaustion and the spreading of infectious disease. The death rate among children and the elderly was particularly high. Of the 134,000 special settlers, 21.7 percent were handicapped, not including children.[12] According to OGPU authorities, 40 percent of special settlers in Western Siberia in February 1931 "lived in makeshift huts, dugouts, barracks, etc."[13] Harsh conditions led special settlers to try mass escapes, which the authorities lacked resources to prevent. One scholar, N. A. Ivnitsky, estimates that more than 100,000 people died in the zones for special settlers in 1930, not including tens of thousands of escapees, many of whom also died.[14]

The government decided to compensate for the disaster of the special exile plans in 1930 by undertaking a more sizable deportation of kulaks the next year. According to the OGPU, 381,173 families (1,803,392 people) were exiled in 1930–31.[15] In 1931 several times more people were exiled. The number of those sentenced to the camps was only slightly less than in 1930, and the number of executions, though cut in half, remained significant (10,651; see Document 90).

In March 1931 a Politburo commission was formed to direct the new deportations. It was headed by Stalin's closest allies, A. A. Andreev and, later, Ya. E. Rudzutak. The commission coordinated the activities of various state institutions dealing with the exile and accommodation of kulaks, and it authorized new repressions, the employment of special settlers in industry, and the allocation of resources. On 15 May 1931 the Andreev commission resolved: "In view of the poor management of the settlers' workforce and their accommodation by economic departments, the economic, administrative, and organizational management of special settlers shall be subordinated to the OGPU."[16] In addition to organizing the deportations, the OGPU was now responsible for the special villages and the exploitation of the kulaks (earlier these functions were reserved for the NKVD, as well as various economic ministries and departments). Special villages, which contained more convicts than the camps did, became an important component of the OGPU penal system.

After taking charge of special settlers, the OGPU leadership acted predictably: it ordered an inspection of the regions of "special migration" in order to demonstrate the terrible conditions under the old administration. The inspection reports were rather candid. A typical report is the 25 July 1931 memorandum by the deputy head of the Gulag, M. D. Berman, on the inspection of the special settlements of Ural province. Berman reported that the forestry administration of the Urals forced special settlers to work for a pittance, provided meager rations, and imposed work targets far exceeding those of the hired laborers. It often transferred special settlers who resisted or were unable to work to penal teams or confined them in the barracks and subjected them to beatings. Special settlers lived in crowded rooms and constantly starved. "The commission witnessed swollen, immobilized children dying of hunger. Hunger has caused a number of suicides. All the grass around the barracks was eaten, as well as the tree bark." As a result, 70–75 percent of all children and 20 percent of the adults were sick.[17]

The situation of hundreds of thousands of kulaks was so desperate that the authorities could no longer ignore it. The main idea of the exile—isolation of the regime's opponents and development of the remote regions using forced labor—did not work. The living conditions caused many deaths and escapes. In a number of cases, wardens of the colonies, unable to prevent mass deaths, encouraged escapes: "If you are able to go and have money, leave at night and disappear so that we don't see you."[18] According to OGPU documents, in 1930–31 more than 1.8 million people were exiled. On 1 January 1932, however, only 1.3 million special settlers were registered.[19] Since healthy peasants were more likely to escape, the proportion of disabled persons grew very quickly. Instead of reaping the benefits of free labor, the state became burdened by the ever-growing numbers of dependents surviving on meager rations. Children in the special villages suffered most. According to the Politburo commission report, in early 1932 the death rate among children under eight "in some places" (i.e., almost everywhere) reached 10 percent in one month.[20] The suffering of children elicited a strong, sympathetic reaction on the part of the local population, which was reflected in numerous letters sent to central government offices.[21]

The authorities were also concerned with the growing social tensions in the exile settlements, no matter how far they were from the center. At least two major protest actions by special settlers attracted Moscow's attention. On 20 April 1931 several hundred special settlers in Nadezhdinsk region, Ural province, took to the railroad and attempted a march on the regional center. Apparently, it was a peaceful action under the slogan "If food is not supplied, we will abandon the settlement." Several days after the event, the OGPU investigation revealed a terrible picture of hunger and abuse of the special settlers by the wardens of the settlement and the foremen of the lumber farms. Many special settlers died of hunger and torture.[22]

A serious riot took place in late July 1931 in Parbig settlement in Eastern Siberia. Between several hundred and two thousand special settlers, armed with axes, clubs, and shotguns, took part in the riot, which was put down by the OGPU and communist volunteer units. Many mutineers fled to the taiga, pursued by the OGPU and the police.[23]

Facing mass escapes, the OGPU took measures to prevent them and to recruit informers among special settlers (their contribution was officially called Cheka servicing). Plans included setting up ambushes on the known escape routes, creating "support groups" from among communists to help capture the escapees, strengthening the guard, and offering bonuses for capturing special settlers. At the same time, the OGPU leaders realized that the most effective means of preventing escapes would be "creating the living conditions that would not encourage escapes."[24]

This obvious truth led to a certain modification of the anti-kulak policy and a stress on the "economic and administrative improvement" of exile. The most important alteration in kulak policy was a decision to stabilize the number of exiled kulaks. On 20 July 1931 the Politburo resolved to discontinue mass deportations of kulak families and to limit further deportations in the areas of total collectivization to "special cases."[25] Although this resolution did not stop repression in the countryside, it reduced the scale of the kulak deportations: 71,000 people were exiled in 1932.[26]

Those deported received no explanation of their crime or what they were to expect. Because the government did not establish the terms of exile or conditions of liberation, at first there were many rumors about prompt release. In the opinion of OGPU leaders, such rumors hampered the kulaks' adjustment to their new circumstances. On 3 July 1931, following the resolution of the Politburo, the Central Executive Committee (TsIK) of the USSR issued a decree establishing that after five years of exile, the kulaks could be reinstated to all rights, including the right to vote, if they "abandon the struggle against collectivized peasants" and demonstrate good work.[27] The resolution intentionally did not mention the right of special settlers to leave exile after five years. However, as long as the exiled peasants did not know about their future, the authorities could consider this document as stabilizing. The OGPU leaders ordered the TsIK resolution posted in conspicuous locations throughout the camps "with the aim of increasing the productivity of labor, bringing down the number of escapees and expressions of dissatisfaction, etc."[28] According to the commission of the Procuracy of the USSR, which inspected the exile locations in 1931, "The decree about the reinstatement of rights after five years of exile had a profound effect on those exiled. They realized that the regime had no intention of physically exterminating them, but had, rather, a focus on the elimination of the kulaks as a class."[29]

A Politburo resolution of 10 August 1931, "On special settlers," based on the semiannual report by the Andreev commission, outlined a quasi-program to "keep special settlers in their places of settlement."[30] The authorities counted on the improvement of living conditions brought about by exiles growing their own produce; also, peasant settlers might be attracted by the chance to work a plot of land. Special settlers received sizable plots for vegetable gardens, as well as seeds, tools, and cattle, as part of a two-year, 40 million ruble credit. If there were 1 million exiles, this amounted to only forty rubles per person. The Andreev commission, realizing that even that money would be difficult to allocate, suggested additional privileges to help mobilize the exiles' resources. They were allowed to purchase horses, cows, and other livestock and to build individual housing without limitations. The exiles working in industry were also allowed to maintain vegetable gardens. All exiles were relieved of all taxes and payments in kind to the state for two years.

The work of special settlers in industry, on state farms, and in the unregulated artels, or cooperatives, was now better organized. The August resolution equalized the salaries, supply norms, and other benefits of the special settlers working on state farms to those of free laborers. Several days earlier, the Politburo had established the output rates for special settlers and free laborers in all enterprises and reduced the deductions from salaries in favor of the OGPU from 25 to 15 percent.[31]

An important part of the program to "strengthen special exile as an institution" was the focused policy toward young people, referred to in the August Politburo resolution as "isolating the youth from the counterrevolutionary influence of old kulaks." Initially young people were granted insignificant benefits, such as the right to organize youth brigades, participate in labor competition (not "socialist" competition, as among free laborers), and join technical, sport, and other activity groups. The only real act adopted by the Politburo on 10 August, allowing young people over eighteen early restitution of civil rights, including the right to free relocation, was rescinded a few weeks later by order of Stalin.[32] But even this nominal separation of young special settlers into a unique group marked the beginning of a process of dilution in the exile experience, which was taken further in later years.

To reduce the pressure of exile, special settlers were from time to time allowed to send "elements incapable of working" (children and old men) to the care of relatives and friends. The 10 August resolution also allowed the transfer of orphaned children from the special settlements to special institutions for children or to the care of local families (including the well-off families of special settlers). Old people who had no relatives to support them were transferred to the state-managed "homes for invalids." According to a circular letter from G. Yagoda, deputy OGPU chairman, by January 1932 more than 3,600 orphans had been identified and more than 2,100 of those had been relocated, although almost no invalids had been sent to invalid homes. Yagoda again demanded steady work to finish the task within one month.[33] Six months later, a Gulag circular letter concerning the use of unemployable special settlers again referred to this problem. Aside from the relocation of invalids and orphans to invalid homes and orphanages or to relatives, the policy statement ordered the establishment of special settlements for families without regularly employable members, such as families of invalids and old men or orphans under twelve years of age. These colonies were supposed to start producing consumer merchandise immediately.[34] Considering that no money was allocated to create these colonies, however, it is unlikely that this order was implemented.

To prevent escapes and reduce the number of state dependents, camp authorities often commuted sentences and permitted kulaks given short terms to move to special settlements and reunite with their families.[35]

On 25 October 1931 separate resolutions on special settlers were compiled into a document of instructions, "Provisional instructions on the rights and duties of special settlers, on administrative functions, and on the rights of the Administration of Settlements in the zones of special migration," which regulated the rights and duties of the special settlers, as well as the administrative offices that oversaw them.[36] According to these instructions, special settlers were employed by orders from the OGPU. They were assigned to particular settlements and houses and had no right even to change apartments without official permission. The instructions reaffirmed many of the earlier orders: the right of special settlers to a salary and goods equal to free laborers'; the right to build individual housing and acquire property, including livestock and tools; the right of their children to study in local schools; the right of homeless children and invalids to social services; and the right of families to transfer their children to outside care. The instructions also established a 15 percent salary deduction to cover the costs of "administrative services" for special settlers.

A clearer elucidation of administrators' rights to punish special settlers (sentences of five to ten days and fines of five to ten rubles) was vital, considering the abuses and crimes committed by wardens and their assistants. In addition to arrests and fines, territorial departments for special settlements could move special settlers to more difficult jobs, relocate them to different settlements, or bar them from work for up to two months. To deny food rations as a punishment was explicitly forbidden. But special settlers were punishable for crimes just as other citizens were. In addition to the instructions, Yagoda recommended the discontinuation of penal teams and penal quarters for special settlers. His circular letter stressed that "the regime in such quarters is similar to the regime in the camps. Beyond this, such illegalities as additional work and denial of salaries are permitted there. This does not and cannot contribute to the [successful] employment of special settlers in industry."[37] A Gulag circular letter of 8 April 1932 urgently ordered the removal of those wardens, assistants, and guards who were recruited from among the convicts: "Life has shown that this contingent of workers is the most prone to committing crimes at work."[38]

A certain diminution of repressive and arbitrary treatment of kulaks, but more significantly the hard work and resiliency of the special settlers, helped to avoid a total catastrophe in the system of special exile. Even so, the situation in the "Gulag peasant zone" remained dismal. In 1932 famine took over the country. Despite the arrival of new exiles, by the end of 1932, according to internal statistics, the number of special settlers had decreased by 175,000 people over the course of the year—down to 1,142,000. Almost 90,000 special settlers were registered as dead, and 207,000, as escaped.[39]

New Camps

As a result of mass punitive actions and the transfer of inmates sentenced to three or more years to the jurisdiction of the OGPU, the network of corrective labor camps grew much faster than originally planned in 1929. The number of inmates in the Solovetsky camp grew from 19,876 to 57,325 between 1 April 1929 and 1 April 1930. The main influx (19,720), which occurred between November and January, prompted the construction of several new camps.[40] By the summer of 1930 such camps as the Northern, Vishersky, Siberian (Siblag), Far Eastern, Kazakhstan, and Central Asian camps were finished or under construction. By August 1930 the total number of inmates in the camps was about 170,000.[41] Still, the future of the camps was unclear. Even the

OGPU leaders originally saw the camp network as a provisional measure, a temporary and inefficient way to house and employ the inmates.

· 6 ·

G. G. Yagoda's proposals to convert camps into colonization settlements
12 April 1930[42]

To Comrades Bokyi, Eikhmans, Messing, Yevdokimov.

The question of the camps must be resolved from a different perspective. Today the camp is a mere gathering of inmates, whose labor we use without any prospects for either the inmates or ourselves. It is essential to make labor more voluntary by giving the inmates more freedom after work. We have to convert the camps into colonization settlements without waiting for the conclusion of prison terms. Reducing a sentence for good behavior, out of philanthropic impulse, is unacceptable and often quite harmful. This also gives the wrong impression that the inmate has been rehabilitated and a hypocritical notion of good behavior, which may be suitable for bourgeois states, but not for us. The whole purpose of transferring inmates to us is to liquidate prisons. It is clear that, under the existing system, their liquidation will take many years, because a camp per se is worse than prison. We have to colonize the North in the shortest possible time.

Here is my plan: All inmates should be transferred to settlements until the end of their terms. Do it this way: a group (1,500 people) of selected inmates from different regions—give them lumber and offer to build huts for them to live in (develop a project; take one from Austrin). Those willing to bring their families should be allowed to do so. [They will be] controlled by a warden, in a settlement of 200–300 houses. During their spare time, after the lumbering season, they (especially the weak) will work in vegetable gardens, raise pigs, mow grass, and fish. At first they will survive on rations, and later—on their own. The settlement could be expanded by adding exiles. All settlements [should be] numbered. In the winter all residents will go lumbering or do work as we indicate. There are colossal deposits of natural resources there: oil and coal, for instance. I am sure that, years from now, these settlements will become proletarian mining towns. Today our prisoners are, for the most part, agriculturalists. They are attracted to land. We now have very few guards and very few escapes. Even if someone escapes, it is unimportant. Those ten–fifteen guards who are now watching over thousands [of inmates] will live by the warden's office. Women should also be allowed to settle and marry. It should be done immediately. We have to find enthusiastic people capable of turning the entire prison system upside down; it has become thoroughly rotten.

I am asking the commission* review this note and carefully investigate these possibilities.

G. Yagoda.

One of the reasons for such plans was the economic difficulties the OGPU faced after processing a large workforce. The way convict labor was organized in the early 1930s demonstrated that mass arrests were not really dictated by economic needs. On the contrary, the OGPU leadership frantically tried, and often failed, to find occupations for the tens of thousands of prisoners. Although the northern camps (primarily Solovetsky and Northern) resolved economic issues by expanding traditional lumbering and road construction work, other camps had more opaque approaches to labor economics. The administrations of the Siberian and Far Eastern camps searched, independently of Moscow, for a useful application of convict labor and signed deals (often of questionable utility) with local enterprises. According to workers in the OGPU central office, the economic plans of the Kazakhstan and Central Asian camps had not been "well developed" and required "serious consideration." In the absence of other opportunities, prisoners in these camps were initially used in agriculture, that is, only part of the year.[43]

The Politburo decision to build a canal between the White Sea and the Baltic Sea using convict labor, which came on 5 May 1930, served as a defining moment for the future of the camps.[44] It was the first large project entrusted to the OGPU, and its completion was anticipated in record time, only two years. The original estimate called for 120,000 workers, which challenged the Gulag's economic planning. In August 1930 the OGPU calculated that building the canal required 276,000 workers, administrative personnel, guards, and service providers (mainly recruited from among prisoners) for the 1930–31 fiscal year. On 20 August only about 180,000 prisoners were available, however, among them 30,000 disabled, sick, and elderly people.[45] Canal construction not only solved the problem of employment for prisoners; it also gave a brand-new direction to the development of the entire penal system. The concentration of tens of thousands of prisoners in camps at such large construction sites proved to be the best form of organization. Subsequently, projects involving settlements for colonists became irrelevant. In the meantime, the decision to build the

---

* It is unclear which commission is referred to. Considering that Yagoda addresses the leaders of the OGPU, it must have been an internal OGPU commission charged with working out proposals to improve the camp system.

canal influenced the reallocation of prisoners between the OGPU and the NKVD and, eventually, the future of both commissariats.

Republican commissariats of the interior, the NKVD of the Russian Soviet Federated Socialist Republic (RSFSR) in particular, also became more involved in economic activity. The NKVD colonies signed contracts with enterprises to provide timber for the Ural metal factories and northern railways. They also supplied lumber for export, developed phosphate mines, built the Saratov–Millerovo railroad, and set up support shops for various enterprises (providing them with packaging materials, fishing nets, etc.).[46]

The OGPU and the NKVD competed for workers. The head of the NKVD, V. N. Tolmachev, opposed the transfer of prisoners sentenced for more than three years and tried to prove that the decision taken in 1929 was provisional. Supported by S. I. Syrtsov (head of the Sovnarkom of the RSFSR) and A. I. Rykov (head of the Sovnarkom of the USSR), the NKVD obtained a government resolution on 18 July 1930 to postpone the transfer of convicts employed at the peat works for a month and a half.[47] This was done without consultation with the OGPU.

The OGPU leaders, presented with a fait accompli, opened a counteroffensive. They insisted on reviewing this issue at a meeting of the Council of People's Commissars (SNK) chairman with his deputies. The deputy chairman of the OGPU, S. A. Messing, and deputy head of the OGPU camp administration, M. D. Berman, sent the following note to the SNK.[48]

· 7 ·

Note from the deputy chairman of the OGPU, S. A. Messing, and deputy head of the OGPU camp administration, M. D. Berman, to the SNK USSR
31 July 1930

Secret.

To the Council of People's Commissars of the USSR.

On 11 July 1929 the SNK USSR adopted a resolution* seeking "to transfer those sentenced by Soviet and republican judicial organs to three

* Refers to the 11 July 1929 SNK resolution "On the employment of criminal convicts" (GARF, fond R-5446, opis' 1, delo 493, listy 210–212), published in M. I. Khlusov (comp.), *Ekonomika GULAGa i ee rol' v razvitii strany v 1930-e gody. Sbornik dokumentov* (Moscow, 1998), pp. 19–20.

or more years to the OGPU corrective labor camps until the end of their terms."

The resolution (paragraph 2) also orders the OGPU to expand the existing corrective labor camps and build new ones to accommodate and employ convicts.

Following this directive, the OGPU organized the economic activities of the camps to meet the needs of the most important and difficult projects related to the urgent government tasks in timber export, railroad and road construction, mining, fishing, and everything else.

Thus, the newly opened northern camps are responsible for constructing, in two years' time, the Ust-Sysolsk–Piniug railway (300 kilometers) and Ust-Sysolsk–Ukhta railroad (290 kilometers). At the same time, they are managing large timber-cutting projects and loading timber for export at the Arkhangelsk port, as well as conducting geological surveys of oil, helium, radium, etc., in the Ukhta and Pechora regions. To successfully complete the above projects, 50,000 workers are required, whereas only 41,000 are available.

The Far Eastern camps are also busy with building the 82-kilometer Boguchachinsk railroad, fishing on the Pacific Coast, lumbering for their own export, and handling export operations for Dalles [Far Eastern State Timber Company]. For these tasks, the Far Eastern camps need 23,000 workers, but only 15,000 are available.

The Vishersky camp specializes in constructing paper factories for the Vishersky chemical plant on an accelerated schedule, lumbering in the northern Urals, and serving in the chemical factories on the Lenva and in Perm (Bereznikovsky chemical plant). These projects require 26,000 people, but only about 20,000 are on hand.

The Siberian camps are building the Tomsk–Yeniseisk railway, producing bricks for Sibkombainstroi and Kuznetskstroi, serving Lenzoloto, and providing timber for Komsevmorput, etc. Timely completion of these projects requires 30,000 workers, but only 24,000 are available.

Finally, the Solovetsk camps are participating in the important tasks of building the apatite railroad, handling independent timber export, building the Kem–Ukhta railroad, working in the fishing industry (processing 40 percent of the catch along the White Sea coast), etc., and require 45,000 people, while only about 40,000 are available.

Today the workforce deficit in the mentioned camp industries is tremendous (about 35,000 workers) and threatens the economic plans of the camps. The situation is worsened by the systematic delays, under different pretexts, in transferring convicts from the NKVD prisons. The latest survey revealed that, in the RSFSR alone, the NKVD failed to transfer more than 20,000 prisoners to the OGPU.

In particular, the workforce crisis worsened in connection with the latest decision by the government to build the canal between the White and

Baltic seas. This task is given to the OGPU directly. To do it as planned, in two years, *120,000 people are required right away.*

It is obvious that to do this task, a significant increase of the camp population is required. At the same time, the current supply of prisoners is insufficient and hardly compensates for the natural decline in camp population as prisoners reach the end of their terms. The only solution to this problem would be the urgent *increase in the number of prisoners transferred from the NKVD prisons, including, in addition to those sentenced to three years, those sentenced to two or more years.*

Resolution no. US080 of 18 July 1930,* which was adopted at the meeting of the chairman of the SNK USSR and his deputies and which delays by one and one-half months the delivery of convicts to the OGPU (the OGPU was not informed about those plans, and its representatives were not invited to discuss them), seriously complicates the situation with the workforce and *threatens to disrupt a number of projects of national importance.*

In connection with the planned meeting of the deputies to review the whole issue, the OGPU believes that, considering the projects of national importance begun by the OGPU, and especially the newly imposed task of building the White Sea–Baltic Sea canal, *any, even temporary delay* in transferring the contingents to the camps would stop the work already under way, in particular the Belomorstroi project.

Likewise, it is impossible and inappropriate to consider canceling the transfer of convicts to OGPU camps.

In consideration of the above, the OGPU offers the accompanying draft resolution to the SNK.†

Deputy Chairman of the OGPU, S. Messing.

Deputy Chairman of the OGPU Camps Administration, M. Berman.

As is evident from this letter, the OGPU leaders blackmailed Sovnarkom by referring to the possible disruption of government tasks on account of an insufficient workforce. The OGPU manipulated the decision to build the White Sea–Baltic Sea canal to obtain maximum concessions. It demanded a transfer to the camps of not only those convicted to three years, as before, but also those convicted to two or more years. In response, the NKVD RSFSR leadership, supported by the chairman of the SNK RSFSR, Syrtsov, offered to reconsider transferring those sentenced for three or more years and to employ some such convicts at the projects under NKVD jurisdiction.[49]

---

* The resolution allowed the NKVD RSFSR to delay the transfer of those sentenced to three or more years for a month and a half and to employ them at peateries (GARF, f. 5446, op. 11a, d. 725, l. 7).

† The document, the main idea of which is summarized in the cover letter, is not published.

On 18 August the SNK USSR created a special commission to resolve this problem. Although the commission made a decision favoring the OGPU, the SNK USSR again supported the NKVD.[50] On 31 August 1930 the meeting of the chairman of the SNK with his deputies resulted in a decision to "retain those sentenced to three or more years with the NKVD, as long as they can be employed at NKVD colonies and factories."[51]

The OGPU chairman, Menzhinsky, then became directly involved in the conflict. On 3 September he wrote a complaint to the Politburo.[52] Stalin unequivocally took the OGPU side. Most likely, his partiality to broadening the OGPU system, as well as his animosity toward Rykov and Syrtsov (both were deposed in late 1930), played a significant role. On 7 September, Stalin wrote to Molotov from his southern vacation residence: "I am told that they want to take criminals (with sentences of more than three years) away from the OGPU and give them to the NKVD. This is an intrigue orchestrated by Tolmachev, who is rotten through and through. Syrtsov, to whom Rykov has been playing up, also has a hand in it. I think the Politburo's decisions should be implemented and the NKVD's should be closed down."[53] On 5 October the Politburo reviewed the question of using convict labor and stood by the 1929 resolution to transfer the "three-year" termers to the OGPU.[54] At Stalin's order, the republican branches of the NKVD were dissolved in December 1930. The OGPU became responsible for most of the convicts. The NKVD colonies became subjects of the republican People's Commissariats of Justice, primarily the People's Commissariat of Justice of the RSFSR. The camps became one of the main elements of the Soviet penal system.

The growing importance of the camp system found its reflection in the transformation of the OGPU Camp Administration (ULAG), created in 1930, into the Chief Administration of Camps of the OGPU (GULAG) in late 1930–early 1931.[55] The GULAG became an integral part of Soviet life and eventually acquired a common name: Gulag.

In developing the camp system, the Soviet leadership encountered certain political problems. Information about new trends in the USSR—in particular, the broad participation of arrested and exiled peasants in timber export—triggered a campaign against Soviet exports in the West. The campaign was even more successful than anticipated in light of the sharpening economic crisis. In the spring and summer of 1930 the United States imposed limits on the import of Soviet goods and completely banned the import of timber. Other countries adopted similar sanctions. The Soviet government denied that it employed convict labor in export industries. On 13 September 1930 the SNK USSR chairman, A. I. Rykov, ordered the following measures regarding the employment of convicts in the lumber industry:

1. Remove prisoners from all loading of foreign ships.
2. Discontinue contacts of inspectors, representatives of foreign companies, and captains of foreign ships with OGPU camp officials.
3. Starting next season, limit the employment of prisoners to woodcutting and lumber removal and conceal all signs of their participation in such work (guards, posters, etc.).[56]

On 20 October 1930, after France imposed limits on the import of Soviet goods, the SNK retaliated by limiting purchases from countries "that establish special limits on trade with the USSR."[57] On 13 February 1931 the Politburo adopted the following proposals, made by one of the most brilliant Soviet publicists, former oppositionist, and then converted Stalinist, Karl Radek: "In response to the slanderous campaign in the bourgeois press about forced labor in the USSR, start a campaign, particularly in *Izvestiia,* around the following issues: a) the socialist organization of labor in the USSR, b) exploitation and work conditions in the capitalist countries, and c) slavery in English, French, and other colonies." The Politburo charged Radek and the head of the Central Committee propaganda department, A. I. Stetsky, with conducting this campaign.[58]

On 5 March 1931, *Pravda* published an article written by the literary giant M. Gorky, "About One Legend." Addressing the workers in Europe and America, Gorky called the statements about convict labor in the USSR "a petty, foul slander" aimed at economically isolating and weakening the USSR. "The Soviet regime does not employ convict labor even in prisons, where illiterate criminals have to study and where peasants enjoy the right to leave for their villages and families during the agricultural season."*

This propaganda campaign was crowned by V. M. Molotov's official statement at the 6th Congress of Soviets ("On 'Forced Labor,'" part of his report, was published in newspapers on 11 March 1931): "They write a lot about our lumber industry abroad. We have 1,134,000 workers employed in it, all of them free laborers. Convict

---

* Gorky went on to script paeans to the White Sea–Baltic Sea canal, at best ignoring the reality of events but providing a valuable and respected intellectual cover for Soviet actions.

labor has nothing to do with the lumber industry." Having admitted the fact of employing about 60,000 prisoners in the northern regions (in non-export enterprises), Molotov claimed that "many thousands of unemployed people would envy the work and living conditions of prisoners in our northern regions." According to archival materials, these topics in Molotov's report were influenced by Stalin. In a note to Molotov, Stalin wrote: "The section on 'forced' labor is incomplete and unsatisfactory. See the comments and corrections in the text."[59]

Despite angry statements in response to critics, the Soviet government was worried about the political and economic price of the foreign campaign against forced labor and made concessions. Apparently, prisoners were no longer used in export operations, and an appropriate law was issued soon. On 27 January 1932 the SNK USSR mandated that the corrective labor codes of the union republics be amended with the following article: "Prisoners and those sentenced to obligatory work (but not in custody) cannot be employed in work related to extraction, production, storage, loading, unloading, or transporting of goods (raw materials, semiprocessed goods, or finished merchandise) that fully or in part are intended for export."[60]

The participation of prisoners in lumbering for export remained a significant part of the Gulag economy. In 1932 six camps specialized in lumbering, and the Gulag's share in the lumber industry was 9 percent. Temnikovsky and Svirsky camps provided about 60 percent of all firewood for Moscow and Leningrad.[61] At the same time, the first steps were taken to employ prisoners in gold mining. Gold was used to purchase materials and equipment abroad. In search of new sources of gold, the Soviet government in the early 1930s turned to the old gold deposits around the Kolyma River. On 11 November 1931 the Politburo adopted a resolution, "On Kolyma," creating a special trust, directly managed by the Central Committee, "to step up the development of gold mining in the upper Kolyma." The OGPU chairman, G. Yagoda, was to oversee and control the trust, and E. P. Berzin, former head of the Vishersky camp, became its director. According to projections, the Dalstroi trust would extract 2 tons of gold by the end of 1931, 10 tons in 1932, and 25 tons in 1933. Free laborers and prisoners would develop the new region.[62]

The plan was frustrated, however. The first group of Dalstroi workers, headed by Berzin, arrived in Nagaevo Bay in February 1932. The Politburo did not approve Yagoda's proposals about resources for

Dalstroi until 16 March. At the beginning of the navigation season, the OGPU was charged with transporting 5,000, and then 20,000 more, "well-equipped" convicts to the region.[63] In April 1932, Sevvostlag, the northeastern camp, was established to support gold mining on the Kolyma River.

The actual work did not start until late 1932, when allocated resources and workers started to arrive. The Politburo projections were not even remotely met. The region produced 276.6 kilograms of chemically pure gold in 1931 and 510.7 kilograms in 1932. Free panners produced all the gold. Regardless, Dalstroi was ordered to produce 15 tons of gold in 1933. It produced only 790.9 kilograms.[64] By late 1932, Sevvostlag housed 11,100 prisoners.[65] The situation in Dalstroi was rather typical. In the early 1930s economic enterprises that later became the Gulag's backbone still met with little success.

In June 1931 the OGPU expedition in Ukhta became the Ukhta-Pechora corrective labor camp, with 2,000 prisoners.[66] (The Ukhta expedition had been searching for oil fields around Ukhta, oil and gas resources in Izhemsk and Pechora regions, and coal deposits and sources of radioactive water in Vorkuta.) By late 1932 there were 13,400 prisoners.[67] On 20 October the Politburo made a decision to establish the Ukhta-Pechora trust under the jurisdiction of the OGPU, with rights similar to those for Dalstroi. Ya. M. Moroz, director of the Ukhta-Pechora corrective labor camp (Ukhtpechlag), became head of the trust, which was supposed to research and develop mineral deposits, build railways and roads, organize river navigation, establish agriculture, and otherwise develop the region.[68] The goals issued for 1933 showed the marginal role the trust had in development: 10,000–15,000 tons of oil, 100,000 tons of coal, 8 grams of radium, and 100 tons of asphaltite. The trust received materials and equipment, and the resolution ordered the transfer of 3,000 families of special settlers to Pechora in the spring of 1933 (an increase in the number of prisoners to 25,000), the mobilization of several dozen specialists from other coal-mining and oil-drilling regions, and the organization in Ukhta and Pechora of professional oil and coal schools (students would be recruited from among graduates of local middle schools and "colonized prisoners"—those freed and allowed to live in exile).[69]

Other OGPU camps also remained insignificant in terms of number of laborers and scale of production. They mainly engaged in lumbering, coal mining (10.3 percent of national coal production in 1932), agriculture, construction, and the production of consumer goods (furniture, toys, agricultural equipment, products made of leftover leather, textiles).[70]

A special category concerned various engineering works controlled by the OGPU. After the Shakhty trial in 1928 and the trial of the Industrial Party in 1930, the repression of "bourgeois specialists" became widespread. Considering the great lack of qualified engineers, the OGPU treated this category of prisoners with special attention and tried to utilize their skills. The economic department of the OGPU created several special design laboratories (OKB). Professor L. K. Ramzin, convicted in the Industrial Party trial, worked in OKB no. 11.[71] Some engineers were sent to construction sites, some to the design bureaus of individual enterprises. It took nine months for convict engineers to build the first Soviet blooming mill at Izhorsk machine-building plant. The president of the Supreme Economic Council (VSNKh), G. K. Ordzhonikidze, announced its completion in the newspapers on 23 May 1931 as a great victory.[72] On 16 December, after a report delivered by the commissar of railways, A. A. Andreev, and the OGPU chairman, V. R. Menzhinsky, the Politburo decreed the construction of an experimental electric locomotive at the Kolomna machine-building plant and at the Moscow Dinamo factory "under the control of and with technical supervision by OGPU officers."[73]

Few archival materials exist about this "intellectual zone" of the Gulag. Below is a document about a group of "engineer-wreckers," who, in April 1930, were sent to the central design bureau of Aviation Plant no. 39, where they constructed several new models of aircraft in just one year.[74]

· 8 ·

Recommendation by K. Ye. Voroshilov and G. K. Ordzhonikidze
to the Presidium of the TsIK USSR for the release and
commendation of a group of arrested engineers
[Before 8 July 1930][75]

Secret.
To the Presidium of the TsIK of the Soviet Union.
In March 1930 the Labor and Defense Council mentioned the particularly sluggish construction of experimental models of aircraft (two–four years) and the unacceptably slow transfer of them to mass production (2–

3 years). The council obligated the NKVM and the VSNKh to speed up experimental construction so that it would be possible to design and introduce new models of military aircraft in 7–8 months.

Subsequent to this decision, Menzhinsky Experimental Plant VAO no. 39 and its central design bureau (the OGPU sent engineers-wreckers there who had been arrested and sentenced to various terms, as well as specialists in aircraft design and weaponry, headed by the designers D. P. Grigorovich and A. V. Nadashkevich) produced, between April 1930 and May 1931, the following experimental models of new aircraft:

	Time Spent Designing and Building a New Model
Single-seat fighter I-5, for engine Iu-6	2 months, 28 days
Two-seat light attack aircraft LSh, for engine M-17	3 months, 24 days
Two-seat armored heavy attack aircraft TSh, for engine M-17	3 months, 5 days
Two-seat fighter DIZ, for engine M-17	3 months, 20 days
Special purpose attack aircraft ShON, for engine M-17	2 months, 19 days
Experimental fighter no. 7, for engine YuP-6	5 months
Heavy bomber TB-5, for four engines YuP-6 (about to go into production)	6.5 months

In addition to such unprecedented acceleration of experimental construction, Plant no. 39 achieved the implementation of mixed construction, that is, building experimental models with welded steel tubes (duralumin with wooden and cloth sheeting), which had not been used in the USSR until spring 1930, and the production of new aircraft with technical capabilities and, especially, armaments comparable to those of the best foreign models.

The Revolutionary Military Council of the [Soviet] Union and the Presidium of the VSNKh believe that the exceptional work of Aircraft Building Plant no. 39 to strengthen the RKKA [Workers' and Peasants' Red Army] Air Force, as well as its exceptional achievements, deserve high reward. Therefore, the RVSS [Revolutionary Military Council of the Soviet Union] and VSNKh petition:

1) To award Plant no. 39 (already awarded the Order of the Red Banner and Labor) the Order of Lenin for meeting and superseding the government plan regarding the speed of experimental aircraft construction and the quality of armaments on new types of aircraft.

2) To grant full amnesty to the following designers-wreckers sentenced by the OGPU collegium to various terms of social isolation, and to reward them at the same time.

The chief designer of experimental aircraft, Dmitry Pavlovich Grigorovich, repented of his previous actions and proved it through his year-long labor—a certificate of the TsIK USSR and a bonus of 10,000 rubles.

The chief aircraft weapons designer, Aleksandr Vasilievich Nadashkevich, created new weapon assemblies that increase the firepower of the Red Air Force—a certificate of the TsIK USSR and a bonus of 10,000 rubles.

The technical director of Plant no. 1, Ivan Mikhailovich Kostkin—a bonus of 3,000 rubles.

The former permanent member of the NTK UVVS [Scientific-Technical Committee of the Administration of the Air Force] RKKA, Pavel Martynovich Kreison—a bonus of 1,000 rubles.

The former VAO engineer, Viktor Lvovich Krovik—a bonus of 1,000 rubles.*

3) To award the Order of the Red Star to the director of Plant no. 39, Comrade Anatoly Grigorievich Gorianov, and his deputy, Nikolai Yevgenievich Paufler, for their initiative and persistence in the creation of the TsKB [Central Design Bureau], their clever organization of its work, their reeducation of engineer-wreckers by means of practical work, and their use of them to increase the might of the RKKA Air Force.

[. . .]†

Chairman of the Military Council of the Soviet Union, K. Voroshilov

Chairman of the Supreme Council of the Economy of the Soviet Union, Ordzhonikidze.

On 8 July 1931 the TsIK USSR issued a decree implementing the recommendations.[76] The resolution reflected new tendencies in the policy toward specialists, proclaimed in the summer of 1931.[77] Many "wreckers" were released from prison and returned to work in industry and transport. However, the successful experiment in using convict specialists obviously convinced the leadership of the effectiveness of forced intellectual labor. *Sharashki*—design bureaus for arrested engineers and scientists, working under police supervision—became an integral part of the Gulag.

---

 * Note at the end of this document: "In addition to the persons mentioned here (former wreckers), I would consider it quite fair to amnesty all those who worked together with Grigorovich and Nadashkevich in the Special Design Bureau. Voroshilov. Ordzhonikidze."

 † The part about rewarding free workers of the plant is omitted.

One of the projects where specialist-"wreckers" worked under OGPU supervision was the White Sea–Baltic Sea canal (Belomorkanal). For the OGPU, the construction of the canal was the first large-scale project involving significant numbers of people, a showcase of the "achievements" of the camp economy. By 1 April 1932 the camp on the construction site, Belbaltlag, had absorbed 26 percent of the entire camp population in the Soviet Union, which then numbered 278,500 strong.[78] The most robust prisoners were selected from other camps and sent to help construct the canal. In early 1933, when work ended, 120,000 people were working there.[79]

Because of this special effort, as well as a reduction in the planned size of the canal, the project was completed in a short time, by the summer of 1933. Whatever the actual importance of the canal, this gargantuan enterprise tested the methods of organizing forced labor that later would be widely used, and created the cadres of chekist entrepreneurs who would play an important role in expanding the Gulag economy in the coming years. In a 15 July 1933 resolution on awarding orders of merit to those who worked on canal construction, the Politburo specially mentioned the deputy head of Belomorstroi, which was responsible for the canal construction, N. A. Frenkel. The attached reference stated that he "was sentenced for swindling and crossing the state border. . . . At OGPU request, this conviction by the TsIK USSR was annulled in 1932. From the beginning to the end of his work at Belomorstroi, which constructed the canal, he organized the work well, secured high-quality construction, and demonstrated good knowledge and expertise."[80] Later, Frenkel was just as active at other Gulag projects. He was head of construction on the Baikal–Amur railway (BAM) and head of the NKVD Chief Administration of Camps for Railway Construction. Frenkel received a rank of general and became (in no small degree, thanks to Aleksandr Solzhenitsyn's book) one of the best-known leaders of the Gulag.

Since Stalin, Kirov, and Voroshilov had toured the canal in July 1933, it fell to Kaganovich and other Politburo members to prepare the 15 July 1933 decrees commending the workers. Awards for the successful completion of the project were given to the top leaders of the OGPU and the construction industry: the deputy OGPU chairman, G. Yagoda; the head of Belomorstroi, L. I. Kogan; the head of the Gulag, M. D. Berman; the head of Belbaltlag, S. G. Firin; and his deputy, Ya. D. Rapoport. These people would later manage the Gulag and its important divisions. Many ordinary workers were granted shortened prison terms and had their convictions rescinded. Newspapers reported these resolutions widely. To maximize the propaganda effect, the Politburo instructed the OGPU to publish a monograph about Belomorstroi.[81] The result of this decision was a tour of the canal by a group of writers and an ill-reputed book, which also was published in the West.[82]

The Belomorkanal experience was clearly taken into account when, in 1932, the OGPU was assigned two more projects. On 23 May and 30 September the Politburo resolved to build the Dmitrovsky canal, from the Moscow River to the Volga, under the auspices of the OGPU. The construction had to be completed within a short period of time (by August 1934) utilizing the workforce, engineers, and equipment that were released from Belomorkanal. The Belomorstroi chief, Kogan, became head of this new project.[83]

On 23 October 1932 the Politburo moved the construction of the strategically important Baikal–Amur railway from the People's Commissariat of Communications (NKPS) to the OGPU.[84] This decision was the result of frustrated plans and a catastrophic situation with the free workforce in the first six months of construction.[85]

The late 1932 resolutions (including the decision to create and develop Ukhtpechlag) profoundly transformed the Gulag. Slowly it was becoming a network of large camps servicing giant economic enterprises. The SNK resolution of 25 October 1932 "On the construction projects under the supervision of the OGPU" established the principle of centralizing the administration of camps. The most important projects for the OGPU were completion of Belomorkanal, construction of the Moscow–Volga canal, the Kolyma, Ukhta, and Pechora mines, and the supply of firewood to Moscow and Leningrad. It was forbidden to give the OGPU additional tasks.[86] However, this prohibition was soon violated.

Life in an Unfinished System

The life of prisoners was only partially regulated by official camp rules. Mostly it depended on circumstances and unwritten laws, which periodically changed, leaving "better" and "poorer" times to be remembered. The early 1930s were characterized, on the one hand, by increased terror and a growing number of victims, but, on the other, by a certain Gulag liberalism, the result of organizational transition.

Between 1930 and 1933 the number of prisoners in the camps almost doubled (from 179,000 to 334,300; see Document 96). Such growth would have caused significant problems for housing and supply even under normal conditions. But some camps were created in regions separated from the European part of the country for long winter months. Because supplies were normally delivered by river, a minor disruption of deliveries during the short period the rivers were not frozen could spell catastrophe. Initially, the camps did not even have meager home-grown food supplies and depended fully on the state for provisions. Worse, camp expansion coincided with the growing famine in the country and the resulting critical decline in centralized supply. This was aggravated by poor management and pilfering by the camp administration.

Despite the worsening food situation, the exploitation of prisoners was constantly on the rise due to high production plans. The immediate result was the physical exhaustion of prisoners, the spread of disease, and high mortality. Typhus, tuberculosis, and scurvy became normal for camp dwellers. According to Gulag medical statistics, 23,066 scurvy patients were treated in local clinics (excluding Sevvostlag) in 1931, and 2,908 were hospitalized. Given that the average camp population was 220,000, one in eight to ten prisoners suffered from scurvy. Most likely, the report figures were incomplete. The number of invalids in the camps was also staggering. As mentioned earlier, by 1 August 1930, the estimated number of exhausted, sick, disabled, infirm, and elderly inmates was 30,000–50,000 out of 180,000 prisoners overall. In the second quarter of 1931, the plan was to release 26,000 invalids, the entire camp population being 230,000.[87]

Releasing invalids was just one of the methods to free camps of the "unemployable contingent." There were several conditions for liberation, including the existence of relatives willing to take the unfortunate prisoners in. In most cases, absent relatives, the old and infirm stayed to die in the Gulag. The most hopeless joined the special "chronic invalid teams" and were allowed to move to exile communities (see Document 23).[88] Some were sent to special camp stations and used for relatively easy work. One such station of the Siberian camp was in the village of Yaia, where 1,350 invalids lived and worked in various shops in August 1932. Their plight so deeply affected a casual visitor that he wrote a letter to the head of the Soviet government, V. M. Molotov.

· 9 ·

Letter from worker S. I. Verkhoturov to V. M. Molotov
5 June 1932[89]

───────────

Dear Supreme Head Viacheslav Mikhailovich.

I, a contracted worker, feel it is my duty to report to you about the situation in our corrective labor camps, [where there are] great abnormalities and injustices. Recently I visited the corrective labor camp in Yaia, Tomsk railroad, Siblag. I saw that the ill old men, the disabled, and the invalids have not been liberated yet. I was struck by their awful looks. There are those who are completely blind, with eyes burnt by mine drilling cartridges, as well as those who are paralyzed, disfigured, and completely mutilated, without hands or legs, and those dying of consumption. In other words, it is awful. The food is very bad; those who are sick and do not work receive meatless pickled-cabbage soup twice a day and 400 grams of bread. They are thin, dark, exhausted. Many of them are crying.

Viacheslav Mikhailovich, these unfortunate infirm old men, mutilated by work and disease, have given the camp all their strength, all their health. They got disfigured while working in the mines and lumberyards; they have more than once paid for their crimes, have lost strength and health, eyesight, and sanity, and should not be reproached with [Criminal Code] articles and [prison] terms. Many of them suffer almost without guilt, slandered by their co-workers and enemy neighbors. They were convicted under articles 58–10, 58–2, 58–11, etc., and they do not even know about such crimes.* Now they are completely disabled and harmless to the Soviet regime. They cannot take care of themselves and urinate or defecate on the spot if not taken to the toilet. It is a nightmare. There is no one to take care of them, and they are scolded, to say nothing about medical treatment or real food.

Viacheslav Mikhailovich, these are fathers, old men, mutilated disabled people. At any time we, the young workers, can get mutilated and become such sick monsters and experience the same thing. We, the workers, feel badly for our disabled old fathers.

We humbly ask you to pay attention to this abscess, to release these miserable invalids to the care of relatives who will take care of them: you don't kick a man when he is down. Here it turns out to be the opposite: invalids and old men mutilated by work in the camp, sick people unable to work, continue to suffer in the Yaia camp of the Siblag, where they were

───────────

* Article 58 of the Stalinist Criminal Code became legendary as a generic category for "political" crimes and had several subsections for specific though imaginative transgressions.

brought from all places. They are dying here of exhaustion and camp mutilations.

We humbly ask you, our dear highest superior, to urgently release these unfortunate, elderly, and disabled people.

Worker S. I. Verkhoturov.

Verkhoturov's letter resulted in an inspection of the camp, but one made by the administration of the Siberian camp, which included the Yaia camp, and the report was favorable to the camp managers. The head of the Siberian camp sent to the Secretariat of the SNK USSR two short memoranda, from the head of the production department and from the head of the medical department of Siblag, which refuted the facts in the Verkhoturov letter: "All disabled [. . .] are working with passion and receive workers' rations"; "Medical assistance is adequate. Food is provided according to existing standards."[90] The case file was sent to the archive.

Any prisoner at any time could end up disabled. The physical conditions of "employable contingents" are reflected in the data about camp outpatient units and hospitals. According to internal statistics (excluding Sevvostlag) from 1931, each prisoner visited the outpatient unit 27 times, on average, and 40 out of 100 prisoners stayed in the hospital for an average of 18.8 days. In 1932 these figures did not essentially change (24.5 outpatient visits per prisoner, while 44 out of 100 stayed in the hospital). It is important to remember that, given the inadequacy of medical centers and a lack of doctors, many prisoners did not receive any medical treatment at all.

According to internal OGPU reports, 7,980 prisoners died in the camps in 1930; 7,238 in 1931; and 13,267 in 1932. These are minimal figures and do not include those murdered by the inmates or the guards. At the same time, as state terror toughened, the lawlessness and arbitrary rule of the camp administrators, as well as crimes in the camps, became more extensive and violent, as was typical in crisis periods. Although we do not possess a large amount of material on this topic, there are reasons to believe that 1929–30 was such a crisis period: mass repression engulfed the country, the camps grew quickly, and maximum exploitation of convict labor became a major state imperative.

The situation in the Solovetsky camp, which was partially exposed by the commission sent from Moscow in 1930, supports this conclusion. The commission discovered such chilling facts of mass violence against prisoners, including murder, that it prosecuted a large group of wardens and other administrative personnel.[91] One of the indictments read: "There were various methods of terrorizing and torturing the prisoners. Besides beating them with poles and *shutilniks* (sticks hardened by fire), in the summer they put prisoners out 'to mosquitoes,' i.e., at attention, naked; made them squat 'on a perch,' i.e., narrow benches, without allowing them to move or make a sound all day long. At night, they gave prisoners only one piece of warm clothing. For minor violations of these rules prisoners were locked up in *kibitkas*—cold wooden quarters—until they were frostbitten. At work, they left those prisoners who failed to complete their tasks in the forest for the whole night, where their extremities became frostbitten. Completely healthy people soon grew exhausted and worn-out and were sent as invalids to Solovki Island. Unbearable conditions at work led to mass cases of self-inflicted injuries—e.g., prisoners hacked off their fingers and toes. It was better to lose a hand or a foot than to suffer at work in the camp. Everybody, from team managers to guards, beat up the prisoners. This was only part of the picture of lawlessness at the Solovetsk camps. There were special cells, 1 meter high, with sharp twigs stuck in the floor, walls, and ceiling. The prisoners locked there could not stand it and 'croaked,' i.e., died.

"They imitated executions by firing squad. At work in the forest, they practiced issuing so-called vacation permits, when a prisoner who failed to accomplish his task was punished by having to carry on his shoulders a 2-meter log for several kilometers to the camp."[92]

The news about the Solovetsk calamity and the changes emanating from the Moscow commission spread among the prisoners. Thus, in 1931, V. I. Smirnov wrote down a story told by a former Solovki prisoner, who was going into exile after serving his prison term: "Until May 1930 conditions were terrible. . . Forced work at lumberyards is extremely difficult. In the summer, for failing to accomplish one's task in time, they often put those guilty out to mosquitoes. It means that a fully naked man is tied up to a tree, so that he cannot move hand or foot, for one or two hours, until he passes out. In the winter, they put naked men on a tree stump. Depending on the temperature, a man becomes frozen in about thirty minutes. He falls down, then they warm him up by the fire and repeat the same operation or make him work. Those who failed to accomplish the task were left in the forest for the night. There were cases when a man didn't get to his barracks for a whole week. Guards changed, and he worked nonstop. The task was such that even strong and experienced woodcutters couldn't accomplish it in less than twelve hours. Many had to work for sixteen, eighteen hours. To evade work that was beyond their strength, many hacked off their fingers or froze their hands. The administration consists of chekists from the criminal investigation [unit], the police, the Red Army. . . .

"A great misfortune befell anyone who arrived well dressed, or if the administration noted that he had some money. Such prisoners were shot from behind—for an 'attempt to escape.' . . . Now these outrages are gone. They feed and dress prisoners at Solovki."[93]

The testimony of the convict and the materials of the commission are similar, proving that rumors not only spread widely in the Gulag but also were quite reliable. Obviously, the chekists themselves were even better informed about the commission's work, which could have influenced the situation in the Gulag in general. According to a report by the Procuracy of the RSFSR, "The situation in the camps has significantly improved compared to 1930, in terms of the general quality of life for the prisoners and in the reduction of administrative abuses of the prisoners, which were quite common in 1930 (especially in the Solovetsky camps). Such surviving Solovki practices were revealed by investigations into the Siberian camps, opened by the Procuracy of Western Siberia, which investigated the Siberian camps at our recommendation. The investigation revealed a number of outrages against prisoners, such as putting them in cold water, 40–50 degrees Centigrade, putting them on a hot stove, and tying them to a pole for several hours. Harsh reprisals by the OGPU Collegium put an end to these incidents."[94]

No available documents prove these statements. The conclusion about the decreased number of crimes by camp administrators contradicts other parts of the same Procuracy report: "The number of malfeasances in office by OGPU officials increased in 1931 over 1930. Among them, such dangerous crimes as abuse of power and exceeding their authority also grew."[95] In the Solovetsky camp in February 1933, members of a large group of convicted criminals and camp workers were sentenced either to death or to long prison terms. According to the special Gulag decree, "for a long time (from the fall of 1931 through late 1932)" they "engaged in the systematic beating of prisoners [. . .], theft and drunkenness [. . .], knife-fights, etc., and eventually grew into an open bandit group completely terrorizing the rest of the camp population."[96] The state punitive policy offered the possibility of a certain alleviation of the prisoners' situation in 1931–early 1932.

The growing involvement of the camps in economic activities and the need to fulfill ever-growing economic tasks put pressure on the camp administration and altered its behavior. Gulag leaders eventually came to realize the limits of the merciless exploitation of prisoners. The 1931–32 economic evaluation of the camps, undertaken by the planning group of the Gulag, offers interesting insights. While constantly stressing the need to increase the output of convict labor and raise its productivity—in part through the shock-work campaign to increase individual productivity through fast, hard, and efficient work—Gulag planners from time to time recognized the limits of over-exploitation. Characterizing the situation in Vishersky camp (directed by E. P. Berzin) in April–May 1931, they wrote: "Prolonged workhours, shock work for months on end without rest, relocating the workforce from one enterprise to another without even a short rest in between, and employing the skilled workforce for unqualified jobs [. . .] has led to a situation in Vishlag where the scale of employment is in inverse proportion to the productivity of labor."[97]

A deficit of workers and the de facto disability of a large number of prisoners (delicately called "exhaustion" in the reports) led authorities to consider merely preserving the camp population. The following circular letter by the camp administration demonstrates such comprehension.

· 10 ·

Circular letter from the GULAG of the OGPU
about teams for exhausted workers
30 November 1930[98]

To the heads of administrations of the OGPU corrective labor camps.

To fully restore the employability of prisoners exhausted by illness or heavy work, it is recommended that camp administrations and their departments create, starting on 1 January 1931, teams for exhausted workers.

1. Teams of exhausted workers should be composed of:

a) those who, after a prolonged illness in the hospital, require a special regimen to restore fully their strength;

b) prisoners exhausted by hard physical work and requiring rest to fully restore their employability;

c) newly arrived prisoners requiring a restoration of health before they can be normally employed.

2. Those prisoners whose health cannot be restored should not be sent to teams for exhausted workers.

3. When considering candidates for the teams, preference should be given to prisoners who performed hard physical work and produced a good impression by their positive behavior and attitude toward work.

4. Prisoners are assigned to the teams of exhausted workers by the head of the administration and the heads of departments via URO [the Accounting and Distribution Department], on recommendation by medical commissions and medical institutions.

5. The term of stay in the teams for exhausted workers is one to one and one-half months.

6. The living quarters of the teams for exhausted workers should be exemplary from the sanitary point of view, equipped, if possible, with trestle beds or one-level bunks, and have bedsheets and towels. Prisoners should have regular baths and changes of bedding and clothes.

7. Food for those in the teams for exhausted workers should correspond to the existing norm: a ration with supplements according to Resolution no. 614879 by the OGPU camp administration, i.e., at least 2,500 calories. Prisoners susceptible to scurvy should receive an additional anti-scurvy ration. It is necessary to pay attention to the variety of food and offer a higher quality of food.

8. Establish in the teams for exhausted workers a strict regimen that includes the afterlunch rest hour, and regularly conduct the work of cultural education and offer light physical exercise.

9. Members of the teams of exhausted workers should care for themselves and perform light work not requiring a lot of physical output for no longer than three–four hours a day.

10. Members of the teams of exhausted workers should be under systematic medical supervision and have personal medical records.

11. After the end of a term in a team of exhausted workers, a prisoner should undergo a medical examination by the medical labor commission, which determined the labor category for each prisoner. In exceptional cases, the commission can extend the stay in the team from two to four more weeks, maximum.

12. The number in the teams of exhausted workers is determined by actual need but should not exceed 1–1.5 percent of the entire number of prisoners.

13. Reports on the work of the teams of exhausted workers for every month should be provided no later than on the fifteenth day of the next month, according to the attached form.

Deputy head of the OGPU Camp administration, Berman

Assistant to the head, Belonogov.

Despite the impossibility of implementing all the ideas in this circular letter, the Camp Administration was demonstrably no longer counting on the influx of new prisoners but concentrating instead on "internal reserves." Refusing those unable to recuperate access to the teams of exhausted workers demonstrates a certain cynical pragmatism.

A focus on economic goals and the need to secure rising productivity contributed to the relaxing of certain camp rules, by allowing large numbers of prisoners to move about unescorted, for example, and permitting those convicted under "counterrevolutionary" articles to occupy administrative positions. Apparently, pressure from below also made Moscow start counting workdays toward the early release of prisoners.

Camp bosses, facing the need to fulfill high production plans, were naturally most interested in searching for stimuli for convict labor. Using force or experimenting with "worker competition" and "shock labor," insisted upon by the central organs in 1930–early 1931, did not provide the required results. The Gulag planning group reported in early 1932 that "the system of shock labor and competition has temporarily lost its stimulating potential mainly owing to the fact that in 1931, for the most part, the extra bonuses given to the prisoners for shock work or to reward them for participating in labor competition were not usable because of the lack of goods in the [camp] stores. In addition to that, shock labor has become a mere formality in some camps. A good example is the state farm "Gigant," where, according to the account, "100 percent [of prisoners] are shock workers, while at the same time the plan was not seen to be fulfilled in all avenues of work."[99]

The best way to stimulate prisoners, as the camp administration knew well, was to offer them early release. Since the law generally referred to such a possibility, local camp administrators tried to promise it based on good work and behavior, but they were criticized by Moscow. The OGPU camp administration head, L. I. Kogan, wrote to local camp bosses in September 1930 forbidding them to "mention the possibility of early release in order not to provide a reason for speculation or hopes for early release." He was rather vague in explaining this: "For various reasons, we currently cannot raise the question of broad implementation of the practice of early liberation."[100]

In less than a year, on 30 July 1931, Kogan issued an order on the possibility of counting workdays toward serving out a prison term. Depending on class origin, prisoners who abided by internal rules and fulfilled or overfulfilled production norms could have three workdays counted as four, or four days as five. This effectively reduced their prison terms. The preamble to the order reveals the pressure by local Gulag managers, who reported on the spread of shock labor and the need to support it.[101]

This order broke the ice, and on 22 November 1931 the Gulag released detailed instructions on how to count workdays toward the reduction of prison terms. The instructions determined three main categories for counting workdays: "a) counting two workdays as three days of a prison term (for shock workers); b) counting three workdays as four days of a prison term, and c) counting four workdays as five days of a prison term." Category *b* was applied for those prisoners who, "before conviction, belonged to the toiling class and socially vital groups of the Soviet population (former workers, peasants, professionals, handicraft workers, artisans, people of free professions) and enjoyed voting rights." Category *c* applied to the rest of the prisoners, such as former traders, clerics, and people in other groups deprived of the right to vote.[102] Compared to similar regulations later, the 1931 instructions were rather moderate.

In addition to counting workdays toward early release, the colonization campaign in early 1931 (transferring prisoners from camps to special settlements) provided a minor alleviation of some prisoners' situation. This campaign was left over from the early projects of mass colonization (see Document 6). According to the Gulag order, it was the "carefully checked prisoners" who were eligible, primarily workers and peasants sentenced for minor crimes and malfeasance who had already served more than half their term.* The main condition was the agreement of the family to move to the colonization region. "Colonized" prisoners and their families received assistance in building houses and finding jobs in industry and agriculture. Until the end of their term, colonists had to deduct up to 20 percent of their salary in support of the camps.[103] Between 1931 and the end of 1932, twelve settlements were created with 6,062 colonists (including 3,570 former prisoners and 2,492 family members). Colonies created by the Far Eastern camp specialized in fishing; those of the Central Asian camp, in agriculture; and those of the Siberian, Vishersky, and Ukhta-Pechora camps, in assistance to industrial enterprises.[104] The campaign of reuniting prisoners with their families at the special settlements near industrial enterprises pursued similar goals.

The relative liberalism of these measures resulted mainly from eco-

---

* However, colonization of "counterrevolutionary elements" was not completely ruled out.

nomic necessity, a fact understood by Gulag bosses. It also reflected certain features of the punitive policy of the state, which should be neither ignored nor overestimated. In the early 1930s the Gulag regime still had not acquired the extreme brutality characteristic of the late 1930s. A certain "punitive idealism" of the revolutionary period still remained. Prisoners from the groups "socially close to the Soviet regime" had a special status. The April 1930 decree on the corrective labor camps, issued by the SNK USSR, divided prisoners into three categories: "The first category includes toilers (workers, peasants, and professionals) who, before conviction, enjoyed the right to vote and who are sentenced to no more than five years for non-counterrevolutionary crimes. The second category includes the same kind of prisoners sentenced to more than five years. The third [category includes] all nontoiling elements and those convicted for counterrevolutionary crimes."[105] The camp administration always had to encourage "class separation of prisoners" and support those "socially close" in order to convert them into "valuable members of the proletarian state."[106]

Three types of regimen were used for prisoners in the camps: basic, alleviated, and favored. "Prisoners on the basic regimen participate in general work, live on the camp premises in special quarters, have no right to leave those quarters freely, and are assigned to work according to the general list. Prisoners on the alleviated regimen are given permanent employment in offices, factories, and industries, live in residences at those enterprises, have the right to short leaves, are assigned to work as employees, and can be rewarded. Prisoners on the favored regimen, in addition to the conditions of the alleviated regimen, enjoy the right to leave the camp premises and to occupy positions in the camp administration and head the work teams."[107]

The latter two categories transformed the prisoners into semi-free people, permitting them to live outside the camp and move about at will, or nearly so. A prisoner in any of the categories could be granted a better regimen. The categories differed only in terms of the minimal application of the basic regimen: six months for the first category, at least a year for the second category, and at least two years for the third. Formally, prisoners in the third category could not occupy administrative positions, that is, enjoy the favored regimen. But in practice, the discrimination against "political" and "socially alien" prisoners was not that strict. In many camps, "counterrevolutionaries" were put on the favored regimen and were used in various administrative positions and in the work of cultural education.[108]

The Gulag leadership at times even displayed a certain religious tolerance.

· 11 ·

Circular letter from the GULAG of the OGPU on changing
the food ration of members of religious sects
20 September 1931[109]

Top secret.

Among the camp population there are individuals refusing to eat animal food (meat, fish, etc.). For the most part, these are sectarian fanatics.

While not encouraging such views, but rather dissuading them through camp cultural and educational organizations, we still should not force them to eat animal food.

The aforementioned individuals should receive natural food rations, with meat, fish, and animal fats replaced by other products totaling the caloric count of the ration.

I am asking you to report on the measures taken to implement this order and amend the rations.

Head of the Chief Administration of the OGPU Camps,
Kogan.

The political regimen, imposed on imprisoned party oppositionists, mainly Trotskyists and members of revolutionary parties opposed to the Bolsheviks, indicates the cruelty of the pre–World War II punitive policy in the Soviet Union. In the early 1930s the political regimen was still in use owing to a certain inertia, as well as to the activity of the Committee of Support for political prisoners headed by Maxim Gorky's wife, E. P. Peshkova, to pressure from public opinion in the West, and to the struggle of prisoners for their rights. An important episode in this struggle was the April–May 1931 mutiny in Verkhne-Uralsk political prison.

· 12 ·

Report on the hunger strike in Verkhne-Uralsk political prison
20 July 1931[110]

Top secret.

To the Secretary of the TsIK USSR, Comrade Yenukidze.

On 25 April of this year, the Trotskyist Yesaian was standing by the window of his cell talking to other prisoners of the Verkhne-Uralsk political prison. A guard shot at him and wounded him, the bullet passing right through his chest.

As a result, all political prisoners declared a hunger strike. Trotskyists also formulated their demands to invite a commission to investigate and prosecute those responsible, and to alleviate the regimen. The hunger strike went on for five days until the administration declared that the commission would come.

Owing to Comrade Krasikov's illness, the commission could not come until after my return from a trip, i.e., on 27 June.

After the Trotskyist prisoners recuperated from the first hunger strike, they organized again and made new demands, including those of a political nature, and declared, on 24 June, another hunger strike "to the death."

While the first hunger strike was supported by prisoners who were members of other political parties, the second one was not supported at all, except by several anarchists.

Upon arrival, the commission had to face a tightly knit collective, and it took a lot of work to undermine it. The hunger strike ended on the eleventh day, with no political demands met and only some minor demands satisfied, as seen from the enclosed list of demands and the directive by the commission.

Attachment: 6 pages.[111]

For the Procurator of the Supreme Court of the USSR, KATANIAN.

· 13 ·

Demands by the striking prisoners of Verkhne-Uralsk political prison
[24 June 1931][112]

Demands to the Collegium of the GULAG of the OGPU.

I. Political part

1. Remove the head of the prison and his assistant.

2. Investigate and harshly prosecute those responsible for the 26 April incident.

3. Provide wounded Comrade Yesaian with special resort treatment.

4. Discontinue physical punishment (beating, tying up, pouring water on, shooting, etc.).

5. Recognize the right to send a collective letter to government organs, and oblige the head of the prison to accept the letter for delivery.

6. Recognize the right to collective representation.

7. Discontinue searches and confiscation of manuscripts.

8. Discontinue rudeness by the administration (including those in the high and the middle ranks).

9. Extend the political regimen to our comrades in pretrial detention and at transfer points.

10. Completely discontinue transporting political prisoners to confinement houses, and from confinement to exile, together with criminals. Provide warm clothes for the journey.

11. Liquidate concentration camps for the oppositionists, and send the Bolshevik prisoners into exile.

12. Count preliminary confinement toward the prison term, and provide timely release for those ending their terms.

13. Permit reading in the cells and during walks, and permit the celebration of revolutionary holidays and days of mourning.

14. Bring a state commission for inspection every six months without exception.

II. Food

15. Improve food rations (greater selection, more variety, more vegetable dishes; exclude oatmeal from the menu and replace it with another second course; provide better-quality fish on seafood days).

16. Improve the quality of food (more calories, fats, and milk) for those receiving special rations for weakness, and increase the rations for weakness to include all those in need of them.

17. Improve the system of purchasing food for money (access to the cooperative store with set prices for soap, sugar, fats, vegetables, and writing utensils).

18. Deliver mailed food packages without delay, and release all impounded products from the warehouse.

III. Other supplies

19. Restore the old quality of cigarettes and increase the daily maximum to twenty.

20. Provide everyone with a uniform, underwear, bedsheets, footwear, and regular changes of underwear on bath days, and provide those suffering from rheumatism with felt boots.

21. Provide winter clothes no later than 1 November.

22. Introduce clothing repair and settle the issue of shoe repair.

23. Provide those comrades in need who are leaving the camp with clothes and shoes.

24. Discontinue the confiscation of products and tobacco from those leaving prison.

IV. Sanitary issues

25. Decrease the number of prisoners per cell. Move all prisoners from twelve–thirteen–person cells into better conditions. Increase the number of solitary units for the communist collective.

26. Cells facing the sun with wooden floors, as well as solitary units, should be assigned exclusively by the doctor.

27. Replace cement floors with wooden floors.

28. Permit prisoners to trade beds, and allow them to move to other cells, provided there is free space.

29. Improve electrical lighting of the cells (replace economy bulbs with half-watt bulbs).

30. Provide all new prisoners with tables and stools without delay.

31. Provide large cells with two dishtowels.

32. Officially allow prisoners to breathe fresh air by the windows.

33. Establish bath days once a week and increase the bath time to one hour.

34. Accept dirty laundry immediately after the bath.

35. Put all newcomers through a disinfecting chamber.

36. Permit weekly use of the barbershop.

37. Make walks longer while at the same time ending the fourth turn and introducing the shift system for walks.

38. Extend the three-hour walk into October and March.

39. Build closets with doors for food in the cells.

40. Regularly disinfect the cells.

41. Allow the use of toilets in emergencies.

V. Cultural services

42. Expand the library; replenish it with periodicals printed in the USSR and, at least, publications by the C[ommunist] I[nternational]. Systematically update the economic, political, and literature sections, and supply literature in the languages of national minorities. Subscribe to at least one copy of each foreign newspaper. Allow the ordering of materials for courses by correspondence. Set up a special cultural fund for this purpose: such funds exist even in prisons for criminals.

43. Allow delivery to the prison of all foreign editions permitted in the USSR, in particular foreign newspapers, including bourgeois newspapers.

44. Allow book exchanges between floors and sections.

45. Provide writing paper in the amount of no less than ten notebooks per person each month.

46. Build monkey bars and parallel bars in the courtyards.

47. Set up radio [loudspeakers].

48. Allow the purchase of light sport equipment (for volleyball, croquet, etc.).

49. Allow the delivery of writing utensils from home.

50. Open learning shops for people in various professions.

VI. Medical care

51. Provide special treatment to seriously ill comrades or transfer them to exile (to places with available medical care and a suitable climate for each individual case) after approval by the medical commission.

52. Treat tuberculosis patients remaining in prison in a separate cell.

53. Improve the medical care, food, and regimen in the prison hospital. Forbid the head of the prison from transferring patients without the approval of the doctor. Give the doctor the right to make professional decisions: to transfer rheumatic and tuberculosis patients and assign them special diets. Allow walks for the ambulatory patients.

54. Distribute emergency medical kits to each cell.

55. Set up a ventilation system in the hospital.

56. Allow patients to use the toilet without limitations.

57. Manufacture dental prostheses for those who have lost their teeth.

VII. Mail and visits

58. Establish real accountability for the failure to deliver priority mail, telegrams, and packages.

59. Allow visits to relatives in exile.

60. Allow comrades without relatives to correspond with the people they indicate.

61. Allow correspondence with relatives living abroad.

62. Allow visits by relatives held in the prison.

Plenipotentiary representatives of the communist collective of the Verkhne-Uralsk political prison—Fyodor Dingelshteindt, German Kvachadze, Gavriil Sayansky.

· 14 ·

Resolution by an OGPU commission on meeting the demands
of the prisoners of Verkhne-Uralsk political prison
[After 27 June 1931][113]

To the head of the political prison, Comrade Biziukov.

Announce to the prisoners that:

1. Investigation into the wounding of Yesaian and the aiming [of guns] at prisoners has been closed. The culprit will be tried in the OGPU Collegium court. The officers of the division have taken appropriate measures to prevent accidents similar to the one investigated by the commission.

2. Prisoners are allowed to use the windows while standing on the floor. It is categorically forbidden to use windows as a means of illegal communication with prisoners from other cells (talking, exchanging notes). Those who break this rule will receive administrative punishment.

3. The commission has discovered cases in which political prisoners have offended the administration. There were also instances of tactless behavior by the junior officers toward political prisoners. In the future, those responsible for offending the administration, by word or deed, will

be held accountable. Similarly, members of the administration who are rude to prisoners will be held accountable.

4. In accord with the opinion of the medical commission, prisoners in need of medical attention will receive appropriate treatment.

5. The caloric level of the food is sufficient, and the products are of good quality. As vegetables and greens grow, the menu will be diversified. The ration of sugar and fats for the sick has been equated with the general ration.

6. The head of the prison allocates inmates to the cells and takes the doctor's recommendations into consideration.

7. Additional insulation for cells 12 and 13 and sanitizing of the cesspit are in the repair plan for this year.

8. All prisoners are to be provided with stools. Tables and enclosed closets will be provided when available. Group cells will be supplied with two towels.

9. Prisoners will receive writing utensils through the prison administration. Utensils received in the mail will be exchanged for those available in prison.

10. A book exchange among prisoners is allowed only through the library.

11. All prisoners are supported by the state. Additional rations at set prices cannot be provided. Prisoners can purchase additional products at the local market at market prices and in the cooperative store at commercial prices.

12. Prisoners will receive bedsheets, underwear, clothes, and shoes as needed and if these items are available in the prison warehouse.

13. All participants in the hunger strike will be given special diet rations for seven days after the end of the strike. During the following seven days, they will receive an additional 200 grams of bread and will be allowed to purchase butter and milk in the cooperative if these items are available.

14. Prisoners are responsible for maintaining their cells and have to clean them at the designated hours. Each month the cells will be disinfected. The doctor's recommendations regarding sanitary issues are obligatory for prisoners.

15. All new prisoners will be put in the quarantine cell, and their personal items will be disinfected.

16. Prisoners will visit the bath once every two weeks for forty-five minutes. Dirty laundry will be collected for washing right away.

17. All non-counterrevolutionary personal statements and complaints related to the facts known by the prisoner in his cell or during his walk will be received by the head of the prison to be delivered as addressed.

OGPU representative—Andreeva

Deputy procurator at the OGPU—Pruss

Head of the prison section of the OGPU—Popov.

In the Stalinist Gulag in the early 1930s, then, prisoners were relatively well-off and free compared to those unfortunate enough to be imprisoned in the later period of starvation, mass shootings, and war. This was not true, of course, for those who, in these "prosperous" years, died of hunger or were killed by irate guards unaware of the "liberal" ideas of the Gulag leaders in Moscow.

CHAPTER 2

Famine

Between the First and the Second Five-Year plans, in late 1932–33, the Stalinist system suffered shocks that resulted in the escalation of terror and a further growth of the system of camps and special settlements. By that time, the social and political crisis resulting from Stalin's "great leap" had peaked. The 1932 harvest was very poor. Forced state procurements in 1932 caused severe famine in the main grain-producing parts of the country: the Ukraine, Northern Caucasus, Volga, and Central Black Soil regions. Ruthless collectivization led to mass deaths among Kazakh peasants, as well as their flight to bordering regions. In general, in 1931–33, according to reliable estimates, between 6 and 7 million people died of hunger.[1] Millions of survivors became chronically ill or handicapped. In the regions most affected by famine, crime spread widely, including such extreme forms as cannibalism. Large numbers of adult peasants and orphaned children moved to the cities, attracted by food rations. Epidemics accompanied hunger, as usual.

The most terrible and tragic event, mass famine, was only one element of the severe crisis that affected every aspect of life in the country. In 1932–33 the Bolsheviks had to face a significant challenge to their power.

Plans for Mass Purges

The Stalinist leadership managed to keep the crisis under control thanks to a policy of severe repression. The dominant methods of grain procurement involved full searches, arrests, executions, and deportations, including the deportation of entire villages. In 1932 the authorities conducted municipal operations against "criminal, socially dangerous, and parasitic elements," which in early 1933 turned into a mass purge connected with the introduction of the passport system. The OGPU fabricated numerous cases of "wrecking" and "counterrevolutionary organizations." The 7 August 1932 law about the protection of socialist property became a contemporary symbol of state terror. Proposed by Stalin, the law called for execution or a sentence of at least ten years in prison for even petty theft. The law, aimed at starving peasants who attempted to take several sheaves of wheat, received the popular moniker "the law of five sheaves."[2]

As usual, the general intensification of state terror led to abuses by local authorities. Millions of people were involved in the vicious circle of criminal proceedings and arrests, and their number kept growing. To house huge new contingents of prisoners and create conditions for a further expansion of punitive actions, in late 1932 the OGPU leaders came up with a plan for creating a new system of isolation: labor settlements in the remote regions of Western Siberia and Kazakhstan. The preliminary plan was to move, in the winter and summer of 1933 2 million people (1 million to each region).[3] The settlers were to engage in agriculture, fishing, and cottage industries. Thus, the OGPU planned to make those settlers self-sufficient in food production within a couple of years, even to the point of obtaining agricultural produce from them. Legally, labor settlers would have the same rights as the special settlers of the first wave, the "kulaks."[4]

The documents explaining the history and justification of the plans to build labor settlements and exile huge numbers of people have not yet been found. Obviously, however, the program reflected the OGPU leaders' skepticism about the camps and a desire to reanimate the idea of concentrating large numbers of prisoners in remote settlements, which made security and maintenance easier than in the camps (see Document 6). Also notable is the SNK resolution of 25 October 1932 strictly limiting the number of permanent OGPU construction sites, the aim there being to stabilize camp "contingents." It is possible that the leaders of the country supported the deportation of a large segment of the population in the European part of the USSR as a means both to reduce social tensions and to alleviate the acute food crisis.

In early February 1933 the OGPU leadership sent instructions to local administrations on the placement of a 2-million-strong contingent of prisoners. This met with harsh opposition from local leaders. On 10 February the secretary of the Western Siberian territorial party committee, R. I. Eikhe, wrote to Stalin in protest: "This proposal is unrealistic and probably was written by comrades unfamiliar with the conditions of the North. Regardless of whatever material resources and assistance come from the center, we can neither bring in and settle so many people nor effect minimally acceptable winterization preparations by the summer of 1933." Eikhe also informed Stalin that even after serious preparation, Western Siberia would be able to receive only 250,000–270,000 people instead of 1,000,000.[5]

After many arguments and adjustments, the OGPU reduced the number of settlers to 1 million. On 10 March the Politburo ratified OGPU suggestions "on creating labor settlements in Western Siberia and Kazakhstan (500,000 people in each territory)" and set up a commission presided over by Yagoda to determine the actual size of the settlements and to prepare a draft resolution on the labor settlements in general.[6] On 20 April 1933, SNK USSR adopted a resolution to establish OGPU labor settlements. The resolution, approved by the Politburo on 17 April, charged the OGPU with creating labor settlements "similar to the existing special settlements." [7] The Chief Administration of Camps of the OGPU was transformed into the Chief Administration of Camps and Labor Settlements (to include the former special settlements of kulaks). M. D. Berman remained head of the administration, his deputy for camps became Ya. D. Rapoport, and his deputy for special settlements, S. G. Firin. Labor settlements were to house the following categories of prisoners:

1. Kulaks and saboteurs of grain procurement
2. Those exiled as a result of cleansing the western border regions (primarily in the Ukraine)
3. Those arrested as a result of issuing passports in the cities (kulaks exposed at industrial enterprises and the socially dangerous elements refusing to abandon the large cities)
4. Those convicted to short terms, from three to five years, but excluding socially dangerous elements

Prisoners in the last category were to be placed in the settlements only if they brought their families with them. In accordance with the earlier

OGPU proposals, the plan was to provide some material resources to create new labor settlements and to use the labor settlers in agriculture, fishing, and cottage industries, as well as equalize their rights with those of the kulaks deported in 1930–31.

Although the resolution did not mention the number of new settlers, it may have targeted 1 million. Even though this constituted only half the initial figure, the realization of the goal would require a complete overhaul of the Gulag structure. The total of almost 2 million in the network of labor settlements (including the old kulak special settlements) would by far exceed the number of prisoners in the camps (as of 1 January 1933 the camps contained a few more than 330,000 people). Plans to transfer to labor settlements those with sentences of three to five years also had potentially lasting consequences. Until then, such prisoners were sent to the camps and made up the majority of the camp population (54 percent as of 1 January 1934; see Document 99). Thus, implementation of these decisions would leave the camps with a small number of particularly dangerous criminals, as well as political prisoners. The basis of the Gulag would be, not large camps exploiting prisoners at major construction sites, but settlements at agricultural, fishing, lumber, and cottage-industry sites with a total contingent of several million state serfs.

One of the first urgent steps in organizing such labor settlements (besides creating space for the victims of further repressive actions) was the emptying of existing prisons. Delays in realizing the plan meant a worsening of the conditions in prisons, jails, and pre-detention holding cells. As a result of mass arrests, the jails held three to ten times more than the normal number of prisoners.[8] Under the conditions of famine and widespread epidemics, this had catastrophic consequences.

According to an OGPU delegate sent to the Ukraine and the Northern Caucasus territory in March 1933, even in large cities (Kharkov, Kiev, and Odessa), non-working inmates in prisons received 100 grams of bread a day, and working inmates received 200 grams. In addition, inmates received water and 10 grams of groats. Sick prisoners in police detention cells received 50 grams of bread a day. "Healthy" prisoners received nothing and "had to rely on parcels or starve" (obviously, they starved, because it was impossible to receive a parcel in hunger-stricken Ukraine). The inspector wrote: "The situation in the Ukraine is such that there are no robust people: absolutely everyone is exhausted." The delegate registered an even worse situation in the

Northern Caucasus, where, in addition to famine, spotted fever raged.[9]
On the average, in early 1933, up to 15 percent of prisoners died of
hunger every month in Uzbekistan; in January, 15 percent of the Tashkent prison inmates died, and in February, 25 percent.[10]

The following OGPU memorandum describes the situation of tens
of thousands of prisoners in police detention cells.

· 15 ·

Memorandum on the preliminary confinement cells of the police
20 February 1933[11]

Starting in 1930, in connection with the decision to make jails self-sufficient, the GUITU [Chief Administration for Corrective Labor Facilities
of the People's Commissariat of Justice of the RSFSR] has closed a number
of unprofitable jails. [. . .]

Closing detention sites while increasing the number of prisoners, a result of expanding the powers of regional courts, has led to the de facto
conversion of police detention cells into jails.

However, police detention cells capable of housing fifteen–twenty people for a short period of time (twenty-four–forty-eight hours) cannot substitute for jails.

First of all, they cannot substitute for jails in terms of size. As already
noted, most of the cells can hold only fifteen–twenty people. Second, they
were designed for brief (twenty-four–forty-eight hours) imprisonment
and are lacking in terms of equipment. Most of them have no bunks,
kitchens, kitchenware, toilets, sanitary equipment, or anything that is necessary to provide normal detention conditions. The cells themselves are
mainly unsuitable for detention or for living: these are old village bathhouses, dugouts, sheds, or, at best, ordinary houses. [. . .]

As a rule, police cells are overcrowded by 200–400 percent and sometimes up to 600–800 percent. Thus, in the Moscow police detention cells,
built for 350 people, 2,341 prisoners were being kept as of 31 January.

As of 1 February, there were 34,794 prisoners in the Northern Caucasus. Regions with only one detention cell keep 500–1,000 prisoners on average. [. . .]

As of 1 January, in the Urals province, cells built for 470 people housed
1,715 inmates. [. . .]

As of 1 January, in the Ivanovo Industrial province, cells built for fifteen
people housed sixty-five people, and cells built for nineteen people had
seventy people, etc.

Similar situations exist in other territories and provinces.

It is important to mention that the overcrowding is only getting worse. The number of those arrested in all territories and provinces is steadily on the rise. [. . .]

Among those kept in police cells, over 50 percent are processed by the NKIu [People's Commissariat of Justice] organs and courts, while 25–30 percent of them have been sentenced to a predetermined confinement.

Prisoners are usually kept from one to three months, but sometimes up to five, six, or even nine months.

Prisoners under the jurisdiction of the NKIu organs and courts are typically kept in confinement for the longest periods of time. Whereas those prisoners that belong to RKM [Workers' and Peasants' Police] organs spend ten–twenty days in confinement, those belonging to the Procuracy and judicial organs spend from one and one-half to three months under arrest.

The overcrowding is exacerbated by the following:

1) The GUITU organs systematically refuse to accept inmates from police pressed by the overcrowding of jails and corrective labor colonies and the associated quarantines there.

As a result, those sentenced to five–ten years in prison are moved 50–150 kilometers back and forth between RKM organs and GUITU organs in Ural province, Western Siberia, Central Volga province, etc. At best, prisoners and guards spend several hours in the cold waiting for the question of transfer to be resolved (Western Siberia, Urals province, etc.).

2) There is a lack of escort guards in RKM organs. [. . .]

The overcrowding is such that the police cells are packed with those arrested. Often prisoners cannot lie or sit down, but have to stand (report by a brigade inspecting the Lower Volga territory).

The inadequate size of overcrowded cells and the lack of necessary equipment result in unsanitary conditions: the cells are filthy and lice-ridden.

Such conditions lead to frequent epidemics. In the latest period, the Northern territory registered eight cases of typhus, the Urals province had forty-two cases, and the Western province had four cases. Moscow had epidemics in five city departments.

The situation concerning the feeding of inmates is no better.

The norm is 17 kopecks per person in police cells. However, given the permanent overcrowding of cells, each ration has to be divided among several people.

Thus, in Belorussia (Gomel), 120 people received rations intended for 50 people; in Bobruisk, 24 rations were divided among 100 people; in Moscow province, products delivered for 5 were distributed among 40 people.

Except in large cities, hot food is not served.

Often regional distribution centers do not provide food for inmates.

Malnutrition and even hunger among inmates in the cells is frequent. There are cases of deaths from hunger (Kazakhstan, Northern Caucasus).

The situation in terms of guarding the inmates is particularly alarming. As noted above, on average, regional RKM departments have only two–three rank and file guards, while some regions have none at all. Therefore, prisoners are guarded mostly by village police officers entirely unprepared for this task.

As a result, the rate of escape from prison has grown enormously.

On 18 December of last year, a total of 29 prisoners simultaneously escaped from a cell in the third police department in Dnepropetrovsk. During three months, 147 inmates escaped in Moscow. During ten months in the Central Black Soil region, 549 people escaped. In the course of twenty days, 15 people escaped in the Western province. On 30 January, 26 inmates simultaneously escaped from a police cell in Armavir. In Tashkent, on 6 January, 6 people escaped from the fourth city [police] department. In the Ivanovo Industrial province, 76 people escaped.

Escapes were accompanied by the murder of police officers and guards (Western province, Northern Caucasus, Lower Volga territory, Central Black Soil region, etc.)

In most cases, escapes were conducted by breaking through the walls, digging under the walls, and cutting the bars. [. . .]

Deputy head of GURKM [Chief Administration for the Workers' and Peasants' Police] OGPU

Makarian.

Hunger, epidemics, high mortality, and escapes were typical for other prisons and detention centers in the country as well. The problems were exacerbated by the abuses and brutality of prison administrators. The case of a detention center in Krasnovodsk, Turkmenia, became widely known.

· 16 ·

Excerpt from the verdict of the military tribunal in the case
of former workers in the Krasnovodsk detention center,
20 April 1934[12]

[. . .] The apparatus of the detention center and the colony [. . .] was engaged in criminal activities: beating the prisoners, arbitrary shootings, appropriation of their products and money. Encouragement of the kulaks, traders, and swindlers has become an everyday norm. [. . .]

As a result of the criminal activity of the overseers, the calorie content of food rations in the detention center and in the colony was below the minimum. The calorie content of rations for individual prisoners employed in outside work could fall to 300–400 calories per day. The administration paid no attention to environment and economic situation of prisoners, who were kept in unsanitary conditions. Medical workers and prisoners repeatedly wrote to Nekrasov* about these abnormalities, but he made no effort to remedy them. All this resulted in mass deaths among the prisoners. Between 1 December 1932 and 1 April 1933, 219 prisoners died of exhaustion. As a rule, those workers, peasants, and social groups close to the proletariat died more often without outside assistance or privileges from the administration. The prisoners were thus forced to escape. There were seventeen successful escapes between December 1932 and January 1933.

To prevent escapes as well as stop the stream of prisoners' complaints about the administration, Nekrasov and the wardens agreed to employ the cruelest measures and "not to spare bullets" so that nobody would be able to leave the detention center or the colony. Having agreed to a collective coverup and having established specific corrective methods (beatings, food deprivation, and "not sparing bullets"), the hired workers of the colony and the detention center, with this goal in mind, began the practice of consciously provoking prisoner escapes and beating and shooting them when captured. The bodies of those shot were displayed in the courtyards, and prisoners were brought [to see them] under escort as a means of terrorizing them and demonstrating to them the impossibility of escape under any conditions. Particularly horrifying were the arbitrary shootings on 25 February and 6 and 27 March 1933.

On 24 February 1933, Meshcheriakov[†] ascertained that prisoners in one cell were preparing an escape by digging a passage under the wall. Meshcheriakov took no legal steps to prevent the escape, as was his duty, but reported it to the head of the colony, Senatov. Senatov called Nekrasov on the phone and informed him of the planned escape. Nekrasov ordered Senatov to follow orders strictly: to bolster the guards, allow the prisoners to escape, and shoot the escapees when they ran. Senatov, having received instructions and approval from Nekrasov, gave the appropriate orders to Meshcheriakov. On 25 February, Meshcheriakov learned that everything was ready for the escape and that it would take place that night. Following Senatov's obviously illegal orders, he took the warden Sharipov and the guard Maltsev (a prisoner himself) with him and set up an ambush near the location of the planned escape. Meshcheriakov instructed Shari-

---

* V. N. Nekrasov was head of the Krasnovodsk detention center.
† I. U. Meshcheriakov was the senior warden of the colony of the Krasnovodsk detention center.

pov and Maltsev to let the escapees leave the underground passage and then shoot them.

In the evening, when it got dark, the prisoners [. . .] were allowed to get out of the underground passage and move away from the wall. Then Meshcheriakov, Sharipov, and Maltsev, without making warning shots, opened fire. The prisoners, fearing that they would be killed, fell prostrate on the ground. Meshcheriakov then ran up to them and shot them each three or four times at point-blank range from his revolver and a rifle taken from one of the guards. [. . .]*

Reports about the critical situation in prisons could no longer be ignored by the top leaders of the country. Especially sensitive was prisons' new status as centers for epidemics, most of all typhus. Therefore, on 11 March 1933, the SNK USSR adopted a resolution, approved by the Politburo, on "discharging" the prisoners.[13] The resolution stressed the transfer of inmates from prisons, jails, and detention centers to camps, new labor settlements, and colonies of the People's Commissariat of Justice and stipulated liberating a certain number of prisoners. These provisions could not be carried out, however, because the camps, too, were overcrowded and afflicted with hunger and epidemics.

The year 1933 witnessed an unprecedented increase in the camp population: almost 50 percent in the first quarter. On 1 January 1933 the camps held 334,000 prisoners; on 10 April, there were 456,000, as well as 41,000 en route.[14] According to the 20 April 1933 report from the head of the Gulag, Berman, to the deputy OGPU chairman, Yagoda, even if the "discharging" goals were met and 55,000 prisoners were liberated and amnestied, the increase in the camp population in May and June would be 255,000 people.[15] This meant that in the first half of 1933, the camps would have to take in more prisoners than in the previous three years. Camps were completely unprepared for prisoners on such a scale. Neither were OGPU labor settlements ready, because plans for their construction mostly remained on paper. The situation in the colonies of the People's Commissariat of Justice, most of which were located in the territories affected by famine, was so desperate that transferring inmates there from prisons and detention centers would only deepen the crisis.

The situation was rapidly deteriorating. By early May there were 777,000 prisoners in crowded prisons, colonies, police detention sta-

* V. N. Nekrasov was subsequently sentenced to ten years in a camp, I. U. Meshcheriakov to six years.

tions, and OGPU jails despite the previous discharges and the very high mortality due to hunger and disease.[16] A further increase of terror was technically impossible.

So the leadership took a rather radical step. On 8 May 1933 the Central Committee and the SNK USSR issued an instruction to party and government workers, OGPU organs, the courts, and the Procuracy forbidding the mass deportation of peasants and limiting the individual deportation of "counterrevolutionaries" to no more than 12,000 households for the entire country. The instruction also forbade unauthorized officials to conduct arrests and banned pretrial arrests for misdemeanors. It established 400,000 as an upper limit for the total number of inmates in the prisons of the People's Commissariat of Justice, OGPU, and Chief Administration of Police (excluding camps and colonies). The government ordered the substitution of imprisonment for one year of forced labor for those sentenced to less than three years, with the remaining two years as parole. The instruction reiterated that those sentenced for three to five years should be sent to labor settlements, and those sentenced to more than five years, dispatched to OGPU camps.[17] To conduct this operation, special commissions were created in all republics, territories, and provinces under the general oversight of the commissar of justice, N.V. Krylenko.

The main difference between the March resolutions and the 8 May instruction on discharging prisoners was that the latter hinted at slowing down the terror and liberating a large number of prisoners. Between 10 May and 30 June more than 363,000 prisoners were liberated, and between 10 May and 6 June, more than 52,000 were transferred to the camps and about 9,000 to labor settlements.[18] On 19 July, Krylenko reported to Stalin and Molotov that as of 10 July all prisons—those of the People's Commissariat of Justice, OGPU (excluding camps), and the Chief Administration of Police—held 397,284 people. Thus, the 8 May 1933 instruction accomplished almost exactly what it intended.[19]

Although the 8 May instruction did not fundamentally alter Stalin's punitive policy, it still signified a retreat from the program of creating a broad network of labor settlements. The mass deportation of peasants was discontinued, and the exile to labor settlements of those sentenced to short terms as well as the "city contingent" was minimized. The change can be explained, first of all, by the complete, early failure of the ambitious plans to organize labor settlements.

The first trainloads of exhausted, sick, poorly dressed, and filthy people started to arrive in the exile areas in April 1933. Those who were alive, barely alive, and dead were unloaded from the cars. Local authorities tried to get rid of these people and often sent them to remote areas, unsuitable for survival. The tragedy on Nazino Island, in the northern part of the Western Siberian territory, became an omen of the nature of exile.

In May 1933 more than 6,000 labor settlers, two trainloads, were brought to the island. These were "lumpen" elements rounded up during the purge of the major cities, mostly Moscow and Leningrad. Since the Nazino tragedy received broad publicity and became a subject of investigation by many commissions, we have access to important documents about what happened next. The most detailed description was made by V. A. Velichko, an instructor in the Narymsk regional party committee, in his letter to Stalin:

> The entire island was virgin land, without any buildings. People were unloaded just as they had been apprehended in the cities and at the train stations: in light clothes, without bedsheets, and often barefoot.
>
> There were no tools on the island, not a crumb of bread. All food had been consumed on the barges, and there was no supply of food nearby. All medical supplies provided for the trains had been confiscated in Tomsk. [. . .]
>
> On the second day after the arrival of the first train, 19 May, there was a snowstorm and strong winds, followed by frost. Hungry, exhausted people, without shelter, tools, and mostly without organized survival skills, found themselves in limbo. Frostbitten, they could only sit, lie, and sleep by the fire, wander around the island, and eat decayed branches, bark, and especially moss. It is hard to tell whether there was another option, for they received no food for three days. Fires spread out of control, and smoke overwhelmed people, who started to die. They were burned alive while asleep by the fire or died from exhaustion and cold, burns, and the surrounding dampness. [. . .]
>
> On the first day after the sun came out, the gravedigger team managed to bury only 295 bodies, having left the rest until the next day. The next day brought new deaths.
>
> After snow and frost came rains and cold winds, but the people still received no food. Not until the fourth or fifth day did they bring rye flour to the island, which they distributed among the settlers, giving them several hundred grams each.
>
> People who got their ration of flour rushed to the river and mixed it with water in hats, foot bindings, jackets, and trousers, after which they ate it. Many of them just ate the powdered flour and suffocated.

For their entire time on the island (ten to thirty days), labor settlers received flour but no dishes. The most resilient ones baked flat cakes by the fire. There was no hot water. Soon cases of cannibalism were registered, at first occasionally and then alarmingly often. At first cannibalism happened in remote corners of the island and then wherever there was an opportunity.

[. . .] Wardens on the island buried thousands of kilograms of flour, which had been stored in the open and rotted in the rain. Even the flour that was distributed did not get to everybody. It was handed over to foremen, i.e., diehard criminals. They claimed flour for their "teams" and hid it in the forest, leaving the teams without food. Inability or unwillingness to organize affairs became evident when they first brought flour to the island and decided to distribute it to the entire 5,000 people individually. This inevitably provoked a rush for flour, and sporadic shots were fired. However, more people died in the stampede, from being crushed in the mud, than from the gunshots.

Most likely, the wardens on the island as well as the military guards had a poor understanding of their tasks and obligations toward the people under their command and were confused by the catastrophe. Only this can explain the system of beating labor settlers with sticks and rifle butts and executing individuals. [. . .]

Such methods of administration and education from the very start contributed to the destruction of all human institutions on the island.

Although cannibalism became the most extreme indicator of degradation there, a more common sign was the creation of marauding gangs and mobs that actually ruled the island. Even doctors were afraid to leave their tents. Gangs had already terrorized people on the barges, appropriating bread and clothes while beating and killing people. Once on the island, they opened a real manhunt for those who had money or gold teeth. Their owners quickly disappeared, and the gravediggers were burying people with hacked-up mouths. [. . .][20]

After the adoption of the 8 May 1933 instruction, OGPU leaders at first tried to achieve just a moderate decrease in the initial million-person quota for the new labor settlements. On 15 May, Yagoda requested resources for 746,000 labor settlers.[21] In June, after a period of accommodation, the quota was set at 550,000.[22]

As the size of the labor contingent decreased, Moscow had to consider changing its composition. The history of the first labor settlements convinced even OGPU leaders that the city lumpen elements were not capable of agricultural work. Overwhelmed with complaints from below, the Gulag leadership reported to Yagoda.

· 17 ·

Report from the assistant to the head of the GULAG of the OGPU,
I. I. Pliner, to OGPU Deputy Chairman Yagoda
28 July 1933[23]

To the OGPU deputy chairman, Comrade Yagoda.

Report.

Most of the lumpen elements sent to OGPU labor settlements from Moscow and Leningrad are repeat criminals, with multiple arrests and convictions.

This contingent, as experience at both the transfer stations and new settlements has shown, cannot be utilized under normal conditions at the labor settlements. They cannot be educated by work, and they demoralize the rest of the prisoners.

According to Comrade Alekseev, the Western Siberian territory PP [plenipotentiary representative of the] OGPU, several attempts to escape and attack the guards took place on the way to the contingent's destination. Upon arrival, they attempted an attack on the guards to steal the prepared daily food ration. There are multiple cases of robbery of the weak by the strong.

In connection to the above, considering your instruction to send the aforementioned contingent to the camps, I request that you order the PP OGPU MO [plenipotentiary representative of OGPU for Moscow province] and LVO [Leningrad Military District] not to send contingents to labor settlements in the future but have the troika of the PP OGPU consider their cases and send them to the camps.

Assistant to the head of the Chief Administration of the OGPU Camps, Pliner.

28 July 1933.

On 7 August 1933, Yagoda instructed the OGPU plenipotentiary representatives for the Moscow and Leningrad regions, the main suppliers of such exiles, to discontinue sending individual criminals and "city lumpen elements" to the labor settlements and to have *troikas* of OGPU representatives sentence them to imprisonment in the camps (this instruction was often later ignored). On 21 August 1933 the SNK USSR issued new quantitative and qualitative quotas for labor exile. The resolution "On the organization of labor settlements" established that 550,000 prisoners were to be sent to the labor settlements of Western Siberia and Kazakhstan in 1933: in addition to 124,000 labor settlers already in place or en route, 48,000 kulaks were to be exiled with their families according to the 8 May instruction, as well as 378,000 of those sentenced to three to five years along with members of their families.[24] The "city lumpen elements" were not even mentioned as a target of exile.

Apparently, the Nazino tragedy completely discredited the labor exile plans in the eyes of the supreme leadership. In September 1933 the V. A. Velichko letter addressed to Stalin arrived in Moscow. In addition to describing terrible deaths of settlers on Nazino Island, the letter raised a broader question about the purge in the cities:

> The trouble is that our elements are occasionally among those sent to labor settlements, mistakenly exiled. Most of them died, being unable to accommodate to the conditions on the island and at the bases. Besides, these comrades were the main victims of arbitrariness, reprisals, and marauding by the criminals on the barges, on the island, and initially at the bases.
>
> It is hard to tell, how many, even WHO [died], because declared documents had been confiscated at the time of arrest, or by police organs at the detention centers, or on the train by criminals who used them to smoke. However, some of them brought their documents with them: party and party candidate cards, Komsomol [All-Union Leninist Youth League] cards, passports, certificates from the factories, factory passes, etc. [. . .]
>
> 1. Novozhilov, Vl., from Moscow. Kompressor works. Driver. Awarded bonuses three times. Wife and child in Moscow. After work, he was getting ready to go the cinema with his wife. While she was getting dressed, he stepped out to smoke a cigarette and was apprehended.
>
> 2. Guseva, an old woman. She lives in Murom. Her husband is an old communist, chief officer of the Murom railway station, who has been working there for twenty-three years. Her son works there as an apprentice engine driver. Guseva came to Moscow to buy a suit for her husband and some white bread. Her documents did not help her.
>
> 3. Zelenin, Grigory. He worked as an apprentice metal worker at the Borovsk weaving factory Krasny Oktiabr and was coming to a Moscow sanatorium for recuperation. His sanatorium authorization papers did not help: he was apprehended. [. . .][25]

Kaganovich, who conducted the work of the Politburo while Stalin was on vacation, ordered the Velichko letter sent to Politburo members. Since the letter was addressed to Stalin, Kaganovich would not have dared to do this without first getting his approval. Signatures on the letter show that, besides Kaganovich, it was also read by Molotov,

Kalinin, Kuibyshev, and Mikoyan. It is hard to tell whether this letter shocked the hardened members of the Soviet supreme leadership. Molotov dispassionately suggested that the Procuracy investigate the circumstances of the case. On 23 September 1933 the Politburo charged a member of the Central Control Commission, the deputy people's commissar of Workers' and Peasants' Inspection, Antipov, with reviewing the case.[26] On orders from Moscow, a special commission of the Western Siberian territorial party committee investigated the case and in general confirmed Velichko's report. As a result, in late 1933 several OGPU workers directly involved in the Nazino events were convicted or reprimanded.[27] As usual, the case ended with the isolation of convenient scapegoats.

According to Gulag statistics, the total number of new settlers in 1933 was 268,091. By 1 January 1934, however, fewer than half of them (116,653) remained in exile. The rest died, escaped, or were transferred to the camps. As a result, between 1 January 1933 and 1 January 1934 the total number of all labor settlers decreased from 1,142,084 to 1,072,546.[28]

Simultaneously, the camps grew much faster than planned, indeed, much faster than ever, despite the high mortality: from 334,300 to 510,307 prisoners between 1 January 1933 and 1 January 1934, excluding those in transit between camps (see Document 97). In spite of the projects occupying the minds of police leaders in 1933—labor exile, special settlements—the camps finally became the backbone of the Stalinist punitive system.

A Deadly Year

Annual records of the camp population on 1 January registered the tragic results of moving the camp population. These cold and impartial figures reflected the numerous and disastrous processes under way in the camps. During the 1932–33 crisis, most of those listed as "departed" actually died of disease and hunger. The number of "incoming" victims of terror easily compensated for the losses.

Despite the increased mortality in late 1932, the OGPU leaders did not consider the situation to be too serious. The Gulag memorandum on the preliminary results of economic activities in 1932, written in early 1933, noted that food supplies "were almost satisfactory." This conclusion was based on the fact that food supplies still remained in 1933 and that a decision had been taken to provide those supplies in

January according to the norms.[29] Besides, the camps apparently had avoided mass epidemics in 1932.

However, the situation was changing rapidly. The first three months of 1933 saw the arrival of 142,000 new prisoners. Most of them were extremely worn down by hunger or had typhoid.[30] It was impossible to supply those transported with food and likewise impossible to comply with orders to avoid sending prisoners infected with typhoid to the camps (to prevent epidemics there). The trains, especially those from the disaster-stricken regions, were indeed death ridden.

· 18 ·

Report from the head of the GULAG of the OGPU, M. D. Berman, to OGPU Deputy Chairman Yagoda on the condition of trains sent to the camps and labor settlements*
8 May 1933[31]

To Deputy OGPU Chairman Comrade Yagoda.

Despite your repeated orders to the PP OGPU of the Northern Caucasus territory about the organization of trains to be sent to the OGPU camps and labor settlements, the condition of the arriving trains is very troubling. Every train arriving from the Northern Caucasus has remarkably high mortality and disease rates, mostly from typhoid and acute stomach diseases.

According to the head of the OGPU Siblag, 341 of the 10,185 labor settlers arriving in Novosibirsk from the Northern Caucasus in trains no. 24, 25, 26, 27, 28, and 29 (3.3 percent) died en route, many from exhaustion. Such high mortality can be explained by:

1. Criminal negligence in selecting the labor settlers, resulting in inclusion of sick and old people unable to survive a long trip.

2. Failure to comply with the directives from higher organs to provide labor settlers with two-months' worth of food. In the aforementioned trains, labor settlers had no food supplies of their own and were provided with only 200–400 grams of bad-quality bread.

3. Failure to provide hot food on the trains, and hot water was provided irregularly. Drinking running water caused mass diseases.

A similar situation exists among camp prisoners sent from the Northern

---

* In the margins, Yagoda wrote: "To Comrade Yevdokimov. I will be forced to stop receiving [trainloads] if you do not urgently improve the situation with transportation. G.Y. 8 May [19]33."

Caucasus. Thus, according to the deputy PP OGPU of the Western Siberian territory, Comrade Shanin, of the 1,400 people arriving to Siblag
OGPU from Bataisk, seven died, nineteen contracted typhoid, and ten
more were removed from the train under suspicion of having typhoid. In
Novosibirsk, they removed two more dead from this train, as well as ten
infected with typhoid and twenty-five typhoid suspects. The train was sent
from Bataisk despite the protest of the train commander, Comrade Shu-
mov, against loading it with suspected typhoid contingents.

Reported for your consideration.

Head of the Chief Administration of the OGPU Camps, Berman.

As the half-alive prisoners were arriving in the Gulag, food rations
there were sharply cut, as was the case elsewhere in the country.

· 19 ·

Memorandum by OGPU Deputy Chairman Yagoda on supplying the camps
31 December 1933[32]

To the Secretary of the VKP(b) Central Committee, Comrade Stalin.

To the Chairman of the Council of People's Commissars of the USSR,
Comrade Molotov.

This year the work of the OGPU corrective labor camps has been proceeding under extremely unfavorable conditions. With the main construction sites being moved to the Far Eastern territory, the situation is becoming even more complicated, for the bulk of the work will be conducted in
the harsh zones of marshes and permafrost. To accomplish the increased
tasks in time, it is necessary to raise the productivity of labor and minimize
the percentage of the sick and the weak in the labor force. Thus, supplying
the prisoners with food, clothes, and footwear becomes extremely important. However, compared with 1932, this year supplies to the camps have
diminished. The existing food rations are significantly less than in 1932.
The strict allowances for material supplies, established by the Committee
of Merchandise Funds, are not observed. The established allowances for
material supplies are greatly reduced. Camp requisition lists, which are
compiled according to existing allowances, are drastically cut.

As a result, the camps did not receive 4 million meters of cotton cloth in
1933, or 300,000 rubles' worth of footwear. Despite the growing camp
contingent, the Committee of Merchandise Funds approved a supply of
goods for the first quarter [of 1934] that is significantly less than that for
the first quarter of 1933. These supplies do not satisfy even minimal camp
demands. For example, the approved 80,000 pairs of shoes is not suffi-

cient even for the contingent of the Far East. This situation can lead to exhaustion and disease in the camps and prevents the utilization of the entire workforce, because part of it inevitably is left without clothes.

Those at the OGPU camps, while working to fulfill construction tasks, persistently labor to create their own food base. Owing to the intensive development of agriculture—livestock husbandry foremost—the camps have quickly (in one–one and one-half years) resolved the meat problem. They are now completely independent of state meat supplies. This year the products of the fishing enterprises begun in 1932–33 fully satisfied the demands of camp contingents. The camps exchange high-quality fish for cheaper kinds from the state to be used for mass consumption. The vegetables grown in the camps cover 70 percent of their demands, which has significantly decreased the state supply of potatoes and vegetables.

For the first time, the camps of Central Asia started producing their own cotton, which will give the state 9 million meters of cloth in 1933. The cotton production in 1934 is projected at 15 million meters, while the camps' demand is 25 million meters. The camps give all cotton wool to the state.

The camps produce a large number of bast shoes for prisoners not employed in earth moving.

Thus, everything possible is being done to make the camps self-sufficient.

I request the following:

1. Review the existing food supply allowances for prisoners and establish the following allowances per person per month (in kilograms):

	Requested Allowances	Current Allowances	Allowances in 1932
Flour	21.0	17.16	23.5
Groats	3.0	2.25	5.75
Pasta	0.5	0.4	0.5
Vegetable oil	0.6	0.3	1
Animal fats	0.1	—	0.15
Sugar	0.7	0.6	0.96
Confectionery	0.5	0.5	0.5
Canned foods, various	¾ can	¼ can	2 cans

The requested allowances are still significantly less than those in 1932.

2. Provide the 4 million meters of cloth and 300,000 rubles' worth of footwear that were not delivered as approved for 1933.

3. Establish the central fund to supply materials for 550,000 prisoners in 1934, according to the 3 February resolution by the Committee of Merchandise Funds.

4. Reconsider the decision by the Committee of Merchandise Funds to supply only 30 percent of the annual supply of cotton cloth and footwear to the camps in the first quarter of 1934.[33]

Deputy OGPU Chairman Yagoda.

As this document shows, according to the 1933 allowances, prisoners received a limited amount of bread and groats from the state. Other products were not supplied, or else their supply was merely symbolic. Food funds were not provided in full, and whatever was supplied was often pilfered. In addition, since the Gulag had no special funds for hired workers, who received supplementary rations, hired workers were supplied at the expense of the prisoners, and they received the scarcest and most desirable products: sugar, confections, canned foods, and vegetable oil. In 1933 there were 45,000 hired workers with families.[34]

Obviously, prisoners could not survive on state supplies. Camps were supported partly by the internal redistribution of foodstuffs, such as meat and fish, by the Gulag itself. In 1933, in addition, the Gulag received funds planned for labor settlements, which did not take off on the projected scale.[35] The most important factor, however, was the ability of the camp administration to organize supplies. Prisoners had the best chance of survival if they were in the camps whose wardens did not plunder too much and if they managed to set up vegetable gardens or livestock farms.

The following selection of Gulag instructions and circular letters reveals to some extent the scale of the famine and the measures made by the Gulag managers to prevent mass deaths of prisoners.

· 20 ·

Circular letter no. 661437 from the GULAG of the OGPU
14 April 1933[36]

Top secret.

To all camps.

Considering the extreme emaciation of the contingents arriving at the camps from the prisons and their resulting inability to work, the GULAG suggests:

1. During the medical examination of the arriving groups, establish, in addition to the existing categories, the category of "the weak," to include

able-bodied prisoners who are unable to work immediately upon arrival owing to emaciation.

2. Prisoners in this group should not be employed in production for fourteen days, but be used for jobs around the camp. They should receive workers' food rations. Note: the aforementioned grace period should not be applied mechanically and universally. After the fourteen days, prisoners in this group should be regularly employed along with the others, but only have to accomplish 60 percent of the daily task to receive full worker's rations. After that period, i.e., fourteen days, this group should be expected to accomplish 80 percent of the daily task for thirty days to receive full worker's rations.

This measure reflects the need to fully and rationally utilize the camp workforce and requires constant oversight by the wardens and department, camp division, and medical center heads to prevent abuses. At the same time, one should avoid mechanical application of the above terms: they represent the maximum limits, not the minimum requirements. You should report to the GULAG every fourteen days on the results of these measures.

I warn you that abuses are possible when quite healthy people are treated as weak or when there is a failure to extend benefits for the time necessary owing to the state of their health. Supply masters and the heads of medical centers and camp divisions will be held accountable for such abuses.

Head of the Chief Administration of the OGPU Camps, Berman.

· 21 ·

Order no. 76 by the GULAG of the OGPU,
"On granting days off to prisoners"
9 June 1933[37]

Secret.

Despite the inadequate sanitary conditions in the camps, which are related to the substandard physical condition of the prisoners and the unsatisfactory condition of new arrivals, as well as the deteriorated living conditions of the prisoners (housing and food), certain camps have not taken necessary measures even to secure adequate rest for the prisoners.

The most intolerable examples are the conduct of work on the weekends disguised as subbotniks [voluntary unpaid work] and various kinds of shock-work initiatives. Such additional tasks, besides making people emaciated, are in the end harmful to production in general because they decrease the productivity of labor.

It is therefore ordered:

1. To observe in all camps a seven-day week with days off. It is permissible to use a seven-day week with no days off on some tasks, but only with permission from the camp administration and with an obligatory twenty-four-hour rest period for each prisoner.

2. To establish the length of the workday for each type of task and to punish those responsible for increasing it illegally.

3. To discontinue the excessive movement of prisoners during lunch breaks by organizing the delivery of hot food to the place of work.

4. By all means possible, to shorten the time to prepare for work and distribute tasks and to provide more time for sleep by improving the system of tool distribution, roll calls, etc., and by making supervisors and administrators responsible for doing so.

5. To eliminate lines during the distribution of food.

6. To grant longer rest time to the weak workers, who have reduced daily work tasks.

Head of the Chief Administration of the OGPU Camps, Berman.

All these measures had little effect, however. The camps lacked sufficient resources and, in any case, despite the famine and the emaciation of prisoners, had to fulfill production plans. For the same reasons, demands by Moscow leaders were contradictory. While demanding the creation of favorable conditions for weak prisoners, they sternly reminded underlings not to take such measures too literally and not to employ them too widely.

For example, not long after issuing a circular letter to improve the health of weak prisoners (Document 20), on 25 May 1933, the head of the Gulag, Berman, wrote a letter "on the frequent cases of fake illness among prisoners to obtain temporary excuses from work or early release from the camps as invalids." The letter stated: "In addition to the usual fake illnesses caused by self-mutilation, self-induced rectum prolapse, and artificial phlegmone, prisoners have lately been affected en masse by stomach disorders and even edemas caused by eating salt or dry coffee and drinking untreated water. There is reason to believe that the cases of fatal poisoning with wild plants in Dmitlag and Balakhna were caused not so much by the desire to add to the ration as by the perceived possibility of getting sick. Attempts to eat refuse from the garbage cans should be treated with the same suspicion."[38] Although such cases were a direct result of severe famine in the camps, demands to step up the struggle against malingerers allowed camp administrators broad discretion in labeling any prisoner dying of hunger or disease as a "simulator."

The early release from the camps of disabled and chronically ill prisoners was an easier and more realistic method than improving living conditions. According to Yagoda's report to Stalin, on 10 April 1933 there were 38,350 sick prisoners in the camps (9.6 percent of the total number) and 12,700 disabled prisoners (3.2 percent), as well as 75,000 emaciated prisoners. Yagoda warned that these numbers would grow.[39] To get rid of the disabled and gravely ill prisoners, the OGPU leaders decided to downsize the camps. Transcripts from sessions of the mobile OGPU troika for the Moscow region, which conducted releases of invalids in the Dmitrovsky camp in April–May 1933, illustrate this process. The majority of those released were people under fifty who lost their health in the camps. For example, F. K. Kubasov, a forty-seven-year-old priest from the Northern territory, convicted of anti-Soviet agitation and propaganda, worked in the camp as a laborer until he was released for "early decrepitude. Invalid." S. S. Koltunov, a fifty-five-year-old peasant from the Northern Caucasus, convicted under the same article, worked as an unskilled laborer on the construction of the Moscow–Volga canal. He was released for "old age decrepitude and acute edema of the lower extremities. Burden to the camp."[40] Altogether, the OGPU leaders planned to release 15,000 disabled and chronically ill inmates in May–June 1933, and 17,000 more in July–September.[41]

Neither approach—improving conditions or releasing incapacitated workers—nor the coming of summer changed the situation in the camps for the better. In some respects, the crisis even sharpened, as is evident from another Gulag circular letter.

· 22 ·

Circular letter no. 669600 from the GULAG of the OGPU
31 August 1933[42]

Top secret.

Despite the downsizing of the camps with the release of unemployable elements (the disabled, the chronically ill, etc.), there are many weak and emaciated prisoners still in the camps. Moreover, there has been a tendency of late toward an increase in the number of sick people, disabled people, and deaths. These occurrences result from an inadmissible attitude of the camp administration toward rationally utilizing the workforce by categorizing prisoners and properly disbursing food rations.

It often happens in the camps that a weak, emaciated prisoner is given a regular work task. By systematically failing to do his job, he receives a smaller ration of food, and, therefore, instead of recuperating, he becomes still weaker. Thus, the OGPU camps create a certain contingent prone to frequent disease.

Considering such a situation intolerable, and in view of improving radically the health of weak and exhausted prisoners and raising the productivity of labor, the Chief Administration of the OGPU Camps suggests that you carry out the following measures:

1. Review the existing practice of allocating the workforce to different jobs so that the healthy workforce is used at heavy assignments, and the weak workforce employed at easy tasks, corresponding to the abilities of each prisoner. Certain individuals, depending on their physical condition, may be assigned reduced tasks for a set period of time. It is important, however, to be wary of simulators and loafers of any sort who avoid work by pretending to be sick.

2. Immediately identify all exhausted prisoners, especially those with edema, and excuse them from work by recommendation of the medical commission for up to fourteen days, depending on their physical condition. Move them to separate barracks and increase their food rations to match the workers' rations.

3. Base the food rationing of these groups on medical necessity, paying attention to the composition of products and the frequency of food service during the day, avoiding long gaps. Each barrack for the emaciated should be put under medical supervision, with an accounting of the condition of each prisoner and his recovery for work.

4. As the aforementioned groups are transferred back to work, they should not be given heavy tasks, but progressively reintegrated into the production process.

5. Immediately after receiving these directives, call a meeting of medical workers and suppliers and establish a plan to implement the outlined measures and personally secure their realization.

Deputy head of the GULAG of the OGPU, Firin.

Since the situation did not improve, the head of the Gulag, Berman, sent out a new circular letter on 5 November 1933: "Some corrective labor camps report that the established [. . .] fourteen-day resting period for those exhausted is insufficient for many of them to recover. Therefore, I permit a prolongation of this period, but only on a case-by-case basis as decided by medical commissions. The number of prisoners granted an extended resting period should not exceed 10 percent of the total number of those assigned to the weak teams. The rest period can be extended by no more than seven–fourteen days."[43]

All these instructions by Gulag leaders show that the camps had a hard time recovering from the famine. The death rate significantly increased in early 1933 and remained high until the end of the year, as shown in the table below, compiled from Gulag sanitary department data. The death toll in the camps did not surpass the 1933 level again until the outbreak of war in 1941 (see Chapter 7). And in fact these figures are too low. First, the sanitary department did not account for Sevvostlag, which held 20,500 prisoners as of 20 August 1933 and about 30,000 as of 1 January 1934.[44] Considering the average death rate (15 percent) and the average number of prisoners, about 3,000 died there. Second, the sanitary department numbers were incomplete, as shown in Chapter 7, excluding as they did those killed by camp gangsters, shot while attempting to escape, and so forth.

Third, the reports did not include deaths en route. Terrible sanitary conditions on the trains transporting sick and hungry prisoners resulted in high mortality (see Documents 18, 20). An even greater number of prisoners were removed from trains along the way. Many of those must have died. As one of the memorandums of the Central Control Commission and the People's Commissariat for the Workers' and Peasants' Inspection (TsKK-NK RKI) stated: "Transporting masses of

The Number of Prisoners Who Died in the Camps

	1932	1933
January	653	3,319
February	569	5,273
March	678	7,251
April	631	7,737
May	592	8,915
June	779	6,590
July	1,137	4,778
August	1,599	5,836
September	1,700	5,334
October	1,540	4,359
November	1,471	4,333
December	1,848	3,562
Total	13,197	67,297
Average annual number of prisoners	275,861	440,008
Percentage of the average annual number of prisoners who died	4.8	15.2

Source: Compiled from materials of the Gulag sanitary department (GARF, f. R-9414, op. 1, d. 2740, 1. 53).

detainees in the winter and summer of 1933 brought about significant losses of people (1,099 sick and emaciated people were removed from the trains before 1 May 1933, and 246 died en route)." The same memorandum gave the increased number of transported prisoners: 797,000 in the first half of 1933 as opposed to 488,000 in the first half of 1932. Almost half of them (366,500) were sent to the camps and OGPU exile, each spending, on the average, ten days en route.[45]

Finally, early release for disabled and chronically ill prisoners offered an easy opportunity to tweak the figures. It is quite possible that many of the released prisoners, in the tens of thousands, never made it to their destinations. Since they did not die in the camps, they did not affect Gulag statistics. Also, Gulag practice could have allowed the inclusion of those already dead among the number of those being released. There may have been other, undiscovered ways of falsifying death statistics. For all these reasons, the official number of 67,297 deaths should be significantly increased.

The situation in the colonies and prisons of the People's Commissariat of Justice was no better. According to the commissar himself, N.V. Krylenko, in the spring of 1933 the prisoners often received "semi-famine or even famine rations"—200–300 grams of bread per day.[46] The exiles who completely depended on state supplies suffered the most, for this supply was cut to a minimum that spring. A letter from the procurator of the Ustkulomsky region, in Komi autonomous province, sent to Moscow in response to an inquiry following up on a complaint from prisoners reveals the situation there.[47]

· 23 ·

Report by the procurator of the Ustkulomsky region,
Komi autonomous province
22 May 1933[48]

To the Secretariat of the President of the VTsIK [All-Russian Central Executive Committee].

I am responding to the complaint of the administrative exiles in Ust-neme village, Ustkulomsky region. I have been receiving similar complaints from almost every village soviet of the region. By the fall of 1933 the number of administrative exiles in the region had reached 3,000. Most of them were elderly people released from the camps. Since June, local authorities have taken them off the supply list several times. The bread ration has been reduced many times. Between November and March the reduction was 10–15 percent for administrative exiles, and after March it reached 50 percent. The allowance is only 3.8 kilograms of flour per month. The region always consumes bread brought in from other locales. Since the population does not have a bread surplus, exiles cannot buy bread to supplement their ration.

After the end of the navigation season, parcels are not delivered, and as a result, each village soviet has been reporting deaths from hunger. For example, in the village of Kerchema, population 480, the death rate has been as follows: October—6, November—10, December—21, January—22, February—34, until 12 March—15. According to the regional OGPU, 480 people have died in four months in 1933.

When traveling, I often witnessed administrative exiles haunting the villages like shadows in search of a piece of bread or refuse. They eat carrion, slaughter dogs and cats. The villagers keep their houses locked. Those who get a chance to enter a house drop on their knees in front of the owner and, with tears, beg for a piece of bread.

I witnessed several deaths on the roads between villages, in the bathhouses, and in the barns. I myself saw hungry, agonized people crawling on the sidewalk. They were picked up by the police and died several hours later. In late April an investigator and I passed by a barn and found a dead body. When we sent for a policeman and a medic to pick it up, they discovered another body inside the barn. Both died of hunger, with no violence involved.

Regional and provincial authorities have been duly informed of these facts. I raised the issue with local leaders but always received one and the same answer: "We barely have enough for workers and employees." I sent an official report to the provincial procurator, but without result. As far as I know, the provincial procuracy has forwarded the report to the territorial authorities.

This situation has led to a sharp increase in thefts from individuals and from organizations. The region faces a real danger from epidemics of spotted fever, typhoid, and other infectious diseases.

Please take appropriate measures.

Regional procurator, Vtrenev.

· 24 ·

Report on special settlers in the lumber industry in connection
with the reduction of rations
14 June 1933[49]

With the transfer of special settlers to the Narkomles [People's Commissariat of Forestry] USSR to be used in the lumber industry, i.e., since

August 1931, the government has established supply minimums for dependent special settlers in lumbering as follows: 9 kilograms of flour, 9 kilograms of groats, 1.5 kilograms of fish, and 0.9 kilograms of sugar per month. On 1 January 1933, Soiuznarkomsnab [People's Commissariat for Supplies] reduced those allowances to 5 kilograms of flour, 0.5 kilograms of groats, 0.8 kilograms of fish, and 0.4 kilograms of sugar.

As a result, the situation of special settlers in the lumber industry, especially in the Urals province and in the Northern territory, has sharply deteriorated:

1. Everywhere in the timber enterprises of the Northern territory and the Urals there are cases of people consuming various inedible surrogates, as well as dead cats, dead dogs, and carcasses of fallen infected animals. This is particularly frequent in the Cherdynsky, Kosinsky, Chusovskoi, and Bereznikovsky timber enterprises.

2. Hunger has caused a sharp increase in disease and death rates among special settlers. In Cherdynsky region up to 50 percent of settlers have fallen ill. Since the beginning of 1933, 1,422 people have contracted spotted fever, 717 have typhoid, and 1,496 suffer from scurvy.

3. Hunger has led to several suicides and an increase in the crime rate and prompted break-ins of kiosks (Gainsky, Cherdynsky, and Krasnovishersky timber enterprises). Besides that, hungry special settlers steal bread and livestock from the local population, especially collective farmers.

4. Inadequacy of supplies has led to a sharp decrease in the productivity of labor. In some timber enterprises the production norms have fallen 25 percent. Exhausted special settlers are unable to fulfill their tasks, get less food as a result, and eventually become unemployable.

There are cases of death in the workplace, as well as upon return from work. In some timber enterprises special settlers are exhausted to the point of not being able to walk to the special settlement after work and have to be transported on carts (the Urals).

5. In some timber enterprises, special settlers who fall ill at work or are excused from work owing to illness are absolutely denied their rations.

6. The arrears in salary payments, which can be up to three–four months in some places, has significantly affected special settlers, who are unable to purchase their rations. In the Urals, on 1 April 1933, wage arrears amounted to 7,136,000 rubles.

7. In this difficult situation, the huge administrative apparatus of the timber industry acquires special importance. It legally steals up to one-fourth of the products intended for woodcutters and squanders a large amount. As a result, only leftover products are supplied to special settlers.

Berman.*

* Initially, the report was prepared for signature by the assistant head of the Gulag, Pliner.

Altogether 151,601 people died in special exile in 1933, according to internal reports. (For comparison, 89,754 people died in 1932.) Considering that, on the average, there were 1 million special settlers, the death rate among them was comparable to the one among camp prisoners—about 15 percent. One has to be cautious, though.

First, labor exile statistics do not include those who died en route. Second, there is evidence that local OGPU leaders attempted to diminish the number of special settler deaths in their reports. For example, managers of the Western Siberian territorial department of labor settlements reported the death of 1,403 "new contingent" labor settlers as of 1 September 1933. However, a commission inspecting one of the regions of Western Siberia in October 1933 found that out of 10,000 labor settlers brought there in 1933, more than 3,000 had died (unconfirmed). (This region drew the authorities' attention by its high death rate in the first place.) V. P. Danilov and S. A. Krasilnikov believe that this discrepancy was caused by attempts to conceal the high death rate by reporting those dead as "escaped."[50] Gulag accounts register 215,856 escapes in 1933.[51]

Gulag statistics registered the death rate among the special settlers of 1933 as significantly higher than the death rate among earlier settlers. On 1 January 1934 the number of people exiled since 1929–32 totaled 955,893; the number exiled in 1933 totaled 116,653. In 1933 there were 129,800 deaths in the first group and 21,801 deaths in the second.[52]

The high death rate was characteristic of those in special exile and can easily be explained. As a rule, new exiles arrived in undeveloped lands, and it took time and huge sacrifices to create conditions for survival: building houses, establishing households, etc. State organs that were supposed to provide the exiles with everything necessary did not do it well enough. Resources were constantly short of supply. The traditional red tape and numerous abuses reduced state support. And in 1933 famine exacerbated the tragedy of the new settlers. They did not receive even those meager means that their "luckier" predecessors arriving in "better years" could count on.

The special settlers of the famine period differed from the settlers of the first wave in another important way. The first group was composed of peasants, experienced in rural life and labor, who came from the relatively well-off countryside and arrived with some food supplies and other resources. The second group was mainly composed of city dwellers, already emaciated from the train ride and unprepared for the hard labor of exile, and criminals, with their specific "skills." Even the kulaks exiled in 1933 differed from their counterparts in the first wave: they were hungry, emaciated, and completely pauperized. These victims of terror could rely only on their jailer, the state.

Prisoners in camps and colonies, as well as exiled kulaks and labor settlers, were among those who suffered most during the terrible famine that peaked in the winter and spring of 1932–33—mainly in the Ukraine, though with repercussions for the entire country. Besides taking the lives of hundreds of thousands of prisoners and labor exiles the famine undermined plans for a huge expansion of the Gulag, conceived in late 1932–early 1933. The Soviet leaders figured out that repression had a limit, beyond which the Gulag would cease to be a means of isolation and exploitation and become instead a means of extermination.

CHAPTER 3

Stabilization of the System

The gradual eradication of famine and the relative improvement of social and political circumstances in late 1933–34 affected even the Gulag. Increased state supplies and in-house agricultural production helped to overcome hunger and mass deaths in the camps. Between 1934 and the autumn of 1936 the Stalinist repressive system and the Gulag stabilized to some degree. Despite surges in terror, especially after Kirov's murder, repression did not reach the scale of the brutally repressive dekulakization nor the subsequent Great Terror. Attention to camp economic functions, as well as certain political concessions to the special settlers of the first wave (mainly youths), demonstrated the potential for "normal" Gulag development, without the excesses of state terror.

Kirov's Murder and the Creation of the NKVD

Until 1933, OGPU leaders had chiefly been preoccupied with mass deportations, the organization of labor settlements, and the prevention of a total loss of camp "contingents." After 1933 they were increasingly involved in solving numerous economic problems. To the existing projects—the Moscow–Volga canal, the Baikal–Amur railroad, gold mining on the Kolyma, and coal and oil work in Ukhta and Pechora—were added new tasks.

In late 1933 the OGPU took over construction of the Tuloma River (Murmansk) hydroelectric power station,[1] the organization of the White Sea–Baltic Sea industrial complex (a network of industrial and agricultural enterprises around the White Sea–Baltic Sea canal),[2] and construction of the Khabarovsk–Komsomolsk highway, identified in the SNK resolution of 10 September 1933 as a goal of "special state importance."[3] A SNK resolution of 27 March 1934 ordered the OGPU to construct a second line of the Karymskaya–Bochkarevo railway in Khabarovsk territory. This task was urgent (to be completed within the year) and rather expensive (334.5 million rubles were assigned to the OGPU for the project). To accomplish the construction of the second line, the OGPU was allowed to transfer prisoners from any other site, unless such inmates were bound by special government decree.[4] The OGPU was not content with this resolution, however. New economic tasks required an ever-growing supply of convict labor.

The only source of additional workers for the camps was the prisons and colonies of the People's Commissariat of Justice, especially the People's Commissariat of Justice of the Russian Federation. Citing the insufficient workforce, G. Yagoda requested that all inmates of the commissariat prisons sentenced to two and more years be transferred to the camps. This suggestion was naturally opposed by the people's commissar of justice of the RSFSR, N. V. Krylenko, along with the procurator of the USSR, I. A. Akulov. Their arguments were persuasive: the transfer of two-year convicts would leave the commissariat with underage criminals and old and disabled prisoners, none of them able to work or support themselves and their jailers. Yagoda had to agree. In early April 1934, Yagoda, Krylenko, and Akulov held a meeting and decided to transfer to the OGPU all inmates of the prisons and colonies, as well as organize special colonies for disabled, old, and sick prisoners. Under the agreement, the People's Commissariat of Justice retained control over those arrested whose cases were still under investigation and review and those sentenced to involuntary labor for up to one year.[5]

Having conceded on the key issue, Yagoda insisted on the immediate implementation of the agreed-on measures by issuing a special government resolution. Akulov again objected, insisting that this issue be tied to the reorganization of the OGPU into the People's Commissariat of Internal Affairs (NKVD) of the USSR, well under way at that time.[6] Facing delays in the reorganization, Yagoda undertook new attacks. In a 4 June 1934 letter to the Sovnarkom, he wrote: "The OGPU camps are experiencing a colossal shortfall of laborers in all projects under their supervision. At the Moscow–Volga canal and the second line of the Trans-Baikal and Ussuriisk railroads alone, the shortage amounts to more than 140,000 people. The transfer of short-term prisoners to the OGPU camps would partly alleviate this gap. I am therefore asking for a prompt review of this question."[7]

Yagoda's pleas were not satisfied. Akulov's point of view prevailed. Nevertheless, discussions about the "ownership" of convicts affected the reorganization of the punitive organs. The NKVD USSR, created in July 1934 and headed by Yagoda,[8] now controlled the prisons of the republican People's Commissariats of Justice, in addition to the OGPU corrective labor camps and labor settlements. The largest of them, the one in the RSFSR, included 548 penitentiaries (259 jails, 90 factory colonies, 89 rural colonies, 23 installations for underage criminals, and 79 general work colonies, which leased out prisoners to various organizations). As of 1 December 1934 these installations contained 212,382 prisoners altogether (140,950 convicted prisoners, with the remainder still under investigation or with their cases under review). About 144,207 prisoners were employed (half of them at the enterprises in the colonies and the other half leased out to other organizations). From the People's Commissariat of Justice the NKVD inherited 781 industrial enterprises, the majority of which were small cottage industries with minimal equipment and, on average, thirty workers. Only a few of them were real plants or factories. These small shops used local materials to produce wooden merchandise, clothes, footwear, and everything else. For the most part, the shops were located in places poorly suited for production, such as outhouses and warehouses. The agricultural enterprises of the People's Commissariat of Justice included 90 state farm colonies and 258 small farms and vegetable gardens, which partly fulfilled the need for food in the colonies and jails.[9]

Obviously, the NKVD did not pay the bulk of its attention to small shops. Former commissariat enterprises were perceived as a source of additional workers for more important projects, as listed in a Gulag memorandum.[10]

· 25 ·

Report on the employment of contingents from NKVD corrective
labor camps as of 11 January 1935
23 January 1935

Top secret.

1. Construction of second lines of the Trans-Baikal and Ussuriisk railroads and the Baikal–Amur railroad—153,547 people.

2. Construction of the Moscow–Volga canal—192,649 people.

3. White Sea–Baltic Sea industrial complex—66, 444 people.

4. Ukhta-Pechora trust works (coal, oil, asphaltite, radium, etc.)—20,656 people.

5. Supplier of firewood for Leningrad (Svirlag)—40,032 people.

6. Supplier of firewood for Moscow (Temlag)—33,048 people.

7. Far Eastern NKVD camp (Volochaevka–Komsomolsk railroad; coal mining at the Artem and Raichikha mines; construction of the Sedansk water supply system; construction of the Benzostroi oil depositories; construction work at Dalpromstroi, the Reserves Committee, and Aviation Construction no. 126; the fishing industry)—60,417 people.

8. The NKVD Siberian camp (Mount Shorskaya railway; coal mining at Kuznetsk coal basin; construction of the Chuisky and Usinovsky roads; leasing out workers to the Kuznetsk steel complex, Novosibirsk Timber Trust, etc.; camp pig-breeding farms)—61,251 people.

9. Central Asian NKVD camp (leasing out workers for construction of the textile factory, to Chirschikstroi, to Shakhtrudstroi, for the Khazarbakh canal construction, to Chuisk Novlubtrest, to the Pakhta-Aral state farm, and to camp cotton farms)—26,829 people.

10. Karaganda NKVD camp (state farms for raising cattle, camp meat supply)—25,109 people.

11. Prorvinsk NKVD camp (fishing industry)—10,583 people.

12. Sarovsky NKVD camp (lumbering and woodcutting)—3,337 people.

13. Vaigach (zinc, lead, fluorspar)—1,209 people.

14. Sevvostlag (Dalstroi trust: Kolyma works)—36,010 people.

15. Akhunsky camp (road construction)—722 people.

Total—731,843 people.

En route—9,756 people.

Grand total—741,599 people.

Of these, more than 90,000 people cannot be employed because of illness. Nonetheless, they cannot be released from the camps for reasons of state security.

Head of the GULAG of the NKVD, Berman.

23 January 1935.

Besides concentrating all prisoners under one jurisdiction, the creation of the NKVD was accompanied by a reform of the Soviet justice system. Most important, the NKVD lost some of its judiciary functions. The powers of the OGPU judiciary collegium were curtailed, and those of the Special Council of the People's Commissariat of Internal Affairs were significantly reduced. Cases investigated by the People's Commissariat of Internal Affairs and its judiciary organs were now sent upon completion of the investigation to "appropriate judiciary organs for conviction according to the law." Cases of state crimes investigated by the NKVD were now, after the investigation, adjudicated by special collegiums of the Supreme Court of the USSR and of union republics, or by territorial or provincial courts. A rather complicated arrangement was established whereby central organs had to approve death sentences.[11]

Thus, the 1934 reorganization of the judiciary system limited the activities of various nonjudicial extraordinary organs. Strengthening the standard judicial process was theoretically justified by the need to use the foremost achievements of bourgeois jurisprudence in the socialist legal system, as well as by the inevitable survival of some elements of bourgeois jurisprudence under socialism.[12]

It is hard to tell how far the Stalinist leadership was willing to go with these reforms. Available documents form a contradictory picture. On the one hand, decisions were constantly contravened, and the Politburo often initiated extrajudicial repressive actions. On the other hand, Stalin supported a campaign for "complying with revolutionary law" in NKVD organs.[13]

The situation changed drastically on 1 December 1934 with the assassination of Sergei M. Kirov, secretary of the Leningrad VKP(b) provincial committee, Politburo member, and one of Stalin's closest allies. Hours after the news of Kirov's death, Stalin personally drafted the TsIK USSR resolution that came to be known as the Law of 1 December. The Politburo formally approved the extraordinary law on 3 December.[14] It instructed that investigations for terrorist acts occur within ten days, that the accused be indicted only one day before trial, that cases be presented without participation of both sides, that all appeals, including appeals for pardon, be denied, and that death sentences be carried out immediately after their announcement. This went radically against the 1934 principles of judicial order and control over death sentences. The Law of 1 December was ideally suited for broad terror campaigns and was actively invoked during the Great Terror of 1937–38.

Stalin used Kirov's murder to eliminate old political foes who opposed him in the 1920s. In the absence of any evidence, Stalin exploited the purported involvement of Zinoviev, Kamenev, and their supporters in Kirov's murder. Several groups of former oppositionists were convicted at closed trials. On 26 January 1935, Stalin signed the Politburo resolution exiling 663 former supporters of Zinoviev from Leningrad to Northern Siberia and Yakutia for three to four years. Another 325 former oppositionists were transferred, by party decision, from Leningrad to work in other regions.[15] Similar actions against the oppositionists of the 1920s took place in other cities.

The exile of oppositionists was part of a broader purge that mostly affected Leningrad. Between 28 February and 27 March 1935 the city was purged of "former people"—those associated with the old regime, such as aristocrats, tsarist officials and officers, clergy, landowners, factory owners, traders, other capitalists, and bureaucrats. During this operation, the NKVD Special Council sentenced 11,072 people to camps, exile, and relocation (4,833 heads of household and 6,239 family members).[16]

Simultaneously, in Leningrad and other cities, a campaign to remove "criminal and lumpen elements" as well as "persistent violators" of the passport regulations was carried out. This operation affected primarily twenty-eight urban centers, the "regulation" cities. To process the huge number of cases, the NKVD and the Procuracy of the USSR organized special local troikas (in different documents named police troikas, passport troikas, or NKVD troikas). With the scale of the operation growing, Yagoda and Vyshinsky sent a letter to Stalin asking to legalize the activities of the troikas "in order to quickly purge" the regulation cities of "criminal and lumpen elements, as well as persistent violators of the passport law." Stalin endorsed the proposition about troikas, but cautioned: "A quick purge is dangerous. We must purge gradually and substantially, without pushing and excessive 'administrative ecstasy.' We should complete the purge within one year."[17]

On 27 May 1935 the NKVD ordered the creation of troikas in republics, territories, and provinces. Troikas included the head of the UNKVD or his deputy, the head of the police division, and the head of the department investigating the case. Presence of the procurator at the sessions was mandatory. Troikas enjoyed the rights of the NKVD Special Council and made decisions to exile, relocate, or imprison for up to five years. Their resolutions had to be approved by the Special Council.[18] There was also a troika of the Chief Administration of Police in

Moscow. According to Yagoda's report to Stalin and Molotov, local troikas and the troika of the Chief Administration of Police passed (and the Special Council upheld) 122,726 convictions in the course of the 1935 operation to "purge the cities" (see Document 94).[19]

Purges of the criminal and lumpen elements were only partly related to the harsh political course after the murder of Kirov. The crime rate in a country going through a sweeping social transformation, combined with the destruction of traditional social structures, was very high indeed. The Kirov murder also served as a catalyst, though not the direct cause, of the purges in border zones, systematically conducted throughout the 1930s.

The main target of the purge in 1935–36 was the Western Ukrainian border zone, a purge instigated by the deterioration of relations with Germany and Poland. In February–March 1935 a total of 41,650 Poles, Germans, and "kulaks" were moved from the western areas of the Ukraine (Kiev and Vinnitsa provinces) to its eastern parts.[20] On 28 April 1936 the Politburo adopted a resolution to transfer 15,000 Polish and German households from the Ukraine to Kazakhstan. The plan was to accommodate them in communities similar to the NKVD agricultural labor settlements. New colonists did not lose their political rights, but were barred from leaving their assigned region. From June–September altogether 69,283 people were relocated.[21]

Other targets of border zone cleansing were Leningrad province and Karelia. On 15 March 1935 the Politburo adopted "measures to step up border defense in Leningrad province and the Karelian ASSR," which included the removal of "unreliable elements" from those regions. The operation was conducted by the new secretary of the Leningrad provincial party committee, Andrei Zhdanov, and the new head of the Leningrad provincial NKVD department, L. M. Zakovsky. The unreliable elements were considered to be "kulaks," other "socially dangerous elements," and Finns, Latvians, and Estonians living in those areas. According to Gulag reports, in the course of this operation 23,217 people were moved from Leningrad province and Karelia to Siberia, the Urals, Central Asia, and Kazakhstan.[22] In 1936, almost simultaneously with the operation in the Ukraine, a new, larger-scale purge was conducted there.[23]

Similar operations aimed mainly against "kulaks" were conducted in Azerbaijan and the Northern Caucasus. On 25 December 1934 the Politburo approved the request of the Azerbaijan communist party CC to "send into administrative exile from Azerbaijan to the concentration camps eighty-seven families of kulaks, inveterate anti-Soviet elements, former large capitalist enterprise owners, and kulaks who escaped from other parts of the [Soviet] Union." In April 1935 a number of people—22,496—were moved from the Northern Caucasian territory to Kazakhstan and Uzbekistan.[24]

Another component of this social unification of the country was the "verification," and subsequent exchange, of party documents. Although technically this was a mere verification of authenticity and exchange of party cards, it was in fact a purge of the ruling party ordered by Stalin, comparable to the territorial cleansing. The party organs and the NKVD conducted the verification. Many of those expelled from the party were arrested. At the December 1935 plenum of the Central Committee, Yezhov, who was in charge of the party purge, reported that, as of 1 December, at least 15,218 "enemies" had been arrested after being expelled, and more than 100 "enemy organizations and groups" had been exposed.[25] At the 25 January 1936 meeting of the Central Committee department of administrative party organs, Yezhov warned that the purge had not been concluded yet and that there were still enemies among those expelled who had not yet been prosecuted. "We must conduct necessary work and oblige the first secretaries of the territorial party committees to get in touch with NKVD organs and to provide us with a list of those to be immediately exiled from the territory."[26] In 1935, 301,000 people were expelled from the party, and in 1936 the number was 134,000. Only 30,600 and 37,000 were reinstated each year, respectively.[27]

After the fatal shot on 1 December 1934, the number of cases falling under the article of anti-Soviet agitation increased sharply, including those implicated in conversations about Kirov's death—whether expressions of approval or speculations about the personal motives of the killer and Stalin's involvement in the murder. In 1935, among the 193,000 people arrested by the NKVD Chief Administration for State Security, 43,700 were charged with anti-Soviet agitation (see Document 90). A distinctive feature of these repressions was that they affected ordinary citizens unrelated to opposition groups.

Repressions became so widespread and threatening to social equilibrium that even the leaders of the repressive machinery became apprehensive. On 31 March 1936 the people's commissar of justice, N. V. Krylenko, who never had been a liberal and who contributed a great deal to the spread of terror after Kirov's death, wrote a letter to Stalin expressing his concern with the dangerous increase in the number of ungrounded convictions for counterrevolutionary agitation:

> To curb this increase, it is necessary for the CC to instruct judicial or-
> gans and organs of the People's Commissariat of the Interior on the
> appropriate limits in prosecuting and serving indictments in such
> cases. Even the formally counterrevolutionary pronouncements like
> those cited ("the Soviet regime leads not to the improvement of life for
> the collective farmers but to their demise," etc.), in the absence of a
> counterrevolutionary past or an explicit socially hostile attitude on the
> part of the speaker, are not a sufficient basis for criminal prosecution.
> Instructions like these coming only from the organs of Soviet power
> and addressed only to the courts would not be effective, because the
> workers of the People's Commissariat of Interior, offended by the ter-
> mination of cases by the Procuracy or by the court, would ask about
> the political attitude of the workers of the court and the Procuracy and
> would charge them with liberalism toward the class enemy. This, in
> turn, could result in party repression of the workers of the courts and
> the Procuracy.[28]

As a result of this letter, the procurator of the USSR, Vyshinsky, was ordered to prepare recommendations on this issue (a copy of Kry-lenko's note with Vyshinsky's marginal notes can be found in the Procu-racy archive). On 16 April 1936, Vyshinsky sent Stalin and Molotov his thoughts on the cases of counterrevolutionary agitation.[29]

· 26 ·

Letter from A. Ya. Vyshinsky to Stalin and Molotov
on counterrevolutionary agitation
16 April 1936

Top secret.
CC VKP(b)—to Comrade I. V. Stalin.
SNK OF THE UNION OF THE SSR—to Comrade V. M. Molotov.
Analysis of the cases of counterrevolutionary crimes between 1935 and early 1936 has shown that the overwhelming majority are about counter-revolutionary agitation. The fact that cases of counterrevolutionary agita-tion form a great majority among cases of counterrevolutionary crimes is understandable, because counterrevolutionary agitation has always been the most common weapon of class-hostile elements in their struggle

against the Soviet regime, and the stepped-up revolutionary vigilance after the villainous murder of Comrade Kirov has naturally accelerated the exposure of class-hostile elements conducting counterrevolutionary agitation. However, the number of these cases and the number of those convicted for counterrevolutionary agitation brought about the need to review carefully the essence and character of these cases.

1. The growth in the number of cases of counterrevolutionary agitation is as follows:

a) In the courts of the RSFSR (according to the People's Commissariat of Justice of the RSFSR):

While the total number of cases of counterrevolutionary crimes brought to court has been rising, the number of individuals indicted for counterrevolutionary agitation in the first half of 1935 was 46.8 percent of all those convicted by the special collegiums of territorial (provincial) courts of the RSFSR for all counterrevolutionary crimes. In the second half of 1935 this number grew to 65.6 percent, and in the first three months of 1936 it grew further: to 81.3 percent in January and 87.2 percent in February. In some territorial (provincial) courts these cases were 91–93 percent of the cases (Saratov territorial court, the main court of the Volga German Republic, etc.).

A study of the social composition of those convicted under this article in the three quarters of 1935 showed that 63.6 percent of them were working people.

b) In the railway transport procuracy:

The growth in the number of cases of counterrevolutionary agitation is no less in the railway transport procuracy. In the third quarter of 1935 the procuracy received 438 such cases; in the fourth quarter of 1935, 800; and in January–February 1936, 823 such cases (excluding two railways).

c) In the military tribunals:

In the military tribunals, since the second half of 1935 there has been a decrease in convictions of military personnel for counterrevolutionary agitation (first quarter—836, second quarter—508). However, the total number of military personnel convicted for counterrevolutionary agitation in 1935 is notable.

In 1935 military tribunals convicted 1,334 regular military personnel of the RKKA for counterrevolutionary agitation, which constitutes 27 percent of the entire number of convictions by the military tribunals.

Among all regular military personnel convicted for counterrevolutionary agitation, 138 people are mid-level, high-level, and senior officers, 79 people are junior noncommissioned officers, 136 people are conscripted junior officers, and 981 are rank and file. In some military districts, many of those convicted are VKP(b) members and candidate members and

VLKSM [Komsomol] members (in the Belorussian military district they form 26 percent of the accused, and in the navy, 31 percent).

A detailed review of 800 cases of counterrevolutionary agitation brought to the Supreme Court of the RSFSR and the military and transport collegiums of the Supreme Court of the USSR showed that in a large number of those cases (30–35 percent) prosecution and conviction for counterrevolutionary agitation was improper and resulted from:

a) an overly broad interpretation by the NKVD, Procuracy, and courts of articles on counterrevolutionary agitation in the republican Criminal Code [. . .] and an unacceptably simplistic approach to investigation;

b) the inability of individual workers to give a correct political evaluation of these cases and to demonstrate sufficient autonomy when termination of a case was required. As a result, the article on counterrevolutionary agitation was applied to mundane chatter, grumbling, expressions of dissatisfaction with the work of individuals or organizations (village cooperative stores, savings banks, etc.), and the singing of anti-Soviet ditties or songs by people who should not be considered counterrevolutionaries pursuing counterrevolutionary goals by singing these ditties or songs.

Here are several examples:

1) A special collegium of the Kursk provincial court convicted A. B. Mezintsev, candidate VKP(b) member, under article 58–10 of the Criminal Code to ten years in prison for saying, in 1934, that "the rural cooperatives work badly" and, in 1935, for speaking at the collective farmers' meeting against selling 500 centners of grain. He suggested selling 200 centners, and the meeting adopted that decision. The Supreme Court overturned the verdict and closed the case.

2) 9 December 1935. A special collegium of the Western Siberian territorial court convicted collective farmer A. I. Vedentsev under article 58–10 of the Criminal Code to three years in prison for criticizing, at a 14 October 1935 meeting, the president of the [collective farm] board over the issue of bread procurement, saying that he was pulling the wool over collective farmers' eyes and that they would be short four kilograms per day. He then asked the RIK representative, Novikov, whether bread procurement was voluntary or obligatory. The latter explained that it was an obligation. Then Vedentsev said, What's the point of summoning us if it is an obligation? and left the meeting. The Supreme Court closed the case.

3) A special collegium of the Kazakh section of the Supreme Court of the RSFSR convicted Saveliev under article 58–10 to two years in prison for suggesting, at the general meeting [of the collective farmers], selling 10 tons of grain to the cooperative instead of 15 tons. The Supreme Court closed the case.

4) A special collegium of the Kazakh section of the Supreme Court of

the RSFSR convicted Meshkov under article 58–10 to three years in prison for saying at the general meeting: "A loan is voluntary. I don't want to sign up for 150 rubles, but I will sign up for 100 rubles." Also, during the report on building a classless society, he remarked: "Under communism there is no lawlessness."* The verdict was overruled.

5) A special collegium of the Western Siberian territorial court convicted collective farmer Zhukovsky under article 58–10 to two years in prison for having said that he refused to work in the kolkhoz, being disgruntled with living conditions. After that he wrote a statement of withdrawal and left to work on a state farm. The Zhukovsky case was closed.

6) The Saratov territorial court convicted a collective farmer, Evdokia Lezneva, born in 1905, for singing anti-Soviet ditties: "I joined the kolkhoz and tried to bring in my wife, but she chastises me: Get lost with your kolkhoz. I am not joining it."

7) The NKVD transportation department of the Moscow circular railway arrested and charged under article 58–10 Aleksandr Koriavin, signal man at the Likhobory railway station, for the inefficient train schedule at the Likhobory station and for pointing out the inadequate system of salary calculation and the need to increase salaries. Koriavin has been working on the railway since 1919 and has been a party member since 1927, a member of the party committee, a shock worker, and the recipient of a Stalinist enrollment badge for exemplary work. He was arrested and detained for two months. The Procuracy closed the case.

8) The operative section of the NKVD transportation department at the Erivan station, Trans-Caucasian Railroad, arrested and charged under article 58–10 the assistant engineers, VKP(b) members Melkopian, Aleksian, and Akopian. During a discussion of the upcoming exchange of party documents in the engineers' class, they had asked the instructor if they would have the right to verify whether members of the Central Committee and the government had themselves successfully passed the verification. All three were expelled from the party and kept under arrest for over four months. The Procuracy closed the case.

It is also important to note that some unscrupulous people used the accusation of counterrevolutionary agitation to get even with others or to benefit in some other way. The organs of investigation, the Procuracy, and the courts are not always able to resolve a case or expose false accusations.

Thus, in 1935, the 52d Cavalry Regiment platoon commander Romantsov was charged with counterrevolutionary agitation in the form of approving the murder of Kirov. Romantsov was arrested and tried by a military tribunal. During the court inquiry, the main prosecution witness confessed that she had slandered Romantsov at the request of her friend,

---

* This was a critical remark, referring to the unjust treatment of the collective farmers.

Romantsov's neighbor. The case was sent for additional investigation, which revealed that there was no basis for indicting Romantsov with counterrevolutionary agitation. Romantsov is a party member and is one of the best party organizers in his regiment. He graduated with honors from the Tambov cavalry school and had received more than ten awards. The Procuracy closed the Romantsov case.

It is necessary to inform you of the above, especially given that a bureaucratic order to the Procuracy would not by itself help avoid such mistakes in applying articles on counterrevolutionary agitation from the Criminal Codes of the union republics. To avoid the unproven indictment of workers for counterrevolutionary agitation, as well as step up the struggle against counterrevolutionary agitation by class-hostile elements, I consider it appropriate to instruct the Procuracy of the USSR, the NKVD of the USSR, and the Supreme Court of the USSR to send a joint order to local organs to bring about a proper approach by the agencies of investigation, the Procuracy, and the courts to applying the articles of the republican Criminal Codes on counterrevolutionary agitation. The said order is to be approved by the CC VKP(b) and by 1 September 1936 the CC VKP(b) is to report on the implementation of this resolution.

In addition, I consider it appropriate for the RSFSR Supreme Court to verify all cases from 1935 under article 58–10 of the Criminal Code of the RSFSR (counterrevolutionary agitation) in the territorial (provincial) courts with the highest rate of indicting the workers with counterrevolutionary agitation (Saratov territorial court, main court of the Volga German Republic, etc.).

A. Vyshinsky.

16 April 1936.

Among the archival materials of the Secretariat of the Procuracy of the USSR, there is a copy of the 11 April 1936 memorandum sent to Vyshinsky by the chairman of the Military Collegium of the Supreme Court of the USSR, V. Ulrikh. The memorandum discusses the situation regarding convictions for anti-Soviet agitation in the Red Army and includes a report on this matter. Ulrikh's note mentions that the issue was investigated at the request of "directing organs."[30] Although no special resolutions on the problem of anti-Soviet agitation were issued, the total number of those arrested for anti-Soviet agitation in the cases investigated by the Main Administration for State Security (GUGB) of the NKVD decreased in 1936, totaling 32,000 people (as opposed to 43,000 in 1935; see Document 90).

Signals from the people's commissar of justice and the procurator of the USSR regarding anti-Soviet agitation aimed at the NKVD marked the broader conflict between these offices in 1934–36. In February

1936, Vyshinsky initiated a discussion of the activities of the NKVD Special Council (see Documents 93–95). In 1935–36, NKVD leaders repeatedly complained to the Central Committee about local courts and procurators who refused to sanction arrests in political cases, acquitted the accused, demanded additional investigation, or passed verdicts that were, in NKVD opinion, too mild.[31] This situation reflected the relative moderation of mass political repression and the "underdevelopment" of the repressive apparatus. In 1937–38 the balance of forces between different repressive organs would be altered, and the courts and the Procuracy would become completely dependent on the NKVD.

In 1935–36 Soviet leaders, including Stalin, had plans both to use mass purges to cleanse the party and the state from "enemies" and to accommodate the millions of "aggrieved" citizens—people who came from the toiling classes or who were too young to remember the tsarist regime or even the prosperous days of the New Economic Policy (NEP). On 31 January 1935, at the height of the repression occasioned by the Kirov murder, the Politburo adopted Stalin's proposal to introduce profound changes in the Constitution. In particular, it endorsed the new electoral system, which replaced unequal, indirect, open elections with equal, direct elections by secret ballot.[32] In the days that followed, this question became the center of a broad propaganda campaign. The government supported promises to introduce the new Constitution with certain liberal acts.

On 26 July 1935 the Politburo adopted a resolution, "On annulling convictions of collective farmers," that affected a large segment of the rural population.[33] The resolution instructed local authorities to "annul convictions of collective farmers sentenced to five years or less (or to other minor punishment) and currently serving their terms, or for those who have been released from prison prior to this resolution. At present, they must work conscientiously and honestly at the collective farms, even though they were individual farmers at the time of committing the crime." Although the resolution did not include those convicted of counterrevolutionary crimes, those sentenced to more than five years, or repeat criminals, it still affected hundreds of thousands of peasants. It took several years to implement this decree. In a 25 April 1936 memorandum to Stalin, Kalinin, and Molotov, Procurator Vyshinsky gave a crude summary of the campaign. Between 29 July 1935 and 1 March 1936 the convictions of 556,790 collective farmers were rescinded (an additional 212,199 collective farmers were pardoned in 1934 by decision of the Ukrainian government). Despite these significant results, Vyshinsky recommended an additional review for regions failing to reduce the high percentage of convictions. The Politburo endorsed this proposal.[34]

Parallel to the campaign to annul the convictions of collective farmers, the government released and pardoned officials convicted of economic crimes in 1932–34. On 10 August 1935 the Politburo approved the TsIK resolution on this matter.[35] In early 1936 the Politburo also agreed to rehabilitate certain categories of those convicted under the law of 7 August 1932 on the theft of socialist property. According to a report by Vyshinsky to the government, by 20 July 1936 a review of the 115,500 cases had been completed. In more than 91,000 instances, the application of the law of 7 August was deemed incorrect. After their terms were reduced, 37,452 people (32 percent of all reviewed cases) were released from prison.[36] A complex array of factors, both internal and external, brought about contradictory policies of terror as well as "reconciliation" and the struggle for "socialist legality" in 1934–36. Many of these factors still await their researchers. Despite the broad scale of the terror, it did not reach the level of the dekulakization campaign or the mass punitive actions of 1937–38. This fragile situation was under constant challenge, however, and was eventually upended in the years of the Great Terror.

Camp Laws and Camp Reality

The political situation in the country directly affected the condition of prisoners. After the Kirov murder and as part of the struggle against "terrorists" and "counterrevolutionaries," the NKVD leaders issued a series of orders to step up vigilance and strengthen the regimen in the camps. On 27 May 1935 the people's commissar of the interior issued Order no. 00193, dealing with "those convicted of terrorism and kept in the NKVD corrective labor camps," which set up new tasks: "The terrorist, as the most dangerous state criminal in the camp, must first of all be put in conditions that completely exclude the possibility of his making connections with the outside world and even escaping from the camp and must, second, be put under constant surveillance to prevent any counterrevolutionary activity on his part." The order instructed that all prisoners sentenced for terrorism be registered and that by 15 July 1935 all those sentenced for "central terror" (i.e., in the cases investigated by the NKVD central organs) be concentrated in two camps, White Sea–Baltic Sea and Ukhta-Pechora. Prior to moving the prisoners, "the most valuable agents dealing with the transferred prisoners" had to be relocated to these camps. The order also toughened the regimen of prisoners convicted for terrorism. As a rule, they were only to be employed on "general work under guard" and not allowed in camp administrative or managerial positions (with the exception of specialists—engineers, agronomists, qualified accountants). Unguarded movement of "terrorist" prisoners was banned, while their mail and the possibility of early release were severely limited. An important element of the new regimen was the requirement to step up the activity of undercover agents, who were the main means of control in the Gulag and provided information on new "counterrevolutionary organizations" among prisoners.

· 27 ·

Excerpts from Order no. 00159 by the people's commissar of the interior,
"On undercover work in the NKVD corrective labor camps"
26 April 1935[37]

Top secret.

The NKVD corrective labor camps hold a large number of extremely dangerous counterrevolutionaries: spies, terrorists, and other anti-Soviet and anti-party elements, who are bitter enemies of the Soviet regime with nothing to lose and who are always ready for the most intense counterrevolutionary actions. Available operative information shows that the internal and foreign White Guard scum are very aware of the weaknesses of the camp regime and the guards and of the number of counterrevolutionary contingents in the camps and perceive the camps as a potential beachhead in organizing an insurgent movement in the USSR. There have been registered specific attempts by foreign White Guardsmen to establish connections to the camps and to prepare them for planned attacks on the guards by subversive gangs at camps near the border.

In view of this very feasible danger of intense counterrevolutionary activities by the White Guard and other counterrevolutionary elements, all but a few camp bosses and heads of third departments* remain passive and neglect to work with the [undercover] agents. These administrators fail to realize that the lack of a reliable agent network and their personal

* Third department—a subdivision within the secret police hierarchy that occupied itself with intelligence and operational work in the camps.

inactivity in working with the agents lead to the escape of the most dangerous terrorists and spies, as well as the creation of counterrevolutionary groups that organize subversive acts in the camps. The lack of experienced agent managers leads to a situation in which double agents provoke the assistant representatives assigned to them, generate "cases" that, upon verification, turn out to be the most insolent fraud, make the third departments and UGB [Administration for State Security] do unnecessary work, and, at the same time, manage to conceal their counterrevolutionary activity. [. . .]

Besides the lack of serious work with agents, some camps have not created a sufficiently harsh regimen for imprisoned counterrevolutionaries. The UGB liquidates the most dangerous criminals, but puts them in camps where they are left without any oversight. Suffice it to say that those convicted for counterrevolutionary crimes are allowed to work in vital areas of camp administration, like the URO. Heads of camps fail to realize that counterrevolutionaries, capitalizing on their carelessness and negligence, assign their people to facilitate practical counterrevolutionary activities.

I order:

1. Heads of the NKVD boards should actively direct undercover work against counterrevolutionaries in the camps. Deputy heads should bear personal responsibility for this work.

2. The NKVD personnel department and the UNKVD personnel departments should, within ten days, strengthen the third camp departments with selected, verified operative officers.

3. Ban prisoners from working in the third departments.

4. Within one month, review all agents in the camps. The review should be personally conducted by the heads of the camps, the heads of the third departments, their deputies and assistants, and the heads of the third sections (divisions). Nobody else should be entrusted to do this work.

5. Review the agents not by formally examining their files and lists but via personal conversation with each agent.

6. The superior reviewing the agents should personally examine the personal and work-related files of each agent and the case to which he [or she] is assigned. Check the number and kind of reports he has provided. Evaluate the necessity of the tasks assigned to the agent. Investigate all connections of the agent in the camp and outside it. Determine whether the agent has been exposed. Give the agent clear and specific future tasks. Taking into consideration the agent's prior work [. . .], create a profile of the agent, and consider the feasibility and form of his subsequent functions. [. . .]

8. Immediately re-subordinate all agents working among the prisoners convicted for counterrevolutionary crimes, as well as those [recruited] among technicians and specialists, to heads of third departments, their

deputies, assistants, heads of sections of third departments, and heads of third sections (divisions). In the future, representatives and deputy representatives should be allowed to manage ordinary informants, not agents.

9. Recruit new agents to secure supervision over all important categories of prisoners (terrorists; spies; anti-party elements; counterrevolutionaries; saboteurs; members of insurrectionist, fascist, wrecking, church, and sect groups and organizations), and wage a struggle against crime in the camps (theft, banditry) and the escape of the prisoners.

10. Discontinue mass agent recruitment. Proceed with recruiting only after careful review and verification of the candidate, using the memorandum of the local departments of the former OGPU or the NKVD, [or] the verdict containing materials concerning his time in the camp. Before recruitment of each agent, explore his connections in the camp and his ability to work with them. Before recruiting the agent, it is essential to formulate the purpose clearly and identify the goals of his work.

11. Centralize up-to-date information on all camp agents in the third department. All changes in the agent network (transfer to other camps, release, escape, acquisition of new agents, etc.) should be properly registered. [. . .]

13. Do not leave unpunished a single case of provocation or misinformation by the agent. Those providing false information or provocateurs should immediately be removed from the agent network, lose all accumulated bonus workdays, be put on a punishment regimen, and, under aggravating circumstances, be prosecuted. [. . .]

15. Strictly enforce accountability in working with agents at all levels of chekist personnel within the camp. The head of the third department and head of the third section (division) should examine all agent reports daily and give relevant instructions personally.

16. Considering the difficulty of recruiting in the camps and the frequent exposure of the agents, the heads of the third departments and sections should secure a system of communication with the agents that would prevent their discovery. [. . .]

19. The third camp department must have information on the behavior and counterrevolutionary activity in the camp of every counterrevolutionary released from the camp. The head of the third department should be personally responsible for the failure to collect both proper and timely operative information on the individuals convicted for counterrevolutionary crimes.

20. To secure the most complete and thorough operative information on the most important counterrevolutionary contingents, GUGB departments should, within one month, provide the GULAG third department with a detailed list of the convicts who require scrupulous agent supervision every day. The GULAG third department should report periodically

to the GUGB departments on progress in collecting operative information on these contingents. [. . .]

24. Establish regular reporting by camp third departments in the form of operational reports sent to the GULAG third department (with a copy to the UGB UNKVD) twice a month (on the 1st and 15th). Operational reports should briefly and clearly outline the progress in agent work, creation of new tasks, supervision of the agents (progress of review, elimination, new agent acquisition), and information on the movement of counterrevolutionary elements.

25. Transfer the most dangerous categories of prisoners to the remote and best-guarded parts of the camp, set up a secure guard, and prevent any possibility of escape. [. . .]

28. Remove from work in the camp URO all prisoners convicted under counterrevolutionary articles. [. . .]

People's Commissar of the Interior USSR, G. Yagoda.

This campaign to toughen the camp regimen affected only some of the prisoners: 118,256 inmates had been convicted for counterrevolutionary crimes as of 1 January 1935 (16.3 percent of the total number of prisoners; see Document 98). More important was the typical arbitrariness of the camp administration. It was not based on instructions or resolutions but more brutal and widespread. Even official documents retain evidence of crimes by the camp administration against prisoners.

· 28 ·

Memorandum by I. A. Akulov on crimes committed by the camp administration
4 June 1934[38]

To the CC VKP(b)—Comrade Stalin.*

Recent analysis by the OGPU Collegium of the cases of workers in concentration camps shows that arbitrary shootings, the beating of prisoners, the rape of imprisoned women, and other grave crimes still happen in the camps. During the past three months the OGPU Collegium has reviewed 130 such cases. The review shows that the crime rate of the camp administration is high and that the efforts by the OGPU Chief Administration of Camps have not reached their goal.

Often junior camp administrators, ignoring OGPU orders and follow-

---

* Note on the first page margin: "Not sent."

ing the principle that everything is allowed, commit excesses without opposition from the heads of camps. [. . .]

Here is, for example, the case of the head of a section of Dmitlag, Aleksandrov, who was in charge of several thousand prisoners. On 4 May
1934, in the presence of a group of prisoners and camp workers, said
Aleksandrov shot dead a twenty-year-old woman sentenced to two years
for violation of the passport regulation. The reason for this shooting was
the prisoner's swearing and her attempt to hit a prisoner overseer. Only after intervention by the Procuracy of the USSR, in June 1934, was Aleksandrov indicted by the collegium for murder. Leaders of the eastern section of Dmitlag not only failed to charge him in a timely fashion but also
had a regional representative announce at a prisoners' meeting the day after the murder that Aleksandrov had been given an award for appropriate
use of arms.

In the same Dmitlag, in the presence of a group of prisoners and collective farmers, a guard shot an escaped prisoner apprehended by collective
farmers, despite the pleas of the collective farmers and the escapee not to
do it. The head of the third department of the Khlebnikovsky region of
Dmitlag closed the guard's case because of his "acute edginess." Later, the
OGPU Collegium sentenced the guard to ten years in prison.

In Svirlag, the guard Derko, in the presence of nine prisoners, the head
of the camp section, and the platoon commander, shot the prisoner
Marchenko, who had refused to walk to the transit center. The shooting
took place half a kilometer from the camp section. The Svirlag administration closed the case, considering the guard's action to have been correct.

In the township where a Bamlag camp section is located, the guard bat-
talion commander and his aide-de-camp, Lilov, apprehended two local
workers. On their way to the police station, Lilov killed one of them without any reason. Though indicted for murder, Lilov was named guard platoon commander and, inebriated, kicked up a row with arms in hand.

The representative of the third department of Dmitlag, Shilkin, received
information about the preparations for an escape by prisoners. Instead of
preventing the escape, Shilkin, instructed by an informer how best to carry
out an ambush, set it up after ordering the political commissar to bring the
best sharpshooters. After being fired at, the escapee returned to his barrack. The organizer of the escape, Shilkin, yelled at the guards who had
missed the escapee and allowed him to go back.

In the said Dmitlag there were scandalous cases of shootings with the
intention to steal. A number of guards, together with prisoner camp workers, prodded prisoners for several months to escape so they could murder
and rob them. What is important to note here is that all these murders of
prisoners over a short period of time did not draw any attention from
camp bosses.

Besides arbitrary shootings, low-level camp workers committed other serious crimes, and they worked without anyone having control over them. These crimes are not immediately exposed, which gives the criminals the opportunity to perpetrate such excesses for a long time. In Ukhtpechlag a group of guards, including the head of the camp section, systematically beat up prisoners and robbed them of their money and belongings. The head of the third department in one of the sections of the Karaganda camps, Egorov, under the pretext of interrogating them, coerced imprisoned women into sexual relationships. He corrupted the entire apparatus and involved his subordinates in these outrages. The case was exposed only after the prisoner Gribanov, jealous of Egorov, shot a revolver five times and killed his mistress, prisoner Musiukova.

A representative of Siblag's third department systematically appropriated prisoners' belongings and drank without restraint in plain sight of the entire camp population. A deputy representative of the third department in Svirlag, Loshkarev, drank voluminously and, using his position to do so, engaged in sexual relations with female prisoners. A representative of the third department of Svirlag, Iliashenko, beat up the prisoners and even set dogs on those who refused to work.

Administrative punishment is completely arbitrary. Thus, in Dmitlag, contrary to the instruction on camps, everybody, including guards, camp elders, and heads of sections, was allowed to isolate prisoners. In a detention cell they found a note written by an investigator among the prisoners: "Receive and lock up in a dark one-man cell. Provide hot food once every four days: 300 grams of bread and cold water. Undress [them] after work."

Instead of a timely and determined struggle against violations of the camp regimen, the low-level camp administration engaged in criminal activities, which was one of the reasons for the spread of banditry in the camps.

In the past several months the OGPU Collegium has sentenced several dozen prisoners to death for engaging in camp banditry, robbery, murders, beatings, etc. Most of those prosecuted for banditry, resistance, etc., are youths born in 1910–16. Thus, among those prosecuted by the OGPU Collegium in twenty-five cases in May, two people were born before 1900, fifteen between 1901 and 1910, twenty-five between 1910 and 1914, and eleven between 1915 and 1917.

These cases also demonstrate the administration's failure to take necessary measures to nip in the bud the spread of banditry in the camps. Thus, as the Sazlag case revealed, a group of prisoners beat up and robbed prisoners for four months in a row, and no measures were taken against them. As a result, prisoners who become victims of robbery are often left completely vulnerable and defenseless. [. . .]

Procurator of the USSR, I. Akulov.

According to a handwritten note on this letter, it was not sent (probably a variant was mailed). However, it obviously reflected the real situation with regard to lawlessness in the Gulag. Although, from time to time, NKVD leaders had to react to cases, they avoided broad generalizations. Thus, on 2 July 1935, Yagoda signed the order "On badgering the prisoners in the Pistsovo corrective labor colony, Ivanovo industrial province." The order confirmed that a review of the complaints by the prisoners in this colony had revealed "outrageous cases of badgering the prisoners." "To force prisoners to work, dogs were set on them. Guards systematically beat the prisoners with sticks and rifle butts." After the order, several colony employees were arrested and tried by a tribunal. The head of the colony was fired and indicted, and other steps were taken. The order, which was sent to all camps, prisons, and colonies, indirectly confirmed that such "badgering" was widespread: "All administrative, chekist, and convoy personnel of the camps, prisons, and colonies herewith are warned that for rudeness toward and badgering of prisoners I will prosecute in the military tribunal not only the direct perpetrators but also those bosses who do not take decisive measures to eradicate this shameful phenomenon."[39]

Despite this threat, only seven months later, on 17 February 1936, Yagoda had to issue another order, "On overcoming the practice of badgering prisoners in the corrective labor camps, prisons, and NKVD colonies." The order gave several examples of "particularly scandalous crimes and arbitrary behavior of low-level camp and prison administrators." Moscow authorities once again announced the need to prosecute several chekists and warned the heads of camps, prisons, and colonies of their responsibility. The Moscow authorities attempted to tighten up control over the camps with a tried-and-true method: information from below. All camp centers, prisons, and colonies were instructed to put up special boxes for complaints to the people's commissar of the interior and the head of the Gulag. "The boxes shall be sealed with the imprimatur of the camp administration and shall be opened only in person by the head of the camp or his deputy (in the camps), or by the head of the OMZ [Department of Corrective Facilities] or his deputy (in prisons and colonies)." All correspondence had to be sent to the people's commissar and "should not be opened under any circumstances." The order instructed that an explanation be given to all prisoners as to the "purpose of these boxes."[40]

Everyday difficulties notwithstanding, prisoners who survived the

Great Terror still remembered 1934–36 as "good" years. Compared to the Terror, all that happened in the Gulag at that time was rather moderate. Camp contingents grew, but "moderately." The death rate, compared to death rates during the famine of 1932–33 and the mass repressions of 1937–38, was "moderate." Also "moderate" was the arbitrariness of the camp administration. G. I. Anfilov, sentenced to five years in the camps in early 1935, wrote to his wife: "My two years in the Far East were marked by a gradual deterioration of conditions. [19]35, compared to [19]37, was a gilded age, an arcadia, of which we say: 'Yes, that was a good time!'"[41] Indeed, everything was relative. Even in that "good time," the Gulag remained a machine of violence and death, to wit, the tens of thousand of people who died in prison without being able to compare the "advantages" of 1935 over 1937.

An important factor determining the situation in the camps in 1934–36 was the relative stability of the number of prisoners. The number increased by 200,000 in 1934 (from 510,000 to 725,000) and by 100,000 in 1935 (from 725,000 to 839,000), and decreased to 821,000, as of 1 January 1937 (see Document 96). This stability, despite the 1935–36 repressions, can be explained by various amnesties: review of the cases of some white-collar employees, liberation of prisoners sentenced under the law of 7 August 1932, and early liberation of shock workers, invalids, and the elderly. As a result, the arrival of new prisoners in the camps in 1936 (431,400 people were transferred to the camps from other installations) only slightly surpassed the number of those freed (369,500) (see Document 97).

The negligible growth of camp contingents, along with a general improvement of the food situation in the country (after 1 January 1935, bread was not rationed, as became the case for other products), helped stabilize supplies for prisoners. According to norms adopted in December 1935, camp prisoners daily received at least 400 grams of rye bread, along with hot dishes for breakfast and lunch. Approximate guidelines for food preparation called for 15 grams of flour per person per day, 60–80 grams of groats, and 500 grams of vegetables. Fish (160–80 grams) was served twenty-two times per month, and meat (70 grams), eight times per month. Prisoners received 350–400 grams of sugar per month. In theory, this meager ration could be increased if the work tasks were completed. Completion of 75–99 percent of a task gave prisoners the right to purchase 200–400 grams of bread each day. Completion of 100 percent of a task or more earned them 600 grams of bread and an "additional dish"—a second breakfast or dinner. Prisoners fulfilling their tasks also won the right to buy goods from the camp kiosks. These rations were not for prisoners who refused to work or who were under investigation. Those prisoners received 300 grams of bread, 35 grams of flour, 400 grams of vegetables, and 75 grams of fish per day, with no meat and only 200 grams of sugar per month.[42] Rations for soap were particularly meager: 300 grams per month, of which 100 grams were for the laundry.[43] No wonder that the reviews consistently discovered the camps to be "considerably lice-ridden."[44]

It goes without saying that the prescribed supply norms were not always fulfilled. Depending on the camp, the situation could vary. As a rule, even the existing foodstuffs were stolen or distributed unfairly. A review of the camps in early 1936 revealed the "insufficient number of kitchens and kiosks, the bad organization of their operations, and the ineptness of the camp administration, resulting in unacceptably long lines. Camp prisoners, after a ten-hour workday, have to spend another one–two hours waiting in the cold for food or to buy such items as tobacco. [. . .] The camp administration does not pay sufficient attention to the distribution of food, nor is it present at the points of distribution, leaving it instead to the cooks. As a result, many prisoners who do excellent work complain that they get worse rations than those who work badly. [. . .] There is no struggle [. . .] against the theft of prisoners' bread and belongings."[45] In general, however, there is no evidence of mass deaths among prisoners caused by hunger in this period. The overall death rate in the camps had decreased (see Document 97).

Economic imperatives and the need to fulfill labor tasks were the main reasons for camp bosses to strive to prevent the emaciation of prisoners. The number of NKVD enterprises grew significantly after 1935 (see Document 25). On 23 June 1935 the SNK USSR endorsed the construction of the Norilsk nickel complex, the largest northern enterprise, capable of producing 10,000 tons of nickel a year. The construction had to be finished by 1938. The government considered this goal a top priority and charged the NKVD to oversee it and set up a special camp.[46] On 28 October 1935 the SNK transferred the previously autonomous Central Administration of Highways, Dirt Roads, and Automotive Transport (Tsudortrans), along with its multimillion-ruble road construction projects, to the supervision of the NKVD.[47] On 14 September 1935 the Politburo approved the Central Committee and SNK resolution to build hydroelectric complexes at Uglich and

Rybinsk using convict labor. Ya. D. Rapoport, former head of Belo-morkanal, was put at the head of it.[48] On 31 January 1936 the SNK charged the NKVD with the construction of the large Segezh pulp and paper complex.[49] On 15 January 1936, to better manage the increas-ing tasks of building warehouses of strategic reserves for the Commit-tee of Reserves of the Labor and Defense Council (STO) of the USSR, the Administration for Special Construction was created within the NKVD. On 25 June 1936 the Sovnarkom approved a plan for the NKVD to build and start up the enterprises of the Committee of Re-serves, assigning a staggering 408 million rubles to do so.[50] By No-vember 1936 the NKVD plan of capital construction had reached 3.5 billion rubles (about 10 percent of all approved capital construction work in the USSR).[51]

Although construction was the most significant part of the Gulag economy, prisoners also produced a large amount of agricultural and industrial output, including timber, gold, coal, oil, and merchandise for mass consumption. After the organizational period was over, such large NKVD enterprises as Dalstroi established themselves and ex-panded their production. In March 1934 the Politburo set for Dalstroi a plan to produce 4.65 tons of gold that year. The actual production was 5.5 tons (compared to 511 kilograms in 1932 and 791 kilograms in 1933).[52]

In early 1935 the Dalstroi chief, E. P. Berzin, reported in Moscow on the progress of work. On 22 February, at a Politburo session, he spoke on the development of the gold industry. The plan for Dalstroi for 1935 called for it to produce 8.5 tons of gold, about 10 percent of the entire national gold production. In view of the successes in the gold-mining industry, the Politburo decided to grant awards to its leaders. A month later, central newspapers published a report on awards given to Berzin and other Dalstroi bosses. For reasons of secrecy Dalstroi was named "Kolymzoloto" in the articles.

The 1935 plan was easily overfulfilled: Dalstroi delivered 14.5 tons of gold. After that, Dalstroi tasks grew fast. For 1936 the plan called for it to produce 24 tons of gold (actual amount, more than 30 tons);[53] for 1937, 48 tons (actual amount, 51.5 tons).[54] Having fulfilled the 1937 plan, Dalstroi produced about one-third of the country's gold. Besides gold, geologists discovered rich deposits of tin ore in the Kolyma Basin. One of the mines at the largest of those fields, Butugy-chag, became widely known thanks to A. Zhigulin's story "Black Stones." Also, there were deposits of wolframite and molybdenite.

The expansion of Dalstroi, which by 1 January 1937 had over 70,000 prisoners, reflected a general tendency in the growth of the NKVD's economic importance, primarily through the development of large construction projects.[55] Foremost among Gulag construction projects were the Baikal–Amur railway (which, as of 1 January 1936, employed 180,000 prisoners, that is, over 20 percent of all camp prisoners),[56] the Moscow–Volga canal, and roads and highways in the Far East.

The transfer to prioritized sites of the most able-bodied prisoners left other camps, those not receiving special attention by the NKVD (especially agricultural camps), with large numbers of weak and sick inmates. In the first quarter of 1936 about one-third of the 300,000 prisoners in these camps were either sick or fully or partially disabled.[57] The sick and disabled, who required resources to support them, undercut Gulag economic achievements. Chekists therefore tried to get rid of them through early release. In 1935–36 the NKVD and the Procuracy issued a number of commutations (with suspension) "in order to rid the camps and penitentiaries of the disabled, the sick, and the elderly."[58]

Unloading unemployable contingents reduced NKVD expenses but did not solve the main problem—a growing deficit in the workforce at a time when economic tasks were growing larger. This situation led to a search for ways to increase the productivity of labor and make the camp economy more effective. According to internal NKVD documents of this period, there were frequent demands to conduct business efficiently and be financially disciplined. An important element of this policy was effective stimulation of convict labor.

On 26 July 1935, the Bamlag prisoner G. I. Anfilov wrote to his wife: "Yesterday I received a shock worker booklet. One page contains the 'Rights.' Here are the rights of a shock worker." Anfilov listed the privileges:

1. The right to register days of shock work as a bonus.
2. The right to the prioritized purchase of specified goods in the kiosk and the receipt of limited-supply merchandise as a bonus when using a shock worker card.
3. The right to receive an extra bonus course and enhanced rations in the canteen and in the café.
4. A prioritized supply of bedsheets.
5. The right to priority use of social-cultural establishments (club, cinema).

6. The right to send two additional letters per month and to [receive] additional money transfers.

7. The right to get one free photo.

He added: "The most important point of this charter of a man and citizen is the first one—bonus days."[59]

The NKVD bosses realized and made full use of the attraction of the bonus workdays, which could be counted toward the prison term. Although earlier Gulag directives stressed the "need to carefully verify bonus workday counts" because of "frequent abuses," the goal of developing this system was established in 1935.[60] Provisional instructions, promulgated on 31 January 1935, standardized the rules for counting bonus days. There were two categories: "a) first-category bonus (four days of the term for three days of work) to be applied to prisoners belonging to the working class before their conviction (former workers, collective farmers, white-collar workers, peasants, artisans not using hired labor, etc.) and enjoying the right to vote; b) second-category bonus (five days of the term for four days of work) to be applied to all other categories of prisoners besides those listed in group 'a' (for example, formerly disenfranchised individuals, traders, clerics, kulaks, etc.)." Shock workers—that is, prisoners who overfulfilled their quotas—had their bonuses raised one notch: for shock workers in the first category, two workdays counted as three days toward serving their sentence, and for those in the second category, three workdays counted as four.[61]

In some remote camps (Bamlag, some sections of Ukhtpechlag, the Tulomsky division of the White Sea–Baltic Sea complex [BBK], Sevvostlag, and Dallag, the Komsomolsk–Khabarovsk railway construction camp), special bonuses, the "super shock" norms, were used because of the difficult climate. "In these camps, the first-category prisoners get three prison-term days for two workdays (shock workers—two prison-term days for one workday). Second-category prisoners get four prison-term days for three workdays (shock workers—three prison-term days for two workdays)." That is, for working a certain number of days, one's prison term was reduced by even more days.

Serious discrimination met those convicted for espionage, terror, subversion, treason, and other such political crimes. A workday count toward early release could be allowed only "by special permission of the GULAG of the NKVD, on a case-by-case basis, as six days of the term for five days of work," with quarterly approval by Moscow. These rules, which resulted from the toughening of the camp regimen after the Kirov murder, nevertheless left the door open for early release of the majority of prisoners.

Another option for early release that was popular among prisoners was colonization, that is, release on condition of staying and working in the neighborhood of the camp. In 1934–36 colonization programs such as the construction of villages for prisoners-become-colonists and preparing the soil for agricultural use were undertaken along the Baikal–Amur railway, at the Belomorkanal complex, in Ukhtpechlag, and in other Gulag divisions. Besides being an incentive to the "good" prisoners, colonization also was a means of developing virgin lands, providing a workforce to the new enterprises, and creating an autonomous agricultural base. According to the regulations, those eligible for colonization were the most productive prisoners from among the workers, peasants, and white-collar workers convicted for petty crimes, malfeasance, and "rural counterrevolution," as well as from among the "socially dangerous elements" (that is, those convicted under nonpolitical articles). A condition for colonization was the readiness of the prisoner's family to move to the colony. In this fashion, "political purity" and long-term commitment to remote regions were guaranteed.

In practice, however, these regulations were often violated. A Gulag circular letter in November 1934 mentioned prisoners' using colonization "to escape the camp regimen and to secure a salary" but with no guarantee of long-term settlement in the colonies.[62] Sometimes, in violation of the rules, prisoners without families and "counterrevolutionaries" were allowed to move to the colonies. Usually they were specialists and managers favored by the camp administration.

Infringement of colonization rules is but one example of how the camps failed to follow strict instructions. Allowing prisoners to go unescorted within the territory of the camp and its enterprises, employing "counterrevolutionaries" as managers, and violating the camp regimen in other ways resulted from economic necessity and from the interests of camp administrators of different rank, who established their own rules and practices. The banditry of criminals, the crimes of guards and chekists, the hunger suffered by working prisoners, the comfort stolen by the so-called imbeciles (*pridurki*—prisoners occupying positions with access to the meager camp resources), everyday ineptitude and its capacity for destroying and sometimes alleviating prisoners' lives, together with the remnants of "liberal" ideas for "reeducating socially acceptable prisoners," were part of camp life. A snapshot of these elements can be seen in a collection of documents describing the life of prisoners in the Dmitrovsky camp, who worked on the construction of the Moscow–Volga canal near Moscow.

· 29 ·

Order no. 217 of the administration of construction of the eastern section
of the Moscow–Volga canal and the Dmitrovsky camp of the OGPU
26 June 1934[63]

Despite the repeated orders issued by the head of the administration and myself regarding the struggle to prevent escapes, a growing number of escapes in the eastern section demonstrates that there has been no radical change in connection with this issue, which is proved by the following figures: 305 people escaped, and 130 have been apprehended over twenty days in June.

This reveals the lack of any chekist prophylactic measures. [. . .] Besides, technical staff of the camp population (including foremen) have not been mobilized to contain escapees. Foremen still do not know their teams and feel no responsibility for the escape of their members. The large number of unescorted escapees shows that the required pass regulation is violated. [. . .] Newly arriving prisoners are not properly searched. The camp administration grants personal visits indiscriminately. As a result, many prisoners have the opportunity to obtain the necessary documents for escape. [. . .] As a rule, the chekist agent network and the VOKhR [armed guards] learn about this or that escape two–three days later, which hampers us in taking adequate countermeasures. [. . .]

I hereby order [the following]:

1. Within three days, sector heads and third section representatives should review [the cases of] all unescorted prisoners and return to escorting all those sentenced to eight to ten years, as well as all the prisoners suspected of or prone to trying to escape. [. . .]

3. Prohibit prisoners in the territory under my command from wearing casual clothes, collect casual clothing, and provide prisoners exclusively with marked uniforms. [. . .]

4. Definitely forbid prisoners to live outside camp territory. All those currently dwelling in private houses should be transferred to the camp zone. [. . .]

Head of the eastern section, Eiduk.

· 30 ·

Circular letter to the heads of the administrations of construction of sections
of the Moscow–Volga canal and the Dmitrovsky camp of the NKVD
7 January 1935[64]

Hard work during the summer and fall of 1934, as well as the lack of adequate attention to preserving the physical condition of the workforce, has caused a sharp increase in the number of temporarily unemployable prisoners. For these people to recover, both central and regional sanitary camps have been created. [. . .] This winter should be fully used to carry out measures to help the workforce recuperate, to create cadres of able-bodied workers capable of fulfilling the 1935 industrial program plans.

To retain the results achieved by each prisoner in the sanitary camp, we order:

1. After leaving the sanitary camps, prisoners should be gradually reintegrated into the workforce by abiding to the following norms:

a) first three days—25 percent of the normal workload

b) next seven days—50 percent of the normal workload

The full workload should be assigned on the eleventh day.

2. For those leaving the sanitary camps, allow for a reduced workday during the first ten days, according to the aforementioned reduced norms, and, upon completion of the series of reduced workdays, promptly send them to their camp sections, unhindered along the way.

3. For ten days after leaving the sanitary camps, prisoners should receive rations equal to the rations of those fulfilling between 100 and 115 percent of the norm.

Head of the Moscow–Volga canal construction, Kogan.

Deputy head of the GULAG and head of the NKVD Dmitlag, Firin.

· 31 ·

Order no. 3 for the Dmitrovsky camp of the NKVD
10 January 1935[65]

Since permission was granted to sell bread openly, there have been cases in which unescorted prisoners purchased it, brought it to the camp, and then engaged in speculation.

I order:

1. Announcing to all prisoners in the camp that they are not allowed to purchase bread in cooperative and state stores.

2. Searching unescorted prisoners at checkpoints. If bread is found, confiscate it and punish the prisoners violating the rules with administrative measures (resume escorting them, deny them a one-month salary bonus, and, for repeat offenders, deny them the right to count off extra workdays [against their prison terms]).

Deputy head of the GULAG and head of Dmitlag NKVD USSR, Firin.

· 32 ·

Excerpts from Order no. 6 for the Dmitrovsky camp of the NKVD
10 February 1935[66]

The newly appointed head of the first section of the Dmitrovsky camp, Comrade Krol, reports that discipline among the prisoners of the section is unsatisfactory. Inadmissible cases of prisoners misbehaving and violating the internal rules of the camp have been registered. Most of the prisoners, especially the technical staff of the combined company living away from the camp, report to their locations at will. They use the lunch break to wander around town, go to town bathhouses, make various purchases, etc., under the pretense of partaking of medical treatment or social activity in the departments of the administration of construction and the camp. [. . .]

Deputy head of the GULAG and head of Dmitlag NKVD USSR, Firin.

· 33 ·

Order no. 31 for the Dmitrovsky camp of the NKVD
25 July 1935[67]

There have been cases lately of the camp section administration preventing prisoners from getting actively involved in the camp press by confiscating manuscripts and persecuting camp correspondents. To prevent such disgraceful actions, I order that:

Section heads shall be personally responsible for immediate delivery to the cultural-educational department of Dmitlag all prisoners' manuscripts for the camp newspapers. The cultural-educational department of Dmitlag shall systematically check on compliance with this order and report all violations of it to me.

Deputy head of the GULAG and head of Dmitlag NKVD USSR, Firin.

· 34 ·

Report to A. A. Gorshkov, deputy head of the Dmitrovsky camp of the NKVD
29 November 1935[68]

Secret.

Prisoner Davyd Abramovich Itskov, petty trader, sentenced by the people's court under article 17–109 of the Criminal Code to two years in prison, works as a kiosk manager in the Vodoprovodny section.

Prisoner D. A. Itskov, seeking to secure early release, by fair means or foul, attempted to coerce workers of the URO apparatus to abuse their position. On 5 November 1935, Itskov approached the head of the release group, asking to speed up his release, but his request was denied. Not content with that, prisoner Itskov pressed the consultant of the attestation commission,* prisoner Pozolotin, to speed up his release.

Itskov received a regular workday count in the fourth quarter. Itskov addressed the consultant of the attestation commission, prisoner Pozolotin, trying to convince him that his workdays should be counted as shock-work days and that the section had counted them as shock work. The attestation commission consultant, without verifying the records, arbitrarily increased the day count by fourteen. Review of the personal file by the release group revealed the illegal increase of the workday count.

For these exploits, I transferred prisoner Itskov to general work and placed the worker of the attestation commission, prisoner Pozolotin, under arrest for ten days.

Considering the above, I am asking to invalidate all of prisoner Itskov's previous workdays and to invalidate prisoner Pozolotin's workday count for two quarters.

Deputy head of the Vodoprovodny section and chairman of the attestation commission, P. P. Chestnykh.

· 35 ·

Statement by prisoner Imapaliev of the Dmitrovsky camp
of the NKVD, sent to the TsIK USSR
10 December 1935[69]

Translation.

To the Central Executive Committee of the Union.

---

* Camp attestation commissions reviewed materials relating to the early release of prisoners.

From prisoner Turdy Impaliev, Dmitlag, third section, town of Tabar.

I herewith inform the committee that in the third section in Tabar there are a number of canal builders. The head of the town administration is a former prisoner, a certain B. M. Krol. The aforementioned Krol engages in unlawful, illegal activities.

1. He illegally puts innocent canal builders under arrest, ordering to strip off all clothing, which leaves them naked in their underwear, and orders that the hands and feet of those refusing to work be tied and that they be placed in water or in . . . (unclear) for six–twelve hours . He does this every day.

2. By order of the town chief, Krol, the personal clothing and money of the arrested canal builders is forcefully confiscated. In the case of a protest, Krol orders the prisoner to be flogged to the point of bleeding, and then confiscates [the personal items]. Krol does not return the confiscated clothing and money but appropriates it.

3. The [town] head, Krol, orders that food be withheld from arrested canal builders for three–four days and thus forces the canal builders to starve for three–four days. Starving, they attempt suicide. There have been several cases of attempted suicide using a knife.

4. The arrested canal builders report to work at 8 A.M. The work is supposed to stop at 4 P.M. or when the task is completed. However, the [town] head, Krol, issues an order that they work from 8 A.M. to midnight. He orders those canal builders who refuse to work upon arrival to be stripped and placed naked in the snow.

5. There are three teams in the town. Canal builders perform shock work between 1 May and 1 November 1935. They overfulfill the norm by 100–150 percent. [. . .] Each (self-financing) team provides 500–1,000 rubles in savings each month. Along with team managers, the [town] head, Krol, keeps the amount of savings secret from the canal builders and appropriates this money for drinking.

6. When the state provides money for shock workers, bosses do not give them the money, but appropriate it, or distribute it among their people, who are not shock workers. They list their people as shock workers but not the real shock workers.

7. Krol passes on to the canal builders only a small share of the clothes (uniforms) supplied by the state. Most of them he appropriates and sells at the market. There are some national minorities in the town. Krol is particularly cruel toward them and discriminates by nationality. National minorities [*natsmen*] have no life. To tell the truth, he does not properly feed them (with acceptable food), and in case there are objections, he says: "You are not in Central Asia here."

8. The above facts have been reported to the superior organs, and the investigation proved them to be true. However, despite the complete proof of Krol's complicity, the Dmitlag administration took no action against

him. On the contrary, those who exposed Krol are now charged under article 58–10 of the Criminal Code. Therefore, Krol decided to ruin the life of those canal builders. These facts can soon be proved by documents.

Therefore, we ask you to look into these cases urgently, because, for reporting these facts to the appropriate organs, I am now charged with counterrevolution under article 58–10.

Therefore, there is no equality (justice) in this camp, to say nothing about reeducation. Simply put, they bother the life out of us. Canal builders are asking you to conduct an urgent investigation and to establish conditions for the reeducation of prisoners.

· 36 ·

Order no. 109 for the administration of construction of the Moscow–Volga
canal and the Dmitrovsky camp of the NKVD
22 May 1936[70]

The acceleration of summer work in the last year of construction,* as well as the high intensity of work, require special attention toward the working prisoners and special care to preserve the workforce. In this regard, special attention should be paid to the newly arriving workers, since they are the most prone to emaciation and various diseases.

At the same time, in several regions (Volga, Tempy, Tekhnika, Iuzhny, Vostochny) there have been instances of blatant violation of the directives on the proper use of prisoners and on the use of that part of the workforce incapable of hard labor, which naturally brings about a rapid emaciation of people and their transformation into invalids.

With no time left, and facing an absolute need to finish all earth-moving and concrete-laying tasks by fall, it is impossible to engage in extensive recuperation activities by removing people from work, as was done last year. Under these conditions, the only recuperation option is the night sanitary camps, where people don't have to be removed from work.[71] [. . .]

Deputy Head of Construction and Head of Dmitlag of the NKVD USSR, Chief Major of State Security, S. Firin.

---

* The Moscow-Volga canal construction was completed in 1937.

· 37 ·

Excerpts from the draft order for the administration of construction
of the Moscow–Volga canal
August 1936[72]

In some districts, malicious and deceptive foremen and team leaders, striving to improve their output figures, have threatened the supervisory foremen and BIK* workers by forcing them to falsify the reported volume of work accomplished. When honest and devoted supervisory foremen and BIK workers did not accede, the fabricators of the crime moved from threats to action. Cases of violence against and the beating of supervisory foremen and BIK workers have been registered again lately in Volzhsky, Orevsky, and Central regions.

For example, on 12 August of this year, in the first section in the Volzhsky region, team leader Urutiunov, unhappy with the controlled measurements of foreman Nikonov, hit him in the face and then grabbed a sledgehammer and tried to hit Nikonov with it, but people managed to wrestle the sledgehammer away from him. Foreman Vasilenko witnessed the assault. The head of the site, free worker Zertsalov, knew about the assault but refused to call the headmaster on duty and even to sign immediately the report of the assault.

On the same day, the foreman of Team no. 3, prisoner Ivanov, attempted to force senior prisoner worker Gagarinov to falsify the report of the amount of his work. Fearing trouble, Gagarinov left to review the work of another team. In the meantime, foreman Ivanov assaulted the supervisory foreman, prisoner Oparinov, and beat him up.

On 22 August, in the first section of the Orevsky region, the foreman prisoner Dzhembailov ran into the supervisory foreman, prisoner Negodiaev, and beat him with a stick for his refusal to approve the report of the work not done by his team. The assault was registered in a report by the clerk of the works, Tsupa, and the deputy clerk of the works, Semykin. There have been multiple beatings in the fourth section of the same region.

In the fourth section of the Central region, the laboratory assistant at the Meneevsky mine (promoter of the quality of gravel), prisoner Levkovsky, was beaten up twice. On 14 August the foreman of Team no. 33–1, prisoner Gasanov, beat up Levkovsky; and on 21 August it was the foreman of Team no. 35–1, prisoner Dzhelamkhan, who beat up Levkovsky. In April the BIK technician Blokhin was beaten in the fourth section. On

---

* Bureau of Instrumental Control Appraisal, which controlled the productivity of work on the Moscow–Volga canal.

29 May someone raided the BIK office and destroyed some of the technical documents.

For the most part, the beatings of and violence against the supervisory foremen and the BIK workers went unpunished, thus creating an atmosphere of impunity.[73] [. . .]

· 38 ·

Order no. 181 for the administration of construction of the
Moscow–Volga canal and the Dmitrovsky camp of the NKVD
8 September 1936[74]

While inspecting the works at the water supply section today, I personally saw that the construction is still plagued with a lack of discipline: dozens and hundreds of people were sitting and lying near the road at the 2d, 3d, and 4th sectors during the workday. Not a single manager made an effort to make these idlers work.

I order:

Giving the head of the water supply section, comrade Usievich, a warning for failure to implement my directive on constant systematic control over those working in production.

Reprimanding the heads of the 2d, 3d, and 4th sectors of the water supply section and warning them that if this phenomenon becomes recurrent, they will be fired.

All heads of sections, sectors, and installations should institute a ten-minute break for rest and smoking each hour and a half, marked by a signal or by raising and lowering a flag. Once the flag is raised or the signal (horn) is sounded, everybody should immediately get back to work and not stop until the next signal. All those violating this order should be put in confinement.

This order shall be announced in every section during roll calls.

Head of the GULAG of the NKVD USSR,
Head of the Construction of the Moscow–Volga Canal,
Commissar of State Security, Third Degree,
M. Berman.

The Dmitrovsky camp was special because it was located in the center of the country, at the outskirts of the capital, and thus fell under the direct supervision of the supreme Gulag leadership. Other camp bosses, whose camps were not only located in remote, inaccessible areas but composed of sections that were sometimes hundreds of kilometers apart, felt themselves much less constrained. For a while, Moscow did not disturb the relative tranquility of the Gulag princes, as long as they fulfilled economic plans. In 1937–38, however, the situation changed as purges among the chekists mounted, and commissions from the center actively searched the camps for compromising materials. One such investigation, undertaken in the Ukhta-Pechora camp in late 1937–early 1938, revealed the practices that had developed there in the previous period of relative stability.

· 39 ·

Excerpt from a report to the head of the GULAG of the NKVD USSR,
I. I. Pliner, on the isolation and regimen of prisoners and the sanitary
conditions of the guards in the Ukhta-Pechora camp
20 January 1938[75]

To the head of the Chief Administration of NKVD Camps on the state of isolation and the regimen for prisoners and on the sanitary conditions of the guards in the Ukhta-Pechora camp.

Top secret.

The Ukhta-Pechora camp occupies a huge territory, with very limited means of communication and transportation, especially in its northern part. The sections of the camp are hundreds of kilometers away from the camp administration, which, given the difficulty of communications, especially in the winter, hampers the direct management of these sections (Vorkuta, Pechora, etc.)

For the most part, the Ukhtpechlag contingent of prisoners are extremely dangerous. Of the 54,947 total number of prisoners (as of 1 December 1937), there are 24,461 prisoners convicted of counterrevolutionary crimes:

Trotskyists	6,080
Spies	3,184
Subversives	466
Traitors	180
Terrorists	1,318
Other counterrevolutionary activities	15,233

In addition to that, the camp houses other categories of dangerous prisoners:

Gangsters	2,950
SOE and SVE*	6,150, etc. [. . .]

The large concentration of extremely dangerous state criminals in the camp required that the camp administration and the third department pay maximum attention to the issue of isolation and to organize a way of guarding prisoners that would be adequate for state security. In reality, the administration of the camp and its third department, having concentrated on production, followed the path of least resistance and forgot about the camp. As will become evident, issues concerning the camp as a place for the isolation of criminals were considered secondary in the Ukhtpechlag. Such an attitude toward camp problems had grave consequences.

First of all, almost everyone the entire camp (95–96 percent) has been left unescorted, which is unheard of in the camp system. Only confinement cells and certain teams or dangerous elements are guarded. Until October 1937 almost the entire camp had not been broken down into zones, and prisoners (especially in the summer) scattered at will after work without any control. Only now are some sections starting to create zones.

None of the camp sections practice daily morning roll calls and work assignments. This makes it difficult (and, in the large sections, extremely difficult) to figure out, after the work has started, who has escaped, how many people have reported to work, and how many refused to work, are sick, lack clothes, etc. Very importantly, none of the camp sections surveyed [. . .] have even the most elementary isolation rules.

This situation has led to frequent escapes and a deterioration of discipline among the prisoners.

In 1937, those escaped from the Ukhtpechlag can be enumerated as follows:

Total escaped	5,253
Escorted	278
Unescorted	4,975
Apprehended	3,778
Remain on the run	1,475

I.e., almost 11 percent of the camp population have escaped. [. . .]

Considering that there has not been even an elementary effort to improve isolation, the number of escapes should be considered "satisfactory," because only the remote location of certain sections and lack of roads can explain why the entire camp has not yet escaped. [. . .]

---

* Socially dangerous and socially harmful elements.

The third department of the Ukhtpechlag made no effort to prevent escapes. It is evident from the following data:

Escapees apprehended in 1937	3,378
Number charged with a crime only	275
Number convicted, among those charged:	
under article 58–6	8
under article 58–8	2
for counterrevolutionary activity	2

Thus, the escapees went unpunished. Moreover, among the 1,138 apprehended escapees from among the extremely dangerous contingent (Trotskyists, spies, subversives, etc.), only a few have been indicted. [. . .]

In addition to the aforementioned shortcomings in escort practices, lack of discipline, etc., camp section heads permitted outrageous things to happen. For example, a top-secret operation plan to prevent escapes was posted in the courtyard of the 5th section office for everybody to see. Last November seven people escaped from Railway Team no. 13. The head of the camp, however, did not call for a search for one month, expecting them "to return."

Remarkably, there is a "tradition" not to regard as escapes cases when prisoners move from one section of the camp to another, even though the sections are hundreds of kilometers apart.* [. . .]

In a situation where elementary rules of isolation are lacking, escort practices are not followed, zones are not established, and escapes are hardly curtailed, to strengthen the regimen and discipline in the camp is almost impossible. It is notable that the camp administration did not seriously and systematically deal with the issue of the camp regimen, and it was completely ignored in the camp sections. Characteristic of the entire camp is demoralization and a lack of discipline among prisoners, and, most notably, the disappearance of a boundary between even the extremely dangerous prisoners and free workers.

Until recently, in Kniazh-Pogost free workers were afraid to go around the camp after dark because of unrestrained robbery and banditry. Moreover, even the VOKhR guards walked at night with their arms drawn. [. . .]

During the celebration of the twentieth anniversary of VChK-OGPU-NKVD organs, all free staff of the fifth department were brought into the zone because the ceremony was held in the club for prisoners. After the ceremony, prisoners—spies and subversives—danced with the wives of the VOKhR commanders and workers of the third department. It is possi-

---

* The reference is to unauthorized relocation by prisoners.

ble to give more such facts. They are characteristic of the style of relations between free workers and prisoners (participation by the wives of free workers in plays with prisoners, etc.). It is important to note that free workers and prisoners quite commonly call each other "comrade" or by first name, even extremely dangerous state criminals.

As mentioned above, a lack of zones and escort practices has led to the effective disuse of isolation. After the NKVD directive to reinforce the regimen for the extremely dangerous contingent, in some camp sections (first, second, and third works), those convicted for espionage, subversion, terror, and other dangerous crimes have been moved into a zone. However, this produced no results, because the entrance to the zone remained unguarded and unattended. Therefore, the NKVD directive to escort the extremely dangerous contingent was not implemented.

In stationary camp sections (first, second, and third works, Kniazh-Pogost, etc.) the prisoners live in three–four apartment houses, where it is impossible to establish order, demand discipline, or, most important, exercise control. [. . .]

The directive by the deputy people's commissar to remove extremely dangerous contingents from management positions is not followed. [. . .]

The GULAG directive to discontinue joint living arrangements is not followed. For example, the spy Rodionov (railroad construction) lives together with his wife and child; prisoner Morozov, sentenced under article 35, lives with his wife, who was sentenced to ten years for treason; spies Orlov, Rozhik (second works) live with families, etc.

In some cases, camp managers ask to maintain joint living arrangements, even though this has no practical justification and, in the case of Ukhtpechlag, violates the interests of state security.

Notable is the extreme lack of discipline among prisoners: most of the prisoners did not stand up when the inspection commission visited their quarters. [. . .]

GULAG Brigade
Head of the Regimen Department of the GULAG of the NKVD,
First Lieutenant of State Security Dibobas.
Head of the Political Department of the GULAG of the NKVD,
Sublieutenant of State Security Kolesnichenko.
20 January 1938.

At approximately the same time, in February 1938, the procurator of the USSR, Vyshinsky, reported on the results of other inspections conducted by the Procuracy: "In Khabarovsk, despite GULAG directives, prisoners in some of the so-called missions (small sections) of the Dallag live de facto as free citizens. A representative of the Procuracy of the USSR visited one of these missions. In one of the barracks he saw a poster, which characterizes the actual regimen of those prisoners. The poster read: 'It is shameful to leave for outside work!' This poster is self-explanatory and describes the regimen for prisoners who are left almost completely unguarded in Khabarovsk."[76]

Most probably, the situations in the Ukhta-Pechora camp and in Khabarovsk were not quite typical of the rest of the Gulag. But neither were they an exception.[77] Many camps conducted operations throughout vast, remote territories. In 1934–37 the number of escapes was very high, between 58,000 and 83,000 each year—testifying to the relative laxity of the regimen (see Document 97). This "liberalism," however, was short-lived.

Colonies for Children

The high crime rate and homelessness among children, a result of the cataclysms that had shaken the country, always worried the government. Many government organs dealt with homeless children and juvenile offenders, employing "pedagogical measures" and repression. Subsequently, homeless children and convicted youth were kept in either regular or closed orphanages or centers, in the People's Commissariat of Justice installations for young criminals, and (usually for those over sixteen years) even in prisons and adult camps.

· 40 ·

Report to the head and the deputy head of the GULAG
of the NKVD USSR on juveniles in the camps
[Before 6 September 1934][78]

To the head of the GULAG NKVD, Com. Berman.*
To the deputy head of the GULAG of the NKVD, Com. Pliner.
Report.
GULAG directive no. 563563 of 29 September 1932 on concentrating

---

* Handwritten in the margins: "We must support those kids seriously so that they get real qualifications and become workers. After giving them qualifications, we will send them to plants and factories in an organized way. Recommend to all camp heads that they send them all to school and provide them with work, and report on them regularly. M. Berman. 6 September"; and "Directives given to concentrate all minors in one camp."

minors in the camp and organizing special work among them has not been fully implemented. There are still intolerable deficiencies:

1. Most of the minors are not gathered together and are staying with adult prisoners, often the inveterate criminals, who negatively influence the children.

2. Most of them are employed in general work. The only difference is a reduction of tasks, but the work (earth moving, lumbering, etc.) does not enhance any of their qualifications.

3. [They] do not receive professional training or education in the team.

4. There is no adequate cultural education, [children] are not given literacy classes, and they are not involved in mass cultural activities.

The aforementioned shortcomings are caused, on the one hand, by the underestimation of the camp administration of the importance of work with minors and, on the other, by the lack of an economic base.

According to KVO [Culture and Education Department] camp reports, partial concentration has been undertaken.

	Camp	[Number of Minors] Gathered Together	Total Minors
1.	Prorvlag	90	96
2.	Siblag	130	237
3.	Temlag	480	647
4.	Karlag	no data	585
5.	Sazlag	no data	79
6.	Dallag	no data	507
	Total	706	2,251

The results in the mentioned camps are not satisfactory given the requirements to reeducate juvenile prisoners. Within the organized groups of minors, theft, card games, hooliganism, failure to report to work, and dismal mass cultural work are commonplace.

In the fifth section of Siblag, only fourteen out of fifty people [juveniles] are working in a makeshift cooperage, with the walls and roof made of brushwood and straw, as in prehistoric times. The rest perform general tasks. Despite the able approach of the supervisor, the collective engages in the following "activity": the loser in a card game gets his teeth broken, or he has to hit a guard or set fire to the toilet. As a result, the toilet is burnt. In the Karlag, juvenile prisoners terrorize the camp, they kick up rows, and sexual perversion is not uncommon. In the Belbaltlag, they had to use armed force to subdue the minors. Similar facts are reported in other camps. This is a result of hastily creating collectives without an adequate economic-production base.

Camps specializing in agriculture are not adequate for work with youth, because youth are not interested in agriculture, and it cannot be a basis for education. Such camps should be considered inappropriate for work with youth.

The results of this work show that the most urgent step would be to concentrate [the young people] in two–three camps with an industrial base. They could serve, after certain additional investment, as a foundation for camp colonies. The most appropriate would be the Temnikovsky camp, which has inherited the tradition of the Sarovskaya commune of the People's Commissariat of Labor and has woodshops, good living quarters, a school building, a club, etc. The Sarovsk section of the Temlag is for invalids, and it would not do any harm to use it as a camp colony for juvenile prisoners.

With an adequate focus on education, this colony could hold 2,000 people, which would almost fully resolve the difficulties of educating juvenile prisoners (up to seventeen years of age). They are currently in the following camps:

1.	Bamlag	451
2.	Dmitlag	420
3.	BBK	438
4.	Ukhtpechlag	7
5.	Svirlag	506
6.	Temlag	647
7.	Dallag	507
8.	Siblag	237
9.	Sazlag	79
10.	Karlag	585
11.	Prorvlag	96
	Total	3,975

Waiting for your instructions.

Attached is a draft resolution on the creation of a special colony for juvenile prisoners.*

Head of the fourth department of the GULAG of the NKVD, Shimko.

The Sarovsk labor colony for juveniles was created in December 1935 on the basis of the Sarovsky camp.[79] By that time, the problem of housing juvenile prisoners had gotten worse as a result of the 1935 anti-crime campaign. Stepping up the fight against juvenile crime brought an increase in the number of convictions.

The spread of crime among children and youth was a natural result of the drastic transformation of the traditional lifestyle of millions of

---

* The draft could not be found.

people, mass repression, the sharp deterioration in living conditions, and famine. Millions of children lost their parents and found themselves on the street. In mid-1934 there were 386,000 children in the orphanages alone.[80] The number of neglected homeless children was astonishing. Young people often committed brutal crimes, typically in a group. Police organs persisted in their criticism of the existing laws, which permitted criminal prosecution only of people more than sixteen years old.[81] Various government commissions discussed the problem of juvenile crime and homelessness in 1934. The decisive factor was, however, the dissatisfaction of the supreme Soviet leadership.

On 19 March 1935, Voroshilov sent to Stalin, Molotov, and Kalinin a letter addressing the facts of juvenile crime in Moscow. In particular, he highlighted the case of two sixteen-year-olds who committed a double murder, inflicted three injuries, and were sentenced to ten years in prison. Soon, however, their term was cut in half because of their age. "Com. Vulf,* with whom I discussed this over the telephone, informed me that this was not an isolated case, and that there were up to 3,000 registered juvenile hooligans, among them about 800 obvious gangsters capable of anything. On the average, he arrests up to 100 hooligans and homeless children every day, and he has nowhere to send them (nobody wants to take them)," wrote Voroshilov. "I think that the Central Committee should instruct the NKVD to organize a settlement of not only homeless but also neglected children and thus protect the capital from the growing problem of juvenile hooliganism. As to this particular case, I do not understand why we cannot just shoot these scoundrels. Do we have to wait until they grow up to be even greater thugs?"[82]

After this appeal, Molotov (having undoubtedly discussed it with Stalin) probably instructed the procurator of the USSR, Vyshinsky, to draft a resolution on the fight against juvenile crime. On 29 March, Vyshinsky sent Molotov the draft, which was later discussed by the Politburo. Stalin showed great interest in the issue and made substantial corrections to the draft. Vyshinsky's original text was rather temperate and contained vague definitions. The first paragraph read: "Juveniles caught systematically stealing, using violence, inflicting injuries, or causing bodily damage should be subjected, at the court's discretion, to medical-pedagogical measures or criminal punishment." Stalin was not satisfied, and corrected the text so that the first para-

---

* Head of the police department of Moscow and the Moscow Region.

graph now read: "Juveniles twelve years old and older accused of theft, violence, inflicting injuries, committing murder, or attempting to commit murder should be prosecuted in the criminal courts and subjected to all forms of criminal punishment."[83] On 7 April 1935 the Politburo approved this resolution, and it was published on 8 April as the TsIK and SNK USSR resolution "On measures to fight against juvenile crime."[84]

On 20 April 1935 the Politburo approved a secret clarification of the resolution to be sent to judicial and procuratorial organs: that "the ultimate punishment (shooting) is also applicable" to children twelve and older. This annulled the old Criminal Code provisions that disallowed death sentences for people under eighteen.[85]

The 7 April resolution led to a rise in the number of juvenile convictions. As usual, punitive organs were particularly active right after the declaration of a campaign. In April–June 1935, according to the police, 9,800 juveniles were registered who had committed thefts or robberies, or had been arrested for hooliganism (before the 7 April resolution, statistics were not kept on juvenile crime).[86] As was typical of all repressive campaigns of the Stalinist period, "excesses" were commonplace at the initial stage of the campaign. For example, children under twelve were prosecuted "for crimes not spelled out by the law: children's pranks, occasional fights, and first-time petty thefts." One Moscow regional court "qualified as an expression of the class struggle the farmer's son's slapping the face of a collective farmer's daughter and sentenced him."[87]

In late 1935 the police apprehended about 160,000 homeless and neglected children, of whom 62,000 were sent to the NKVD child reception centers and 10,000 were arrested. The rest were sent home to their parents or to orphanages.[88] In 1936 the number of unattended juveniles apprehended was 156,000 (no data were provided on homeless children, whose number actually decreased).[89] Although not all apprehended juveniles were indicted, the number of sentences is rather significant: in 1935 courts sentenced 6,725 juveniles between twelve and sixteen, and in 1936, they sentenced 15,031.[90]

Mass arrests of homeless and neglected children and growth in the number of juvenile convictions made it necessary to reorganize the penitentiaries. The 31 May 1935 SNK and Central Committee resolution "On eradicating children's homelessness and neglect" provided for several types of children's institutions. The NKVD was in charge of isolation wards, reception-distribution centers, and labor colonies.[91] Next, the People's Commissar of Internal Affairs issued, on 7 June, an order, "On organizing work to eradicate children's homelessness and neglect," that created, within the NKVD USSR, a department of labor colonies for juveniles (as well as similar local departments). This department was put in charge of reception-distribution centers and labor colonies—which had been managed by the republican People's Commissariats of Education and the local organs of power—and the Gulag juvenile labor colonies.[92]

A 25 June letter from Yagoda to the leaders of the republican, territorial, and provincial NKVD departments summarized the official view on the tasks of the labor colonies: "Develop all details regarding the organization of production and education in the labor colonies so that they are not converted to either prisons or social security departments. The goals are to teach juveniles to work and produce merchandise that will pay for the maintenance of the colonies, to avoid spending state money in the future, and, right now, to reduce organizational costs."[93]

In fact, the principles "isolation—self-sufficiency—reeducation" were applied toward regular NKVD camps, not just children's colonies. Children's colonies were different because of their lighter regimen and less demanding labor. In addition, there were occasional attempts to educate the children by encouraging self-organization. According to the NKVD juvenile labor colony instructions, the colonies housed "juvenile criminals aged twelve–sixteen and homeless children aged fourteen–sixteen." Officially these "ward students" had to study as well as work so that they had a specialty by the end of their term. One of the most acclaimed methods of education was self-government, with children serving on the general assembly of the colonists and on the commissions in charge of various aspects of colony life (production, conflicts, culture, economy, etc.).[94]

Reality defied the proclaimed principles, however. Even internal NKVD inspections routinely exposed multiple violations of the regimen and crimes by both the juvenile colonists and the administration. Contrary to the rules, children under twelve were sent to the colonies. Often the colonists did not work, and their living conditions were terrible. Theft, drinking, and card games were commonplace. Colony bosses imposed harsh punishments, beat the children, and employed privileged nonworking "leaders" and "managers" to keep the rest of the ward students in check instead of using the organs of self-government. The appalling living conditions and the absence of armed guards resulted in frequent escapes.[95]

Soon the NKVD bosses rejected the principle of reeducation and tightened the regimen for juveniles by expanding the network of guarded special-regimen colonies. The first such colony was created in July 1935 in Arkhangelsk.[96] On 2 November 1935, in response to the difficult situation in the colonies, Yagoda signed a directive to heighten "juveniles' responsibility for crimes committed in the colonies." "Inveterate colonists" under sixteen were to be sent to the Arkhangelsk or Tobolsk guarded colonies; those over sixteen, to the Gulag camps.[97] In May 1936 three more guarded colonies were established, and the next year, another four.[98] Their number grew further in the years thereafter.

As of 1 January 1937 there were 38,000 juveniles in the labor colonies.[99] The colony workshops manufactured machine tools, fire extinguishers, trailers, metal beds, spoons, furniture, knitted garments, musical instruments, and photographic paper, to name just a few products.[100] The children who did the work had various destinies. Some of them won their freedom, and some were sent to camps, continuing their grievous journey through the Gulag.

Old and Young in "Kulak Exile"

In early December 1935, one year after the Kirov murder, Stalin, at a meeting of combine operators, initiated a fervent propaganda campaign. At the meeting, a Bashkir collective farmer, A. Gilba, said: "Although I am a son of a kulak, I will sincerely struggle for the cause of the workers and peasants and for the construction of socialism." Stalin then made his famous remark, "A son is not responsible for his father," which became one of the best-known political catchphrases in Soviet history.[101] It also hinted at the problem of the regime's relations with the many children of the "former [ruling classes]" and the kulaks. Discrimination and persecution based on family background threatened to generate more and more enemies of the Stalinist regime. The children of the many "enemies" and the "dekulakized" were growing up and forming a substantial part of the young and active labor force.

The authorities, who realized this problem at the beginning of the dekulakization campaign, followed a policy of separating the exiled youths from the older "counterrevolutionaries and kulaks" (see Chapter 1). In the early 1930s campaigns for the restitution of civil rights for limited numbers of special settlers (which included the right to leave exile) were popular as an important means to prevent mass escapes and to create division among the deported "kulaks." The creation of an "exile aristocracy"—that is, special settlers "who had proven their loyalty to the Soviet regime with their honest, productive work and good behavior"—contributed to a certain stabilization and helped to resolve the thorny issue of relations between the state and the second generation of kulaks.

These goals were part of the 27 May 1934 TsIK resolution that legally allowed the restitution of civil rights for "the most distinguished special settlers, particularly the youths." The restitution of civil rights and permission to leave exile could even be granted early, before their automatic application after five years in exile.[102] This liberalism was short-lived, however. In early January 1935, M. D. Berman, head of the Gulag, in response to the political currents after the Kirov murder, sent the following document to G. Yagoda.[103]

· 41 ·

Report from the head of the GULAG, Berman, to Yagoda
January 1935

To the People's Commissar of the Interior of the USSR,
Comrade Yagoda.
Report.
Reports from local sources show that there are cases of mass restitution of the civil rights of exiled special settlers who did not settle in their places of residence [in exile] and that after restitution many of them abandoned the labor settlements. A similar situation exists for those whose civil rights were restored on an individual basis. For example:

From the time of the creation of labor settlements to 1 November 1934, civil rights were restored to a total of 8,505 families (31,364 people). Of those, 2,488 families (7,857 people) stayed in the labor settlements—that is, 25.1 percent of those whose civil rights were restored.

Additionally, in November 1934, in the gold-mining industry in the four regions of the Sverdlovsk province, 900 families (3,240 people) simultaneously had their civil rights restored. This constituted 50 percent of the total number of those working in gold mining in this province. Of the 588 families in the Isovsky region whose civil rights were restored, 30 families have left, and 80 families are considering leaving. On 5 November 1934 [a total of] 1,689 people working in gold mining and at the

Karugol enterprises in Kazakhstan had their civil rights restored. In the Northern territory, of the 9,621 cases of restitution, in only 968 did the people remain in the labor settlements. A similar situation exists in some other territories and provinces.

To prevent similar incidents in the future, I suggest that NKVD administrative chiefs be instructed:

1. To forbid a mass restitution of civil rights for special settlers.

2. To restore civil rights individually, and only for special settlers who have settled in their prescribed areas of residence.

3. To start mass work among special settler–candidates for restitution to convince them to stay voluntarily in the labor settlements.

4. To prevent special settlers whose civil rights have been restored from returning to their home regions. [. . .]

Head of the Chief Administration of the Camps of the NKVD,
M. Berman

After reviewing this report, Yagoda issued an order, on 5 January 1935: "It is essential to send an urgent instruction that the restitution of civil rights does not give the right to leave [the labor settlement]. If there is no [such] law, we should bring it to the attention of the CC or the TsIK. Write a memo and cite these figures."[104] On 10 January, Yagoda signed an order to the heads of the NKVD administrations not to allow those whose civil rights had been restored to leave their labor settlements.[105] On 17 January he wrote to Stalin asking him to issue an addendum to the 27 May 1934 resolution, stating that "restitution of civil rights does not give labor settlers the right to leave their place of residence." On the margins of Yagoda's note, Stalin wrote: "Exactly." Poskrebyshev, Stalin's assistant, sent the document "as is" to the secretary of the TsIK USSR, Yenukidze.[106] On 25 February 1935 the TsIK USSR adopted the appropriate resolution.[107]

The new law showed the resolve of the country's leadership to prevent the dilution of the "kulak exile," and it bound labor settlers to exile indefinitely. Nevertheless, they still retained a small legal way to obtain freedom. According to the 15 March 1935 NKVD circular letter, the TsIK law of 25 January did not include young people not yet recruited, invalids sent to their relatives for care, or women labor settlers with restored civil rights who married free citizens, if their husbands moved to another region.[108] Later the list of the exempt categories was expanded.

In the spirit of the political campaign under the slogan "A son is not responsible for his father," the government adopted numerous decisions alleviating the situation of several categories of special settlers.

Thus, the SNK and Central Committee resolution of 15 December 1935 on schools and labor settlements allowed the admission of special settlers' children to the regular middle and high schools and to colleges.[109] A circular letter from the people's commissar of internal affairs that accompanied the resolution sent to the heads of NKVD administrations specified that the young special settlers admitted to the technical colleges and institutes, whether in the territory of exile or in other territories and provinces, were liberated and would no longer be considered special settlers.[110] Although the NKVD sabotaged the implementation of this resolution, it significantly changed the situation of the exiled youths.

Having discerned a new trend, local leaders started sending Moscow their proposals on how to reorganize the kulak exile. In December 1935 leaders of the Western Siberian territory sent the following memorandum.[111]

· 42 ·

Memorandum by the secretary of the Western Siberian territorial VKP(b)
committee, R. I. Eikhe, and the chairman of the territorial executive committee,
F. P. Griadinsky, on measures to strengthen,
both organizationally and economically, the collective farms
of the northern regions of the Western Siberian territory
[Before 26 December 1935]

To the CC VKP(b), Com. Stalin
To the SNK USSR, Com. Molotov
[. . .] Since the majority of the special settlers have embraced honest labor decisively and are working sincerely to establish nonofficial agricultural cooperatives, it is possible and advisable at this time to accelerate the restitution of civil rights for those labor settlers who have demonstrated in practice their active participation in the organization of nonofficial cooperatives and who have broken with their exploitive past. In particular, this should be applied to young people.

It is also important to clarify the issues of everyday life for the special settlers who have had their civil rights restored. Currently, the restitution of civil rights does not allow free movement or change of residence for special settlers. We consider it appropriate to somewhat soften this limitation on movement and to allow the special settlers whose civil rights have been restored to move freely between the districts of the Narymsk region. In addition, they should be given the prospect of becoming rightful citizens of the Soviet Union by establishing that, if they work honestly for five years, they will be allowed to move to any region of the USSR, except for the one from which they were exiled. In our opinion, this would not negatively affect the colonization of the North, because after five years most of the settlers settle and adjust themselves to northern conditions and would be unwilling to move to another region of the country.

Also, it is necessary to clarify the situation of the children of those labor settlers whose civil rights have not been restored. We think that the children of the special settlers who reach adulthood before their parents' civil rights have been restored should automatically receive their civil rights if they have broken with their parents and are independently and productively working. In real life, it does not always happen so. Special settlers' children who came to the settlements as little kids are still considered labor settlers after they reach adulthood, even if they break with their parents. Thus a system of hereditary labor settlers is being instituted.

We believe that it is generally important to step up our work to reeducate the children of settlers and to make them rightful citizens of our Soviet country, true laborers of a classless socialist society. It is essential to improve the role of schools and the Komsomol in achieving this task. In particular, we consider it necessary to allow the organization of pioneer groups at the schools attended by the children of labor settlers and the admission to the VLKSM [Komsomol] (with the approval of each case by the territorial Komsomol committee) of certain young men and women whose parents have had their civil rights restored and who have proved to be shock workers at work and activists in the social organizations and voluntary societies.

It is also necessary to resolve the question of unemployable and elderly special settlers who have no children or other relatives in the labor settlements. If we leave them in the labor settlements, we will have to create nursing homes for them and support them at the expense of the state. This would be quite inexpedient. We believe that the territorial procuracy and the territorial NKVD administration should be allowed to release from the labor settlements old men and women without children or other relatives in the labor settlements and permit them to move in with relatives who agree to take care of them (except relatives in Moscow or Leningrad).

Since the process of employment of special settlers is coming to an end, and some of them have had their civil rights restored, NKVD workers hope to start the transfer of authority over the special settlements to the local soviets and regional executive committees and of the economic administration of labor settlers to People's Commissariat of Agriculture organs. We believe that at this moment, this action is inappropriate and could negatively affect the whole process of colonization of the North by labor settlers and the foundation of the labor settlers' economy. This measure should be postponed until the labor settlers are all employed and the nonofficial cooperatives are completely in place. [. . .]

Secretary of the Western Siberian territorial VKP(b) committee, R. Eikhe

Chairman of the territorial executive committee, F. Griadinsky

The letter from Eikhe and Griadinsky was sent to the interested departments for consideration. The procurator of the USSR, Vyshinsky, wrote a positive response but suggested disallowing "free movement of the labor settlers whose civil rights have been restored between the districts of Narymsky region." However, Vyshinsky also made an important recommendation to extend the measures proposed for the "kulaks" of Western Siberia to other regions of the country.[112] The NKVD bosses generally took a similar position. In a response to the memorandum of the Western Siberian leaders, Yagoda also recommended extending the proposed measures to the entire country. He, however, did not support sending elderly labor settlers to their relatives for care. Instead, he suggested the creation of special nursing homes in exile, to be paid for by the labor settlers.[113] Yagoda's radical stance can be easily explained. Indeed, as the Western Siberian leaders pointed out, the NKVD was trying to completely rid itself of the labor settlements and to subordinate them to the local authorities. Yagoda had been promoting these ideas in the government since mid-1935[114] and used the Eikhe-Griadinsky memorandum to promote his plans: "The Eikhe and Griadinsky letter describing the good economic situation of the labor settlers supports the proposal to transfer the labor settlements from the authority of the People's Commissariat of Internal Affairs to the authority of the sovnarkoms of the union and autonomous republics and the territorial and provincial executive committees."

After the Politburo reviewed the memorandum, responses, and supporting materials, the Central Committee and the SNK issued a resolution, on 17 January 1936. It endorsed the Eikhe-Griadinsky proposals with the exception of the permission to leave exile after five years. It also rejected Yagoda's request to remove the labor settlements from the jurisdiction of the NKVD.[115] Thus the supreme leaders proved to be more conservative than the NKVD and the Procuracy, both of which supported the proposal to allow free movement after five years. The Central Committee and the SNK also vetoed Yagoda and Vyshinsky's proposal to extend the approved measures to other regions. As a result, only some of the labor settlers in Western Siberia whose civil rights had been restored were allowed to move freely within Narymsky territory, but their children received civil rights, and the unemployable elderly people were freed from exile.

The preparation of the 17 January resolution demonstrated that the supreme leadership of the country lacked clear ideas about the future of "kulak exile." While realizing the need for certain changes, the leaders were aware that the system of labor settlements could crumble, the exiled "kulaks" could leave en masse, and they preferred gradual and partial liberalization to those contingencies. Another testament to this position was the reaction to the letter of the leader of another region with a high concentration of labor settlers.[116]

· 43 ·

Letter from the secretary of the Igarsky VKP(b) city committee
(Eastern Siberia), V. Ostroumova
25 May 1936

To the CC VKP(b), Com. Stalin

To the SNK USSR, Com. Molotov

Considering rather specific working conditions in the North (Igarka), I am asking for your support in resolving the following questions.

[How to deal with] the special settler youth:

1. Over the course of seven years, there arose in Igarka (in the factories) a large segment of young people—children of the special settlers whose civil rights had been restored. These young people are the backbone of the Stakhanovite movement* (high productivity, good social habits). The best of these young people are eager to become Komsomol members. It would be good if, in individual cases, the most tried and distinguished Stakhanovite workers from the special settler children were allowed to join the Komsomol.

[How to amend] the draft resolution:

Allow the Igarsky city party and the Komsomol committee to admit to the Komsomol the most reliable Stakhanovite workers from among the children of the special settlers. Each individual case shall be approved by the territorial party committee.

2. The existing rules do not allow the Igarka special settlers (mostly young) whose civil rights have been restored to leave Igarka. The right to

---

* Refers to the campaign centered on A. Stakhanov, who officially set a labor productivity record by overfulfilling his quota by 14 times in 1935.

move at least within the polar regions would, on the one hand, raise the political morale of those with restored rights and would, on the other hand, force the managers of Igarka and other localities to fight for better services for the workers in order to attract them with superior living conditions and cultural entertainment and not by binding them administratively.

[How to amend] the draft resolution:

Allow the Igarka city soviet to permit the special settlers whose civil rights have been restored to move freely within the Enisei polar region: to the south, Turukhansk, Kureika; to the north, Potapovo, Dudinka, Ust-Port, Dikson, Khatanga, Nordvik.

3. The decree allowing entrance to institutions of higher education without regard to social background* was met with enthusiasm by Igarka youth. The city soviet and the city [party] committee received a number of applications from those finishing seven or ten years at school to enter institutions of higher education, including music schools. However, territorial organizations ([specifically,] the People's Commissariat of Internal Affairs) explained that the children of special settlers whose civil rights have been restored in the Krasnoiarsk territory are allowed to enter institutions of higher education no farther away than Krasnoiarsk, and then only on a case by case basis with the permission of the territorial People's Commissariat of Internal Affairs (there is not a single university in Krasnoiarsk).

[How to amend] the draft resolution:

Allow the Igarka city soviet to permit the children of special settlers whose civil rights have been restored and who excel in their studies to travel to any city in the [Soviet] Union to enter an institution of higher education.

4. It would be expedient to give the city soviet the right to restore civil rights to the most tried-and-true Stakhanovite youths.

[How to amend] the draft resolution:

Allow the Igarka city soviet to restore civil rights to the most trustworthy Stakhanovite workers from among special settlers' children under twenty-five years (who have spent at least five years in Igarka).

5. Approximately 15,000–18,000 people are living in Igarka (a census has never been conducted). About two-thirds of them are special settlers. According to current practice, marrying a Stakhanovite woman whose civil rights have been restored, or even a daughter of a special settler who was never disenfranchised, is incompatible with being a Komsomol member.

[How to amend] the draft resolution:

Consider inappropriate the existing practice in Igarka, where marrying

---

* Refers to the 15 December 1935 resolution on schools in the labor settlements.

a young person (a child of special settlers) who was never disenfranchised or who had their civil rights restored is considered incompatible with being a Komsomol member. [. . .]

Secretary of the Igarka VKP(b) city party committee, head of the political department of Glavsevmorput, V. Ostroumova

25 May 1936.

Ostroumova's letter is reproduced from Molotov's copy. He wrote "agree" next to each proposal to broaden the special settlers' rights. On 22 June 1936 the Politburo endorsed Ostroumova's proposals.[117]

Taken altogether, these resolutions, though not changing the situation in the labor settlements significantly, created preconditions for other changes and provided a legal foundation for gradual dilution of the "kulak exile," a dilution that accelerated in later years. Also, many illegal factors contributed to the eventual transformation of exile, the most important of them being the escape of labor settlers.

Difficult living conditions were the main reason for the escapes. Living in the harsh climate of semicolonized regions that constantly lacked vital resources was a daunting trial, even after the problem of famine and mass deaths had been overcome, and relative improvement of living conditions through house construction and agricultural development had taken place. Forced hard labor quickly crippled or otherwise incapacitated labor settlers, especially those employed in industry and at timber yards. As a rule, labor settlers had no living quarters of their own and stayed in dugouts or barracks at the factory, mine, or yard. Delays in salary payments were quite frequent, too, which doomed these remote labor settlers to a hungry existence.[118]

Mass escapes presented a major problem for the authorities. On the one hand, escape was a crime, and the perpetrators had to be captured and severely punished. On the other hand, hundreds of thousands of "kulaks" had escaped from exile from its inception through the mid-1930s, settled in various regions of the country, married, and found jobs. Their identification, conviction, and return to exile was politically challenging and economically inexpedient. Therefore, the authorities were rather flexible in dealing with the escapees, which accorded with their appeasement of young labor settlers.

· 44 ·

Circular letter no. 94 from the NKVD and the Procuracy of the USSR,
"On indicting labor settlers who escape from the settlements"
15 October 1936[119]

To all heads of the UNKVD of the republics, territories, and provinces
To the procurators of the republics, territories, and provinces
Here is a response to inquiries from local executives:

1. As a rule, labor settlers that escape from the settlements should be charged under article 82 of the Criminal Code of the RSFSR and related articles of the Criminal Codes of the union republics and punished by imprisonment, the term not to exceed three years.

2. Labor settlers convicted under article 82 of the Criminal Code of the RSFSR, upon completion of their prison terms, shall be returned to their labor settlements with no exceptions.

3. If family members of escaped labor settlers have underage children, the family members shall provide a written promise to come to the labor settlement where the escape had occurred. Local police organs shall secure their departure for the labor settlement.

4. Escaped labor settlers who are invalids, unemployable elderly people, underage children, or families without able-bodied men, as well as women burdened with small children—shall not be sent back to exile but left in their place of residence in the care of relatives and friends.

5. If escaped underage children of labor settlers have, by the time of their arrest, come of age and been engaged for a number of years in productive labor, or attended schools and colleges, they shall be neither indicted nor sent back into the exile.

6. Those labor settlers who, after escaping, have established families and are engaged in productive labor shall be neither indicted nor sent back to the labor settlements.

7. Heads of the local UNKVD, depending on the circumstances of specific cases (when an escaped labor settler has been engaged in productive labor for a number of years, and nobody is left in exile, etc.), are permitted to release such labor settlers and, if the local procuracy does not object, lift the charges against them.

8. The UNKVD resolution not to send escaped labor settlers back to the settlements shall be immediately communicated to the UNKVD in charge of each escaped person in order to stop the search and to clear that person's record.

Deputy People's Commissar of the Interior of the USSR, Commissar of state security, Third Degree, M. Berman.
Procurator of the USSR, A. Vyshinsky

All the legal and illegal ways to escape from exile altered its nature. By 1 September 1936 the NKVD had 1,845 labor settlements with 278,700 families (979,017 people) living there. In addition, there were 77,616 labor settlers whose civil rights had been restored. As a comparison to the 1 January 1934 figure of 1,073,000 labor settlers shows, despite new deportations and more births than deaths, the number of people in special exile had shrunk over the course of three years.[120] Data on labor settlers' movements in 1936 shed more light on these trends.

Between 1 January and 1 September 1936 the population of the labor settlements increased by 121,000 people. About two-thirds of them were new exiles; more than 18,000 were newborns, and the rest were exiles who returned to the settlements (forcefully or voluntarily) after escaping. In the same period, labor settlements lost more than 125,000 people (more than 14,000 died, more than 18,000 escaped, 4,000 were liberated, and more than 86,000 were transferred to nursing homes, orphanages, and the care of relatives).[121]

The resolutions of late 1935–early 1936 led, then, to the release of about 90,000 people and the transfer of children and invalids out of exile. Escapes became less frequent (for example, there were 200,000 in 1932 and the same number in 1933). This can be attributed to better living conditions in exile, the smaller scale of deportations, and changes in state policy that now opened certain legal avenues for restless youths prone to escape. Kulak exile decreased even more in later years. In 1937–38, however, escaped "kulaks" and labor settlers who stayed in exile fell victim to the Great Terror.

CHAPTER 4

The Great Terror

Never in Stalin's time was state terror small-scale or insignificant. The years 1937–38, however, saw an upsurge in the extent and cruelty of state repression. "Great Terror"—the term applied to those years, coined by Robert Conquest—has been accepted and used by generations of historians. New archival documents related to state repression in 1937–38 have not altered our understanding of the period, but they have clarified the essence and mechanisms of the Great Terror. It is now understood that the seemingly chaotic mass repressions were in fact a series of centrally directed punitive actions against various groups that the Soviet leaders perceived as real or potential enemies. These operations started in July–August 1937 and were ordered to stop around November 1938. They included bloody actions and mass shootings unparalleled in the entire sweep of Soviet history. The preceding period, from approximately August 1936, had been marked by a broadening of the purge campaigns. Although this prepared the ground for the Great Terror, it did not make it inevitable.

The Terror devastated the country and worsened the situation in the Gulag. Prisoners, including those arrested before the Terror, became its main victims. Mass executions, an unprecedented escalation of violence, starvation, and an increased mortality rate characterized the Gulag in those years.

Plans

Often the mass repressions of 1937–38 are called the *Yezhovshchina,* after Nikolai I. Yezhov, people's commissar of internal affairs from late 1936 to late 1938 and one of the main organizers of the Terror.[1] Historians usually associate him with the radicals of the Stalinist faction, who are believed to have inspired and promoted the Terror. Many try to discern what in the "bloody dwarf's" personality would account for the brutality of the repressions. Some even attribute his behavior to his physical ugliness: he was slightly less than one and one-half meters tall, with an unattractive face and figure, evident even in touched-up official photos. As much evidence shows, however, Yezhov was little more than a faithful executor of Stalin's will, cruel and enterprising though he was.

Yezhov's time came in late 1934, when Stalin selected the forty-year-old party worker, who had risen from secretary of the provincial party committee to the head of a department of the Central Committee, to undertake a special mission. The assignment was to oversee the falsification of charges against Kamenev and Zinoviev in the Kirov murder. Yezhov accomplished this task and, in early 1935, became secretary of the Central Committee and chairman of the Party Control Commission. After that, at Stalin's order, Yezhov worked together with the NKVD in conducting the repression against the "Trotskyists" and "Zinovievites," which culminated in the August 1936 open trial of Zinoviev, Kamenev, and other former oppositionists. This trial signaled the intensification of repression against everybody who had supported, directly or indirectly, any political opposition.

On 25 September 1936, Stalin and Zhdanov, who were in Sochi on vacation, sent a telegram to the Politburo in Moscow: "We consider it absolutely essential to appoint Com. Yezhov as people's commissar of internal affairs. Yagoda was obviously not up to the task of exposing the Trotskyist-Zinovievite bloc. The OGPU is four years late in [accomplishing] this task. All party workers and the most provincial internal-affairs representatives are saying so. Agranov should be retained as Yezhov's deputy at the commissariat."[2] The next day, the Politburo adopted a resolution making Yezhov the people's commissar of internal affairs and demoting Yagoda to people's commissar of communications.[3] Soon after that, Yagoda was arrested and, in March 1938, sentenced to be shot.

Stalin's telegram contained general instructions for the chekists: the

OGPU was four years late in exposing the "terrorist organizations" of former oppositionists. Under Yezhov, the fabrication of new cases picked up steam. On 23–30 January 1937 a second major trial, of the "parallel anti-Soviet Trotskyist center," took place in Moscow. Seventeen defendants (including such prominent statesmen as Yu. L. Piatakov, G. Ya. Sokolnikov, Karl Radek, and L. P. Serebriakov) were sentenced to be shot or were sentenced to long prison terms. The late February–early March 1937 plenum of the CC VKP(b) summarized the results and ordered a continuation of the purge. Yezhov reported on the former leaders of the "right deviation," N. I. Bukharin and A. I. Rykov (another leader of the faction, M. P. Tomsky, committed suicide in August 1936). The plenum considered them guilty of creating a de facto terrorist organization and endorsed their subsequent arrest. In March 1938 these leaders were tried, along with another group, in the third major public trial, and sentenced to be shot.

As was typical, the Moscow trials incited falsification in many cases of "rightist terrorist organizations" throughout the country. On 25 May 1937 the Politburo endorsed a resolution to exile from Moscow, Leningrad, and Kiev former oppositionists and former communists expelled from the party, as well as family members of those former oppositionists who were sentenced to death or to imprisonment for five or more years. A 15 June 1937 NKVD instruction toughened these measures further. It added Sochi, Taganrog, and Rostov-on-Don to the list of cities targeted for cleansing and ordered into exile the families of former oppositionists expelled from the party.[4]

The prophylactic nature of the purge was demonstrated by the broad sweep of repression in the army and defense industry. On 29 March 1937 the Politburo issued a resolution mandating retirement or dispatch to civilian work for Red Army officers who had been expelled from the party for political reasons. This was only the initial stage of the purge in the army. Arrests of Soviet military leaders started in 1936 and culminated in the June 1937 trial of the "anti-Soviet Trotskyist military organization." Many high-ranking generals, including the deputy people's commissar of defense, M. N. Tukhachevsky, were sentenced to be shot. Arrests at the top led to multiple arrests in the army in general.

The "exposure" of counterrevolutionary organizations led to purges within the party and government apparatus, including purges of secretaries of regional party organizations accused of lack of vigilance or even direct participation in the conspiracies. Changes of personnel that were particularly drastic prompted the party apparatus in late

1937 to respond forcefully to orders from the center to step up the struggle against enemies and demonstrate its initiative and unconditional support for the new shift in the general line.

Purges of cadres and structural reorganizations affected the NKVD as well. Frequent personnel shifts and arrests in the central apparatus of the NKVD, in the people's commissariats of the union republics, territories, and provinces, and among rank-and-file operatives were precursors of the Great Terror. The threat of being sacked and arrested was the best way to shake up the chekists and promote effective and determined workers. A letter from Yezhov to Stalin asking permission to nominate A. I. Uspensky* the head of the Orenburg department evinces the criteria used to select new NKVD leaders: "This is the first time that we recommend Com. Uspensky for a position of leadership. He is well trained and will, no doubt, master the operative work. He has one shortcoming: he is rather rude with his subordinates. However, I believe that he will overcome this shortcoming once promoted to a responsible position."[5]

The repressions that initially hit former oppositionists and the politically unreliable (from Stalin's point of view) sectors of the Soviet bureaucracy were accompanied by a general toughening of punitive policies and the spread of repression to broad sectors of the population. In July 1937 the Soviet leadership adopted decisions that revealed its intention to spread the purge to all "unreliable" social and national groups. The circumstances and immediate imperatives that led to these decisions remain unclear. Perhaps the best explanation of the spread of the purge was given by Bukharin in his 10 December 1937 letter to Stalin, which he wrote from his prison cell: "There is something great and bold about the political idea of a general purge. It is (a) connected with the prewar situation and (b) connected with the transition to democracy. This purge encompasses (1) the guilty; (2) persons under suspicion; and (3) persons potentially under suspicion."[6]

Apart from the unavoidable praise and mention of democracy, this letter is worthy of serious attention. Bukharin knew Stalin and the realities of political life in the 1930s very well. Throughout the early 1930s a large part of the population had been constrained in various ways (see Chapter 7). Stalin and his supporters viewed them as "guilty," "under suspicion," or "potentially under suspicion."

---

* A. I. Uspensky, who later became people's commissar of internal affairs in the Ukraine, was one of Yezhov's strongest supporters.

The very first move toward broadscale repression—the Politburo resolution of 2 July 1937, "On anti-Soviet elements"—indicated that the leaders of the country aimed at the physical elimination of a potential fifth column, given the danger of a looming war.[7] At that time, the purge encompassed former kulaks who had escaped from exile and criminals (no further explanation was given). The resolution instructed that the following telegram be sent to the secretaries of the provincial and territorial party committees and the republican Central Committees:

> It has been observed that a large number of former kulaks and criminals deported at one time from various regions to the North and to Siberian districts and then returning to their regions at the expiration of their period of exile are chief instigators in all sorts of anti-Soviet crimes, including sabotage. This has occurred both in the kolhozes and sovkhozes as well as in the areas of transport and in certain branches of industry. The CC of the VKP(b) recommends to all secretaries of regional and territorial organizations and to all regional, territorial, and republican representatives of the NKVD that they register all kulaks and criminals who have returned home in order that the most hostile of them be forthwith arrested and executed by means of a troika and that the remaining, less active but nevertheless hostile elements be listed and exiled to districts [*raiony*] as indicated by the NKVD. The CC of the VKP(b) recommends that the names of those comprising the troikas be presented to the CC within five days, as well as the number of those subject to execution and the number of those subject to exile. Secretary of the CC, I. Stalin[8]

While preparations were under way for this operation, it was decided to conduct a series of smaller operations of the same kind. On 24 July 1937 the NKVD was ordered to start "a special purge of the personnel of the water stations (especially the filtration systems), bacteriological stations, research institutes, and laboratories dealing with microbiology." The following categories of workers had to be immediately arrested: all foreign nationals, naturalized foreigners, "individuals related to foreign countries, [and to] foreign intelligence and its agents," and "active anti-Soviet elements."[9]

On 25 July 1937, Yezhov signed an operative order from the People's Commissariat of Internal Affairs, no. 00439, which read: "Recent operative and investigative materials have proven that the German General Staff and the Gestapo are organizing broadscale espionage and subversive work at the most important, primarily defense, industrial enterprises by utilizing German nationals who have taken root there. Agents among the German nationals, who are already engaged in wrecking and subversion, concentrate on organizing subversive acts at a time of war and prepare cadres of subversives for that purpose." Local NKVD administrations, within three days upon the receipt of this order, had to send to Moscow lists of all German nationals working at military plants and enterprises with defense subdivisions, and on the railroads, as well as those who had previously worked at such enterprises but stayed in the USSR after leaving those jobs. Starting on 29 July, all those listed had to be arrested within five days. The order urged "particular carefulness" in conducting investigations, "full exposure of the still-hidden agents of German intelligence," and the immediate arrest of new "spies, subversives, and terrorists" exposed in the course of the investigation. Similarly, the order instructed that by 1 September (by 15 September for Eastern Siberia and the Far East), all German nationals be accounted for who worked at nonmilitary enterprises, in agriculture, and in other offices, along with those who had taken Soviet citizenship and used to work in military enterprises. Each case had to include a memorandum summarizing the compromising materials and the decision to make an arrest. Similar memorandums on German political émigrés who had worked in military enterprises and accepted Soviet citizenship had to be presented by 5 August.[10] The operation against the Germans opened a series of similar actions against other nationalities that became an important part of the Great Terror.

On 31 July 1937, after consultations that took much more than the five days established by the 2 July directive, the Politburo reviewed the draft operational order by the People's Commissariat of Internal Affairs, "On the operation to repress former kulaks, criminals, and other anti-Soviet elements." Yezhov's NKVD deputy, M. P. Frinovsky, was put in charge of this most significant action of the Great Terror. Order no. 00447, a voluminous document, has been published many times in Russian and other languages, including English,[11] because it became the core of the mass repressions of "anti-Soviet elements" in 1937–38.

Order no. 00447 initiated operations "to repress former kulaks, criminals, and other anti-Soviet elements," starting between 5–15 August (depending on the region) and concluding in four months. It named the "contingents to be repressed," which included all who in some form opposed the Soviet regime or had been a victim of state terror: the kulaks who had completed their terms of exile or who had escaped; former members of anti-Bolshevik parties (Socialist Revolutionaries, Georgian Mensheviks, Mussavatists, Dashnaks, etc.); former White Guardsmen; surviving tsarist officials; "terrorists" and "spies" from previous years; political prisoners in the camps, and on and on. Criminals occupied one of the last places on this list.

The order separated those repressed into two categories: those to be immediately arrested and shot and those to be sent to a prison or camp for eight–ten years. Each province, territory, and republic was assigned quotas for both categories. In total, the order commanded the arrest of 268,950 people, of which 72,950 (including 10,000 camp prisoners) were to be shot. The order allowed local administrations to request additional quotas. Beyond that, families of the repressed people could be sent to the camps or exiled. Special troikas decided the fate of those arrested in the republics, territories, and provinces. As a rule, a troika consisted of the people's commissar or head of the NKVD administration, the secretary of the local party organization, and the procurator of the republic, province, or territory. Troikas enjoyed the extraordinary right to pass verdicts unilaterally and carry them out, including death sentences.

Soon after the beginning of the operation to exterminate anti-Soviet elements, on 9 August 1937, the Politburo endorsed another NKVD order, "On the liquidation of Polish subversive espionage groups and organizations of the POW [Polish Military Organization]."[12] The Polish operation came second after the German and was followed by more than ten operations against other "counterrevolutionary national contingents." Besides Poles and Germans, the repressions targeted Romanians, Latvians, Estonians, Finns, Greeks, Afghans, Iranians, Chinese, Bulgarians, and Macedonians. A special operation was conducted against the so-called Kharbinians (workers on the Chinese Eastern Railroad who returned to the USSR after the railroad was sold in 1935).[13] The Stalinist leadership viewed all these groups as fertile ground for spies and collaborators.[14]

The Polish operation was not only one of the largest; it also became a model for conducting similar national operations. NKVD Order no. 00485 on repression of the Poles established a new procedure for conviction, which was used in other actions. According to this procedure, each case was summarized in a short memorandum. Individual memorandums were put together and typed in a list. A *dvoika* (a two-person committee composed of the UNKVD head and the local procurator) reviewed these lists ("albums") and decided on the sentence: death or five–ten years in a camp or prison. After that, the albums were sent to People's Commissar of Internal Affairs Yezhov and Procurator Vyshinsky in Moscow for them to approve the verdicts and return the albums so the sentences could be carried out.

Another group perceived as potentially dangerous comprised families of the enemies of the people. Another operation was conducted to isolate them, though on a smaller scale than those against anti-Soviet elements or the national operations. According to the 15 August 1937 order by the people's commissar of internal affairs, no. 00486, the wives of traitors had to be arrested and sent to the camps for five to eight years, and children over fifteen who were "socially dangerous and capable of anti-Soviet actions" had to be sent to camps, corrective labor colonies, or special orphanages. The order furthermore commanded the transfer of orphaned children of enemies of the people to an orphanage or to the care of relatives.[15]

These operations, which made up what later would be called the Great Terror, were conducted with varying intensity until November 1938. Complementing them were the regular activities of the Soviet punitive organs, which became more active in this period. In addition to the troikas, which oversaw the mass operations, there were courts, military tribunals, and the Military Collegium of the Supreme Court, all of which contributed to the Terror. There are many descriptions of the numerous trials that were conducted throughout the country. In contrast to the closed troika sessions, open trials played an important propaganda role, and their proceedings were widely publicized.[16] The Politburo directly sanctioned the most important trials, especially in late 1937. It also usually determined the outcome. Between 8 August and 17 December 1937 the Politburo sanctioned approximately thirty-five trials in various parts of the country.[17] The trials of the Great Terror were notable for the frequency of conviction and the harshness of the sentences (usually the death penalty).

In late 1937 a purge of the border regions was renewed. The most significant aspect was the deportation of Koreans from the Far East to Kazakhstan and Uzbekistan in September–October, following a 21 August resolution of the SNK and the Central Committee, "On the deportation of the Korean population from the border regions of the Far Eastern territory," which aimed "to stop the penetration of Japanese spies in the DVK [Far Eastern territory]."[18]

· 45 ·

N. I. Yezhov's memorandum on the deportation of Koreans
from the Far Eastern territory
29 October 1937[19]

Top secret.

To the Chairman of the Council of People's Commissars of the USSR,
Comrade Molotov.

On 25 October 1937 the deportation of Koreans from the DVK was
completed. In total, 124 trains with Koreans have departed, containing
36,442 families, or 171,781 people. Only about 700 people are left in the
DVK (Kamchatka, Okhotsk, special settlers); they will be removed by an
additional train before 1 November of this year.

The Koreans sent to the Uzbek SSR number 16,272 families, or 76,525
people. Those Koreans sent to the Kazakh SSR number 20,170 families,
or 95,256 people.

Seventy-six trains have arrived and been unloaded, while forty-eight are
en route. The NKPS successfully conducted the transfer, and the trains
moved on schedule, with rare exceptions. Some confusion took place at
the destination points through the fault of the receiving organizations
(SNK of the Kazakh and Uzbek SSRs), which in some places failed to prepare for the arrival of the deportees.

The situation in the Kazakh SSR and the Uzbek SSR regarding the
placement and economic use of the deportees is clearly unsatisfactory and
threatens to place the last parties of deportees in very difficult situations.
Gosplan and the republican people's commissariats should be involved in
settling the deportees: the People's Commissariat of Land [should] deal
with agriculture, irrigation, and the organization of the MTS [machine
tractor stations]; People's Commissariat of Education, with organizing the
Korean school network; and the People's Commissariat of Internal Trade,
with organizing stores in the areas of settlement.

People's Commissar of Internal Affairs of the USSR, General Commissar of State Security, Yezhov.

The NKVD orders guiding the mass operations in 1937–38 show
that the Great Terror was a centrally organized punitive action,
planned in Moscow, against a potential fifth column perceived as capable of stabbing the country in the back in case of war. Substantial evidence shows that the author of these purges was Stalin and that he initiated the operations. The Politburo approved all important orders.
The punitive operations were centrally financed through special reso-

lutions, as with any other planned state enterprise or economic undertaking (see Document 48). The main elements of the 1937–38 operations—identifying the categories of those to be repressed, creating troikas and the reporting system, and so forth—had already been used in previous campaigns, such as dekulakization.

Skilled in conducting mass punitive actions, the Soviet leadership was well aware of the inevitable and self-evident desire of local leaders to overfulfill the plans set in Moscow and to demonstrate their initiative and vigilance. The directives from Moscow supported these initiatives as an important means of conducting and expanding the operations by establishing additional quotas. The center, as a rule, fully controlled local NKVD organs. Up to a certain point, Moscow turned a blind eye on the excesses committed by rampant chekists. Excesses, while violating the directives, were important to the plans for repression. On the one hand, they were an effective means of escalating the purges; on the other, they allowed the leadership to terminate the mass operations by condemning the excesses but preserving the main results of the Terror.

In any case, local initiative and excesses did not mean that the center was not on top of the situation, nor that the repressions had spun out of control. The main parameters of the operations, and the signals to start and end them, came from Moscow and were adhered to locally. Excesses would not have happened without orders from Moscow. The circumstances in which mass operations were conducted in 1937–38 support this conclusion.

Mechanisms

Although the Politburo approved Order no. 00447 on 31 July 1937, heads of the local NKVD administrations had apparently been informed about it earlier. The UNKVD of the Western Siberian territory, for instance, held a meeting on 25 July at which the draft order was read. Participants were informed that the draft was being reviewed by "higher authorities"—that is, by the Politburo. Still, plans for the repressive campaign were disclosed, along with an explanation for the reviewing of cases by the troika.[20] The rush to divulge information about an order that had not been formally approved shows that the issue had been resolved before 31 July (Yezhov would not have dared to send out the draft order without Stalin's approval) and that Moscow was trying to accelerate preparations for action.

From the very beginning, the mass operations were designed to exceed the quotas established by the center, as was made clear by the procedure in Order no. 00447 for requesting additional numbers. All the procedures anticipated escalation of the operations and an increase in the number of arrests.

After receiving quotas from Moscow, provincial and territorial NKVD administrations convened meetings of municipal and district NKVD bosses to distribute tasks in connection with the arrests. Local NKVD offices created lists of anti-Soviet elements. The former head of the NKVD department in Kozhevnikovsky district (Novosibirsk province), in a 1956 memorandum, described how the lists were created: "I reviewed all the materials (agent information, etc.) available at the district department and made up a list of I do not remember exactly how many—I believe 150 or 160 people. The list included former kulaks, active anti-Soviet clerics and sectarians, former participants in the Kolyvansk counterrevolutionary uprising, some exiles, former White Guardsmen, etc., who conducted anti-Soviet agitation and exhibited an insurrectionist and terrorist disposition."[21]

Making up lists using existing files and information from agents was apparently typical at the initial stage of the operations. At times, when such preliminary data were missing, the chekists resorted to more creative methods. For example, when the head of the Belozersk operative sector of the Vologda province UNKVD, Vlasov, and his assistants were told to "investigate and expose kulak and anti-Soviet elements engaged in counterrevolutionary activity," they "went to corrective labor colony no. 14 pretending to be a medical commission to select and send prisoners to other colonies. Having selected 100 prisoners, Vlasov and his men fabricated transcripts of their interrogations, at which the prisoners supposedly admitted having committed grave crimes against the state. They obtained signatures on the transcripts by presenting them as medical forms." The fabricated cases were prepared for nonjudicial review by the troika of the Vologda province UNKVD, and all 100 people were shot.[22]

After making arrests, NKVD organs created investigative files for the troikas. The investigative files usually consisted of confessions of espionage, membership in underground terrorist organizations, statements against others arrested, and similar "evidence." No further proof of guilt was necessary. It was not always easy to obtain confessions, however, because many prisoners refused to slander others or take blame. Various districts used different methods to extract confessions, described in many documents and memoirs.

The most humane was the direct falsification of interrogation protocols: the investigators wrote and signed transcripts themselves without ever talking to the prisoners. Since verdicts were usually passed without even bringing the accused to a troika session, such falsifications could not be exposed. Another widespread practice was adding testimony to previously signed protocols. Provocateurs and false witnesses ready to give any evidence were often used as well. The NKVD recruited "activists" among the prisoners, who engaged in "cell work": they pressured inmates who refused to sign confessions, tried to scare them, and advised them to alleviate their situation by confessing, playing up to the prosecutors, and so forth.[23] The chekists called these agent provocateurs "clowns."[24]

Living in overcrowded, unsanitary prisons on meager rations was a torture in itself that broke many people. But often it was not enough to obtain confessions, so the NKVD turned to physical torture. There are many documents and published testimonies about this.[25] Memoirs and archival documents show a gruesome picture of crimes committed in NKVD prisons. One of the most frequent forms of interrogation was the "conveyor" method, where several investigators took turns in the nonstop interrogation of a prisoner for several days without sleep, forcing the prisoner to stand or sit in uncomfortable positions. Often such conveyor interrogations involved beatings and other forms of torture. Descriptions of NKVD tortures could fill many pages. Some evidence is extremely depressing and difficult to read.

For example, an investigation of the NKVD administration in Chita conducted by the VKP(b) party control commission in late 1939 revealed multiple cases of falsification of evidence and torture in 1937–39. "Investigator Trofimov systematically beat" prisoner K., arrested in December 1937. He "knocked K.'s teeth out and kicked her. As a result, he damaged [her] spine, and K. could only 'stand' on her hands and knees." K. survived and even got back her freedom, and was able to tell about her interrogation. According to the investigators, "she was a broken invalid, unable to move on her own, with a shaking head, dislocated cheekbone, and shattered nervous system." At the time of this memorandum, Trofimov was still working in an NKVD organ.

Another victim of the Chita chekists, prisoner Sh., was arrested in

April 1938 and continuously interrogated for twenty days, including eleven days without sleep. Besides being forced to hold uncomfortable "stances," Sh. had to sit on the edge of a chair with extended hands and legs while investigators hit his legs with rulers. On 17 April 1938 "his head was squeezed between the steel bars of a sink, and he was beaten with sticks on his back and legs for two days and nights. After the beating, he was put in a stance and beat on the head with a paper-weight, a bottle [. . .], a chair leg [. . .] until unconscious, and then thrown in a lockup."

Another example is the case of the Vologda chekists, mentioned before. On 27 December 1938, Vyshinsky forwarded to Stalin and Molotov a copy of the statement by a worker of the Vologda UNKVD, I. V. Anisimov, who reported the 1937 violations by the agents of the NKVD department in Belozersk. Anisimov claimed that they "applied fascist methods of interrogation and murdered, through physical violence, those who sternly refused to sign the minutes prepared in advance. [. . .] They broke the nose of one accused man with a metal hook, poked out his eyes, and then dumped him under the floorboards. [. . .] They killed [. . .] two citizens with a sledgehammer and buried them under the floorboards."[26]

This and several other high-profile cases were fully prosecuted in 1939. After the investigation, nine people from the Belozersk regional department and the Vologda provincial administration of the NKVD were arrested. The Vologda chekists were accused of falsifying cases and convicting the innocent. In a report to Stalin and Molotov, Vyshinsky suggested that three of the arrested be shot and the rest sentenced to long prison terms.[27]

Such determined measures against NKVD agents were exceptional, even though crimes in the NKVD prisons were routine. Abundant evidence shows that cruel tortures were used almost everywhere on a regular basis. Aside from never being gentle, Soviet punitive agents were at that time members of one of the most criminalized and brutal security services in history.

Confessions extracted by torture provided new names for arrest. Also, from the very beginning of the operation, the government expected a high volume of flashy revelations. Following the example of the Moscow show trials, local authorities tried to fabricate as many collective cases as possible in order to expose a large number of counterrevolutionary organizations. The people's commissar of internal affairs in Tataria, V. Mikhailov, gave his deputy, M. Sheludchenko, the following written orders (which became known after the arrest of both of them in 1939): "The case is worth nothing unless we connect it to foreign countries, in particular Japan, Germany. [. . .] We need facts proving preparation for terrorist activity. [. . .] All attention is paid to group cases connected to the center or abroad. [. . .] Apprehend the rank-and-file immediately, connecting them to a group of 150–200 people. [. . .] Arrest individuals only as a last resort; do not overload yourself with individuals. [. . .] I think that in the category of counter-revolutionary nationalist formations alone, we should take 2,000–3,000. I will ask for 5,000–8,000,* because we have been working in-effectively and have not really started on that sector."[28]

The resolve to fabricate big cases involving counterrevolutionary centers and far-flung organizations was characteristic of all NKVD divisions in those years.

· 46 ·

Statement by prisoner P. A. Yegorov
20 December 1938[29]

To the CC VKP(b), Moscow, Comrade I. V. Stalin.

From Pavel Andrianovich Yegorov, former chekist, imprisoned for five years in the Ust-Vymsk Corrective Labor Camp, under article 193–17, paragraph *a,* of the Criminal Code of the RSFSR.

One cannot overestimate the merits of the UGB NKVD organs in destroying and physically eliminating the enemies of the people, Bukharin, Rykov, and their associates—Trotskyist-Japanese-German agents. In general, the merit belongs to you and the party, under whose leadership the UGB organs successfully began and completed this extremely complex operation, having shown the entire world the monstrous and traitorous essence of the Trotskyist-Bukharinist hirelings, who were unprecedented in the history of humankind. The entire progressive world rightfully admired the work of the UGB in 1937–38 and esteemed the punitive organs of proletarian dictatorship. This esteem was cultivated in the minds of the workers by the party and our press. Along with these glorious acts, that have forever found a place in the history of humankind, some local UGB

---

* Mikhailov refers to his request for Moscow to increase the quota for arrests and executions.

organs, having ignored your repeated reminders about showing love and concern toward humanity, took the wrong path of fabricating false cases of arrest. Unlike the hostile elements, these people were selflessly devoted to you and the party, true compatriots, who had never thought of any hostile actions against the Motherland. They arrested honest employees, artisans, and ordinary citizens whose interests did not go beyond their families. Many thousands of such people ended up being shot or imprisoned in the corrective labor camps.

I myself am a former chekist, having worked for sixteen years, from 1922 until the time of my arrest, on 25 January 1938, in ChK [Cheka]-OGPU-NKVD organs in Siberia. In 1937, I took an active part in liquidating the hostile elements in Novosibirsk province and the Altai territory. Lately I have worked as head of the special UGB NKVD office in Tomsk, at the rank of lieutenant major of state security.

We received the first NKVD USSR directive to prepare for a mass operation in July 1937. This directive made us put together lists of all counterrevolutionaries, socially alien elements, and criminal recidivists dangerous to society. After that a signal came to start the operation and organize judicial UNKVD troikas to review those cases. Thus, the main strike against the counterrevolutionary and criminal elements registered in our files was delivered in August 1937.

The successive directives from the leaders of the NKVD administration, delivered at the meetings and in the reports, implied the need to associate the entire operative contingent registered in our files with counterrevolutionary organizations, different in name but similar in goals, connected to the foreign intelligence of hostile countries as well as white émigré centers abroad. The operative workers of the organs interpreted these directives as calling for the immediate physical liquidation of all counterrevolutionaries, including passive manifestations, that served as the basis for various insurgent formations. Vigorously following these directives, the agents fully comprehended the historic necessity of purging our country of this contingent.

The starting point in accomplishing this task had to be the headquarters of these organizations, and operative groups were dispatched to different locations with the goal of finding these headquarters. Lieutenant Major Popov, temporarily filling in as head of the fourth department of the UNKVD, was sent to the Narym district in command of an operative group. Upon arrival in Narym, he buried various weapons in different locations and then arrested a group of former White officers headed by former Colonel Mikhailov. In the course of contrived investigative procedures, Popov elicited their admission to the existence of the Russian General Military Union (ROVS) in Siberia. Those arrested "pointed" at the hidden caches of arms, which were discovered in the presence of witnesses from

Soviet and social organizations. The arrested "center" of the organization provided extensive testimony about the supposed organization having a large number of members.

A junior lieutenant of state security, Golubik, head of the third department of the UNKVD, was sent to the Kuzbass region with a similar task and conducted an equally successful operation there.

Following the examples of Narym and Kuzbass, the UNKVD brigade and the local apparatus of the city department discovered a ROVS in Tomsk. There they created a "headquarters" using our agents, the former White officers Sitnikov and others, who were told that the Motherland required that they give such testimony and that they would be temporarily arrested to conduct operations inside prison cells with people arrested as members of this "organization." Later they were all shot.

In the Biisk and Altaisk branches, the apparatus of the third UNKVD department successfully conducted an operation against an insurrectionist Japanese espionage organization, headed by the former leader of the Altai partisan forces, Tretiak. This operation obliterated all the leaders of the partisan movement from the reactionary rule of [Admiral] Kolchak in Siberia, as well as a large number of Red partisans.

The individual counterrevolutionaries arrested, as well as separate groups and whole organizations under our investigation, were concatenated into entire networks with sizable branches.

Until approximately late September or early October 1937, this operation had merely been a matter of destroying all counterrevolutionary cadres and did not affect the population at large. Since September 1937, however, demands started pouring in to step up the operations, and cipher telegrams ordered the arrest en masse of all deserters, Poles, Latvians, Iranians, and people arriving from the KVZhD [Chinese Eastern Railroad] (Kharbinians), etc.

The UNKVD started allocating to the periphery the "minimum control figures" for arrests, which indicated just the starting point. For example, Tomsk repeatedly received control figures of 1,500, 2,000, 3,000, etc., [which encouraged] competition to arrest even more.

To assist the cadre workers in the [security] organs in this colossal, unprecedented operation, a large number of police, mid- and higher-ranking officers of internal and border troops of the NKVD, Komsomol members, the heads of special sectors of various offices, former chekists, etc., became involved.

In late September–early October, after we finalized all our calculations, the operation came down on innocent people who had never taken part in any anti-Soviet or counterintelligence affairs and had never compromised themselves through any such connections.

Many of us failed to understand the reason for continuing this operation, which scared us. But only the CC VKP(b) or you could stop the wild tempest of it.

The sincere efforts of some chekists to save innocent people only resulted in their arrest and death. The number of suicides among the chekists soared.

At that time in Tomsk, a certain Pushkin conducted the cell work. [. . .] Pushkin's "assistance" was enormous. [. . .] It was done as follows. Heads of the investigative groups divided the arrested into groups of five to ten people each. For the most part, these people had not known each other prior to arrest. They were then distributed among different investigators. The investigators, after receiving assurances from Pushkin that the arrested were ready to sign anything that the investigators would give them, called them in, filled out personal information questionnaires, got lists of friends from them, and sent them back to the cell. At the second meeting, investigators asked for their signature on the standard statement about their membership in the ROVS or a similar organization. Thus, according to the official papers, five–ten people who had not known each other turned out to be well acquainted, and had been recruited by one another to join a certain counterrevolutionary organization of which all the friends of the arrested also became members.

In Novosibirsk a similar approach was used, along with other techniques. For example, the third UNKVD department, headed by Junior Lieutenant of State Security Ivanov, used big, thick, old albums with heavy bindings, steel rulers, etc. All these objects were categorized as "first degree," second degree," and "third degree." They used these objects as a brutal means of beating those arrested. They widely utilized the technique of positioning the arrested on their feet for several days, often tying them to safes and doors to keep them from falling down, until they signed the protocols and wrote a confession about membership in the [counterrevolutionary] organization. A certain Malozovsky, who worked in the third department, conducted investigations of Germans, Latvians, and Lithuanians. He only put on paper what he considered necessary for the investigation and read to the arrested, off the top of his head, that they were devoted people, and asked to release them. Malozovsky always ended these protocols with the slogans "Long live Soviet power!" and "Long live Comrade Stalin."

They were then made to sign blank sheets of paper, and [Malozovsky] wrote the protocols [or] forged the signatures on the protocols.

The majority of those arrested were shot.

They used various methods to hunt down the Poles, Latvians, and other national minorities subject to mass arrests. They reviewed the lists of workers in offices, address lists at registration centers, etc. They often arrested people unlucky enough simply to have Polish, Lithuanian, etc., names but who had nothing to do with that particular nationality. Such people were listed as members of monarchist insurrectionist organizations (however, an oral instruction came from Novosibirsk not to mention nationality on troika agendas in such cases). A former peddler or artisan became a large trader or proprietor, an accountant became a tsarist official, agent provocateur, etc.

In the Altai territory, a troika reviewed cases without properly processing the paperwork. The investigation methods there were even more terrifying.

A huge operation was conducted in railway transport. The head of the sixth department, Captain of State Security Nevsky (aristocrat, former officer), boasted that he managed, through confessions, to nail a member of the Central Committee.

In general, it became fashionable for some of the chekists to attempt to bring down the big people. In the process of fabricating accusations and forcing the arrested to sign them, many chekists included the names of high-ranking party and government officials in the statements. The practice was considered of great merit, and such people quickly rose and advanced professionally.

This statement clearly described the main stages of the operations in 1937, as well as the relations between Moscow and the regions. The mass fabrication of group cases, encouraged by the NKVD leadership, caused a chain reaction. Each falsification brought in new cases and added new names to the lists of counterrevolutionary organizations. In case the confessions did not provide enough material to arrest a sufficient number of enemies, the chekists used roundups and indiscriminate street arrests. Such methods are described in a review of the Turkmen NKVD in 1939.

· 47 ·

Report on the mass operations in Turkmenia
23 September 1939[30]

Top secret.

To the Procurator of the USSR, Com. M. I. Pankratiev.

To the Chief Military Procurator of the RKKA, Brigade of Military Justice, Com. Gavrilov.

[. . .] The NKVD TSSR [Turkmen Soviet Socialist Republic] apparatus started mass arrests in August 1937, i.e., after the announcement of

NKVD USSR Order no. 00447. [. . .] After they used up the meager operative list of anti-Soviet elements, they started mass unjustified arrests only
to fulfill the quotas established by Nodev and Monakov. At the time of the
arrest, neither the age nor the past and present activities of the person were
taken into account. One could go to the market and be indiscriminately
rounded up, arrested, and interrogated, accused of anti-Soviet activity—
espionage, membership in a counterrevolutionary organization, etc.

The inquiry into the activities of the former workers of the third NKVD
department of the TSSR [. . .] revealed that, to fulfill the quotas, the workers of the third department repeatedly organized roundups at the markets
of Ashkhabad, Kizyl-Arvat, Mary, etc. During the roundups, all suspi-
cious-looking people were arrested. At the time of a roundup, they did not
check documents, and after that, the arrested were put on a "conveyor"
and beaten, and they provided information requested by the investigator.
[. . .] In the course of the roundups in February–May 1938, [. . .] 1,200
people were arrested, most of them workers, including party members,
deputies of the soviets, etc.

On the eve of the May Day celebration in 1938, Monakov gave special
quotas for arrests. These quotas specified the exact number of people to be
arrested but did not give a list of them. As a result, to fulfill Monakov's assignment, the workers of the third department, operative groups of the
UPVO NKVD, etc., started arresting people on the streets whose appear-
ance seemed suspicious for some reason. As a rule, arrests were conducted
without the sanction of the procurator. Without the appropriate procurator's sanction they arrested VKP(b) members, high-ranking Soviet and
party workers, scientists, and specialists—college and university professors and teachers, engineers, agronomists, etc. [. . .]

II. Illegal methods of investigation

The NKVD TSSR, city and regional NKVD departments employed
beating, the "conveyor," and other refined tortures to extract confessions
from the arrested, on a wide scale bordering on provocation. Investigators
beat and put on the conveyor all the arrested without exception, irrespective of the kind of material that the investigator had on them. [. . .]

In February 1938 the NKVD TSSR for the first time introduced the
"mass conveyor." After a while, owing to the high effectiveness of this interrogation method, the mass conveyor was adopted by other people's
commissariat departments. [. . .] For the mass conveyor, dozens of arrested people were lined up facing the wall in a special room. A designated
person on duty for the conveyor prevented them from falling asleep or lying down until they agreed to give the testimony required by the investigator. The stubborn individuals under arrest were also subject to beating,
handcuffing, or bonding. A large number of cases have been uncovered

where the arrested were kept on the conveyor for thirty–forty days without sleep. [. . .]

At these mass conveyors, also called conferences, drunk officers periodically beat the arrested without distinction, often with great cruelty. For example, the investigation revealed that the head of the fifth department, Glotov, inebriated and accompanied by other workers, repeatedly beat the arrested on the conveyor with an airplane cable. He insisted that they all confess to espionage. [. . .] Sadist Glotov went so far as to scoff at the arrested on the conveyor by making them dance a *barynia* [Russian dance], "cheering up" those who danced badly by pricking them with a hot awl. [. . .]

The third department put on the conveyor women with babies, professors, and scientists [. . .] and even arrested Iranian and Afghan consular officials without the imprimatur of the NKVD and the Procuracy of the [Soviet] Union. In the NKVD department of the Kerkinsk district, its chief, Lopukhov, and officer Ovcharov systematically beat inmates on the conveyor. According to his own testimony, Ovcharov, while drunk, broke two stools over the heads of prisoners, and within one hour made all fifteen people confess to espionage.

Agents from the roads and transportation department of the GUGB NKVD of the Ashkhabad railroad, Alekseenko, Semendiaev, and others, while exhorting confessions from the arrested, pulled out hairs from their heads and beards, pierced their fingers with needles, pulled out toenails, etc.

The beatings of the arrested often ended in murder. The investigation revealed about twenty cases of murder during interrogation at the departments of the People's Commissariat of Internal Affairs of the TSSR and on the periphery. [. . .] To conceal the murders of the arrested in the apparatus of the NKVD TSSR, the physician of the medical ward, Nikitchenko, who also took part in torturing the arrested, wrote false death certificates. On the periphery, officers wrote false certificates themselves, without the help of doctors, and stamped them with seals stolen from medical installations. Sometimes [. . .] they fabricated a case, reported it to the troika, and then used the troika resolution to create a false report on the execution performed.

One of the most outrageous means of exhorting confessions was, of course, interrogating those arrested "at the ditch." This meant [. . .] taking a detainee who, despite the conveyor and beatings, obstinately refused to confess, out of town to a place of execution, alongside those sentenced to death, and starting to shoot those sentenced to death in his presence and threatening to shoot him if he did not confess. [. . .] Such interrogations usually resulted in the slander of tens and even hundreds of mostly innocent people. In addition, the NKVD operative groups and the central apparatus of the NKVD TSSR widely employed "cell work" with those arrested. This involved one or several inmates beating or intimidating other inmates to make them behave as the investigator desired. [. . .]

The Maryisk operative group used one of the arrested Afghan consular workers for cell and conveyor work with the arrested. He was also a headman of the conveyor. Normally, when an arrested person was brought to the conveyor, this man met him and showed him his back and buttocks, red and black from beating. He recommended making all confessions and statements required by the investigator to avoid beating and other tortures.

The roads and transportation department of the NKVD of the Ashkhabad railroad maintained a "wet cell" where heavily beaten inmates were kept. To pressure a resistant prisoner, he was put in the wet cell to intimidate him.

Obviously, cell work with those arrested led them to slander themselves and tens of other people mentioned in the investigator's notes. [. . .]

III. Provocation, forgeries, and falsification of investigative materials and cases

Criminals among the former leaders of the people's commissariat, in order to fabricate cases, widely used beatings, the conveyor, interrogations at the ditch, cell work, interrogations of "staff witnesses," and "corrections" of the statements of the accused—i.e., adding to the protocols, on behalf of the accused, the most unreal and fantastic of inventions.

Lower-ranking agents, less experienced with such provocations, used cruder forgeries. They wrote interrogation protocols on behalf of nonexistent witnesses and signed them. They created fictitious protocols of searches and discoveries of large sums of money, weapons, etc. They wrote false affidavits on the social and material situation of the accused, converting collective farmers and former poor and middle peasants into kulaks; workers into former White Guards, members of anti-Soviet parties, etc. [. . .]

Cases of "individual anti-Soviets" were fabricated by the hundreds, and the process was rather simple. As a rule, to prove the "guilt" of the arrested, two–three fake witnesses were interrogated, who provided no relevant information but signed the protocol already prepared and composed by the investigator. A forged affidavit about the social background of the accused was added to the file, the accused was interrogated, and the case was submitted to the troika for review.

The investigation of cases involving violations of socialist legality uncovered hundreds of "staff witnesses," who, pressured by threats, deceit, or sometimes money, provided testimony against any person, as instructed by the investigator. [. . .]

Group cases, fabricated by officers-provocateurs, deserve special attention. [. . .] The entire Greek population of Ashkhabad—forty-five people—was arrested in the case of the "Greek insurrectionist organization in Ashkhabad." [. . .] A foul slander that was the basis [. . .] for this action asserted that the forty to forty-five Greeks living in Ashkhabad, including teenagers and the elderly, were planning to start an armed struggle against military units spread throughout Ashkhabad, to disarm and exterminate those units, and to overthrow Soviet power. In practice it was supposed to look like this: the Greeks purchase hunting and small-caliber weapons in the Dinamo stores; having armed themselves with small-caliber rifles and shotguns, they start an armed confrontation with the infantry division and the NKVD military units in Ashkhabad. [. . .] The character of any "testimony" from the arrested participants of the insurrectionist organizations [and] their plan of action does not require any commentary.

In June 1938 there was a fire at the Bairam-Aliisk butter factory. The cause of the fire was unknown, and the plant was brought to a halt for six days. Monakov, Balanda, and Akimov went to Bairam-Ali and arrested the entire shift that was working in the shop at the time of the fire, and then Balanda and Akimov set out to fabricate an SR organization at the factory. After heavy beatings, the arrested named over 100 workers and employees at the factory as members of counterrevolutionary organizations. They were immediately arrested. Among them were forty party members, i.e., 65 percent of the entire factory party organization. The investigation of the case of the agents of the third department undoubtedly proved the provocative nature of the case of the "subversive SR organization in Bairam-Ali." Of the 103 people arrested in this case, 101 were released, one died in prison, and one was charged with malfeasance. [. . .]

Military Procurator of the NKVD troops of the Turkmen border district, Military Justice First Degree, Kosharsky.

The CC VKP(b) reviewed the case of the Turkmen chekists in 1939 as part of a hypocritical campaign to "restore socialist legality" (see Chapter 5). Although we do not possess similarly detailed investigative materials for other regions, it can be said that the Turkmen chekists' crimes were rather typical. The growing scale of the repressions and the activity of the local NKVD bosses were inspired by the position of the supreme leadership of the country and the NKVD, who spurred the advancement of the mass operations and eagerly issued additional quotas for arrests and executions. By 1938 more than 500,000 people had been convicted under Order no. 00447.[31] This meant that the original figures, established in July 1937, had been significantly surpassed. As Order no. 00447 stipulated, local NKVD departments requested additional quotas on arrests and executions from Moscow. According to available documents, only a few additional quotas were approved by the Politburo. The majority of the approvals were issued by Yezhov without the formal approval of the Politburo but with Stalin's consent. On 15 August 1937, for example, the head of the NKVD administration for Omsk province, Gorbach, sent Yezhov a telegram reporting that as of 13 August, 5,444 people had been arrested in the first category,[32] and requested the increase of the first-category quota to 8,000 people. Yezhov forwarded the telegram to Stalin, who scribbled on it: "To C. Yezhov. I support [*za*] the increase of the quota to 8,000."[33]

Arrests and executions reached such a large scale in 1937 (see Document 91) that the mass operations seemed to have reached their peak, especially since they had been planned for late 1937. Nevertheless, on 31 January 1938 the Politburo adopted two new resolutions that determined a new surge in terror in 1938.

First, the Politburo allowed the NKVD "to extend through 15 April 1938 the operation to destroy the espionage-subversive contingents among the Poles, Latvians, Germans, Estonians, Finns, Greeks, Iranians, Kharbinians, Chinese, and Romanians—both foreign and Soviet citizens. [. . .] Recommend that the NKVD, until 15 April, conduct a similar operation to destroy the cadres of Bulgarians and Macedonians, both foreign and Soviet citizens."[34] Second, the Politburo endorsed the NKVD proposal "to set an additional number of former kulaks, criminals, and active anti-Soviet elements to be repressed." The resolution instructed that by 15 March (1 April for the Far East) an additional 57,200 people be repressed and that 48,000 of them be shot. The powers of the troikas were extended accordingly to fulfill this task.[35] Thus, the operations based on Order no. 00447, originally meant to be concluded in four months (by December 1937), were extended by another four months. On 1 February 1938 the Politburo also approved a quota for executions for the Far Eastern camps— 12,000 people—and, on 17 February, allowed the NKVD of the Ukraine "to conduct arrests of kulaks and other anti-Soviet elements and have those cases reviewed by the troikas, having increased the Ukrainian NKVD quotas by 30,000."[36]

There were two reasons for the extension of the mass operations into 1938: the inability of the chekists to cope with the sheer number of those arrested or earmarked for arrest in 1937, and a new set of goals and targets. The 1938 operations were not just an extension of the 1937 repression: they had their own goals and involved new categories of people whom the leaders of the country considered to be potentially dangerous. Stalin gave appropriate instructions to the NKVD. On 17 January he wrote to Yezhov:

> The SR line (both left and right) has not been fully uncovered. [. . .] It is important to keep in mind that there are still many SRs [Socialist Revolutionaries] in our army and outside the army. Can the NKVD account for the SRs (the "former") in the army? I would like to see a report promptly. Can the NKVD account for "former" SRs outside the army (in civil institutions)? I also would like a report in two–three weeks. [. . .]
>
> What has been done to expose and arrest all Iranians in Baku and Azerbaijan?
>
> For your information, at one time the SRs were very strong in Saratov, Tambov, and the Ukraine, in the army (officers), in Tashkent and Central Asia in general, and at the Baku electrical power stations, where they became entrenched and sabotaged the oil industry. We must act more swiftly and intelligently.[37]

Stalin thus provided new targets for repression and ordered the continuation of the operations. Most likely, there are other letters of this kind still to be found. According to the following memorandum by Yezhov, the NKVD had been actively planning for large-scale operations under Order no. 00447 to continue at least until mid-1938.

· 48 ·

Letter from Yezhov to Molotov on financing mass operations
18 February 1938[38]

Top secret.

To the Chairman of the Council of People's Commissars of the USSR, Com. Molotov.

In my letter, no. 63072, from 24 December 1937, I requested that you give instructions to provide the People's Commissariat of Internal Affairs of the USSR 22 million rubles to cover the costs of the operation to repress former kulaks, criminals, and anti-Soviet elements and 8 million rubles to cover surplus spending in 1937.[39]

The 22 million rubles allocated for 1938 is not enough to support the entire operation.

Preliminary calculations show that, in the first quarter, 47,000,000 rubles will be needed, including:

Maintenance for 167,000 people, at 2 rubles per day	30,000,000 rubles
Transfer of 100,000 people, at 100 rubles each	10,000,000 rubles
Escort, automobile and carriage transport, etc.	7,000,000 rubles

For the second quarter, the estimated expenses will be 46,100,000 rubles, including:

Maintenance for 108,000 people, at 2 rubles per day	19,400,000 rubles
Transfer of 217,000 people, at 100 rubles each	21,700,000 rubles
Escort, automobile and carriage transport, etc.	5,000,000 rubles
Total expenses for the first and second quarters	93,100,000 rubles

Considering the already allocated 22,000,000 rubles for 1938, an additional 71,100,000 rubles are needed, including:

In the first quarter	25,000,000 rubles
In the second quarter	46,100,000 rubles

I am asking you to order an allocation for this amount.
People's Commissar of Internal Affairs of the USSR,
General Commissar of State Security, Yezhov.*

On 25 February the people's commissar of finances reported to the government that, for 1938, the NKVD received 70 million rubles to conduct the operation "to repress former kulaks, criminals, and anti-Soviet elements."[40]

Apparently, the operation under Order no. 00447 did not proceed as broadly in 1938 as in 1937, even though it took twice the allocated time (the Politburo approved additional quotas for the repression of "anti-Soviet elements" repeatedly, and again in August 1938). That year the most significant operations were those against "national counterrevolutionary contingents." They were so extensive that Moscow had a hard time approving the large number of albums, the lists of those arrested. So it was decided to abandon the practice of approving the album verdicts at the center and to give local NKVD organs the power to approve the verdicts. On 15 September 1938 the Politburo endorsed the NKVD proposal to establish local special troikas, consisting of the first secretary of the territorial and provincial party committees or Central Committee of the national party, the head of the appropriate NKVD administration, and the procurator of the province,

---

* The document was signed by Yezhov's deputy, Frinovsky, who was responsible for the operation under Order no. 00447.

territory, or republic. The troikas had the authority to approve the remaining albums within two months (until 15 November) without sending them to Moscow. The resolutions of the special troikas were carried out immediately.[41] Between September and November 1938, special troikas sentenced 105,000 people, among them 72,000 to death. According to the Memorial society, in the course of the "national operations" between 25 August 1937 and 15 November 1938, a total of 335,500 people were convicted, and 247,200 among them were shot.[42]

The end of the mass operations was ordered from the center, just as their beginning had been. On 15 November 1938, Sovnarkom and the Central Committee forbade the review of cases by the troikas.[43] On 17 November, Sovnarkom and the Central Committee forbade "mass operations of arrests and deportations."[44] On 24 November, Yezhov was relieved of his duties as people's commissar of internal affairs. The Great Terror was over.

Victims

Thanks to the high level of centralization and the regular delivery of reports, the NKVD office in Moscow amassed extensive information about the victims of the various operations. These figures provided the basis for a secret compilation of reports for the Soviet leaders after Stalin's death. The archives have allowed access to these reports in recent years (see Document 91). According to these memorandums, in 1937–38, NKVD organs (not including the police) arrested 1,575,259 people, 87.1 percent for political crimes. Of those arrested in cases investigated by the NKVD, 1,344,923 people were convicted in 1937–38.* More than half of them (681,692) were shot (353,074 in 1937 and 328,618 in 1938). These figures probably reflect the true scale of the operations of the Great Terror. A careful examination of documents in different archives, mainly the Federal Security Service (FSB) archive, by Memorial Society activists increased these figures only marginally: "In only two years of the Great Terror, all NKVD organs (excluding the police) arrested more than 1,600,000 people."[45] There are no reasons not to trust these secret figures, which were used by NKVD leaders. Apparently they accurately reflected information com-

---

* The difference of 200,000 between the number of those arrested and those convicted is due to some people being convicted in later years, having died during the investigation, or being released.

ing from the provinces and regions. Of course, it is not clear how accurate the local reports were.

Data about those physically eliminated during the Terror need to be updated. Besides those officially executed, others died under torture or of extremely harsh living conditions, or both. Some of those deaths were evidently backdated as executions (see Document 47), but many were registered as caused by illnesses. Of the 13,044 people arrested for political crimes in Novgorod province in 1937–38, for example, 6,183 were listed as executed and 102 as having died during the investigation.[46]

Executions and murders during investigation characterized the Great Terror, setting it apart from other bloody events of Soviet and world history. If we assume that 700,000 people were executed or otherwise killed in August 1937–early November 1938, on average 1,500 people were exterminated every day. Even hardened chekists could not always effectively maintain this bloody pace. For the most part, the executions were individual. According to existing documents, no means of mass extermination (such as gas chambers) were used. However, regular shootings were sometimes supplemented by various sadistic methods of execution.

· 49 ·

Memorandum about the former people's commissar of
internal affairs of Dagestan, V. G. Lomonosov
30 December 1954[47]

Former Commissar of Internal Affairs of Dagestan ASSR Vasily Georgievich Lomonosov was sentenced to the ultimate penalty on 26 September 1939 by the Military Collegium of the Supreme Court of the USSR. At his 25 March 1939 interrogation on the violations of socialist legality in the NKVD Dagestan ASSR, he testified:

"I plead guilty to the fact that in 1937–1938 a series of crimes and hostile actions took place in the People's Commissariat of Internal Affairs of the Dagestan Republic, for which I, as the former head of the commissariat, bear full responsibility at the state level. These crimes are as follows:

"1. A violation of revolutionary legality by replacing, on my personal orders, in October–November 1937 in two operative groups, in Kizliar and Khasaviurt, the legally established extreme penalty—shooting—with killing by strangling for those sentenced to the ultimate penalty during a fake medical examination. I personally was in charge of this operation. In the Khasaviurt district we thus strangled 120 people and buried them in two ditches in the yard of a house in the center of town, where workers of the Khasaviurt RO [district] NKVD lived. [. . .]

"The accused were summoned as if being prepared for a transfer; I conducted a brief questioning about the indictment materials and the social background of the accused; then it was announced that to prevent escape during the night trip to the railway station [the accused's] hands would be tied. After that, the accused was moved to a room next door and strangled there with a thin wire in a matter of seconds. Then the body was moved, through a hole in the wall, hidden behind a piece of felt, to a shed. From there, once the bodies accumulated, they were put in ditches near the shed." [. . .]

The former head of the Khasaviurt RO NKVD, Viktor Anukhovich Makhaev, sentenced to the ultimate punishment, testified:

"Lomonosov decided to strangle with ropes those sentenced in the first category and to bury them in the yard where my family lived. [. . .] It was organized like this: The arrested was led to a room, and there was another empty room next door, the so-called headquarters. [. . .] Our task was to tie the hands of the accused. Lomonosov personally reviewed each case one more time, despite the existing troika resolution, and always talked to the arrested while reading the file. Thus, we announced to the accused that he would be loaded in carriages no. 2, 4, etc. Then he was led through one room into another, where the actual stranglers, Sergeant Boychenko and Top Sergeant Romanenko, were waiting.

"They put the prisoner in a chair and asked him: If you are ill, tell us. One worker told the accused: Lift your head, show your neck. Why don't you have clean underwear? At that time, the other—Romanenko—put a loop [around his neck] and strangled him. Each person took about five minutes. [. . .]"

Those arrested by the regular police were not among the 1.6 million listed as arrested by NKVD organs. Most of them were sentenced by courts of regular jurisdiction and by police troikas. In 1937–38, according to statistics from the organs of justice, regular courts processed the cases of about 2 million people, and sentenced 730,000 of them to prison terms (others were sentenced to corrective labor, received suspended sentences, or were acquitted, or their cases were remanded, etc.).[48] Only a small portion of these people were arrested for political crimes by organs of state security. There are no data about the activity of the police troikas in 1937–38. In 1935 these troikas sentenced 123,000 people (see Document 94).[49]

Apparently, in 1937–38 about 2.4 million people were arrested.

Various nonjudicial organs and courts dealt with about 3.5 million people (a large number of those given a suspended sentence or sentenced to corrective labor had no previous arrests). In the course of these two years, more than 680,000 people were sentenced to death, and 1.5 million to various prison terms.

The number of those deported and exiled in 1937–38 also needs adjustment but probably totaled several hundred thousand people. The largest of the actions, the deportation of Koreans from the Far East, involved more than 170,000 people (see Document 45).

About two-thirds of those sentenced to death or prison in 1937–38 were convicted for political crimes. That does not mean that the rest were ordinary criminals. It was difficult to distinguish ordinary criminals among the victims of Stalinist punitive system because of its extreme brutality and injustice, especially in the periods of mass terror. Even NKVD documents provide some indirect evidence for this. For example, an order by the people's commissar of internal affairs dated 21 May 1938 on the work of police troikas (created to fight crimes) mentioned convictions of "collective farmers who, though with a history of prior arrests and convictions [. . .], were not engaged in criminal activity and were not connected to criminal groups."[50]

According to the many regional martyrologies and books of memory (lists of those shot in 1937–38) that have been published in recent years, the majority of victims of the Great Terror were not the bosses, as it was sometimes said, but ordinary people accused of political crimes only because the leaders of the country decided to conduct mass operations. "Aleksandr Dmitrievich Abanin, born in 1878, [. . .] non-party member, Russian, blacksmith in the fourth mining section of the Kirov mine [. . .]"; "Pavel Fyodorovich Abbakumov, born in 1885, [. . .] non-party member, Russian, inspector in the ninth section of the financial department of the Kirov railroad [. . .]"; "Aleksandr Abramovich Abramov, born in 1882, [. . .] non-party member, Russian, individual peasant," etc. These are the first entries of the *Leningrad Martyrology,* a compilation of information about 40,000 people shot in Leningrad and Leningrad province between August 1937 and November 1938.[51]

Besides the direct victims of terror (those imprisoned, shot, deported, etc.) there were many people affected indirectly. Hundreds of thousands of people, while not being arrested, lost their jobs or were expelled from universities, the party, or the Komsomol. The reason could be "connections to the enemies of the people," relatives living abroad, an "alien" social background, or something else equally tenuous. The fate of these outcasts was dire. They suffered not only economic setbacks but also grave psychological stress, being under the constant threat of arrest.

Children of those repressed were always the first victims of the Great Terror. The principle "the son is not responsible for his father," proclaimed about two years before the Great Terror but never truly implemented in practice, was replaced by another principle: isolation of and discrimination against all close relatives of the arrested. According to the 15 August 1937 order by the people's commissariat of internal affairs, wives of "traitors" and their children over fifteen were to be arrested. A large number of young orphaned children were either taken in by relatives or sent to orphanages.[52]

· 50 ·

Note from Yezhov on sending the children of repressed parents to orphanages
1 June 1938[53]

Top secret.

To the Chairman of the Council of People's Commissars of the USSR, Com. V. M. Molotov.

In accordance with the CC VKP(b) resolution, from the beginning of the operation* through 10 May of this year, the NKVD has sent 15,347 children of repressed parents to the People's Commissariat of Education orphanages in Moscow and in the [Soviet] Union.

As suggested by the NKVD USSR, up to 5,000 more people should be apprehended and accommodated. To accommodate this contingent, [republican] Commissariats of Education should provide additional space: in the RSFSR, for 3,000; in the UkSSR [Ukrainian SSR], for 2,000, for a total of 5,000 people.

Owing to an increase in the size of the contingent, the NKVD will require additional funds to conduct the transfer of children to the People's Commissariat of Education orphanages in the amount of 1,525,000 rubles, according to the attached calculation. [. . .][54]

People's Commissar of Internal Affairs of the USSR,
Commissar General of State Security,
N. Yezhov.

---

* Refers to the operation against the families of traitors conducted in compliance with the 15 August 1937 order by the people's commissar of internal affairs.

Branded as offspring of enemies of the people, these children could not enjoy a normal life; indeed, they could face arrest after coming of age. Mass repressions were one reason for the growth in the number of homeless children and the surge in juvenile crime. Thus, in 1936 judiciary organs convicted more than 15,000 juveniles aged between twelve and sixteen; in 1937, more than 17,000; in 1938, more than 20,000; and in the first half of 1939, more than 13,000. The number of juveniles arrested for going about unattended was 156,000 in 1936, 159,000 in 1937, 175,000 in 1938, and 91,000 in the first half of 1939.[55]

The majority of the population of the country was, in various forms, strongly affected by the bloody terrorist policies in 1937–38. As was typical in an age of terror, both mean and mediocre people, as well as scoundrels, had a better chance of survival, even promotion, than ordinary, decent people. This factor was of great significance for the consequent development of Soviet society.

Extermination Camps

Although the 1937–38 operations were aimed at the physical liquidation of anti-Soviet and counterrevolutionary elements, as well as potential wreckers and spies, the majority of those arrested were sent to camps, colonies, and prisons. The influx of many new victims of the Great Terror swelled the numbers of inmates and, consequently, brought a sharp deterioration in the already dismal living conditions and helped spread arbitrariness and repression in the Gulag.

Like the rest of the population, inmates in the prisons and camps were targets of repression and purges. Order no. 00447 specified that 10,000 people in the camps had to be shot. The quota increased with time, along with regional quotas. As part of the operation against anti-Soviet elements, Yezhov ordered, within two months from 25 August, "an operation to repress the most active counterrevolutionary elements in the GUGB prisons": all of them had to be shot. The quota for the Solovki prison was set at 1,200.[56] Between October 1937 and February 1938 more than 1,800 Solovki prisoners were shot.[57]

Many former prisoners remember stories about executions in the camps and how they amplified fear. Particularly terrifying memories were left by the mass shootings in 1937–38 in the Kolyma Sevvostlag, dubbed the Garanin shootings after the head of the camp, Colonel S. N. Garanin. According to A. G. Grossman, Garanin brought "several armed guards with him from Magadan to the mines and asked the camp administrator about the best workers who fulfilled the plan. Naturally, there were political prisoners among the best [workers]. He ordered the camp administrator to take those prisoners beyond the perimeter of the camp, where they were taken and shot. This was done at night, when all prisoners were asleep. The news spread to other camps, which produced great panic among the prisoners, who literally hid under the bunks, fearing for their lives."[58]

E. M. Lvov recalled that "Garanin had a headquarters. Farther down, the highway bends like a serpent. Near one of the turns, away from the road, there was an ordinary prison barrack encircled by barbed wire. The entrance to the zone was guarded. This mini-camp was called Serpantinka. There the Garanin troika convened. There it handed out prison terms, which were called Garanin [terms]. They also passed death sentences, which were carried out on the spot. All the Kolyma prisoners talked about it."[59]

These testimonies are supported by evidence. In 1938 alone, the Dalstroi troika sentenced 12,566 people, of which 5,866 were sentenced to death.[60]

Besides executions, Gulag bosses toughened the regimen and denied prisoners the small privileges that they had retained. In May 1937 the NKVD issued two circular letters: "On measures to strengthen the regimen in prisons and colonies" and "On the isolation and strengthening of the regimen in the camps for particularly dangerous prisoners."[61] The letters ordered lockups in all prisons and colonies, regular searches of prisoners, and harsh punishments even for small violations of the regimen. All political prisoners had to be removed from administrative and managerial positions. Exceptions were made only for technical managers (foremen, taskmasters, supervisors). Even they had to be guarded at all times, en route to work and at work. All political prisoners who, out of economic convenience, had previously enjoyed certain privileges and a relative freedom of movement within the camp, were now escorted. Unescorted movement around towns was prohibited for all prisoners, regardless of their crime. Prisoners who had been lent out to other enterprises and who were not guarded had to be returned to the camps, and so on.

The arrival in the camps of a large number of new prisoners, exhausted by incarceration and torture, ill, and often without clothes, had catastrophic consequences. Since the mass operations started in August 1937, the peak of the new arrivals came in the winter. Contrary to the rules demanding that only physically fit and employable prisoners be sent to the camps, the new contingents were mostly sick and unable to work. In late 1937 large groups of elderly, disabled, and emaciated people arrived in Bamlag, and 953 inmates of Ukrainian prisons were sent to the Kaluga camp. When the train arrived, on 6 October 1937, it carried 200 emaciated prisoners and 77 disabled and sick people among the rest. The arriving prisoners had no clothes (89 people wore only underwear) and were lice ridden. Often the provincial and republican penitentiary departments in charge of prisons and colonies sent to the camps more prisoners than the instructions from Moscow required.

All these facts were cited in a 19 December 1937 special order by the people's commissar of internal affairs, "On violations of the instructions on selection and transfer of prisoners to the NKVD camps." The order threatened that charges, "including criminal prosecution," would be pressed against the heads of prisons and colonies for permitting such violations.[62] The threats, however, had no effect, and a new order was issued on 17 April 1938. The order stated that, in Bamlag alone, in the last quarter of 1937, more than 10,000 new prisoners were unemployable because of health problems.[63] This order was not complied with either. A memorandum from the accounting and distribution department of the Gulag, written soon after that, registered several new instances in which large numbers of sick, lice-ridden, and unclothed prisoners were transferred from prisons to the camps. Among the 986 prisoners sent from the Ukraine to Arkhangelsk, none had underwear, and 197 had no shoes. From Mari ASSR and Tataria to Soroka camp were sent "elderly people aged fifty-seven to seventy-two, unable even to move."[64] Sending large numbers of emaciated, sick, and disabled people to the camps, as well as exceeding the set quotas, were natural results of the general disorganization of the entire Gulag system in the years of the Great Terror. Overcrowded prisons and colonies tried to get rid of prisoners, but the camps could not accommodate them.

The Siberian and Far Eastern camps faced a real crisis. Many prisoners, sent to a completely ill-prepared Bamlag in the last three months of 1937, found themselves in terrible conditions. Mass deaths and the spread of typhus put a stop to sending prisoners there. Ten thousand prisoners rejected by Bamlag in October–December 1937 were taken off trains in Novosibirsk and sent to Siblag, the Siberian corrective labor camp.[65] This, however, led to the overcrowding of Siblag and epidemics of typhus there.

· 51 ·

Memorandum from Vyshinsky about epidemics in the Siberian camp
27 February 1938[66]

Top secret.
CC VKP(b)—to Comrade I. V. Stalin.
SNK USSR—to Comrade V. M. Molotov.

An inspection by the Procuracy of the [Soviet] Union has established that eight sections of Siblag are affected by typhus. As of 24 February, 314 people are infected, and another 203 are suspected of having typhus. At the Mariinsky distribution center, there were 110 infected people and 157 suspected of being infected. The problem is exacerbated by the fact that the Mariinsky distribution center, with a maximum capacity of 3,000 people, keeps 10,000 people under guard.

In sending along this information, I am asking that you instruct the NKVD to take immediate and urgent measures to prevent a further spread of typhus among those imprisoned.

Procurator of the USSR, A. Vyshinsky.

The instruction by the Gulag administration to move some of the prisoners from the Siblag to other camps had to be called off because typhus patients were found on the very first trains carrying them away. The epidemics spread to the Far Eastern camp, Ushosdorlag, and to Sevvostlag. Several inspections made in early 1938 showed that the old camps were overwhelmed by the newly arriving prisoners.

· 52 ·

Memorandum from Vyshinsky on the results of the
inspection of the NKVD camps
19 February 1938[67]

Top secret.
To the People's Commissar of Internal Affairs of the Union of the SSR, Commissar General of State Security, Comrade N. I. Yezhov.

The inspection of the prisoners' conditions in the Baikal-Amur, Far Eastern, Ussuriisk, and Ukhta-Pechora camps, conducted by the Procuracy of the Union, has established that in some camp divisions the prisoners' conditions are unsatisfactory and, in some cases, absolutely intolerable.

For example, there are 500 prisoners in the fifty-second unit of the seventeenth division (near Bikin station, eight kilometers from the border with Manchuria). They live in cold, dirty barracks with dirty bunks. In the absence of a classification of prisoners at the time of their placement in the barracks, the most reprehensible inmates have established the best conditions for themselves and have taken the best bunks (near the furnace), and they continually rob the working prisoners of food rations and clothes. As a result, prisoners have no incentive to report to work: 222 prisoners completely fail to report to work. Of those, 98 people do not work because they have no clothes or shoes at all. Among the prisoners there are some so ragged and lice ridden that they pose a sanitary danger to the rest. These prisoners have deteriorated to the point of losing any resemblance to human beings. Lacking food (on a punishment ration), they collect orts and, according to some prisoners, eat rats and dogs. The head of the unit informed me that only one dog (belonging to him) was left alive around the unit. As a result of inadequate food rations, there are extremely emaciated prisoners in the infirmary, and prisoners with frost-bitten extremities. [. . .]

In his 26 January 1938 letter, the procurator of Bamlag informed me about the situation of prisoners in the fourteenth division of that camp: "In the infirmary, there are prisoners lying naked on long bunks, literally packed like sardines in a barrel. They are not taken to the bathhouse for weeks owing to the lack of underwear and bedsheets. In some rooms, women are lying on the bunks in the same room as men. A syphilis patient lies side by side with a tubercular patient. In a common room, there are patients with erysipelas (infectious) packed with stomach patients. Tubercular patients, with surgical patients. They take people who froze to death off the arriving trains (Moscow train).

"Those arriving have no underwear, nothing but rags. The terrible thing is that there is not a single change of underwear, boots, or clothes in the Bamlag. Their bodies are covered with scabs, but they do not take a bath, because they are not provided with underwear. Their tatters are full of hundreds of lice. There is no soap. Many have nothing to put on to go out to the bathroom. The so-called recovering team is in fact [. . .] in a dark barrack. People there completely lack underwear and pea jackets and only have ragged light jackets. They resemble humans or, more likely, savages, or people of the Stone Age. And new trainloads of people without clothes keep coming, and people go on the road barefoot, unclothed, and we have minus twenty to minus fifty degrees Centigrade here. There are no houses. There is nothing to build houses with, no tools, no saws or axes. What is to be done? Typhoid patients arrive with the recent trainloads. Somebody—obviously hostile—is arranging for people to die en route and to die upon arrival.

"In order not to hold up cars and in order to prevent a jam on the railroad, zealous bosses of the fourteenth division decided to have the arriving people walk seventeen kilometers. As a result, in the first group of 750, five people died of cold, and ninety-two were frostbitten (mostly their feet). In the second group, forty-two people were frostbitten, and in the third, thirty.

"Fats are not supplied for long periods of time. Patients with weak stomachs eat from the common cauldron. There is no sugar in the infirmary (fourteenth division). The food situation is catastrophic. Now, 60,000–70,000 prisoners will be placed deep in the taiga in winter, with only one month's worth of food. People may find themselves without food, separated from the rest of the world by impassable marshes until November. Hundreds of telegrams sent to the GULAG about the catastrophic situation in the camp go unanswered. People become brutalized, and some are nearly insane. There are no fresh vegetables. In two–three months, scurvy may start, but new prisoners keep coming and coming. In three and a half months, 75,000 arrived, and the same number on wheels." [. . .]

Inspection of the Ukhtpechlag has shown that the living conditions of prisoners in this camp are also clearly unsatisfactory. Only 60 percent of prisoners have a place to live. The rest stay in tents, which are not adequate for living during the winter. Prisoners are not getting even 50 percent of the required warm clothes and shoes. As a result, during the 4 November 1937 transfer of 2,086 prisoners from the Sindor camp center to Tobys division, ordered by the Ukhtpechlag chief engineer, Maksimovich, sixteen people got frostbitten on the way and died of cold and exhaustion. The camp procuracy has indicted Maksimovich and other perpetrators of this crime. [. . .]

Procurator of the USSR, A. Vyshinsky.

· 53 ·

Report on the results of the inspection of the
Ukhta-Pechora camp of the NKVD
20 January 1938[68]

Top secret.

[. . .] The living conditions of the prisoners (except at the first and second works) are exceptionally appalling. Particularly unsatisfactory is the state of affairs in the camp divisions at the construction of the Kniazhy Pogost–Chibiu railway and the Chibiu–Krutaia highway.

The filth is extensive and overwhelming and, in some camp centers (Sidiu, fifth, sixth, etc.), simply catastrophic. There are almost no bed-sheets, and prisoners sleep on bare, dirty bunks. In some camp centers (Sidiu, fifth, fourth, etc.) the stink in the barracks is unbearable because people almost never go the bathhouse. With rare exceptions, underwear is dirty, not laundered for months. Camp divisions have almost no changes of underwear, and thus where people go to the bath, bathing does not ful-fill its purpose. Clothing is badly insufficient, and in some camp centers many prisoners cannot work because they lack clothes.

In the camp divisions with emaciated prisoners (Sidiu, Tobys, twelfth, fifteenth, and sixteenth divisions), the conditions are such that they can become havens of infectious disease and mass death (in December thirty-eight people died at the twelfth camp center).

In most camp centers on the Krutaia–Chibiu highway, prisoners are so crowded in the barracks that they sleep on top of one another. There is no extra space either on the bunks nor under them.

Foods supplied to the prisoners are exceptionally bad. Almost all kitchens are unsanitary. Throughout December, most camp centers did not receive meat, fish, or fats, and in some places soup was made without vegetables (by adding flour—so called blending). Some camp centers bake underdone bread that is almost impossible to eat. In some camp centers (sixth camp center, twelfth camp center, and sixteenth camp center) pris-oners have no spoons or bowls, which literally brutalizes them.

The ill (the scabbed, diarrheal, and venereal patients, etc.) stay in com-mon quarters with other prisoners (at the railroad and highway construc-tion sites, etc.).

Naturally, this situation has led to catastrophic physical conditions for the camp population and the minimal employment of prisoners. [. . .] Even the Ukhtpechlag sanitary department, in its report on the physical condition of prisoners from 1 December 1937, which gives far from the real state of affairs, shows a rather unpleasant situation:

Second category*	17,831
Third category†	11,132
Disabled	1,332
En route	471
Emaciated and sick	6,656
Total	54,947

As a result, the employment rate of prisoners in the camp is very low. [. . .]
The administration believes that the growth of group C [third cate-

---

* Prisoners capable of medium-rated labor.
    † Prisoners capable of just limited work or unemployable (including invalids, the el-derly, and the emaciated).

gory] is a result of GULAG authorities sending to the camp a large number of sick prisoners and disabled ones in 1937. However, while it is true in general, the decisive factor is the appalling living and sanitary conditions, which lead to the growing numbers of emaciated people. [. . .]

The difficult situation in the old camps was easy to foresee. Even before mass operations started, it was clear that the existing camps would not be able to accommodate an influx of prisoners. The 31 July 1937 Politburo resolution that approved Order no. 00447 ordered the construction of an additional network of camps "in remote regions of Kazakhstan," in the forests of the North, in the Urals, and in Siberia. Plans to build camps in Kazakhstan were never implemented owing to insufficient funds. The main effort was concentrated on organizing a network of forest camps.

There were several reasons to select the timber industry as an area of employment for the new prisoners. First, it was relatively easy to set up forestry farms quickly and with minimal investment. Second, the timber industry was experiencing certain difficulties. On 6 June 1937 the chairman of the State Planning Committee (Gosplan), G. I. Smirnov, reported to Stalin and Molotov that in the first half of 1937, timber production by the People's Commissariat of Forestry had achieved only 48 percent of the amount specified in the annual plan; because of the seasonal nature of the work, the amount was normally 75–78 percent. According to Smirnov, the production of the People's Commissariat of Forestry during the first eight months of 1937 had decreased by 6 percent, compared to the same period in 1936.[69]

According to the governmental decree, the Gulag had to establish, by 1 January 1938, seven timber camps with 103,000 people in them.[70] As a result of hasty decisions connected with mass repressive actions, along with insufficient funding, the prisoners who were brought into the new forestry regions found themselves in an extremely difficult situation. Gulag statistical reports on the new camps provide some scanty information about the tragedy that took place in the forestry regions of the North and Siberia.[71]

For the first two months after the organization of the seven new camps (October–November 1937), the reports registered a large number of escapes (more than 700) and a relatively small number of deaths (532).[72] The arriving prisoners, forced to fight for survival, still had strength to escape. The weather conditions also contributed. In December the death rate went up, and the number of escapes decreased. Later (we have data for only January–March 1938) this trend became more pronounced. The winter left the emaciated prisoners little chance of survival if they escaped, nor even if they stayed. As of 1 January 1938 there were 91,500 prisoners listed in the seven new forest camps. Among them, 41,200 were able to perform heavy work, 20,700 could do medium-level work, and 22,700 could only do light work or were altogether unemployable (including 4,900 invalids). Quite a few prisoners, 6,900, were not categorized at all, which probably means that they were also sick. The death rate among the new camp prisoners was astonishing. According to the report, in December 1937 the number who died was 2,415; in January 1938, the number was 3,343; in February, 3,244; and in March, 3,040. On average, the number was slightly less than half of the entire number of prisoners who died in all the camps (about 26,000 between December 1937 and March 1938).[73]

Creating the new camps had horrifying consequences. In the first six months more than 12,500 died, 1,272 escaped, and more than 20,000 were unemployable, including 5,000 invalids. The original plan to place 103,000 worker prisoners in the camps by 1 January 1938 proved to be unachievable. The new forest camps, organized in 1937, became in fact provisional death camps. Soon afterward, four of them were closed and one was relocated; only two survived for a while.[74]

As was evident from the situation in the old and new camps in late 1937–early 1938, the Gulag was unable to support the mass operations as planned. As of 1 February 1938, there were 1,126,500 prisoners in the camps (including those en route), compared to 786,595 prisoners as of 1 July 1937, before the start of the mass operations. In addition, there were 545,331 inmates in prisons and 339,872 in the colonies.[75] The majority of the prisoners had to be transferred to the camps. With these plans in mind, the government decided, in late December 1937, to organize six more forest camps to accommodate 150,000 prisoners.[76] By March 54,000 prisoners had been brought to those camps, and 22,000 were on the way.[77] According to February 1938 calculations by the Gulag accounting and distribution department, just the excess camp prisoners and prison inmates to be transferred to the camps amounted to 200,000 people, whereas the camps could accommodate only 57,000–60,000.[78]

The excess 140,000 prisoners were created during the first stage of the Great Terror. Even though a large number of prisoners were shot, the Gulag did not have the capacity to support the four-month operation planned for mid-1937. The scale of the repressions in 1938, however, surpassed the scale in 1937. Despite the executions, which were in large degree a result of overcrowding in the camps, 800,000 new prisoners arrived at the camps in 1938, while only 330,000 were released or transferred to other prisons. Consequently, as of 1 January 1939 there were 1,317,195 prisoners in the camps, 355,243 in the colonies, and 352,508 in prisons. The total number exceeded the number of all prisoners on 1 January 1938 by almost 150,000.[79]

These numbers would have been bigger had it not been for a high death rate in the camps, colonies, and prisons, which, in 1938, far surpassed the death rate of previous years (except during the 1933 famine). According to the NKVD, 25,376 people died in the camps in 1937, and 8,123 died in prisons and colonies. In 1938 these numbers were 90,546 and 36,039, respectively.[80]

However large these numbers are, the Gulag reports were incomplete. First, because of the leap in the number of prisoners, there was more opportunity for falsification. The number of prisoners officially listed as "departed for various reasons" grew rapidly, for instance. In earlier years this category included, on average, 1,200 to 2,700 people. In 1938 there were 16,500 (see Document 97).

Second, during the period of mass repressions and mass movement of prisoners, deaths en route greatly increased. We do not have sufficient data for analysis, but Gulag statistics show not only a large number of prisoners being moved from prisons and jails to the camps but also a significant movement between camps. In 1937 about 215,000 prisoners were transferred between camps; and in 1938, more than 240,000. There was also a reverse movement from the camps to colonies and prisons: about 44,000 in 1937 and almost 56,000 in 1938 (see Document 97). For prisoners, these moves were sheer hell. Congestion, filth, terrible heat in the summer and extreme cold in the winter, and the presence of ill (and sometimes dead) fellow passengers contributed to the spread of disease and high mortality. People died on the trains, on the road from the railway stations to the camps, and along every step of the way. Although Gulag documents do not provide a compilation of deaths en route, the difference between the number of prisoners sent and the number received is telling. In 1938 the difference was 38,000 (see Document 97).

High mortality was not the only manifestation of the crisis in the camp system as a result of the Great Terror. A large number of prisoners were on the verge of death and were listed as unemployable or full invalids. According to Gulag reports, in 1938 (mainly in the third and fourth quarters), over 9 percent of the camp population (100,000-plus people) could not work owing to illness, emaciation, or disability.[81] It is possible that this number was artificially reduced. In April 1939, L. P. Beria, the new people's commissar of internal affairs, reported to the government that, besides invalids, there were up to 150,000 "emaciated and disabled workers" (see Document 61).

Another category of prisoners that revealed the crisis in the camps was the group of the unclothed. One can only imagine what being officially unclothed meant in the Gulag, where nobody was well dressed. The lack of clothes was caused by administrative excesses, theft, and the general shortage of consumer goods in the country. In the long line of those waiting to obtain the limited clothes and footwear, prisoners were among the last. The NKVD regularly prepared, and People's Commissar of Internal Affairs Yezhov signed, petitions to the government to provide additional textiles and footwear for the many new prisoners. These petitions were only rarely satisfied. By September 1938 the number of prisoners in prisons and colonies had reached 2,000,000, whereas they received (in early 1938) only 422,000 pairs of shoes and 213,000 pairs of felt boots. "This situation impedes full utilization of the workforce owing to the resulting lack of clothes," wrote Ezhov to the head of the government, Molotov.[82]

Gulag statistics distinguished the *otkazchiks,* prisoners who refused to report to work, from other nonworking prisoners. In 1938 about 1 percent of the camp population were otkazchiks.[83] Among them could have been ill or unclothed prisoners. As gang crime spread, the number of otkazchiks reflected the regimen in the camps. With the mass repressions, the cruelest and most aggressive criminals increased their influence, terrorized the political prisoners, and often imposed their own rules.

An important indicator of the situation in the camps was the rate of escapes, always closely watched by the leaders of the country and the NKVD bosses. Despite draconian measures to prevent escapes of most of the prisoners, the number who managed to flee remained significant—58,200 in 1937 and 32,000 in 1938. According to camp reports (not quite reliable), most of the escapees were apprehended (see Document 97). As a rule, the camp administration blamed the escapes on a guard system overtaxed by the massive increase in the number of prisoners. As of 1 August 1938, there were 55,300 camp guards (including 12,800 prisoners). This number represents 4–5 percent of the total number of prisoners. The NKVD bosses considered it essential to increase the number of guards to 90,000 (7 percent of the total number of prisoners).[84]

But for the leaders of the country, the main sign of trouble in the camps was their failure to fulfill economic tasks. The plans for industrial production and capital construction, imposed on the NKVD, continued to grow in 1937–38. In August 1937 the NKVD was charged with the construction of the Kyibyshev hydroelectric complex on the Volga River and of similar projects on the Kama,[85] as well as the construction of the 5,000-kilometer-long section of the Baikal–Amur railway, between Taishet and Sovetskaya harbor.[86] On 5 September 1937 construction of the Ulan Ude–Naushki railroad was added to this list.[87] In April 1938, as a result of increased railroad construction in the Far East, the government resolved to establish a railroad building department of the Gulag in the Far East, which would include six railroad camps.[88] In February 1938 the NKVD assumed administration of the Raichinkinsky and Bukachachinsky coal mines, previously under the auspices of the People's Commissariat of Heavy Industry.[89] In May 1938 the NKVD was charged with the construction of ten sulfide cellulose plants (to be opened no later than February–April of 1939),[90] the Arkhangelsk and Solikamsk paper-cellulose industrial complexes,[91] and other projects. As a rule, those were complicated tasks, which the people's commissariats of industry had failed to carry out.

In almost every case, the NKVD was ordered to accelerate construction. Theoretically, the new tasks and the expansion of the existing enterprises were supported by rapid growth of the camp population. In reality, however, the expected production growth and new capital investments could not be achieved because of the disorganization of the camp system and the emaciation of the workforce. The NKVD proved unable to meet the construction plans for the new projects and usually blamed it on the lack of workers.[92] Some internal NKVD documents are more straightforward and shed light on the true reasons for the economic failures.

· 54 ·

Memorandum on the situation at the construction sites
of the GULAG of the NKVD
[Before 17 November 1938][93]

To the Head of the Political Department of the GULAG of the NKVD
USSR, Brigade Commissar Comrade Vasiliev.*

Since I was dispatched to work in the GULAG of the NKVD in late
1937, I have encountered in my practical work in the planning and financial department, as well as in the entire GULAG, a number of rather suspicious facts, which I consider imperative to report to you:

I. The work to realize capital investments in 1937, and the work of the
majority of the construction sites in general, has been ineffective and quite
unsatisfactory.

The 1937 plan was fulfilled by only 71.6 percent. In particular:

a) Hydrotechnical works—80.5 percent

b) Railroad construction—62.7 percent

c) Industrial construction—63.2 percent

At almost all GULAG construction sites, the main work is expensive,
and the productivity of labor is low. [. . .]

III. The cost of the main types of work is as follows:

	Measurement Unit	In the Plan	In Reality
1. Volgostroi			
a) earthworks	cubic meter	2 rubles, 86 kopecks	4 rubles, 61 kopecks
b) concrete	cubic meter	106 rubles, 10 kopecks	177 rubles, 71 kopecks
c) provisional civil construction	cubic meter	18 rubles, 35 kopecks	22 rubles, 47 kopecks
2. Second railways			
a) building of the main route	kilometer	50,040 rubles	76,960 rubles

[. . .]

---

* On 17 November 1938, the head of the Gulag political department forwarded this
note to the deputy people's commissar of internal affairs, Filaretov, and on 22 November, to Yezhov.

V. At some construction sites, overhead expenses are enormously high, especially to support administrative staff. For example:

	Plan	Reality
1. Volgostroi		
All construction overhead expenses		
a) in relation to direct expenses	21%	22%
b) including support of administrative staff	8%	13.5%
2. Second railways		
Administrative expenses	8%	11.73%
—Overspending here alone came to		
12,767,000 rubles		

[. . .]

VI. In addition to the high cost of work, low productivity, and extremely high overhead expenses, almost all construction sites have a low ratio of utilization of the workforce and an excess of the latter [the workforce]:

	Plan	Reality
1. Volgostroi		
Group A*	89.2%	80.5%
Groups C and D (resting)†	2.2%	10.1%
2. Second railways		
Group A	77.5%	75.3%
Groups C and D (resting)	10%	12.25%

[. . .]

VII. Use of mechanized equipment.

The use of mechanized equipment and vehicles in 1937 was quite unsatisfactory. As of 1 January 1938, 87 percent of the machines went unused. Construction machines and transport vehicles were used as follows:

a) Excavator yield:

1. At Volgostroi—77%
2. At Southern Bay—44%
3. On secondary route—65% [. . .]

b) Auto transport yield:

1. At Norilskstroi—54%

---

* Refers to those working in production.

† Group C—those who are ill, emaciated, or disabled. Group D—those not working for other reasons (in this case, resting).

2. On line no. 2—80%

3. At Segezhstroi—81%

4. At Southern Bay—87%

A similar substandard situation can be found with other construction machines and equipment and at other construction sites.

VIII. Losses.

Because of the awful work at the construction sites, the GULAG spends more than the planned, or even estimated, capital investment. In total, the GULAG overspends 240,400,000 rubles against the planned cost. [. . .]

IX. Overstocking.

In addition to the above, and thanks to the awful work (to say the least) at the construction sites, which is evident, construction materials were supplied irrespective of the fulfillment of construction plans. As a result, several sites received deficit materials, supplies, and foodstuffs not according to plan, thus withdrawing such resources from circulation. [. . .]

XII. Why all this happens?

Most important, the GULAG does not conduct an adequate fight to improve the work at the construction sites, to eradicate and liquidate the consequences of wrecking. Often in the GULAG, things happen that are virtually indistinguishable from real acts of wrecking. For example:

1. It is obvious that the enemies of the people had their filthy hand in planning capital investment at GULAG construction sites: capital investments are outlined in varying figures, the control figures are provided late, the structure of capital investment is frequently modified, etc. All this led to undermined construction work because of a lack of finances and materials or because of overstocking, locking up funds in unnecessary equipment, materials, etc.

Thus, in 1938 the GULAG changed the capital investment plans for Volgostroi (specifically, to 660, 610, 550, 300, and 330 [million rubles]). The situation is similar at other construction sites. [. . .]

Similar planning took place in 1937. As we have already pointed out, thanks to such planning methods, most construction sites locked up capital investment in materials and closed their current accounts because of the lack of finances. [. . .]

Only nine out of twenty-eight GULAG construction sites have approved technical plans and financial appraisals. The rest are working without these. Technical plans take so long to create that the construction is almost over by then. For example, the construction of the Moscow–Minsk highway will be completed by November 1938, but they do not have a technical plan yet. Financing of construction sites is secured by special resolution of the government.

Most of the GULAG construction sites, because of their scale and importance, are considered special-quota sites and are under special governmental control. As such, according to the 23 October 1934 SNK resolution, their plans and financial appraisals can be approved only by the SNK. This SNK resolution established a special procedure for approval of plans and appraisals, forbade uncontrolled spending of state resources, and required that the Sovnarkom approve each alteration of the capital investment [plan].

The GULAG leadership, i.e., Pliner, decided to overlook this resolution. To obtain money not involving the government, he reassigned a number of construction sites, which had to be under SNK control, as lower-priority projects, thus permitting the head of construction to approve construction plans and financial assessments. The head of construction transfers his rights to the chief engineer of the construction site. Thus, financial assessments that had to be approved by the government ended up not being reviewed by the party committee, the GULAG administration, or even the head of construction, but were entrusted to the chief engineer of the construction site.

Party bureau organizer [of the financial and planning department of the GULAG],

Chugunikhin.

On the whole, failure of the Gulag to achieve the intended industrialization goals was inherent and predictable. The Gulag economy was never effective, and it survived only through the massive, uncontrolled exploitation of forced labor. The Great Terror, though mainly shaped by political goals, exacerbated these tendencies. The 1937–38 repressions converted Soviet camps into extermination centers instead of promoting productivity by supplying additional workers.

CHAPTER 5

Beria's "Reforms"

On 17 November 1938 the Politburo adopted a resolution, "On arrests, procuratorial supervision, and investigative procedure," that terminated the punitive actions of the Great Terror in the same centralized fashion as they were started. "The mass operations engaged in crushing and eradicating hostile elements, carried out by organs of the NKVD during 1937–38 and involving a simplified procedure of conducting investigations and trials, could not help but lead to a host of major deficiencies and distortions in the work of the NKVD and the Procuracy."[1] In other words, having forbidden further mass operations and deportations, the leaders of the country blamed the NKVD for the excesses of the Great Terror.

These accusations heralded another campaign, "to restore socialist legality," and a new purge of the NKVD cadres. The NKVD entered this period with a new leader, Lavrenty P. Beria, who was appointed as the new people's commissar of internal affairs on 25 November 1938. Beria's main task was to strengthen the punitive mechanisms disorganized during the Great Terror and to conduct a purge of the chekist cadres with minimal losses. Beria acted accordingly. He revealed himself to be a full supporter of harsh terror and the expansion of the Stalinist repressive machine and the Gulag economy.

The Legality of Torture

In August 1938, Beria, who was thirty-nine years old at the time, was recalled from his position of leader of Georgia to become the deputy people's commissar of internal affairs of the USSR, and soon after that he replaced Yezhov as commissar. He was probably Stalin's best choice. Beria was tough, experienced in political games, and talented administratively (in Stalin's view). Between 1921 and 1931 he had worked in VChK-OGPU organs, reaching the position of chairman of the Trans-Caucasian Chief Political Administration (GPU) before Stalin transferred him to do party work.[2] For a number of years, Beria was one of Stalin's favorites, and from March 1939 he enjoyed Stalin's support in his capacity as a Politburo candidate member. Stalin's encouragement and Beria's connection with the punitive organs determined Beria's aggressive style as people's commissar. Chekist corporate solidarity, damaged by the 1939 turn in the general line, eventually prevailed, in no small degree thanks to Beria's efforts.

One of Beria's main tasks was to conduct a purge of the commissariat to remove Yezhov's people and replace them. (Every major reorganization of the secret police involved this general sequence of events.) The new purge unfolded under the traditional slogans "Restoring socialist legality" and "Liquidation of wreckers [among the chekists]." Recent studies show that the scale of this purge was quite large. However, we should not overestimate it. Altogether, 7,372 officers of state security were fired that year (23 percent of the total), and 937 of those were arrested.[3] Yezhov was arrested in April 1939 and shot in February 1940.

No studies attempt to explain the logic behind selective repressions in the NKVD. To strictly follow the slogan "Restoring socialist legality," all state security workers would have had to be arrested, including Beria, because nobody could remain uninvolved in the crimes committed by that organization. Naturally, under those conditions, the new NKVD leadership had to balance punishment against retaining the effective core of the punitive organs. A major challenge was dealing with the campaigns to review verdicts passed during the Great Terror and have cases previously reserved for the troikas examined by regular courts.

According to Beria's order of 26 November 1938, all cases in which the investigation had been completed, as well as cases that had been reviewed by the troikas but whose sentences were not yet carried out, had to be processed as regular criminal cases and sent to the courts or the Special Council of the NKVD USSR.[4] On 26 December 1938, Beria and the procurator of the USSR, Vyshinsky, issued a directive to the republican-level people's commissars of internal affairs, heads of departments of the provincial and territorial NKVD divisions, procurators of the republics, territories, and provinces, military districts, and others, ordering the review of complaints about the troika resolutions. Wherever the verdict was deemed incorrect, the case was closed and the prisoner freed.[5]

For NKVD workers, this came as an unpleasant surprise. Previously, the cases reviewed by the troikas or the Special Council were approved through the so-called simplified procedure (with confessions and statements extracted by beating). Despite the proclivities of the Stalinist court system and the Procuracy, it was not easy to move obvious falsifications through the courts. Between 1 January and 15 June 1939, the Procuracy and the courts returned over 50 percent of all cases for additional investigation to NKVD organs.[6] In some cases, the courts acquitted the accused. Equally unpleasant to the NKVD was the campaign to review the verdicts issued by the troikas in 1937–38. So blatant was the falsification and use of torture that the courts and procurators reviewing the complaints, despite their general sympathy with the NKVD, could not turn an entirely blind eye. In these cases, NKVD agents who remained in their positions were indicted.

As a result, chekists were frequently pitted against the prosecutors and judges. In December 1938, the head of the Leningrad province UNKVD, S. A. Goglidze, complained to Beria about the procurators.

· 55 ·

Report by S. A. Goglidze on inappropriate actions by the Procuracy
23 December 1938[7]

Top secret.
To the People's Commissar of Internal Affairs of the USSR,
Commissar of State Security, First Degree,
Comrade L. P. Beria.
Moscow.
The new important role of procuratorial supervision and the responsibility laid on the organs of the Procuracy for the arrests and investigations

conducted by the NKVD, stemming from the 17 November 1938 resolution by the SNK USSR and the CC VKP(b), were interpreted incorrectly by the workers of the Leningrad provincial procuracy.

The procuracy of Leningrad province simplifies its role as a supervisory organ while refusing to adequately participate in the investigation and often interferes with the normal course of the investigation.

The 9 December visit by the provincial procurator, C[omrade] Baliasnikov; his deputy, Dorofeev; and other workers of the procuracy to the special building of the OMZ [Department of Corrective Facilities] prison, where those under investigation of the UGB UNKVD LO [Leningrad province] are kept, offers a case in point.

The procurator visited the cells where interrogations of prisoners were conducted, interrupted the interrogations, and offered those arrested a chance to speak about how the investigators were conducting the interrogation, whether they applied illegal methods of investigation, were rude, etc. In cases where the arrested complained about their rough treatment, Procurator Baliasnikov, there in the presence of the arrested, sternly reprimanded the officers.

In some cases, Com. Baliasnikov stopped the interrogation of the detainee by two officers, as he considered that the presence of the second agent would hinder the normal course of investigation. In addition to that, Com. Baliasnikov, in the presence of the prisoners, demanded that inmates be treated politely and gently.

Similar cases of distortion by procuratorial supervision can also be found on the periphery.

On 11 December Procurator Com. Shatalov inspected the cells of the Pskov prison. In one of the cells, containing more than 100 prisoners, he persistently elicited from the prisoners facts about rude behavior by the officers, as well as their names. As a result, certain prisoners provocatively concocted facts, thus slandering the NKVD organs.

This could not but very negatively affect the behavior of those under investigation. Using inappropriate actions by the procurator, prisoners adopted the practice of totally recanting their previous statements. Moreover, under interrogation, prisoners now behave defiantly, refuse to give statements, demonstratively demand the replacement of the investigators, the presence of the procurator, etc.

By reporting the aforementioned facts, I am asking you to consider explaining to the procurator of the Leningrad province, Com. Baliasnikov, and the procuracy in general their tasks that stem from the 17 November 1938 resolution of the SNK USSR and the CC VKP(b).

Head of the NKVD Administration for Leningrad province,
Commissar of State Security, Second Degree,
Goglidze.

Vyshinsky sided with the chekists and sent a letter to Baliasnikov in which he demanded an explanation and warned that "the procuratorial supervision over investigation must be conducted in such a manner so as to exclude any encouragement of the prisoners to deliberately slander the investigation."

The situation in Leningrad province was not an exception. Many local NKVD bosses asked Moscow for help. Their position was articulated in a letter to Beria from the deputy people's commissar of internal affairs in the Ukraine, A. Z. Kobulov: "Concerning the previously existing practice of physical methods of interrogation, I believe that the investigators who treated beatings as the main method of investigation and who maimed prisoners in the absence of sufficient proof of their anti-Soviet activity have to be strictly punished. But that does not mean that all NKVD workers who used physical methods during interrogation should be prosecuted. It is important to consider that such methods of investigation were cultivated and encouraged by the former hostile NKVD leadership in the Ukraine."[8]

Beria fully supported this position. On 5 January 1939 he forwarded the Kobulov letter to Vyshinsky, asking him to clamp down on the procurators mentioned in it.

The problem for the chekists was complicated by the fact that, besides procurators and judges, agents were attacked by the secretaries of regional party organizations. Local party bosses tried to strengthen their position by joining the campaign to restore socialist legality, and to regain control over local NKVD departments, which had usurped enormous power in the years of the Great Terror. The provincial party committee secretaries confronted the chekists, accusing them of falsification and torture. To protect his subordinates from such attacks, Beria had to appeal directly to Stalin. Probably as a result of these appeals, Stalin assumed responsibility for the use of torture by the NKVD. On 10 January 1939 he signed a telegram to be sent to the secretaries of the provincial, territorial, and national communist parties, to heads of NKVD administrations, and to republican-level people's commissars of internal affairs that read:

> The CC VKP(b) explains that the application of physical methods by the NKVD was allowed from 1937 by the CC VKP(b). [. . .] It is common knowledge that all bourgeois intelligence services use physical methods with representatives of the socialist proletariat, and use it in the most barbaric forms. The question is, Why should socialist intelligence be more humane with inveterate bourgeois agents, rabid ene-

mies of the working class and collective farmers. The CC VKP(b) believes that physical methods should continue to be used, as an exception, with open and unrelenting enemies of the people. It is a completely proper and appropriate method.[9]

The style and contents of the document leave no doubt that it was written personally by Stalin, although the original draft has not been found (most likely, it was destroyed).

Because the use of torture was the only charge on which NKVD workers could be indicted, Stalin's telegram proved to be a de facto absolution for the majority of chekists. Having received Stalin's powerful backing, Beria issued new demands to the procurator of the USSR, Vyshinsky, and the people's commissar of justice, Rychkov, sending them identical letters:

· 56 ·

Memorandum from L. P. Beria on the inappropriate actions
of the workers in the Procuracy and the courts
2 March 1939[10]

Strictly secret.

To the People's Commissar of Justice of the USSR, Com. Rychkov.

According to information from the NKVDs of union and autonomous republics and from the heads of the provincial NKVD departments, some workers of the procuracy incorrectly interpret the 17 November 1938 SNK USSR and CC VKP(b) resolution "On arrests, procuratorial supervision, and investigative procedure."

According to the people's commissar of internal affairs of the Dagestan ASSR, Com. Panteleev, the procurator of the republic, Filatov, and the deputy procurator of the republic, Musaev, have adopted an erroneous and harmful stance in liquidating the distortions of legality in the conduct of the investigation.

These procurators visited prison cells and photographed suspect bodily areas of the prisoners, looking for signs of beatings. Deputy Procurator Musaev was particularly active in visiting prison cells and prison hospitals. He personally gave prisoners paper to write statements revoking their confessions. As a result, all prisoners, whether minor offenders, spies, terrorists, or saboteurs, insolently declare: "We are innocent people, arrested by enemies, and we confessed under duress."

In addition to that, plots and organized hunger strikes take place in the prisons.

Besides individual workers of the procuracy, certain court officials have adopted an incorrect line on the aforementioned question. Thus, according to the deputy people's commissar of internal affairs of the Ukrainian SSR, Com. Gorlinsky, the president of the Southwestern railway court, Gapon, does not objectively review cases of counterrevolutionary crimes. [. . .]

During the hearings of several cases by the railway court, the president of the court, Gapon, conducted the questioning of witnesses in a biased manner and confused them during their testimony while limiting the interrogation of the accused to a mere formality. [. . .]

The deputy procurator of the railway, Zadoin, who was state prosecutor for these cases in the court, took no measures to unmask provocation by the accused and did not familiarize himself at all with the materials of the cases with which he worked in the court.

According to the head of the Saratov province UNKVD, Com. Kiselev, the chairman of the military tribunal of NKVD internal troops, Korotkin, follows a clearly provocative line in his work of investigating NKVD organs. In reviewing cases at the sessions of the tribunal, Korotkin consistently downplays some crimes and compromises the investigation. He often remands cases on the basis of only the slanderous statements of the accused and sometimes acquits and frees prisoners on the same basis. [. . .]

I am asking [you] to give appropriate instructions to the local organs. Please inform the NKVD USSR about the action taken.

People's Commissar of the Interior of the USSR,
Commissar of State Security, First Degree,
L. Beria.

Encouraged by Moscow's support and having overcome the initial scare, NKVD agents acted more insolently and defiantly. On 21 December 1939 the new procurator of the USSR, M. I. Pankratov, wrote to Beria: "I have repeatedly reported to you about the numerous facts of the violation of law by the investigative departments of the NKVD and the UNKVD while conducting investigations. [. . .] For example, on 20 April 1939 the special department of the Kiev military district sent an order by telegraph to its subordinate special departments that prisoners could be freed only with the permission of the special department of the district, whether or not the local procurator issued a resolution to this effect. In other words, the special department usurped the function of endorsing or confirming resolutions by the procurators. [. . .] Some local and central NKVD agents have assumed that by protesting the resolutions issued by the procurators, they can block the procurators' resolutions to close cases and free prisoners, which is against the law."[11]

Such protests changed nothing. Moreover, in early 1940 the NKVD managed through the adoption of bylaws to establish a self-serving order concerning the release of prisoners who were acquitted by the court in counterrevolutionary cases or due to be released when the Procuracy threw out their cases. From then on, all court acquittals and procuratorial resolutions to close cases had to be approved by the NKVD. "Individuals acquitted by the court of counterrevolutionary crimes," read the 20 March 1940 order by the people's commissariat of justice and the procurator of the USSR, "cannot be immediately released by the courts, but shall be returned to the places of their imprisonment, from where they were brought to the court. [. . .] The aforementioned individuals can be released only after the NKVD organs confirm that they have no objections."[12] This resolution was so clearly unconstitutional and illegal that some justice officials objected to it. The people's commissar of justice of Belorussia, S. Lodysev, wrote to Stalin: "It turns out that even though there is no legal justification to keep a person acquitted by the court under arrest, he will still remain in prison, and his fate will be decided by an administrative organ."[13] The letter was forwarded to Vyshinsky (who had become deputy chairman of the SNK USSR), who explained Lodysev's mistake to him.[14]

Similar attempts to restore the omnipotence of the NKVD could be discerned in the campaign to review verdicts issued by the troikas in 1937–38. From the outset, the review was very limited. The authorities did not intend to reverse the results of the Great Terror. Most problems were related to cases in which the death sentence had been handed out. Even in those few cases where the verdict was reviewed and falsification became evident, the reversal of the verdict was politically dangerous. Without clear guidelines, bureaucrats turned to an extensive exchange of letters.

· 57 ·

L. Yachenin's inquiry about the procedure for reviewing cases
of those sentenced to be shot
28 December 1939[15]

Top secret.

To the Procurator of the USSR, Com. M. I. Pankratiev.

Following your instructions, the organs of the procuracy of the Ukrainian SSR requested for review a large number of cases concerning complaints from relatives of those sentenced to the ultimate punishment.

Most of these cases consist of a protocol of the interrogation, during which the arrested confesses to committing grave counterrevolutionary crimes or espionage, and a troika resolution to shoot [him].

Such cases are very difficult to review. However, I would like to inquire about other cases in which the materials and a careful review determine that the troika resolution was wrong and that a person was sentenced to be shot for no reason whatsoever. What should the procuracy do in such cases?

If we consider annulling the troika resolutions, what would be the consequences, considering the fact that we never tell the relatives about the death sentence? Obviously, we cannot declare the case closed when the troika resolution is deemed wrong.

Please give us guidance on how to deal with this situation, because we are making no headway with these cases, and they in fact find no resolution here.

Procurator of the Ukrainian SSR, L. Yachenin.

Pankratiev ordered a response to Yachenin that the question about reviewing the cases of those wrongly sentenced to death by the troika had been raised with the "directing organs." Indeed, overwhelmed with similar requests, Pankratiev sent a letter to Stalin and Molotov in which he defended the idea of a limited review of the death sentences.[16] Apparently his recommendations were not accepted. Under pressure from NKVD organs, only a few of the relatives' complaints were reviewed. In May 1940, Pankratiev responded to an inquiry from a procurator about how to respond to the relatives of those shot: "Your response should be approved by the NKVD. A practice has been established to inform them about the conviction and a prison term in remote camps."[17] In September the new procurator of the USSR, V. M. Bochkov, instructed all the procurators "to discontinue, until further notice, the review and examination of cases of those sentenced to the ultimate punishment, in response to relatives' complaints."[18]

A total disregard for complaints about cases with a death sentence was but an aspect of the general trend to refuse exoneration for the victims of the Great Terror. In April 1940 the self-serving chekists' desire to squelch a review of the cases received an official boost. On 23 April the people's commissar of internal affairs and the procurator of the USSR issued an order permitting a review of troika verdicts only by the NKVD Special Council, thus not only complicating the procedure but putting it under the full control of the NKVD.[19] The chekists were ordered to investigate their own crimes. This meant nothing good for the victims of terror.

According to Gulag reports, a total of 223,622 people were released from the camps in 1939 (see Document 97). Most likely, the majority of them were criminals, with only a small percentage of political prisoners. In any case, the number of those imprisoned for counterrevolutionary crimes in the corrective labor camps shrank by more than 10,000 between 1 January 1939 and 1 January 1940, from 454,432 to 444,999 people (see Document 98).

Prisoners who were still under investigation in late 1938 had a better chance to be freed. Since most of the cases were fabricated, and some chekists who took part in falsifications had also been arrested as enemies, prisoners had a hope of being considered victims of the enemies in the organs of state security. The authorities more easily freed those arrested who had not yet been sent to the camps than those who had already passed through the doors of the repressive system.

The actual results of Beria's "restoration of socialist legality" fully reflected the desire of the supreme leadership and of the chekists themselves to minimize policy changes while preserving, and even strengthening, the punitive machine. For Stalin and his comrades-in-arms, the mass operations of 1937–38 were unquestionably beneficial, having strengthened the defense capacity of the country right when war loomed.[20] Most of the torturers of the Great Terror stayed with the NKVD and pursued successful careers. Tortures and falsifications of cases continued (although on a smaller scale than in 1937–38), encouraged by Stalin in the January 1939 directive.

On 9 February 1939 the head of the Chita province UNKVD department, Feldman, beat up a prisoner during an interrogation. The victim ended up in the hospital, and the case was investigated. The procurator of the province questioned the victim in Feldman's presence. Feldman did not deny the beating and declared that he had "beat [prisoners] in the past and will continue to beat [them] in the future." Soon Feldman was transferred, with a promotion, from Chita province.[21] The head of the special department of the Black Sea Fleet, Lebedev, responded to the protests of the fleet's procurator about the beating of the arrested: "I have beaten in the past and will continue to beat. I have a directive from Com. Beria in this regard."[22]

"New Order" in the Camps

Beria inherited from Yezhov a rather disorganized camp economy. The mass arrests of camp bosses, the mortality and disability rates among prisoners, and the destruction of the traditional and relatively effective organization of labor and the camp economy had resulted in the NKVD's failure to meet economic plans. It was vital for the new management to demonstrate its abilities to Stalin by achieving quick economic success.

One of Beria's first acts in his new position was the creation of the Special Technical Bureau, supervised by the people's commissar of internal affairs. On 8 January 1939 the Politburo approved Beria's draft resolution to create this bureau, and on 10 January an appropriate NKVD order was signed. According to the resolution, the bureau was organized to "make use of the prisoners possessing special technical knowledge and skills" in order "to construct and produce new armaments for the army and the navy." Beria personally took charge of the Special Technical Bureau.[23]

An inquiry conducted after Stalin's death revealed that Beria played an important role in determining the fate of the leading aviation engineers,[24] who were arrested in 1937–38 and used in the famous Central Construction Bureau no. 29.[25]

· 58 ·

Memorandum by the Procuracy, the KGB, and the administrative department
of the Central Committee of the Communist Party on the
rehabilitation of specialists in the aviation industry
23 February 1955[26]

Top secret.

To the Secretary of the CC CPSU, Com. Khrushchev.

In accordance with your instruction, we reviewed the investigative cases
of A. N. Tupolev and other imprisoned prominent specialists in the aviation industry. [. . .]

As a result, it has been established that:

Tupolev and other prominent workers of the aviation industry were arrested by the NKVD in 1937–38. The NKVD had no specific materials to
indict the prisoners, and the investigation was based only on statements
by the prisoners in which they accused each other.

For example, Tupolev stated that he had organized an anti-Soviet group
among TsAGI [Central Institute for Aerodynamics and Hydrodynamics]
workers, whose members supposedly engaged in sabotage in the early
years of the Soviet regime and later set up a hostile organization that sabotaged the construction of almost all aircraft.

Soon after Tupolev's arrest, such leading workers of the TsAGI as Mia-
sishchev, Petliakov, Nekrasov, and others, were also arrested. All of them
confessed during interrogation that they supposedly were engaged in anti-
Soviet activity.

Later, most specialists in the aviation industry recanted their confessions as being false and stated that they had been forced to take the blame
by the forbidden methods of investigation.

In 1938 all of them, without being convicted, were sent to work in the
Special Technical Bureau of the NKVD USSR, and their cases were sent to
the archive without being reviewed by the court.

At the time of his ascension in the NKVD USSR, to create the impression that arrested specialists were being put to good use, Beria managed,
by deception, to secure the approval of "instances" [that is, the Politburo
or Stalin] for the sentencing in absentia of 307 aviation specialists to various prison terms. He insisted that "reviewing these cases in a usual manner is disadvantageous, because it will distract the specialists from work
and will threaten the work plans of the Special Technical Bureau."

In presenting these far-fetched and unsubstantiated arguments, Beria
also claimed that the guilt of arrested specialists in committing state
crimes had been proven and that bringing the accused to a court session

would prove nothing, since they had been in close touch for a long time and would have already agreed on any future statements. In his letter Beria also asked for permission to create a special commission, composed of himself, the procurator of the USSR, and the chairman of the Military Collegium of the Supreme Court of the USSR, which would determine, in absentia, the degree of punishment for each of the arrested specialists, in the form of imprisonment for five to fifteen years.

The KGB archive also has the protocols of sessions from the aforementioned commission during which the commission determined the punishment for all arrested specialists. In May 1940 the Military Collegium of the Supreme Court reviewed in absentia the cases of the arrested specialists and determined their punishment in accordance with the resolution of this commission.

Thus, all the arrested specialists were convicted. Later, in 1940–44, at the request of the NKVD, the Presidium of the Supreme Soviet of the USSR freed many of them and cancelled their convictions. [. . .]

Although the Special Technical Bureau required only a small number of prisoner specialists, the fulfillment of gargantuan NKVD plans, mainly for construction projects, depended on the availability of hundreds of thousands of able-bodied prisoners. Such were difficult to find in the camps. A January 1939 Gulag memorandum revealed that, among the 1,130,955 prisoners for that month, 789,534 people (70 percent) worked in production; 117,353 prisoners (10 percent) were employed in camp services; and about the same number (117,896 people) did not work owing to disability, illness, or emaciation. Another 106,172 people (slightly more than 9 percent) constituted group D— prisoners who, from the point of view of the camp administration, were capable of working but did not work for a number of reasons. Among them were the "contingents" en route to and between camps, the otkazchiks (13,885 prisoners who refused to work), prisoners who did not work because they lacked clothes (16, 625), prisoners who did not receive work tasks because of stalled production (15,126), and others.[27]

The low percentage of able-bodied workers made it impossible to fulfill economic plans. Besides, NKVD bosses realized that the figures did not reflect the true picture. In March 1939 the second Gulag department (in charge of prisoner registration) drafted a memorandum to the NKVD leadership that signaled serious problems.

· 59 ·

Memorandum about NKVD requirements for the GULAG workforce
March 1939[28]*

Top secret.

To the Deputy People's Commissar of Internal Affairs of the USSR,
Division Commander, Com. Chernyshev.

As per the adopted plan of capital investment for 1939, according to the
GULAG of the NKVD planning department, the workforce needs at the
construction camps for the month of April of the current year has been determined to be 1,420,000 people. As of 1 April the projected availability
of prisoners (including the approved quotas and those en route) will be
1,304,000 people.

To maintain the workforce (given natural diminution), the camps and
construction sites will require 143,000 people in April alone, including:

ZhDSU† in the Far East	30,000 people
Sevvostlag	33,000 people
Dallag	10,000 people
Construction no. 211	4,000 people
Ushosdorlag	11,000 people
Yagrinlag	5,000 people
Agricultural camps	10,000 people
Forest camps	15,000 people

The Far Eastern camps and construction sites alone will require at least
90,000 people in April.

The main source for making up the deficit in the workforce would be
prison inmates, with the partial transfer of prisoners from subordinate
and partner colonies.

a) Availability of prison inmates:

Although the total number of prison inmates, as of 1 March, was
101,500, only 32,000 can be sent to the corrective labor camps. The rest
can be divided as follows:

Awaiting response to cassation appeal	39,000 people
In transit	6,400 people
Sentenced to prison	3,000 people
Sentenced to corrective labor colonies	21,000 people

* The document is reproduced from an undated copy.
† Administration of Railroad Construction.

Among the 32,000 [who can be sent to corrective labor camps], 15,000 were sentenced for counterrevolutionary crimes. The 32,000 also includes juveniles, the disabled, the partially handicapped, and those in other categories that make them ineligible for transfer to the camps.

Therefore, the number of prison inmates does not satisfy the workforce needs of the railway construction board according to Order no. 00173 from the people's commissar of internal affairs,[29] let alone the workforce needs of Sevvostlag, which requires just physically fit prisoners capable of hard labor.

b) Availability of prisoners in the colonies:

As of 1 March there were 346,000 prisoners in the colonies.

The 1939 plan for contractual projects requires 215,000 people; for proprietary projects, 281,000. This leaves a gap of 150,000 people.

Of the total number of prisoners in the colonies, 39,000 are invalids and people who are partially handicapped. There are 258,000 able-bodied workers in the colonies (including 41,000 awaiting replies to cassation appeals), and most of them are short-term. The regular delivery of inmates from the prisons does not offset the natural departure of prisoners from the camps.

In response to the existing situation in the supply of a workforce to the construction camps, I suggest a series of measures that, while not resolving the problem in general, would somewhat alleviate the situation regarding the workforce:

1. Satisfy the initial labor demands of the construction camps that are working, at your orders, on important state projects. As a priority, send prisoners there.

2. Discontinue sending prisoners to all other camps, and announce that there will be no delivery of an additional workforce in the coming months.

3. After this, instruct all camps and construction sites to maximize the employment of prisoners, improve the organization and mechanization of work, raise the productivity of labor, and substantially improve the living conditions of the prisoners (lodging, food supply, clothing, etc.).

4. Allow the construction camps to retain former prisoners as free workers.

5. Take a series of measures to strengthen the so-called emaciated contingent with the aim of getting them back to work.

6. Review the colonies for proprietary projects with the aim of reducing in size and liquidating a number of colonies, and move prisoners to the camps.

7. Allow the dispatch to Sevvostlag of those sentenced to prison.

8. Rescind Order no. 016 about sending to Sevvostlag only those able to perform hard physical labor, and permit those able to perform physical labor to be sent.[30]

Reporting the aforesaid, I am asking for your instructions.

Head of the Second Department of the GULAG of the NKVD,
Lieutenant of State Security, Granovsky.

Recommendations summarized in this letter later became even more
imperative. On 31 March 1939 the SNK and the CC VKP(b) adopted
a resolution about broadscale railroad construction by the NKVD in
the Far East involving an additional capital investment of over
280,000,000 rubles.[31] On the same day, the SNK charged the NKVD
with another large project: a railroad connecting Kirovskaya railway
and the Northern (Soroka–Obozerskaya) railway. These resolutions
prompted Beria to come up with some important proposals for the
government.

· 60 ·

Beria's note about discontinuing the early release of prisoners on parole
9 April 1939[32]

Top secret.
To the Chairman of the SNK of the Union of SSR,
Comrade V. M. Molotov.
In the Third Five-Year period, the workforce of the corrective labor
camps of the People's Commissariat of Internal Affairs received the task of
managing important construction works, totaling up to 12 billion rubles.
This poses to the commissariat the most serious task of securing the most
efficient use of the camp workforce.

At the same time, the general status of the NKVD corrective labor
camps as a means of combining corrective labor practices with the employment of its contingents at economic, industrial, and construction sites
is such that it makes it extremely difficult to fulfill this task without adopting rather decisive and serious measures.

An unsatisfactory supply of food and work clothes to those laboring in
the camps has not allowed the possibility of employing fully all the physical capacities of the prisoners.

The existing GULAG of the NKVD USSR food ration of 2,000 calories
is designed to support a nonworking prison inmate. In reality, supply organizations reduced this low ration by 65–70 percent. As a result, a significant percentage of the camp labor force end up in the emaciated category and are hence useless for production. As of 1 March 1939, there were
200,000 emaciated prisoners in the camps and colonies. Thus, in general,
no more than 60–65 percent of the workforce is used.

No less important is the issue of the mechanization of production and construction work done by the camps. The leadership of the people's commissariat, spoiled in the past by the abundance of workers, did not address the questions of rationalization and mechanization of work. A double and even triple number of workers compensated for the machines. Today, when the number of available workforce is 20–25 percent below that required, and will decrease in the future, the camps cannot complete their tasks without a high level of mechanization at work. The people's commissariat is contemplating the question of technical support to GULAG projects and will report its considerations to the government in the coming days.

At the same time, the practice of early release on parole, allowed by the current [criminal] codes of the RSFSR and other union republics, leads to the situation where prisoners in the camps are, as a rule, if they are working well, released halfway or sometimes one-third of the way through the term established by the court; i.e., a prisoner sentenced to three years often gets out in ten–eleven months.[33] Such is the current practice of all judicial bodies, which rely too liberally on article 124 of the corrective labor code of the RSFSR.

The practice brings to naught the effectiveness of the corrective labor punishment, nor does it contribute to the fight against crime. It also creates an extremely high fluctuation of the camp contingent and negatively affects the organization of production cycles and the productive work of the camps in general. For example, in 1938 up to 90,000 of the 260,000 in the entire contingent in Bamlag were released. A substantial percentage of those released were released on parole or through the counting of workdays. A similar situation exists in the other camps.

These three factors—a bad food supply, a low level of mechanization in production, and the fluctuation of the workforce as a result of early release practices—lead to a situation in which the criminals fail to get rehabilitated and the workforce is quite poorly managed.

The People's Commissariat of Internal Affairs considers it necessary to undertake the following measures:

1. Reject the system of release on parole of the camp contingents. Those sentenced to the camps should serve the full term of their punishment as determined by the court.

Instruct the Procuracy of the USSR and the courts to discontinue reviewing cases for release on parole, and Internal Affairs to discontinue the practice of counting one workday for two days of the prison term.

2. The main stimulus for increasing labor productivity should be improved food rations for good workers demonstrating a high productivity of labor, monetary bonuses to this category of prisoners, and less restrictive custody along with improvements in their living conditions.

Prisoners who are exemplary workers demonstrating high labor productivity for a long period of time can be released early on parole by the decision of the Collegium of the NKVD or the NKVD Special Council if they have a special commendation from the head of the camp and the head of the camp's political department.

3. Harsh coercive measures should be used against absentees, those refusing to work, and wreckers: more restrictive custody, detention cells, worse living conditions, and other disciplinary methods. The most inveterate wreckers should be subject to harsher judicial punishment, including the ultimate penalty.

Every time such measures are used, they should be broadly announced to the prisoners.

4. Supply food and work clothes to the camp workforce to utilize fully the physical capabilities of the camp workforce at any enterprise.

Sovnarkom should review and approve the allowances for food and clothing supply to the camp workforce.

People's Commissar of Internal Affairs of the Union of the SSR, L. Beria.

· 61 ·

Beria's note on supplying NKVD construction sites with a workforce
24 April 1939[34]

Top secret.

SNK USSR to Comrade V. M. Molotov.

In 1939 the NKVD USSR was charged with managing capital construction for the most important projects: railways and highways of strategic importance, construction of the NKO [People's Commissariat of Defense] and NKVMF [People's Commissariat of the Navy] airports, special projects of the NKVMF, the Arkhangelsk factory, three integrated pulp-and-paper mills, five special cellulose pulp mills, a deepening of the Amur River, the Kuibyshev and Rybinsk hydroelectric power stations, the design of the Solikamsk [power station], Norilskstroi, and Dalstroi, the harvesting of 51 million cubic meters of timber, and a number of other important projects, totaling over 5 billion rubles—not including the value of gold, fish, agricultural produce, and consumer products.

To fulfill this program of work, 1,550,000 camp workers are needed. In addition to that, camps provide up to 80,000 people for other commissariat projects. As of 1 April 1939, there were actually 1,264,000 people (excluding invalids), which is 330,000 less than required. The monthly decrease in camp contingents (the difference between the newly convicted and those released) was 23,000–25,000 people in the first quarter of 1939.

In addition, among the existing camp workforce, there are up to 150,000 emaciated and partially employable workers owing to poor food supply in the camps. This results in an actual shortfall in the workforce of 400,000. All this seriously threatens the completion of the program of works delegated to the People's Commissariat of Internal Affairs.

Particularly serious is the situation with regard to the workforce at NKVD projects in the Far East, where Dalstroi, railroad and highway construction, special construction for the TOF [Pacific Fleet] and the army, a deepening of the Amur River, timber harvesting, coal [mining], fishing, and other works, totaling 1,900,000,000 rubles, require 680,000–700,000 people, whereas only 200,000 are available.

At some construction sites, the NKVD is forced to resort to hiring free workers (Volgostroi, the Arkhangelsk factory, the Kuibyshev hydroelectric project, highways), which considerably complicates maintaining the camp regimen when [both groups] work together. While it is more or less possible to hire workers for central construction sites, the Far East requires the delivery of just camp prisoners.

Based on the current balance of the workforce and considering the urgent need to add to the workforce in the Far East (especially construction site no. 206, BAM, and Dalstroi), the People's Commissariat of Internal Affairs requests approval for the following measures:

1. For 1939, stop the expansion of construction works remanded to the NKVD, and stop dispatching its workforce to other organizations.

2. Order that the NKVD supply, in May and June, 120,000 people for the construction of highways and railways in the Far East and to Dalstroi, for which purpose allow that the NKVD:

a. withdraw 60,000 prisoners from the contractual works where the NKVD alone supplies the workforce (see attached list); and

b. transfer 70,000 people sentenced to two years or less to the camps from the corrective labor colonies.

3. The NKPS should secure, in May–June, the transfer by train of 120,000 prisoners to the Far East, at NKVD request.

4. The Economic Council of the SNK USSR, beginning with the second quarter, should increase funds for provisioning the GULAG of the NKVD USSR based on an average ration for an industrial worker.

5. In accordance with the aforementioned organizational measures, the NKF [People's Commissariat of Finance] USSR and the NKVD USSR should revise the SNK USSR plan, the new plan for financing [the projects], and the amount of funding for the GULAG and the NKVD.

Hereby asking for your resolution,

People's Commissar of Internal Affairs of the USSR, L. Beria.

Attachment.

Memorandum on the numbers of prisoner workers provided to the people's commissariats.

People's Commissariat	Actual Allocation of the Workforce	Number to Be Withdrawn
1. People's Commissariat of Ferrous Metallurgy	22,403	15,000
2. People's Commissariat of Nonferrous Metallurgy	5,499	2,000
3. People's Commissariat of the Chemical Industry	1,176	—
4. People's Commissariat of Ammunitions	17,282	7,000
5. People's Commissariat of the Aircraft Industry	9,141	4,000
6. People's Commissariat of Armaments	2,850	1,000
7. People's Commissariat of Shipbuilding	2,200	1,000
8. People's Commissariat of Defense	2,644	1,000
9. People's Commissariat of Machine Building	5,424	3,000
10. People's Commissariat for the Collection of Agricultural Products	693	—
11. People's Commissariat of Agriculture	10,145	5,000
12. People's Commissariat of Communications	5,395	3,000
13. People's Commissariat of Forestry	10,346	5,000
14. People's Commissariat of the Fuel Industry	10,197	5,000
15. People's Commissariat of Electric Power Plants	6,326	3,000
16. People's Commissariat of the Food Industry	888	—
17. Other People's Commissariats and Local Organizations	20,654	15,000
Total	133,739	70,000

Deputy People's Commissar of Internal Affairs of the USSR, Division Commander V. Chernyshev.

Thus, in his April memorandums, Beria proposed rather drastic measures of his own to reorganize the NKVD economy: increasing the allowances for food and clothes for prisoners, rejecting early release on parole, toughening repressive measures (including capital punish-

ment) for "absentees, those refusing to work, and wreckers," freezing
the number of NKVD construction works in 1939, discontinuing the
supply of workers to other commissariats, and transferring to the
camps those in the colonies with sentences of up to two years.

As usual, prior to adopting such important measures, the SNK leadership forwarded Beria's letters to various institutions. Some proposals
(like increasing food supplies to the prisoners and financing the Gulag)
met no objections.[35] However, such issues as early release on parole
and applying the ultimate punishment to prisoners caused debate.
Procurator of the USSR Vyshinsky and People's Commissar of Justice
Rychkov spoke up against these measures. In their letters to Sovnarkom, they argued that early release on parole should not be dis-
carded (though it should be "improved"), not only because it was allowed by law but also because it had a positive effect on discipline and
the productivity of labor. As to applying the ultimate punishment to
"inveterate wreckers of camp life and production," Vyshinsky and
Rychkov insisted on observing the existing laws. In Beria's proposal
they discerned, not without reason, an attempt to legalize execution by
shooting at the NKVD's will. The ultimate punishment should not be
used if the prisoner did not commit crimes for which the Criminal
Code allows shooting, wrote Vyshinsky and Rychkov.[36]

Initially, the position of the Procuracy and the People's Commissariat of Justice received support in the government. On 7 June 1939 a
meeting of deputies of the chairman of the SNK USSR, presided over
by Molotov (with Beria present), resolved not to discuss the issue of
early release or the issue of the ultimate punishment.[37]

It is still unclear what steps Beria took after that. He probably ap-
pealed directly to Stalin and secured his support. This was all the easier to do since Stalin, in August 1938, had expressed similar thoughts
about discontinuing early release, though in relation to an individual
case.

· 62 ·

Stalin's speech at a session of the Presidium of the Supreme Soviet of the USSR
"On the early release of prisoners who distinguished themselves in the
construction of the second railway line from Karymskaya to Khabarovsk"
25 August 1938[38]

I. V. STALIN: Were you right to present a list of prisoners to be released?
They leave their workplace. Could we think of some other way of assess-
ing their work—awards, etc.? We are doing the wrong thing, and we are
disrupting the work of the camps. These people, of course, should be released, but from the point of view of the state economy, it is bad.

We should find 10,000 such people, but only 2,000 have been found so
far. The best people would leave, and the worst would stay.

Is there a way of doing it differently, so that these people stay at work—
by giving awards, maybe orders? Otherwise, we will release them, and
they will return home, again fall in with criminals, and follow the beaten
path. The camps have a different atmosphere; it is difficult to get spoiled
there. I am talking about our decision. If, following this decision, [prison-
ers] get early release, these people will again follow the beaten path.

What if we put it this way: lift their punishment early in hopes that they
stay at the construction site as free workers? But the previous decision is
not good for us.

Let's not approve this draft today, but charge the NKVD with thinking
of other means to make people stay in place. Perhaps put it this way: a pre-
mature annulment of their conviction so as not to impel them to leave.
They should be allowed to bring their family, have the regimen changed
for them, and maybe even be considered free laborers. As we used to refer
to a voluntary-forced [state] loan, here is a voluntary-forced stay.

In view of Stalin's attitude, it is no wonder that, several days after
Sovnarkom refused to deal with the problems formulated by Beria, the
Politburo fully supported the NKVD leaders. The 10 June 1939 Politburo resolution "On the NKVD camps" literally repeated Beria's 9
April proposal to discontinue release on parole and to punish the
wreckers (including shooting). It also charged Sovnarkom with reviewing the allowances for food and clothes at the camps.[39] On 15
June 1939 the Presidium of the Supreme Soviet of the USSR issued a
decree, "On the NKVD camps," that was based on the Politburo resolution. It rejected early release and urged that repression be increased
in the camps. On 4 July the SNK Economic Council approved the new
food and clothing allowances for the camp prisoners. These new allowances also generally satisfied, with minor modifications, the requests by the NKVD leadership.[40]

At the same time, after several months of red tape, Beria's proposals as outlined in his note of 24 April 1939 (Document 61) were approved. On 17 June 1939 the SNK USSR adopted a resolution on supplying a workforce for NKVD projects in 1939. The NKVD was allowed to stop providing prisoners to other commissariats and departments and to move 120,000 prisoners to the Far East in June–July 1939. By 1 January 1940 the NKVD had to reclaim all prisoners previously provided to other commissariats and departments.[41]

Concessions to the NKVD were accompanied by the rejection of one of the main components of Beria's program—stabilizing and limiting the economic plans of the People's Commissariat of Internal Affairs. During 1939 the plan for NKVD capital construction was increased by over 1 billion rubles, that is, one-third more than the amount targeted by the original plan for 1939.[42] This increase was a result of the expansion of old NKVD projects and the beginning of new construction. Capital investment in Dalstroi and the Norilsk steel industrial complex increased dramatically. The amount of work on NKVD railway construction was so large that, on 2 January 1940, the Politburo approved the organization, within the NKVD, of the Chief Administration of Camps for Railroad Construction.[43]

The growth in the amount of work to be performed by the NKVD, given a relative stagnation in the number of "camp contingents," complicated the task of the new bosses of Internal Affairs, especially since the hard-won promises of the government to allocate resources and to move prisoners from other projects were, as usual, not fully realized.

The new rations, approved by the government, came into effect in the fourth quarter of 1939 but were not backed by sufficient funds. The total need for food in the camps greatly exceeded the available resources (see Document 63). And only part of those supplies reached the prisoners: much of it got delayed en route, rotted, or was stolen. A similar situation existed for the clothes allocation. Even though most camps were located in regions with an unfavorable climate, a significant number of prisoners lacked basic clothing, much less winter wear. According to the Gulag supply department, in 1939 the Gulag received only 54 percent of the cotton cloth, 62 percent of the blankets, 74 percent of the leather shoes, and a meager 26 percent of the felt boots that were needed. Since the Gulag leaders considered clothes and bedsheets to be "objects crucial for the completion of the work tasks," most of those were sent to the camps engaged in construction and servicing key projects. The camps attempted to alleviate the problem with their own resources. Often shoes were made out of salvage and waste materials, such as old tires. Thick cotton stockings (*bakhily*) substituted for felt boots, and tin cans were used as plates.[44]

In general, compared to the previous period, despite the freeze on mass repressive actions and a certain stabilization in the number of prisoners, the difficult living conditions of the prisoners improved only marginally. The rates of death and illness remained high in the camps. Emaciated though the prisoners were, the demands on them grew, which eventually incapacitated or killed them. A Gulag special communication of 23 July 1939 about the situation in the Yagrinsky camp stated, "Many leaders of camp sections have adopted the practice of forcing those who were ill and emaciated to do hard work, which leads to the early exhaustion of the workforce, deaths, and the spread of an unhealthy mood among the prisoners." That camp had more than 10,000 prisoners suffering from scurvy. The camp administration called them "inveterate slackers" and put them in detention cells.[45]

The situation in the Yagrinsky camp was typical. A Gulag directive, from 16 September 1939, highlighted attempts by "some camps" to solve the problem of fulfilling work tasks "mechanically" by "making prisoners work for fourteen–sixteen hours until they fulfill their work tasks and by organizing work on the weekends." Such practices, the directive went on, "leads to the emaciation of prisoners, an increase in the disease rate, and, in the end, a failure to fulfill the planned tasks."[46] Another Gulag order, on 5 November 1939, prohibited the inclusion in the "refusers" category of work "those without shoes or clothes, emaciated prisoners, disabled [prisoners], or sick prisoners, unless they are simulators," or those who "temporarily are unable to fulfill the norm for reasons beyond their control."[47] As a rule, however, such complaints merely drew attention to the situation without any real consequences. As the following report by the Gulag sanitary department mentions, it was commonplace in 1939 for "prisoners with a reduced ability to work to receive full work tasks." Unable to complete their tasks, they are given reduced rations, their health worsens, and the disease and death rate rises.

· 63 ·

Preliminary report on the activities of the GULAG sanitary department in 1939[48]

By 1939 the sanitary and living conditions in the camps were rather poor. Prisoners were crowded together, with an average living space of 0.5

to 2.5 square meters [per person], with a cubic capacity of between 1.5 and 5.6 cubic meters per person. The previous food rations were clearly inadequate, both in volume and in the amount of protein and fats. The systemic unavailability of vegetables seriously affected the supply of vegetables to the camps. Some camps received only 20–30 percent of the required amount. The entire situation was aggravated by food reserves that were insufficient to satisfy the calculated norms. As a result, almost every camp suffered from an irregular supply of meat, fish, fats, and vegetables.

The clothes allowance was rather strained. Camps received only 35–50 percent of the required bedsheets. A change of bedsheets was everywhere lacking, and the supply covered only 35 percent of the demand.

The problem of using prisoners at work regardless of their physical condition remained unresolved.

Such difficult conditions made the camps clearly vulnerable to epidemic diseases. The spread of scurvy was a threat, as was the physical deterioration of the camp population. [. . .]

I. Hospital network

Medical assistance. As of 1 January 1939 the ITL [corrective labor camps] had 1,171 hospitals and casualty wards, with a total of 39,839 beds, or [enough for] 3.4 percent of the entire population of the corrective labor camps.

As of 1 October 1939 the number of beds in the ITL hospitals was 38,360, or [enough for] 3.66 percent of the population.

As of 1 January 1939 the entire network of detention facilities (prisons and corrective labor colonies) had 16,885 beds ([enough for] 1.99 percent of the population). [. . .]

Non-hospital facilities. These consisted of outpatient departments attended by doctors and nurses. The dynamics of the non-hospital facilities are represented in the following table.

	As of 1 January 1939		As of 1 October 1939	
	Outpatient Departments Attended by a Doctor	Outpatient Departments Attended by a Nurse	Outpatient Departments Attended by a Doctor	Outpatient Departments Attended by a Nurse
In corrective labor camps	247	1,782	398	2,099
In corrective labor colonies	415	631	185	373

[. . .] A decrease in the number of outpatient departments attended by doctors and nurses in the corrective labor colonies is related to the trans-

fer of medical facilities from the detention centers to the Chief Administration of Prisons.[49] [. . .]

In regard to the supply of medical facilities with both hard and soft
stock,* it is most important to note the insufficient delivery of bedsheets
and pillowcases, as well as towels and robes for the patients and the medical staff. [. . .]

All camps are fully supplied with medicines and bandages, according to
the existing allowances for medical supplies.

The variety of food supplied to the hospitals is not adequate. Particularly frequent are delays in the delivery of milk, fresh meat and fish, butter,
and dietary grains. A lack of these products, or the prolonged interruption
of their supply, significantly degrades hospital rations and retards healing.

II. Loss of workdays to sickness

The question of prisoner employment remains unresolved. Prisoners
with a limited ability to work are given full tasks. As a result, because of
their inability to fulfill norms, their rations are reduced and their physical
health deteriorates. This, in turn, results in an increased disease and death
rate. [. . .]

The food allowances introduced in the fourth quarter of 1939 have not
had a positive effect. It is important to stress, however, that the food allowances in all places are not supported by adequate food reserves, and
the actual caloric value of the rations does not correspond to the allowances owing to continual interruptions in the food supply.

Analysis of the disease rate shows that most illnesses are related to living conditions, food rations, and employment. These are the skin and sub-
cutaneous cellular tissue diseases, avitaminosis (scurvy, night blindness,
pellagra), tuberculosis, and both non-work-related and work-related injuries. The latter are quite frequently due to inadequate safety measures
and, in some camps, badly organized work. [. . .]

III. Death rate

Compared to a similar period in 1938, the death rate in the eleven
months of 1939 was significantly lower, as seen from the following figures
[percentages of the total number of prisoners]:

	1938	1939
Agricultural camps	7.17	2.76
Forest camps	10.37	3.5
Construction camps	5.02	2.54
Average	6.69	2.91

---

* Hard stock is equipment and furniture; soft stock is towels, sheets, and so on.

A notable decrease in the death rate can be explained by the broad implementation of health measures to restore the workforce by organizing work teams; expanding the number of beds, which allowed for timely hospitalization; improvement in the quality of medical care; and, finally, a lack of epidemics in the reported period.

The highest death rates among the agricultural camps are in Sazlag (4.71 percent) [and] Siblag (2.79 percent).

Among the forest camps, the camps most notable for a high [death] rate are Ustvymsky camp, with 12.64 percent, then Usolsk camp (6.85 percent), Viatka camp (4.82 percent), [and] Lokchimsky camp (4.07 percent). The lowest death rates are at Ivdel camp (1.94 percent) [and] Taishet camp (2.29 percent).

Among the construction camps, the highest figures are at the Eastern railway camp (7.73 percent), Northern railway camp (7.33 percent), [and] Ukhta-Izhemsky camp (5.38 percent). The lowest [are] in the group of camps around Moscow, construction [site] no. 200 (0.3 percent) [and] Solikambumstroi (0.61 percent).

The highest proportion of disease-related deaths involves the diseases resulting from the insufficient quality and quantity of food. In some months in the forest camps, deaths from these diseases account for 50 percent of all deaths (Viatka camp, etc.). [. . .]

The NKVD leaders, as they had earlier that year, complained about the inability of many prisoners to work. In a 14 September 1939 report to the government, the deputy people's commissar of internal affairs, Chernyshev, noted that there were up to 50,000 invalids and up to 150,000 partially employable prisoners, that is, prisoners who were extremely emaciated or seriously ill.[50]

The aim of boosting the number of workers by relocating them from other commissariat sites was not realized. The 17 June 1939 SNK resolution infringed upon the interests of powerful economic departments that utilized the available prisoners and were unable to replace them promptly with free laborers. The government was bombarded with requests to retain prisoner workers at different projects. In many cases, Sovnarkom leaders supported these requests. In a 14 July letter to Molotov, Beria reflected on this situation: "SNK Resolution no. 882/143 of 17 June 1939 to transfer the NKVD workforce from the construction sites of other commissariats is being implemented rather slowly. All commissariats petition the SNK USSR to exempt them from the SNK USSR resolution. The Economic Council [. . .], on a case-by-case basis, released the People's Commissariat of Nonferrous Metallurgy from that obligation and extended the deadline for timber cutting and timber rafting. As a result, the transfer of the workforce to the F[ar] East is proceeding very slowly."[51] The impediments, noted by Beria at the very earliest stage in the implementation of the 17 June resolution, did not go away. The transfer of all prisoners from non-NKVD sites, planned for 1 January 1940, was not realized. The Gulag allowed its prisoners to stay at other commissariat sites in the years to come.

To fulfill the ever-growing plans, NKVD bosses returned to tried-and-true methods—the merciless exploitation of prisoners and increased repression of the "wreckers of production and disorganizers of camp life."

The Fight Against "Wreckers" and "Spies"

The appointment of a new people's commissar of internal affairs encouraged Gulag leaders to redouble their efforts to "instill order" and "strengthen the regimen" in the camps, colonies, and prisons. The new bosses (as well as the old ones who retained their positions) had to demonstrate their administrative effectiveness and their persistence in the struggle against "the results of wrecking in NKVD organs." On the other hand, the situation in the Gulag after the Great Terror was critical, as demonstrated by failures to fulfill economic plans and a large number of unpleasant incidents in the camps and colonies.

In late 1938–early 1939 a wave of disturbances hit the juvenile colonies. Vyshinsky reported to Stalin and Molotov that on 29 December 1938 "there was a riot of 490 prisoners in Valuy labor colony. Insurgents destroyed the building in which they stayed, injured seven guards, and looted the liquor store. Some prisoners escaped from the labor colony."[52] On 22 December 1938 the people's commissar of internal affairs issued an order in connection with a mass revolt of juvenile prisoners in the Severouralsk camp. According to the order, armed force had to be used to quell the revolt.[53] On 1 April 1939 the commissar issued another order, "On the results of the investigation of disorders that took place in the Ostashkovo, Valuisk, and Chepetsk NKVD labor colonies (for juveniles)." The order identified the terrible living conditions of juvenile prisoners as the cause of the disturbances, which resulted in "the destruction of and damage to some tools and property, destruction of some buildings, the looting of warehouses and stores, with total damages amounting to tens of thousands of rubles." "Residence areas are filthy, the apprentices had not visited the bathhouse for a month and a half. [. . .] Many apprentices had no clothes or shoes and had to walk to school and work barefooted. Some of them walked to the dining hall barefooted in the snow. The food in the dining hall is insufficient and of low quality. There were cases of worms, cockroaches, etc., getting into food. [. . .]" In addition, prisoners were subjected to beatings, lockup in detention cells, etc., just for complaining about the quality of food and the living conditions.[54]

Still, among the Gulag population, juvenile prisoners received the best protection from arbitrariness (which explains, in part, why they rioted so easily; there is no evidence of similar disturbances in the camps). The situation of most prisoners was much worse. Hunger, exhaustion, disease, and a high mortality rate went hand in hand with arbitrariness and criminal behavior by low-level camp administrators. Camp managers and their friends among the staff embezzled meager resources, and criminals terrorized the rest of the prisoners. The number of escapes remained significant. All this not only clouded the NKVD's reputation in the eyes of national leaders but threatened to undermine the foundations of the Gulag.

NKVD bosses anticipated a negative backlash from the curtailment of the system of early release on parole. This measure radically altered the situation in the Gulag by denying prisoners their main stimulus to adapt and be loyal to the camp system. To understand better the impact of this decision, it is important to remember that in the years of the Great Terror the number of prisoners sentenced to long terms grew significantly. On 1 January 1937, the share of camp prisoners with sentences between five and ten years was 26 percent; on 1 January 1939 their share had grown to nearly 45 percent (those sentenced to more than ten years steadily constituted about 1 percent of the total number of prisoners; see Document 99). Prisoners sentenced to long terms who had accumulated a large number of bonus days, whether by fair means of foul, were particularly frustrated and angry.

Fearing the consequences of ending the system of early release, the NKVD tried to take preventive measures. On 15 June 1939, the same day the decree by the Presidium of the Supreme Soviet of the USSR was signed, Beria issued an order "on suspending the practice of counting workdays toward the early release of prisoners on parole." The order stated that from this time forward, the main stimulus for raising the productivity of labor would be "improved supply and rations for good workers who demonstrate a high productivity of labor, monetary bonuses to this category of prisoners, visits by close relatives, and less restrictive custody, along with an improvement in their living conditions." The order also emphasized the intensification of repression. "Absentees, those refusing to work, and wreckers of production should be subjected to harsh measures—a more restrictive regimen, detention cells, more difficult living conditions, and other disciplinary measures. The most inveterate disorganizers of camp life and wreckers should be subjected to even harsher measures—criminal prosecution. [. . .] Heads of camps and the heads of political departments should widely inform the prisoners about each case requiring such judicial measures."[55] Gulag instructions issued after the 15 June order paid special attention to the prevention of escapes, which were anticipated from prisoners with long sentences.

The third department (security service) of the Gulag evaluated the situation in the camps just weeks after the new rules were implemented.

· 64 ·

Circular letter no. 148 from the third department of the GULAG, "On stepping up the struggle against escapes and violations of the camp regimen"
31 July 1939[56]

Top secret.

To all heads of the third departments of the NKVD camps and the third divisions of the OITK [Department of Corrective Labor Colonies] and UITK [Administration of Corrective Labor Colonies].

According to reports sent to the third department of the GULAG of the NKVD from the third camp departments and the third divisions of the OITK, Order no. 0168 by the people's commissar of internal affairs of the USSR, of 15 June of this year, discontinuing the practice of counting workdays toward early release on parole, has been met with stout resistance from the most spiteful group of prisoners.

These reports also demonstrate that this resistance is manifested through:

a. an increase in the number of escapees

b. malicious, conscious wrecking in order to undermine the fulfillment of production tasks

c. provocation of conflicts and insubordination

It also has been established that prisoners who were sentenced for anti-Soviet crimes conduct constant agitation among hard-working prisoners, causing them often to refuse to work and fulfill tasks without a chance for early release.

It also has been established that the leaders of some camps and OITK have not yet restructured their work in accordance with paragraphs 3 and 4 of this order—that is, to improve living conditions and provide benefits, as outlined in the order of the people's commissar, for the prisoners who do excellent work.

The third camp departments do not efficiently and quickly enough implement paragraph 5 of this order, which is to indict the most inveterate wreckers of production and disrupters of camp life.

Hereby it is ordered:

Within ten days of the receipt of this directive, to reveal:

1. Those most maliciously refusing to work and those consciously refusing to fulfill prisoner tasks

2. The organizers of group escapes and conflicts

3. Those conducting malicious agitation to hamper production work

4. Other disrupters of camp life and production

Prisoners implicated in committing the aforementioned crimes should be immediately arrested and prosecuted in strict accordance with the Criminal Code and NKVD Order no. 00762 of 1938.[57]

The court verdicts in these cases should be sent to the third department of the GULAG to be published as announcements.

Deputy Head of the Third Department of the GULAG of the NKVD, Second Lieutenant of State Security, Trofimov.

On the same day the third department issued another circular letter demanding a stiffer regimen and picturing a near-riot situation in the camps.

· 65 ·

Circular letter no. 146 from the third department of the GULAG,
"On conducting systematic searches of prisoners in the corrective labor camps and corrective labor colonies of the NKVD"
31 July 1939[58]

Top secret.

A simultaneous search of all prisoner barracks, initiated by the third department of the Temnikovsky NKVD camp, revealed a huge number of items that it was forbidden to store.

For example, the search retrieved 111 axes, 11 crowbars, 38 saws, 110 hammers, 828 knives, 52 razors, 34 mock grenades, 7 dumbbells, 2 passports, and 12,983 rubles. Also, two underground passages for group escapes by prisoners were discovered.

Considering the unsatisfactory situation in regard to the regimen and the isolation of prisoners in other NKVD camps, I suggest that at least once a month, under the guidance of the third departments, the guards and camp administration conduct surprise searches in the prisoners' barracks in order to retrieve various prohibited items and documents that can be used for escapes and attacks on the guards.

Please inform us about the results of the searches.

Deputy Head of the Third Department of the GULAG of the NKVD,
Second Lieutenant of State Security,
Trofimov.

Knowing NKVD methods and the NKVD's particular interest in exposing plots, it is possible that such frantic letters did not adequately reflect reality. Although it is certain that the situation in the camps became more difficult after the cancellation of early release, there has been no evidence of mass or active protests. Apparently the majority of prisoners channeled their frustration into complaints and statements. The number of such letters was so large that in December 1939 the deputy head of the Gulag sent the following directive to camp bosses and the heads of departments in the corrective labor colonies: "The people's commissar of internal affairs of the USSR, the procurator of the USSR, and other officers have lately received a large number of open letters from the prisoners in the NKVD camps and colonies asking for a reinstatement of the counting of workdays. [. . .] I hereby suggest that from now on, open letters from prisoners asking to reinstate the counting of workdays not be accepted, no matter to whom they are addressed."[59]

The wave of discontent was neutralized mostly by repression and terror. On orders from Moscow, camps conducted a prolonged battle against those refusing to work and against the "wreckers." Several thousand people were prosecuted, and some of them were shot.

· 66 ·

Memorandum on the number of camp prisoners sentenced
for disrupting camp life and wrecking
29 April 1940[60]

As of 20 April, the operative chekist camp departments had indicted and prosecuted a total of 4,033 people for disrupting camp life and wrecking. Compared to the total number of NKVD camp prisoners (1,327,031), this constitutes 0.3 percent.

The largest number of indictments for the aforementioned crimes were in the following camps:

Sevvostlag	1,068 people
Belbaltlag	377 people
Ustvymsky camp	187 people
Nizhne-Amursk camp	173 people
Vorkuta camp	117 people, etc.

At the same time, there are camps where the number of those prosecuted for disorganizing camp life and wrecking is in the single digits. For example:

Ivdel camp	3 people
Segezh camp	4 people
Luzhky camp	6 people
Khimki camp	7 people
Usolsk camp	9 people, etc.

Of the total number of those prosecuted, 201 people were sentenced to the ultimate penalty. Of these:

Shot	56 people
Ten years substituted for the ultimate penalty	63 people
Fifteen years substituted for the ultimate penalty	1 person
Awaiting approval of the sentence	81 people

Also, among those prosecuted for disrupting camp life and wrecking, 2,155 people were sentenced to an extension of their prison term to ten years; there have been no cases of extending the term for more than ten years.*

A number of cases—1,250—are at the litispendence stage, and 339 people are under investigation.

The Deputy Head of the Special Department of the NKVD USSR,
Captain of State Security,
Gertsovsky.

These repressive actions were usually announced to the prisoners of the camps where those shot or sentenced were held. Occasionally, special orders by the people's commissar of internal affairs or general Gulag

---

* The extension of prison terms in such fashion proved to be exceedingly arbitrary, a fact that inmates waiting for release often noted as the most demoralizing aspect of camp life.

announcements used the execution of the "disrupters" as part of a prisoner intimidation campaign.[61] Below is an example of one such order.

· 67 ·

Order no. 721 by the people's commissar of internal affairs, "On sentencing
prisoners for persistent refusal to work and self-injury"
31 October 1939[62]

Cases of persistent refusal to work by the prisoners have lately become more frequent in some NKVD camps.

In the South camp UZhDS [Administration of Railroad Construction] of the GULAG of the NKVD in the F[ar] E[ast], a group of fifteen prisoners, on the initiative of prisoners Kovalev and Silaev, have for a long time persistently avoided work by engaging in self-injury.

On 23 September of this year, the judicial-criminal collegium of the Supreme Court of the Buriat-Mongol ASSR reviewed the case of those in this group refusing to work and sentenced the instigators of self-injury, Kovalev and Silaev, to be shot.

The remaining thirteen prisoners were each sentenced to ten years in prison.

In the Birsk forest camp, a group of [female] prisoners headed by prisoner Zakarian conducted an anti-Soviet campaign among the prisoners, and incited them to refuse to work. Some members of the group did not report to work for sixty–seventy days.

All members of the group were prosecuted. The court of the Jewish Autonomous Region,* after reviewing this case, sentenced prisoner Zakarian to be shot. Other prisoners were sentenced to various prison terms.

I order:

That all heads of camps and administrators of NKVD corrective labor colonies announce this order to the prisoners and explain to them that in the future, not only those refusing to work and engaging in self-injury will be prosecuted but also those individuals who incite other prisoners to commit these crimes.

Deputy People's Commissar of Internal Affairs of the USSR, Division Commander,

Chernyshev.

---

* The Jewish Autonomous Region, an area on the Amur River near Khabarovsk in the Soviet Far East, was a grand project of the Soviet government to create a Jewish homeland in the USSR in the late 1920s and 1930s. Its capital and largest city was Birobidzhan.

Apparently, self-injury (intentionally getting sick or even mutilating oneself) mentioned in this order became widespread in the camps. Often not working, being admitted to the hospital, or even gaining one's freedom as an invalid was the only way to survive in the extreme conditions of the camps. Gulag bosses sent special instructions demanding that the camps fight against the practice of "simulation and self-injury."

· 68 ·

List by the sanitary department of the GULAG of some methods and techniques of simulation and aggravation used by prisoners in the camps and colonies
21 February 1939[63]

To get a release from work, a transfer, or a release from the camp under article 458 of the Criminal Code of the RSFSR, prisoners sometimes use methods and techniques that create pathological conditions similar to those of grave illnesses or an illness that serves as an excuse to get a release from work, a transfer, or an early release on parole.

The most common methods listed below are only typical and do not reflect the full array of techniques practiced by the prisoners. Therefore, each new case has to be carefully studied and made known to free medical workers of the camp where the incident occurred, as well as reported in detail to the GULAG of the NKVD.

The most characteristic techniques of the simulators are:

a. Artificially induced symptoms of myocarditis, heart disease, or nephritic disorders

The most frequently used agents are dry or diluted cooking salt, salted fish, etc., eaten along with drinking large amounts of water, tea [. . .], ersatz coffee (dry and strong brews), tobacco or shag infusions. [. . .]

b. Artificial gastro-enterocolitis

The most common causes: ingesting soap or soapy water, kerosene, a large amount of [household] soda, poisonous raw mushrooms, roots, refuse from garbage pits or garbage cans, as well as raw meat, fish, or water in order to induce diarrhea, etc.

c. Artificial boils or reopening and irritating wounds

Artificial boils are usually created by puncturing the skin and underlying tissue of an extremity with a needle and a thread soaked in kerosene, turpentine, or petroleum or by infecting wounds, scratches, cracks, or abrasions. The puncture is usually made at the mid- or lower shin, at the front, on the edge of the tibia. Sometimes they inject so much kerosene that if the boil is opened soon after that, its contents can burn.

Any unusually slow-healing sores, abrasions, cracks, or wounds should be suspected as the result of artificial irritation. The various agents used for irritation are salt, kerosene, turpentine, cinders, chemical fertilizers, urine, etc. The delay in healing is also caused by mechanical irritation. [. . .]

d. Simulation of fever

Fever is often simulated by a temporary localized increase in temperature at the bodily site where measurements are taken. An armpit with local irritation and inflammation (caused by rubbing in salt, applying a rag soaked in kerosene, etc.) leads to a localized increase in temperature. By measuring under the armpit, the thermometer registers a localized increase in temperature, and an inexperienced medical worker can interpret it as a general fever. If the measurement is conducted in the absence of a medical worker, prisoners can tamper with the reading by quickly rubbing the thermometer on a cloth or by shaking it.

e. Simulation of feebleness and arrhythmia

If one puts under his armpit an object of an appropriate size (a potato, a wooden ball, a thick fold of a jacket) and squeezes his arm to his body, the resulting pressure on the armpit artery allows him to control the strength and rhythm of his pulse, including its complete disappearance. A similar effect can result from applying bandages to a hand above the wrist joint. This simulation is easily exposed by examining the arm and the armpit and by measuring the pulse in a hand spread away from the body.

f. Simulation of venereal diseases

To simulate gonorrhoeal urethritis with secretion, prisoners often directly irritate the urinary tract by injecting soap or kerosene, which leads to symptoms similar to those of acute gonorrhea: secretion, redness of mucous membrane, etc. [. . .]

g. Since it is difficult to describe all cases of simulation and aggravation, the aforementioned serve only as the most typical examples. [Prisoners] often skillfully simulate various mental illnesses, epilepsy, traumatic neurosis, pull out (with their fingers) the mucous membrane of a rectum to simulate prolapse, aggravate illnesses of internal organs, simulate and aggravate the immobility of joints and muscle contractions, blindness, deafness, etc.

h. The most frequent cases of self-injury are:

1. hacking off fingers and extremities

2. freezing the extremities

3. artificial irritation and reopening of wounds, rashes, scratches, and other actions preventing prompt healing

4. chemical burns of the skin and underlying tissues

5. injuries, traumas, etc.

Head of the GULAG Sanitary Department, Chalov.

One of the tasks of the Administration of Gulag Security, created in 1939, was to deal with "those refusing to work and wreckers." Another task was to increase the number of armed guards and replace inmate guards with hired civilian guards. Security was always a sore problem for the Gulag. There were never enough people willing to do this dirty work, especially in the extreme conditions of remote camps. Therefore, camps and especially colonies often used guards from among the criminals—which again reveals the official Soviet favoritism toward actual criminals, although the lack of laborers in the Gulag meant that at times even political prisoners served in a number of "civilian" positions. As of 1 January 1939 there were 70,161 armed guards in the NKVD camps, including 60,839 hired rank-and-file guards and junior commanders and 9,322 prisoner guards. In the colonies there were 24,760 armed guards, 9,059 hired guards, and 15,701 prisoner guards.[64]

Naturally, inmate guards often violated the rules, abused their power, and committed grave crimes. Compared to them, hired civilian guards, although not distinguished by lofty morality or discipline, seemed to be a lesser evil. For that reason, NKVD leaders tried, while increasing the number of guards, to replace prisoner guards with civilians. In December 1938 the Gulag apparatus prepared a memorandum for the government asking to raise the number of hired armed guards at the NKVD camps from 60,000 in late 1938 (that is, equivalent to 4.6 percent of the total number of prisoners) to 80,000 in 1939 (5.7 percent).[65] On 21 March 1939 the People's Commissariat of Internal Affairs issued the order "On replacing inmate VOKhR officers and prisoner guards of the corrective labor camps and colonies of the GULAG of the NKVD with hired civilian guards." The order set a 1 June deadline to complete this overhaul in the camps and a July deadline for the colonies. Guards were to be recruited from among demobilized soldiers, junior army officers, and NKVD troop officers. The order allowed the continued use of inmate guards, but without weapons.[66]

Not all these plans were realized. As of 1 January 1940 there were 70,264 hired officers in the camps and 15,309 in the colonies. Despite the resolution to replace prisoners with free hired officers by mid-1939, only some of the prisoner guards had been replaced by 1 January: 3,256 remained in the camps and 8,859 in the colonies. The number of armed-guard positions amounted to 5.8 percent of the number of prisoners in 1940 (5.05 percent in 1939). The new quotas, along with the need to replace prisoner guards, meant that camp security was undermanned by 11,279 rank-and-file guards and officers as of 1 January 1940 (by 8,553 in the camps and 2,726 in the colonies). In addition, there were civilian guards with expiring contracts to be replaced in 1940. All this taken together constituted a serious problem. In 1939 a great effort was required to hire 19,077 guards among the discharged army soldiers and officers.[67]

One of the goals of strengthening security was to prevent escapes, which had become very frequent in the previous period. According to Gulag reports, the number of escapes in 1939 significantly decreased. In 1938 a total of 31,322 people escaped from the camps, and 22,586 (72.9 percent) of them were captured. In 1939 there were 12,250 escapees, and 9,807 (80 percent) were captured. In 1939 a total of 6,092 prisoners escaped from the colonies, and 3,468 were captured. (The numbers for 1938 were not registered.)[68] Even considering that the data on escapes were incomplete (the camp administration had a natural desire to conceal negative statistics), a certain tendency is evident. Beria's NKVD established order with an iron hand, apparently successfully.

In the years of the Great Terror, the number of political prisoners in the camps significantly increased. As of 1 January 1937 there were 104,826 political prisoners, and two years later, as of 1 January 1939, there were 454,434—a jump from 12.8 percent of the total number of prisoners to 34.5 percent (see Document 98). Many were listed as members of "right Trotskyist counterrevolutionary organizations," as terrorists, and as spies. According to Soviet punitive doctrine, these were the most dangerous categories. Such prisoners were kept on a special regimen in the camps and were not allowed to occupy various positions (in reality, these restrictions were often ignored). Political prisoners were the first targets of additional repressions in the camps. In the years of the Great Terror, they constituted the majority of those shot during punitive operations in the camps. Although mass shootings were curtailed under Beria, fabricated charges of an "anti-Soviet underground" in the camps persisted. The fight against the underground was an important element in establishing the new order in the Gulag. There were several actions along those lines in 1939.

· 69 ·

Circular letter no. 124 from the third department of the GULAG,
"On establishing the centralized intelligence network 'the Chain'"
13 July 1939[69]

Top secret.

To the heads of the third departments of the NKVD USSR corrective labor camps, third departments and sections of the corrective labor colonies
of the republican NKVDs, and the UNKVDs of territories and provinces.

The development of the intelligence network "the Chain" by the third
department of the Northern railway camp of the NKVD USSR has exposed efforts to create an anti-Soviet group among the prisoners of this
camp with the goal of organizing a mass escape of prisoners and their
[subsequent] clandestine struggle against the Soviet regime. The inspirer
of this group was prisoner Pliako, a Trotskyist, sentenced to ten years.

According to his own statement given to an undercover agent, he maintained personal relations with Slutsky and Rakovsky.

Prisoners sentenced for anti-Soviet activities, primarily Trotskyists,
were recruited to join this group.

One of the active members of the group, a former VKP(b) member sentenced for espionage, Vishnevsky, told the agent that until the day of his
arrest, he had maintained personal contact with Radek and Sokolnikov.

The leader of the group, Pliako, raised the question of creating a mili-
tant group to disarm the camp guards as its immediate practical goal.

To avoid exposure, this anti-Soviet organization was built of five-member cells so that no cell knew about the existence of the others. Thus, in
case one cell was discovered, the others would remain unexposed.

Lately the network has registered active attempts by this anti-Soviet
group to find ways of establishing connections with the outside as well
and preparations to produce anti-Soviet leaflets and develop the program
of the group.

On orders by the people's commissar of internal affairs of the USSR,
Com. Beria, the intelligence network "the Chain" has been engaged.

Pliako, arrested in this case, testified that he was the leader of this anti-
Soviet organization, which he had created among the prisoners of the
Northern railway camp. The organization called itself the Northern
Communist Union and had a goal of uniting former communists con-
victed for anti-Soviet activity with individuals at large who had been ex-
pelled from the VKP(b).

According to Pliako, this anti-Soviet organization was preparing a mass
escape of prisoners and was developing its program. One of the members
of a five-man cell, sent to Cheliabinsk after a review of his case, had or-

ders, while keeping in touch with the cell, to supply information about the popular mood and to prepare secret meeting places for members of the organization who escape from the camp.

Members of this organization who escaped from the camp had the practical task of establishing cells of this anti-Soviet organization and pursuing active anti-Soviet work and anti-Soviet propaganda with the idea that "the Leninist portion of the party is repressed and the remaining group has degenerated and carries out improper policies."

The final goal of the anti-Soviet work of this organization was the overthrow of the current leadership and government.

Considering the fact that similar anti-Soviet Trotskyist formations with secret five-member cells exist in other camps, the third department of the GULAG of the NKVD USSR established a centralized intelligence network, "the Chain."

Considering the above information, you should:

1. Review the agents' reports on the Trotskyists in your camp and, if signs of an anti-Soviet formation similar to the one exposed in the Northern railway camp are detected, open an undercover investigation nicknamed "the Chain."

2. Urgently select appropriate people and recruit agents capable of providing information on such formations.

3. Pay special attention to discovering lines of communication between the Trotskyists who are targets of "the Chain" network in different camps and those who have been released.

4. Aim at a quick operative engagement of the intelligence people involved in "the Chain" network.

Please immediately pass all new intelligence information to the third department of the GULAG of the NKVD USSR.

Deputy head of the third department of the GULAG of the NKVD, Senior Lieutenant of State Security, Trofimov.

· 70 ·

Circular letter no. 224 from the third department of the GULAG,
"On the development of the intelligence network 'Wisemen'"
1 November 1939[70]

Top secret.

To all heads of the third departments of the NKVD camp administrations.

The "Wisemen" intelligence network established by the third department of the White Sea–Baltic Sea industrial complex [BBK] of the NKVD has exposed an anti-Soviet group among prisoners of the BBK headed by the former *petliurovets** Godunov and Menshevik Soltanov, who in the past was connected to Shliapnikov and Preobrazhensky.

In this case, twelve people have been arrested. They confessed their crimes.

The anti-Soviet organization had a goal of disarming the armed guard and fleeing to Finland "in order to establish connections with foreign anti-Soviet organizations to conduct a struggle against the Soviet regime" (Soltanov's testimony).

Besides the prisoners, members of this organization planned to draw in special settlers living in the camp's vicinity.

It has been established that the inmate guard Khropach participated in the anti-Soviet organization and informed Godunov about the number of guards and their weapons. Together with Godunov, Khropach participated in working out a plan to disarm the guards.

Undercover agents secretly recovered anti-Soviet leaflets manufactured by the members of the group that were to be distributed among prisoners and special settlers. [The group] also made a poster with an anti-Soviet slogan. Members of the group made attempts to acquire a compass, binoculars, weapons, and a map of Karelia.†

To stir up discontent among the prisoners, [the group] disseminated defeatist propaganda and provocative anti-Soviet insinuations.

The investigation fully confirmed the reports of the intelligence network "Wisemen," [the success of which] was mainly due to:

1. a well-organized planting of able internal agents into the anti-Soviet group

2. a quick probe, which took a little over a month

3. a timely acquisition of evidence by retrieving, via agents, the anti-Soviet leaflets

However, the operations of the network were not well thought through. In particular, such an important question as removing agents from the network was not seriously addressed.

Arrests in this case were conducted simultaneously. Those arrested were not separated from each other but put in one room and transported in one carriage or car. Since two internal agents were not arrested, Godunov was able to correctly identify them.

Because of incorrect instructions given to the agents by the intelligence officers leading this case, a mutual exposure of agents took place.

Agents "Afoniushkin" and "Kievsky" received similar orders. As a re-

---

* *Petliurovets*—follower of Symon Petliura, head of the independent Ukraine (1917–18), who supported Poland in its war against Soviet Russia (1919–20) and eventually fled with his government to Paris.

† Karelia was on the border with Finland and thus escape was theoretically possible.

sult, their behavior at the secret meetings of the anti-Soviet groups was identical in some cases, which led each of them to suspect the other as an agent of the third department.

In view of the fact that similar formations exist in other NKVD camps and considering the above information, you should:

1. Carefully review all files and agent reports related to the subjects who are or could become (given their former activities) organizers of anti-Soviet activity in the camp.

To focus on this contingent, it is necessary to select trustworthy agents carefully and to provide systematic guidance for their work.

2. Step up agent work among the armed guards to discover the nature of their connections with prisoners. The agents should pay special attention to, and work closely with, the inmate guards.

3. In the future, when conducting operational activities aimed at anti-Soviet organizations and groups, always create an operational plan indicating how to extract the agents from the operation.

The operational plan should be submitted for approval by the third department of the GULAG.

This circular letter must be discussed at an operative meeting of the department.

The head of the third department of the GULAG of the NKVD,

Captain of State Security, Trofimov.

Knowing the NKVD's style, it is possible that the majority of these cases were fabricated. This is not to say that some organized groups of political prisoners did not exist in the camps. There are no data about this, nor about the true scale of the chekist operations against the "anti-Soviet underground" in the camps. The third department of the Gulag summed up the results of these operations in its 16 December 1939 circular letter: "Operational activities of the agents of the third departments in the corrective labor camps, stepped up owing to measures undertaken in the second half of this year, have revealed that members of anti-Soviet formations in the camps (Trotskyists, rightists, SRs, etc.) conduct active work to create anti-Soviet formations among the prisoners and use every means possible to get out of the camp and restore their ruptured connections [once] in the outside world."[71] This was a nice proof of vigilance to report.

The Case of the Krasnoiarsk Camp

Between 29 October and 26 November 1939 an inspector from the Gulag security administration in Moscow, Lieutenant of State Security

Yasson, studied the situation in the NKVD camp in Krasnoiarsk. The inquiry resulted from a letter by prisoner Arkhangelsky about the arbitrariness of the camp administration. Deputy People's Commissar of Internal Affairs Chernyshev took note of it and sent Yasson to Siberia.

Such close attention to the Arkhangelsky letter was accidental. Moscow bureaucrats, who received hundreds of thousands of letters from prisoners and their relatives, were rather immune to such pleas. A review by the Gulag bureau of complaints in 1938 revealed "months-long red tape in processing citizens' complaints and statements sent to the GULAG of the NKVD from the prisoners." An order that followed this inquiry stated: "In this situation, with a large number of statements and complaints (over 20,000 letters each month), the GULAG apparatus has not yet worked out a system for reviewing the complaints and responding to their authors. As a result, many letters go unanswered, which, in turn, leads to multiple repeat complaints."[72] Nevertheless, NKVD leaders encouraged prisoners to write, seeing the letters as a source of information about, and a way to exercise control over, the situation in the camps. Every once in a while these statements triggered inquiries and the punishment of camp administrators to serve as an example. Such was the case with the Arkhangelsky letter.

The Krasnoiarsk camp, which became the focus of investigation, was not a large Gulag unit. This typical timber camp was created in February 1938, at the height of mass repression, near the town of Kansk, Krasnoiarsk territory.[73] It held 10,000 people in April 1938 and more than 15,000 in January 1939. The composition of prisoners reflected the trends of the Great Terror. As of 1 October 1938, of the 17,500 prisoners in the camp, 9,800 were political prisoners, and 3,900 were so-called socially dangerous and socially harmful elements.[74] By the time Yasson arrived in November 1939, there were about 15,000 prisoners in the camp. The head of the camp was Captain of State Security S. I. Shatov-Lifshen.

Yasson's inquiry is important because he, in addition to reviewing camp paperwork, interviewed prisoners and civilian personnel. He summed up the results of his investigation in a memorandum sent to Chernyshev.[75]

· 71 ·

Memorandum on the violation of revolutionary legality and the condition
of prisoners at the Krasnoiarsk corrective labor camp of the NKVD
8 December 1939

Top secret
To the Deputy People's Commissar of Internal Affairs of the USSR, Division Commander Com. Chernyshev.
Memorandum
On the violation of revolutionary legality and the condition of prisoners in the Krasnoiarsk corrective labor camp of the NKVD.

Following your orders, the deputy head of the OITK UNKVD of the Krasnoiarsk territory, Com. Lykhin, and I conducted, between 29 October and 26 November 1939, an investigation of the condition of prisoners in the Krasnoiarsk corrective labor camp and verified the facts of arbitrariness in the camp, referred to in the statement by prisoner Arkhangelsky.

We inspected the Nizhne-Poiminsk section and the Kansk, Ilansk, and Ingash camp divisions, containing 10,277 of the inmate contingents, with a total registered number of 14,993 prisoners (as of 25 November 1939).

1. Violations of revolutionary legality

In the course of the review of prisoner Arkhangelsky's statement and the questioning of a large number of prisoners and some civilian employees, we have uncovered a direct violation of revolutionary legality in the Krasnoiarsk camp in the form of systematic beatings of prisoners by the heads of the camp sections, armed guards, and inmates employed in the low-level camp administration.

The following facts support this conclusion.

On 20 July of this year, guards Noskov and Nikolsky captured prisoners Chuguev and Zhelomsky, who had escaped from camp section 4. At the time of the arrest, Noskov set a dog on them that bit them badly and tore their clothes. Upon Chuguev and Zhelomsky's arrival at the command post of camp section no. 4, guards Kulesha and Mikhailov beat them up badly. The beatings were witnessed by about fifteen civilian employees, including the head of the camp section, Astashenko, the platoon political instructor, Liashenko, several guards, and their wives. Kulesha and Mikhailov have been prosecuted. Liashenko was never punished for allowing the beatings and never reported the incident to the superior commanders of the armed guards. [. . .]

On 2 June of this year, prisoners N. A. Ivanovsky and Giliam Mirzaev escaped from camp section 5. On the same day, they were captured by guards Shulga, Lazin, and another one, whose identity has not yet been established. The last one, according to Shulga, hit Ivanovsky with a rifle butt.

While under escort en route to the camp section, Ivanovsky and Mirzaev were met by the platoon political instructor, Gontovoy, who had set out to search for the escapees, accompanied by a group of guards and two civilian tractor drivers. They all attacked Ivanovsky and Mirzaev and beat them with sticks and rifle butts. They beat them so hard that they were brought to the camp section semiconscious.

In July, Ivanovsky was transferred to camp section 4, where armed guards Lutsik and Voloskov and the head of the detention cell, prisoner Kamolov, beat him up. In the process, Lutsik cracked Ivanovsky's skull with a revolver handle. [. . .]

On 25 September, prisoners Ya. E. Archivasov, A. Z. Dmitriev, and Prokhor Ribtsun escaped from camp section 4. On the same day, they were arrested by the dog handler, Noskov. At the time of the arrest, all three were beaten up and bitten by the dog.

Beatings of prisoners in camp section 4 are commonplace. [. . .]

The head of the detention cell, Kamolov, is closely connected with repeat criminals, whom he shelters from work in the cell. He passes food from the barracks to those in detention, sets up card games in the cell, engages in a sexual relationship with the prisoner Vishnevskaya, who is under investigation and is kept in detention, and maintains a close connection with armed guard Antipin, via whom he connects with his wife in Kansk (he has been removed from this position and sent to general works).

Assistant warden Popov is also closely connected with repeat criminals and has organized thefts in the camp section. In 1939, while head of the detention cell, he assisted in the escape of six prisoners and received 80 rubles for it (he has been removed from this post and sent to general works). [. . .]

In the same camp section, in the summer, armed guard Mitin unexpectedly used a firearm at point-blank range and seriously wounded prisoner Ya. V. Podgaets. Mitin has been indicted. Podgaets is undergoing treatment in the hospital.

In October armed guard Ivanov illegally used a weapon and shot prisoner A. S. Kirillov in the Tinsky work zone.

Ivanov will be tried by the revolutionary tribunal.

In August the juvenile prisoners A. A. Chei and A. P. Trunin escaped from camp section no. 2. On the same day, they were arrested by the platoon commander, Fefelov (assigned to the school), and guards Ditkovsky and Eprintsev. The latter is currently a secretary of the Komsomol committee of the Nizhne-Poiminsk division. During the arrest, Chei and

Trunin were stripped naked and beaten, and Chei was also made to munch earth. Materials on the beating of Chei and Trunin are filed in the third section of the Nizhne-Poiminsk division, but those responsible have not yet been indicted. [. . .]

The case of the group beating of prisoners on 20 October in the detention cell of the camp section is exceptionally outrageous. The circumstances of the case are as follows.

One of the prisoners disassembled the furnace in the detention cell, climbed into the corridor, opened the cells, let all the prisoners into the corridor, and locked the outside door. (The detention cell is in the camp zone).

Having learned about this, the guard on duty, Maleta, sounded the alarm. The head of the camp section, Beba, platoon commander Briuzgin, and a group of armed guards arrived at the camp section. They armed themselves with axes and shovels, broke into the detention cell, and started beating all the prisoners there. [. . .]

On 25 October, in the Tugusha work zone of the Ilansky OLP [separate camp section], guard Shevtsov, while escorting Tolstopesov's team to work, uttered an anti-Semitic remark to prisoner M. L. Shulshraiber. In response to the latter's remark that anti-Semitism was inappropriate for a Soviet guard, Shevtsov made Shulshraiber sit on a tree stump for five hours dressed only in a padded jacket, in the 30° C cold.

Upon returning to the camp, Shevtsov submitted a report saying that Shulshraiber had wrangled with him during work. The head of the work zone, Com. Tsapik, did not look into the truth of the matter and put Shulshraiber into a detention cell for three days. [. . .]

The violation of revolutionary legality in Krasnoiarsk territory has its own history.

Starting in 1938, in several camp sectors (Punchet, Perezha, etc.), aside from beating the prisoners, such forms of torture as exposing semi-naked prisoners to mosquitoes and putting them on tree stumps for several hours half-naked were practiced. Those responsible were at some point indicted, and their cases reviewed by the military tribunal. [. . .]

2. The situation with the camp regimen

The prisoner regimen in the camp is extremely unsatisfactory.

GULAG orders to prepare the camp for the winter have not been followed. They only started repairing barracks and insulating tents for the prisoners in November.

For the most part, camp sections are in an unsanitary condition. Prisoners are lice ridden, and the barracks are filthy and bug-infested.

The camp contingent is crammed together. In the Nizhne-Poiminsk section (section chief—Kashpitsky), up to 7,000 prisoners have 0.84 square meters per person, while the norm is 3 [square] meters. A large number of prisoners sleep under the bunks and on the floor.

No more than 30–40 percent of the prisoners have bedsheets.

Some camp sections (Kansk OLP, third camp section, Aksha work zone) did not have bathhouses, which they have only now started to build. The capacity of the existing bathhouses is insufficient.

As a rule, camp sections have no dryers. Prisoners' clothes and shoes do not get dry, which leads to colds.

Supplies, especially of winter clothes, are far from adequate. Prisoners are already not taken to work owing to their lack of shoes and clothes. [. . .]

The third camp section (head—Novikov) is in an exceptionally unsanitary condition. It is so crowded that in some barracks the space per prisoner is 0.61 square meters. There is no bathhouse. The food is inadequate for the healthy prisoners and those undergoing treatment in the hospital.

The existing hospital, housing more than 100 prisoners, is not fully provided with both a soft and a hard inventory. Room no. 7, with over forty patients (most of them with chronic tuberculosis) has two-tier bunks. The patients have no bedsheets and stay on bare bunks for months.

The mortality rate at the camp section is high. Given that fifteen–twenty prisoners die there each month, the section head, Novikov, had already by September prepared 150 graves for the winter. By the time of this investigation (4–5 November), there were 108 graves [left]. Prisoners also dig the graves.

The food supply for prisoners is unsatisfactory. The newly introduced food rations for prisoners have not been implemented in some camp sections (third, fifth, Ingash, Tugusha, etc.) owing to the lack of a sufficient assortment of products.

There are no fats in the camp at all. Meat and fish are supplied to the camp sections intermittently. For five months prisoners received no sugar.

3. The situation regarding camp discipline

Camp discipline is very poor. There is no opposition to any refusal to work. With rare exceptions, persistent refusers and disorganizers are not prosecuted.

In just four camp sections (Ingasha, Karagansk, Komendantsky, and no. 6) 909 workdays have been lost owing to refusals. [. . .]

Brigandage, robberies, thefts, hooliganism, knifing, open resistance and threats to the camp administration and guards, gambling, drinking, and other criminal activities flourish in the camp.

In some camp sections (4, 5, Karagan, etc.), gangster and criminal elements undermine camp discipline and terrorize the rest of the prisoners.

Robberies and thefts are commonplace. At the same time, the fight against crime and against violators of the camp regimen is very weak.

The actual practice is such that, even for open gangsterism, managers of the camp sections put a prisoner in a detention cell for only several days.

Workers of the local third department do not pay sufficient attention to crime and do not prosecute repeat violators of the camp regimen.

The following fact serves as an illustration. At the second camp section, prisoner Kopka categorically refuses to work, disrupts the entire camp contingent, engages in gangsterism and gambling, systematically offends camp administrators and the guards, and offered armed resistance to the camp section administrator on duty and the supervisor when they tried to put him in a detention cell. On 17 October he, armed with a knife, forced his way into the office of the head of the camp section, Com. Turovsky. On 25 October he injured prisoner Shakirov with a knife.

Instead of isolating and prosecuting Kopka as an active bandit and disrupter, he was appointed head of the team of juvenile criminals, according to the camp section boss, Com. Turovsky. This came at the suggestion of the workers of the third section of the Nizhne-Poiminsk division (head of the third section—Com. Yankovsky).

4. Detention practice.

The detention regimen, regulated by the provisional instruction on ITL prisoner management, is systematically violated in the camp.[76]

Prisoners are put into detention cells in groups of fifteen–twenty, often as entire work teams, without adequate formalities and often for no reason.

In the fourth camp section (head of the camp section—Astashenko), during the third quarter, 720 people were put in detention. In October alone, out of a total number of 800 prisoners, 285 were put in the detention cell. Those put in the detention cell are stripped of warm clothes (quilted and padded jackets), which the cell manager keeps until the prisoner leaves it—in winter conditions.

Prisoners are put into the so-called eighth cell, which has no bunks or heat, dressed similarly.

At the time of the investigation of the fifth camp section, there were twenty-four prisoners kept in the detention cell for refusing to work. Twenty-two of them were kept in a chamber only 4.6 square meters big. After the inquiry, the provisional head of the camp section, Pavlov, had to release most of the prisoners as detained for no reason.

On 28 October, at the third camp section, prisoners Kim and Kremnev were put into a detention cell for refusing to report to work. Both were sick and had a doctor's release from work.

At the Karagansk camp section, they put nursing mothers with children in detention cells (Ponomareva, Sukhikh).

Such things happen because it is guards and prisoners (supervisors, deputy supervisors, team leaders, etc.) more often than camp bosses who put people in detention and are, in fact, masters of the situation and capable of pursuing their own policy because of the lack of control on the part of the civilian staff.

The head of the sixth camp section, Shlykov, started to subject the regimen violators to such punishment as putting them in "the cold one" (a cell that is still under construction and has no heat at all). [. . .]

As head of the first camp section, Shlykov badgered invalid prisoners. On 22 June he ordered all invalids to line up, stripped their upper bodies of clothes, inspected them, and selected seventy-eight people for hard labor, including all invalids with sedentary tasks and some complete invalids. He ordered them all to work in the forest on 23 June.

The next day, twenty-two people failed to report to work, and all were put in detention cells. [. . .]

5. The situation of juvenile prisoners.

[. . .] The 170 juvenile prisoners in the camp[77] are distributed in small groups in most camp sections. Their living conditions are inadequate, and most of them have no bedsheets. Newspapers and books are very scarce. There are no educational or cultural games.

In some cases, juvenile prisoners live with the adults, usually in the worst barracks.

Regular juvenile working hours are observed only in the second, fourth, and Karagan camp sections and the Tinskaya work zone. In other camp sections, they work the same hours (ten–eleven) as the adults.

There has been extremely weak cultural and educational work conducted among the juvenile prisoners, and their constant contact with the criminal element, because of inadequate living conditions, fosters theft, hooliganism, gambling, and sexual corruptness.

In the Karagansk camp section and the Tinskaya work zone, homosexuality is widespread among juveniles. In the Tinskaya work zone, seven people (with Cherevatov as their leader) are being prosecuted for sexual coercion, rape of prisoners, [. . .] and gangsterism.

6. Work at the camp.

In the course of the review of the camp regimen, materials on the antistate practice of systematic falsification in timber harvesting came up. Thus, in the former Ilansk division (head of division—Barats), in the fourth quarter of 1938, in the former Kasianovsky camp section alone, 20,000 cubic meters of timber were falsely added to the timber delivery report.

Such falsifications were made in other camp sections and were balanced out in the first days of January 1939.

A similar situation was found regarding fulfillment of the plan for the first quarter of 1939. The former head of the division, Barats, received instructions to falsify the first quarter plan from the camp administration head, Com. Shatov, and the head of the production department, Kravchevsky, and gave appropriate orders to the heads of the camp sections. For the Tugushinsky camp section, the falsification amounted to 8,000–10,000 cubic meters; in the Karagansk camp section, up to 5,000 cubic meters.

The falsification of the production plan for the first quarter of 1939 was balanced out in the first days of April 1939.

The camp administration, however, reported that the plan for the first quarter of 1939 had been fulfilled, and several workers, including Com. Shatov, received rewards for fulfilling the plan. [. . .]

The head of the second section of the regimen department
of the Security Administration of the GULAG of the NKVD,
Lieutenant of State Security Yasson.
8 December 1939.

Yasson focused primarily on the crimes that were under official investigation. Obviously, the camp administration preferred to remain silent about the majority of crimes and abuses. Still, those few facts that Yasson reported demonstrated the poor results of NKVD attempts to "restore order" in the camps.

The Kraslag situation was typical. The camps had their own laws and regulations. Administrators preferred to delegate prisoner management to guards and low-level supervisors who were prisoners. Particularly valuable were the ruthless gangsters like prisoner Kopka, who was assigned to supervise a team of juveniles in the Krasnoiarsk camp. Such camp tyrants maintained order with their own methods, and camp administrators were mainly interested in results. For that reason, there were privileged prisoners in many camps (for the most part, criminals), and the chekists turned a blind eye on their crimes in exchange for their help in securing order.

Campaigns to strengthen the regimen and intimidate prisoners, directed from Moscow, untied the hands of camp administrators and encouraged arbitrariness and violence. The brutal beating of captured escapees (despite the risk of prosecution) was considered to be a more effective method of preventing escapes than planting agents and stepping up vigilance, as required by NKVD orders. The camps responded to NKVD demands to increase the number of working prisoners and fight against the "disruption of camp life" by branding sick, unclothed, and handicapped prisoners as those refusing to work, locking them up in detention cells, and forcing invalids to do hard labor. Isolated in remote regions, working in extreme conditions on the verge of death, hundreds of thousands of prisoners were bound by the various twists in punitive policy as well as by petty local bosses, who excelled in adapting orders from Moscow to the reality of the camps.

CHAPTER 6

Mobilization and Repression

From the outbreak of World War II in September 1939 to the German invasion of Russia on 22 June 1941, Soviet punitive policy was significantly influenced by new territorial acquisitions (western Ukraine, western Belorussia, Bessarabia, northern Bukovina, the Baltic states) and the war with Finland, as well as accelerated military preparations. These factors influenced the character and goals of terror and also stimulated the expansion of the NKVD economy.

Though not officially at war, the Soviet Union got actively involved in the territorial reshaping of Europe. One of the main concerns of the Stalinist leadership was a swift purge of the occupied territories with the urgent goal to "sovietize" them. According to Memorial Society historians, the key targets of the security organs in the prewar years were the newly acquired countries and territories: 52 percent of the 206,600 people arrested by organs of state security in the USSR between September 1939 and June 1941 were from the western Ukraine and western Belorussia.[1] Arrests were also made in the Baltic states and in Moldavia.[2] The purges involved mass deportations of the "unreliable" population. In 1940–early 1941, there were four large-scale deportations from western Ukraine, western Belorussia, the Baltic states, and Moldavia, which placed about 370,000 people in exile in remote areas of the USSR.[3]

The bloody liquidation of the "fifth column" in the new territories included the notorious Katyn case. On 5 March 1940 the Politburo resolved to shoot 25,700 former Polish officers, clerks, landowners, industrialists, gendarmes, and other members of the Polish elite in prisoner-of-war camps in the Ukraine and Belorussia. In April–May 1940 a total of 21,857 people were shot.[4] Stalin obviously was trying to thwart any potential attempts to restore the prewar Polish state.

In the rest of the USSR, arrests of "anti-Soviet elements" had declined since 1939 (see Document 92). However, from mid-1940, several million Soviet citizens were affected by an extraordinary labor mobilization. A 26 June 1940 decree by the Presidium of the Supreme Soviet of the USSR established prison terms of two to four months for leaving work without permission and up to six months of corrective labor at one's workplace with up to a 25 percent salary reduction for absence from work without proper cause. In the less than a year before the outbreak of war, more than 3,000,000 people were convicted under this decree; 500,000 of them were sentenced to prison terms.[5] There were other similar campaigns. On 10 August 1940, for example, the Presidium of the Supreme Soviet of the USSR adopted a resolution toughening punishment for petty theft at the workplace and for hooliganism—up to one year in prison.[6]

The escalation of terror contributed to the expansion of the network of camps, colonies, and prisons. On the eve of war, the NKVD was one of the largest economic entities in the country, entrusted with the urgent construction of projects of military and strategic importance. Hundreds of thousands of prisoners, shifted from one site to another, could not fulfill all the tasks given to the NKVD. Gulag bosses were in a constant and frantic search for additional workers and compensated for labor shortages with an intensified exploitation of prisoners.

Supplying a Workforce

"Reestablishing order" in the camps in 1939 only marginally mended the disastrous consequences of the Great Terror. The situation in the Gulag remained very difficult, and NKVD bosses knew it from the realities of economic failure (not the deterioration of humane conditions in the camps). In November–December 1939, while drafting economic plans for the next year, it was discovered that in fulfilling capital construction plans for 1939 only 3.6 billion rubles had been spent—84 percent of the planned 4.3 billion rubles. The industrial production plan would be fulfilled by 88 percent. The production of timber and coal was also far behind.[7] Dalstroi's production of pure gold was 66.6 tons in 1939, although the goal had been set at 79.9 tons (this goal was originally inflated: in 1938, Dalstroi produced only 62 tons of gold).[8]

These pressing circumstances determined the position of NKVD leaders in discussing capital investment strategy. The People's Commissariat of Internal Affairs drafted a plan of capital works for 1940 in the amount of 4.5 billion rubles, which was only 200 million rubles more than the plan for 1939. In a letter to the government on 3 November 1939, Beria stressed that "the GULAG did not have a sufficient workforce" to accomplish certain important projects and that the 1940 capital investment funds would be used primarily "for accelerating and completing the construction of projects scheduled to be launched."[9] After arguments with Gosplan, which insisted on providing the NKVD with only 3 billion rubles, the chekists finally succeeded in securing 3.4 billion rubles.[10] They could not limit their tasks to finishing existing projects, however. For a year and a half before the outbreak of war, the NKVD received an avalanche of new and urgent tasks.

Railroad construction was by far the largest enterprise in 1940. Parallel to the work in the Far East, the NKVD was increasingly involved in the construction of strategically important railroads in the northern part of European Russia. On 25 December 1939, after approving the plan of capital investment for 1940, the Politburo significantly increased (by 130 million rubles) the 1940 financing of the Soroka–Obozerskaya line. To accelerate the work there, authorities resolved to transfer up to 50,000 prisoners along with equipment and machinery from other NKVD sites.[11] The government paid special attention to this 350-kilometer line, which connected the Kirovsk and Northern railway lines near the Soroka (Belomorsk) port on the Northern Sea, among other places. In July 1939 the secretary of the CC VKP(b), A. A. Zhdanov, on Stalin's orders, requested from Beria a report on the progress of construction. Beria responded, using the opportunity to request additional assistance.[12] Apparently capitalizing on Stalin's special attention to that line, Beria managed to get sizable resources for its completion.

On 9 May 1940, in agreement with plans to increase significantly the extraction of coal in the Vorkuta-Pechora mines—one of the most important mining regions in the Soviet Union and thus a major Gulag site—the Politburo adopted a resolution ordering the NKVD to accelerate the construction of the Northern Pechora railroad linking Kotlas and Vorkuta (the decision to build this road was made in October 1937). This very long line, stretching 1,560 kilometers, would connect the coal-extracting regions with the coal-consuming northeastern parts of the USSR. The resolution ordered that the Kotlas–Vorkuta railroad be finished "in the shortest time possible": limited use was to commence in December 1941, with full operations scheduled to start between December 1943 and July 1944. Plans provided for 160,000 construction workers.[13] Another NKVD railroad project, the 367-kilometer Konosha–Kotlas line, also became extremely urgent. The SNK and the CC VKP(b) issued an appropriate resolution on 12 September 1940, stating that limited use was planned to start in December 1941. The NKVD had to transfer 55,000 prisoners there from other railway construction sites.[14]

Second in volume were the NKVD hydrotechnical projects—canals, hydroelectric power stations, ports. In mid-1940 the government focused on accelerated construction of the Volga–Baltic and Northern Dvina waterways, connecting the Baltic, White, and Caspian seas via the water systems of the Volga and Sheksna rivers, White Lake, and Northern Dvina. On 23 September 1940 the Politburo adopted the appropriate resolution by the SNK and the CC VKP(b).[15] The NKVD had to start work immediately to complete the project by the 1943 navigation season.

The year 1940 became crucial for yet another NKVD industry—the production of nonferrous metals. On 31 January 1940, Beria sent a letter to the SNK about Dalstroi plans; in it he suggested a drastic acceleration of development for this industrial complex. To offset the failure of gold production plans in 1939, Dalstroi would produce 80 tons of pure gold and 2,000 tons of tin concentrate, according to Beria's ambitious draft plan. He suggested moving up to 50,000 more prisoners and the necessary equipment to Kolyma by early 1940.[16] On 10 February 1940 the Politburo approved these proposals.

Soon thereafter, the NKVD acquired new extraction and metallurgical works in addition to Dalstroi. In late 1939 the government ordered Beria to investigate the possibility of augmenting the output of the northern nickel complex in Murmansk province, which belonged to the People's Commissariat of Nonferrous Metallurgy. On 29 December 1939, Beria reported to Stalin and Molotov about the possibility of boosting the production of nickel there from 1,500 tons in 1939 to 7,000 tons in 1940 (the plan called for 3,000 and 5,400 tons, respectively). He was skeptical about the ability of the People's Commissariat of Nonferrous Metallurgy to ensure such progress and suggested that the complex and all supporting construction groups be put under the aegis of the NKVD. Beria said that unifying the management of the two largest centers of nickel production (Norilsk Nickel and Northern Nickel) would facilitate the development of the complicated technology for processing the Kolsk and Norilsk ores and increase the production of nickel, copper, and platinoids.[17]

On 13 January 1940, two weeks after Beria's letter, the SNK and the CC issued a decree transferring the Northern Nickel complex (producing copper and nickel), the construction of the Kandalaksha aluminum plant, and the Kolstroi trust to the NKVD "in order to secure a considerable increase in the production of nickel, as well as an accelerated construction of enterprises due to be launched in 1940–41." The NKVD nickel complexes and the construction of the Kandalaksha works were categorized as top-priority strategic projects, and the delivery of supplies for them, as military freight.[18]

Several other projects of the People's Commissariat of Nonferrous Metallurgy were also put under NKVD management. The Dzhezkazgan brassworks was transferred to the NKVD on 19 March 1940,[19] and the Verkhoiansk and Yakutia tin mines were transferred on 11 October 1940.[20] On the same day, the Politburo reviewed and approved the program defining the NKVD role in the production of aluminum and magnesium.[21]

In 1940, the NKVD also was given the task of building hydrolytic and sulfite alcohol plants,[22] securing a substantial increase in oil production in the Ukhta-Pechora oil region, creating a new oil base in the northern part of European Russia,[23] and building aircraft plants in Kuibyshev province, constructing highways, and more. To accomplish all this, the initial plan for NKVD capital construction for 1940 was increased by 1.1 billion rubles, for a total of 4.5 billion rubles.[24] NKVD bosses seem to have accepted all new economic tasks enthusiastically, as if to compensate for economic failures in the past and to demonstrate the organization's importance and potential. To a great degree, the new tasks were related to the general situation in the country: after World War II broke out, the government urgently adopted multiple resolutions on the construction of military enterprises. The huge increase in capital construction placed high demands on resources, infrastructure, and related industries. To continue and, more important, finish the construction of those enterprises, enormous amounts of capital were needed, more than the state budget could supply. This problem became particularly visible during the discussion of the plan for 1941.

· 72 ·

Beria's memorandum on the draft capital construction plan for 1941
20 November 1940[25]

Secret.
To the SNK USSR,
Comrade V. M. Molotov.
On 2 November the NKVD USSR presented to the SNK USSR and Gosplan a blueprint for capital construction in 1941 in the amount of 9,158,000,000 rubles.

The plan was drawn up in accordance with effective resolutions of the SNK USSR and the CC VKP(b) regarding the amount of and timeframe for construction works managed by the NKVD USSR.

Gosplan drafted a plan of works for the NKVD USSR in the amount of 5,470,000,000 rubles. Based on this plan, Gosplan then allocated material resources.

The amount of work for the NKVD projected by Gosplan does not cover the majority of prioritized construction projects. Among these sites are the Volga–Baltic route, with 300 million rubles allocated instead of 700 million; the Northern Pechora railroad, with 420 million instead of 550 million rubles; Ukhtaneft, 120 million planned instead of 340 million required; hydroelectric power stations, 400 million planned, with 1 billion requested; Dalstroi, 300 million planned, with 470 million required.

A similar situation exists for other construction sites.

The situation regarding the supply of equipment and materials is no different. Gosplan projected that supplies do not satisfy the needs at the construction sites even at the 5,470,000,000-ruble estimate. For example:

Machine tools—10,841 required (including 6,418 for aircraft plants), 2,597 planned

Boilers, regular and high pressure—646 required, 97 to be provided

Locomotives—42,564 required, 27,613 to be provided

Compressors—817 required, 279 to be provided

Armored cable—2,100 kilometers required, 590 kilometers to be provided

Barbed wire—4,000 tons required, 900 tons to be provided

Gosplan has already allocated funds for January 1941 based on these figures, which are clearly insufficient to our needs.

[. . .] Considering the drastic difference between the NKVD USSR plan and Gosplan's proposals, the NKVD USSR asks you to order a special review of the NKVD USSR plan for 1941 and its material support.

People's Commissar of Internal Affairs of the Union of the SSR, L. Beria.

Upon receipt of this letter, Molotov wrote to his deputies, Mikoyan, Voznesensky, and Bulganin: "We would have to set up a special meeting. I think, Saturday, 23 November at 3 P.M." The meeting took place on 25 November, and it took a specially appointed commission several more weeks to deliberate on the issue. Finally, in January 1941, a compromise variant of the plan was adopted: the NKVD received 6,850,000,000 rubles in 1941.[26] This plan of capital construction mostly included the projects that had been started in the previous period—the Volga–Baltic waterway, hydroelectric power stations, Northern Pechora railway, extraction of oil in Ukta, and production of gold in the Kolyma, among others. However, just as in 1940, the plan was quickly enhanced after approval. In January the NKVD received several additional nonferrous metal plants to run; in February, capital investment in the Volga–Baltic and Northern Dvina waterways was increased for 1941 in order to accelerate their construction.[27] By 8 March 1941 the amount of capital construction that the NKVD had to perform that year had reached the gigantic figure of 7.6 billion rubles (including capital investments allocated via other ministries).[28] Still, the transfer of additional factories and construction sites to the NKVD continued until the outbreak of war.

The most important of the tasks—the building and reconstruction of airports for the People's Commissariat of Defense in 1941—was conferred on the NKVD on 24 March 1941. To accomplish this extremely urgent task, the NKVD had to supply 400,000 prisoners, and the People's Commissariat of Defense had to assemble one hundred 1,000-person construction battalions.[29]

It was impossible to manage this huge economic-punitive machine from the central Gulag office. Gradually, specialized NKVD structures, responsible for various sections of the camp economy, started to appear: first within the Gulag and later as independent chief administrations (Dalstroi was one). On 4 January 1940 the Chief Administration of Camps for Railroad Construction was created, with N. A. Frenkel as its head. On 13 September 1940 the Chief Administration of Camps for Hydrotechnical Construction was formed, headed by Ya. D. Rapoport. The expansion of NKVD economic functions led to its general reorganization. On 3 February 1941 the Politburo issued a resolution dividing the NKVD into the NKVD per se and a new People's Commissariat of State Security. Beria remained the people's commissar of internal affairs, and his former deputy, V. N. Merkulov, became the people's commissar of state security. This reorganization accelerated the process of creating new administrations. On 26 February 1941, the Chief Administration of Camps for Industrial Construction was created within the NKVD. This body managed the construction of defense factories, cellulose and paper mills, and hydrolysis plants, among others. The same decree created the Chief Administration of Camps for Metallurgical Plants and Mines (in charge of the Norilsk and Northern Nickel industrial complexes and other enterprises involving nonferrous metallurgy). On 24 March, following up on the decision to start massive airfield construction, the NKVD Chief Administration for Airport Construction was created.[30] Finally, shortly before the war, on 21 May 1941, Beria came up with a suggestion to the government to organize a chief administration of camps for special construction in the oil industry. The government issued an appropriate decree on 5 June, but it was never implemented owing to the outbreak of war.[31]

As a result of the reorganization, the Gulag became just one of several NKVD chief administrations, although it continued to play a key role. Remaining a symbol of the punitive system, the Gulag managed several branches of NKVD industry (timber, fuel) and continued to administer camps, colonies, and labor settlements. It accounted for and distributed prisoners, maintained their regimen, and conducted operational activities at the detention facilities and at places of internal exile.

One of the Gulag's functions was to supply prisoners to other economic commissariats. The commissariats, preferring to fulfill government tasks with the help of cheap and mobile camp contingents, successfully beat back all NKVD attempts to reclaim prisoners. The 1939 resolution to remove all prisoners from commissariats besides the NKVD, starting on 1 January 1940, could not be implemented by 1940. As of 1 April 1940 various commissariats accounted for more than 90,000 prisoners. The main consumers of convict labor were the People's Commissariat of Construction (more than 22,000 prisoners), the People's Commissariat of Forestry (16,500), and the People's Commissariat of the Aircraft Industry (more than 14,000).[32] Even after issuing this resolution, the government went against it by ordering the supply of new "contingents" for various projects. The pressure from numerous commissariats was so strong that even Stalin had to speak out. At the July 1940 Plenum of the Central Committee, he said: "You have noticed that the commissariats very often ask the NKVD to provide people from the GULAG, the criminals. I must say that if we consider all our construction sites, one-third of the entire workforce at the remote northern construction sites consists of criminal elements. [. . .] We must have reserves instead of borrowing people from the GULAG. It's a shame, it's an unwelcome phenomenon. It's acceptable to use the GULAG in some remote corners, but in the machine industry, in the cities, where criminals work side by side with noncriminals, I really don't know. I'd say it's very irrational and not quite appropriate."[33] Stalin's remarks had no serious consequences, and he himself probably did not count on it. In 1940 and in early 1941 commissariat requests for prisoners soared. Many of them were granted—an admission of economic reality, for the commissariats likely could not meet their labor needs without a supply of prisoners.

On the eve of war, the NKVD's critical task was to find a workforce to support the snowballing economic assignments. The task was all the more difficult because, after the Great Terror, there were no mass repressive actions to augment the workforce. Between 1 January 1939 and 1 January 1940 the number of prisoners in the camps increased by only 27,000 (see Document 96). In 1940 the NKVD managed to fulfill the plan mainly by shifting prisoners between projects. In May 1940, in connection with the decision to build the Northern Pechora railroad, the government allowed the NKVD to transfer inmates of prisons and colonies to the camps and construction sites, regardless of the term of their sentence.[34] The capacity of the colonies and prisons to supply a workforce was also limited, however.

The situation started to change in late 1940 after the laws on labor discipline (26 June) and petty thefts and hooliganism (10 August) had been implemented. Those convicted under these laws received short sentences—four months or one year accordingly. In the past, the chekists had neglected such "contingents" because of their short terms and consequent small economic value. Where there was a severe deficit of workers, however, one could not be too picky. This was especially the case because the short terms were balanced by the large number of those so convicted.

As of 1 January 1941, nearly six months after the implementation of the 26 June order on absenteeism, nearly 2.1 million people had been convicted, of which 320,000 were sentenced to prison (85 percent received two- to four-month terms).[35] It was tempting to unload the crowded prisons and also to utilize the hundreds of thousands of additional hands at NKVD construction sites and other projects. On 10 September the government allowed the NKVD to use the *ukazniks*—those who had violated the decree (*ukaz*) on labor discipline and thefts—"in the corrective labor colonies and camps under a strict labor regimen and with a ten-hour workday while extending to them the differentiated GULAG rations based on their output."[36]

Initially, the idea was to keep the majority of convicts in the same province where they were sentenced and to send them to colonies (only occasionally to camps). For that purpose, it was planned to expand the so-called counteragent colonies, which performed contractual work for various organizations.[37] Because the ukazniks were sentenced to short terms, it was inexpedient to transport them a great distance. The growing labor shortage changed the situation. On 12 November, Beria signed an order to transfer to the camps, before 20 December, 120,000 prisoners sentenced to ten months and more under the 10 August decree. Another 50,000, sentenced under the 26 June decree, were to be transferred.[38] This was one of many similar actions that drastically altered the composition of the camp population. As of 1 January 1941 there were 37,800 camp prisoners sentenced to under one year (many more than in previous years) and almost 387,000 (a quarter of the total number of prisoners) sentenced to one to three years (see Document 99).

Even though prisoners were regularly released, there were almost 488,000 inmates as of 15 January 1941 (compared to 190,000 on 15 January 1940).[39] The number was growing along with the rise in convictions under the decrees of 26 June and 10 August. On 1 February 1941, Beria signed a new order on the relocation of 170,000 inmates to the camps and colonies.[40] By 1 June 1941 the number of prisoners in colonies had reached 516,500 (compared to 315,600 on 1 January and 425,600 on 1 December 1940).[41] At the same time, the colonies now played a more important role in accomplishing the main economic tasks of the NKVD, instead of fulfilling their traditional functions of secondary support. The short-term prisoners thus became an important source of forced labor.

In the prewar period, it was typical to use "semifree contingents" at NKVD construction sites. In March 1941, for instance, the government allowed the NKVD to use those sentenced to more than four months of corrective labor without imprisonment in the construction of airfields, in addition to camp and colony prisoners. Such convicts usually continued to work at their regular jobs but received a reduced salary. By 15 June 1941, many people sentenced to corrective labor— 52,000—had been sent to construct airfields.[42] The Chief Administration of Airport Construction also utilized people mobilized in the so-called labor battalions of the People's Commissariat of Defense. According to a government decree, 100,000 people had to be mobilized to labor battalions in May 1941 for NKVD use. All citizens born between 1914 and 1921 and "not drafted into the Red Army for moral-political or other reasons" were to be mobilized.

Camp Mobilization

Despite the employment of all possible resources, there were still not enough prisoners for all NKVD projects. A chronic deficit of workers, characteristic of the forced-labor economy, was exacerbated by the particular problems of prewar mobilization. The tremendous increase in the number of capital projects, the mass relocation of prisoners, the growing disorganization of the camps and colonies, arbitrariness by the administration, guards, and criminals (officially called criminal-gangster elements), and the traditional shortage of food and clothing, made worse by the rapid growth of camps and colonies, drove down the already low productivity of convict labor. In typical Gulag fashion, this problem was solved mainly through the brutal exploitation of prisoners.

From July 1940, Gulag construction sites and enterprises officially adopted an eleven-hour workday (instead of a ten-hour workday), with three days off per month. This measure merely legalized existing practice and encouraged bosses to prolong workhours even further. In 1941 additional workhours per day were introduced for the workers, technical and engineering (IT) staff, and other employees of airport-related enterprises.

The key feature of the prewar camp mobilization was the intensification of forced labor and repression. Having deprived the camp economy of basic material rewards, such as counting workdays toward early release, the NKVD and the government now fully relied on increased repression. To give an example, the 10 May 1940 SNK and CC VKP(b) resolution on the construction of the Northern Pechora railroad yet again included the following statement: "To intensify the struggle against those refusing to work, as well as violators of labor discipline and the camp regimen, create tribunals at administrative offices of construction sites to review the cases of, and pass sentences on, inveterate prisoner refusers and disrupters of production."[43] This resolution, though issued for just one, albeit large, camp, reflected the general situation in the Gulag, as is evident from many other documents.

· 73 ·

Circular letter no. 23 from the NKVD
28 January 1941[44]

Top secret.
To all heads of administrations in NKVD camps and corrective labor colonies.

In late 1940 twenty-six prisoners were prosecuted for violating the camp regimen and for systematically refusing to work.

The supreme tribunal of the NKVD troops sentenced twenty-one of the accused to the ultimate penalty of capital punishment—shooting (the verdicts have been carried out). The other five prisoners have been sentenced to ten years in prison.

To prevent violations of the camp regimen by prisoners and to fight against those stubbornly refusing to work, I order that:

In the future, all verdicts passed by the military tribunals and courts for similar crimes be formally announced to the prisoners of the camps and corrective labor colonies.

Deputy People's Commissar of Internal Affairs of the USSR, Chernyshev.

Chekists in the camps readily enforced such orders. A harsh response to "refusers" and "disrupters" was for them the easiest way of demonstrating their professional competence, as well as a way to fix progress reports. Whereas the existence of emaciated, unclothed prisoners or prisoners unable to work for other reasons could bring reprimands, transferring them into the "refusers" category made the administration look good as well as responsive to the instructions from above. In the end, the arbitrariness of camp administrators and the overexploitation of prisoners in disregard of their physical condition attained such a scale that the NKVD leadership felt obliged to react. On 15 February 1941 a Gulag order on violating the rules on accommodating prisoners was issued. In particular, it stated: "In some camps and colonies of the NKVD USSR [. . .] there have been cases of putting in detention cells, and assigning reduced food rations to, prisoners who could not report to work or fulfill production tasks owing to a lack of clothes or shoes, illness, or [poor] physical condition." The order instructed that "all prisoners in detention cells and receiving reduced food rations be subjected to a medical exam," that those who were sick or who refused to work owing to a lack of clothes or shoes not be punished, and that a monthly review be conducted of the regimen in the detention cells, and that the correctness of the practice of assigning reduced rations as punishment also be reviewed monthly. The order explained this "liberalism" by stating that the number of such abuses "reduces the general productivity of the contingents and results in a growing number of emaciated and sick prisoners."[45]

According to documents, the 14 February order had no practical effect. On 23 May 1941 the Procuracy of the USSR reported to the NKVD on "the facts of the violation of revolutionary legality" in the camps of Leningrad province. This prompted the following NKVD resolution.

· 74 ·

Resolution by Deputy People's Commissar of Internal Affairs S. N. Kruglov
on inspecting the camps of Leningrad province
6 June 1941[46]

Top secret.
To the head of the NKVD Administration for Leningrad province,
Sr. Major of State Security, Com. Lagunov.
Leningrad.
According to the Procuracy of the USSR, many instances of violations of revolutionary legality have been registered in several camp divisions in Leningrad province. For example, in camp section no. 2 of Podporozhsky district, sick prisoners are forced to work and are subjected to beatings if they refuse. [. . .] Healthy prisoners capable of doing hard work are assigned to easy tasks on account of bribes. There were prisoners in the detention cell arrested for refusing to work. Medical examination of these "refusers" revealed that they were sick.
In camp section no. 7, Tikhvinsky district, the head of the camp section, Grigoriev, arrested prisoners without any reason, did not issue formal or-

ders, and locked up prisoners, stripped of outer clothing and shoes, in cold quarters in the winter. He personally beat up prisoners. [. . .] He forced sick prisoners with fever to work.

On Grigoriev's orders, those who refused to work were taken off the camp territory and made to run in snow or water, put in the snow and kept in the cold until evening, and put in a detention cell for the night.

Incidents of bribes to give prisoners easy work have been registered in this camp section. Grigoriev is personally responsible for squandering 3,000 rubles.

In the Ust-Luzhsk camp section of Kingisep district, the deputy head of the camp section, Khitrikov, appropriated prisoners' personal belongings. In barracks no. 42 and 55 of this camp section, foremen routinely took bribes for fictitiously inflating the percentage of work accomplished.

There are also cases of the confiscation, by administrative personnel, of products destined for prisoners.

In that camp section, between October 1940 and March 1941, there were ten cases of fatal accidents and about a thousand more with less grave outcomes.

I order a careful investigation of the aforementioned facts, and should they be confirmed, prosecution of those responsible must follow. Please report on the results.

Deputy People's Commissar of Internal Affairs of the USSR,
Commissar of State Security, Third Degree, Kruglov.

About the same time, the Chief Administration of Camps produced a memorandum indicating that the facts noted by the procuracy in Leningrad province were commonplace.

· 75 ·

Memorandum on the incorrect classification of prisoners as refusers
and their number in the first quarter of 1941
2 June 1941[47]

Secret.

To the Head of the Chief Administration of Corrective Labor Camps and Colonies of the NKVD USSR,

Senior Major of State Security,

Com. Nasedkin.

A review of reports from the first quarter of 1941 on cultural and educational work has demonstrated that the administration of camp sections and colonies in some camps and corrective labor colonies does not pay sufficient attention to the fight against those refusing to work.

At the same time, there are still instances of blatant violation of the main directives about the struggle against refusers [. . .], [instances] when sick, emaciated, unclothed, shoeless prisoners, prisoners in transfer, etc., are automatically branded as such. As a result, the total number of losses to refusals in the first quarter is over 1 million workdays.

For example, in Dzhezkazgan, [. . .] fifty prisoners who had been evaluated and listed as refusers turned out to be sick and emaciated, whereas only six of them were true refusers.

In Onega camp, besides the incorrect listing of prisoners as refusers, there is no proper accounting for the latter (seventh separate camp section). For example, according to the KVCh [Culture and Education Division] of the sections, there were 10,532 man-days lost to refusers; according to the URO, 17,000; and according to the materials of production departments, 24,636 man-days.

On 24 February 1941, at the court session reviewing the cases of refusers in the same eighth camp section, it was established that the signatures of the KVCh head on the resolutions about the refusers had been forged.

In the Nizhne-Amursky camp, the administration of the colony incorrectly listed prisoners as refusers. As a result, in this camp, on average, there were 1,239 refusers every day, i.e., 2.4 percent of all the prisoners in the camp.

The situation in such camps as the BBK is no better. Owing to the poor work of the low-level administration and the cultural-educational sections, the average number of refusers was 2,607 each day.

In the Northern Urals camp, the number of refusers amounts to 29,227 man-days. For the most part, this is a result of the camp management keeping aloof from the fight against refusers and leaving this serious issue to the KVCh alone, as well as incorrectly listing prisoners as refusers. For example, in the fifth section, six prisoners who had accomplished 80 percent and 100 percent of the norm, were listed as refusers. In the seventh camp section, twenty-eight prisoners, locked up in the detention cell for ten days for theft and gangsterism, were not sent to work and were listed as refusers.

In the same camp (thirteenth section), during February and March, 377 light-labor prisoners were used at hard work. [. . .] They systematically failed to accomplish their tasks and, as a result, received reduced rations, grew emaciated, and were transferred into the "refusers" category. During daily lineups in the camp sections, team leaders created lists of all the prisoners who stayed in the camp zone and sent those lists, without verifying them, to the planning department. The latter mechanically listed them all as refusers. [. . .]

This work is completely unsatisfactory in the Vladivostok camp. The number of refusers there has more than tripled compared to the fourth quarter (fourth quarter—11,854, first quarter—42,039 man-days).

There were instances of listing prisoners without clothes or shoes as refusers in the colonies in Irkutsk, Chkalovsk, and other provinces. [. . .]

Head of the KVO [Culture and Education Department] of the Political Department of the GULAG of the NKVD, Kuzmin.

On the first page of this document Kuzmin scribbled: "To file. 19 June 1941." Most likely, the memorandum was never sent to Nasedkin, or else it was ignored by the Gulag heads.

The growth in the number of prisoners and their increasing exploitation, coupled with the endemic lack of resources, led to a continual deterioration of living conditions in camps and colonies. Monthly and quarterly summary reports on the use of labor resources in the NKVD camps in 1940 showed a high percentage of prisoners employed in production and a large share of disabled, chronically ill, and emaciated prisoners and prisoners without clothes or shoes. The share of disabled and sick prisoners in most camps was around 7–10 percent (up to 15 percent in Vorkuta camp and Belbaltlag).[48] These reports were based on data provided by the camp administration, which naturally tried to conceal the real extent of the problems by listing sick prisoners as "refusers" and manipulating the numbers in other ways. There was also an "others" category, which contained no explanation of failures to report to work. So grave was the situation that in October 1940, Moscow required that a "five-month campaign to recuperate the workforce" be conducted in the camps.[49]

The growth of economic plans in 1940–41 brought about more frequent transfers of prisoners between different sites. While the total number of prisoners was more or less stable, transfers between camps significantly increased (from the already huge number of 347,000 in 1939 to 563,000 in 1940; see Document 97). The high number of transferred prisoners signified terrible suffering for hundreds of thousands of people.

As a rule, each new construction project and the camp attached to it were started from scratch. Living conditions in the new camps were unbearable even by Gulag standards. The established camps, which had to provide prisoner workers to the new sites, naturally tried to get rid of the sick, emaciated, and disabled prisoners and ignored Moscow's instructions to deliver "quite healthy, employable prisoners." A typical example was the transfer of prisoners to the construction of the

Northern Pechora railroad. Despite the high priority of this site, in June–July 1940, at an early stage of camp formation, over 3,000 prisoners in the Arkhangelsk and Kotlas prisoner assembly centers were identified as sick, "partially employable," or disabled. A list of such prisoners on a train that arrived in Kotlas in late June mentioned prisoners "lacking or with immobilized extremities—fifty-eight people; highly emaciated—nineteen people; lacking one eye and with reduced vision in the other—nine people," and so on.[50] Considering that, on average, there were 3,851 prisoners in the Northern Pechora camp, we can estimate that half of the arriving prisoners were removed from the trains in poor physical condition.[51] The relocation of thousands of disabled and sick prisoners inevitably led to a high death rate en route. However, there are no relevant statistics available on this point (see Chapter 7).

All attempts to secure healthy prisoners for the construction project failed, strict orders notwithstanding. Relatively healthy prisoners arriving at the Northern Pechora camp often died or became invalids because of brutal treatment. Indeed, this construction project is a glaring example of how prisoners were exploited. Hard work, ten–twelve-hour workdays, and extreme weather conditions resulted in 3,586 deaths in the first seven months of its existence (data as of 1 January 1941).[52] Although the Pechora camp had more than 37,000 prisoners in January 1941, only 53 percent of them were actually employed. Disabled, sick, and emaciated prisoners made up 21 percent of the total, and those without clothes or shoes, "refusers," and other nonworking prisoners made up 14 percent.[53] By May 1941 the situation had apparently improved. Of the nearly 76,000 prisoners, 76.5 percent were employed, and the share of nonworking, sick, and disabled prisoners was down to 9 percent.[54] There are reasons to believe that these figures were manipulated, however, and that the exploitation of prisoners, regardless of their physical condition, increased. The inspection of the Pechora camp in late May revealed the following picture.

· 76 ·

Report on the Northern Pechora camp
23 May 1941[55]

Top secret.
To the People's Commissar of Internal Affairs of the USSR,
Comrade L. P. Beria.

According to the operations department of the Northern Pechora camp of the GULZhDS [Chief Administration of Camps for Railroad Construction] NKVD, the leadership of the Pechora camp, ignoring the lessons of the past year, does not take adequate steps to create normal living conditions for the prisoners. Prisoners are led to work in felt shoes and old tarpaulin boots. They stay in cold water and mud from the spring thaw for days on end, which results in a large number of colds.

As of 10 May, in the southern section of the Pechora camp NKVD alone, there were 1,361 bedridden patients. Every day the number of patients is growing. The number of scurvy cases has increased precipitously. As of 10 May, there were 8,389 scurvy patients in the southern section of Pechora camp. Among them, 3,398 people had a second-grade illness; and 4,991 people, a first-grade [illness]. The number of scurvy cases is rising.

The columns' [units'] need for dryers, bathhouses, and disinfecting chambers has been only 5–10 percent satisfied. In the absence of water boilers, people have to drink unprocessed water. The need for dishes in the columns had been only 40 satisfied.

The barracks and tents are kept in unsanitary conditions. There is a great lack of bedsheets and underwear. Up to 70 percent of prisoners are lice-ridden.

The leadership of the Pechora camp has mandated nonobservance of the twenty-one-day quarantine obligatory for all newly arriving groups.

Those arriving at Kanin Nos are sent to their destination [on foot], walking 150 kilometers in felt boots through mud and water.

Head of the GULAG of the NKVD USSR,
Senior Major of State Security, Nasedkin.

Apparently, the situation in the Pechora camp was rather typical. According to the Gulag sanitary department, in December 1940–January 1941 the death rate grew sharply.[56] In early 1941 the camps and colonies were ravaged by tuberculosis, pellagra, scurvy, and venereal diseases.[57]

· 77 ·

Memorandum on the prisoner regimen in the Middle Belsk camp
10 March 1941[58]

As of 1 March 1941 the camp population of the Middle Belsk camp is 4,622 people.

According to the information available to the GULAG of the NKVD USSR, only 18 percent of prisoners are provided with living quarters. The rest of the camp contingent stay in dugouts and tents, which are inadequate for living.

In the commander's camp section, in the third and fourth divisions, prisoners sleep on bare bunks in summer clothes.

About 3,000 prisoners do not have warm clothes and shoes.

As a result of the lack of clothes and shoes, there are cases of prisoners refusing to work. In the third division alone, the daily number of refusers can reach 100, and for the entire camp, 200–300.

The supply of food to prisoners is poorly organized. There were mass refusals by prisoners to eat low-grade food (in July and August 1940).

No cultural and educational work is conducted with the prisoners owing to the lack of space.

To inspect and assist the camp administration in rectifying the shortcomings, on 1 March 1941 a team of GULAG of the NKVD USSR workers was sent to the Middle Belsk corrective labor camp. [. . .]

Head of the GULAG of the NKVD USSR,
Senior Major of State Security, Nasedkin.

· 78 ·

Report on the Middle Belsk camp
17 May 1941[59]

Top secret.
Special communication.
To be delivered to:
Com. Kruglov,
Com. Nasedkin.*
According to the operative-chekist department of the ULAG UNKVD for the Khabarovsk territory, the regimen in the Middle Belsk camp of the NKVD has not changed despite the inspection by the GULAG commission.

Of the 4,000 camp prisoners, 1,795 are not under escort. One-third of the prisoners live outside the camp zone.

Prisoners sentenced for counterrevolutionary crimes are still kept with the prisoners sentenced for ordinary crimes.

Unescorted carriage drivers, loaders, and forwarders, who can freely leave the camp grounds, deliver letters to the outside world. Prisoners maintain contacts with the locals who live nearby.

Until now, prisoners sentenced for embezzlement, theft, and swindling under the 7 August 1932 law are allowed to be employed in the camp administration apparatus and in the sections at work related to guarding merchandise and other valuables.

As a result of allowing this category of prisoners to have access to valuables, the camp suffered embezzlement, theft, and waste [*promot*] in the amount of 204,000 rubles in 1940.

Living conditions in the camp are very difficult. The camp is provided with living quarters for only 23 percent. The appalling overcrowding results in lice everywhere. Fifteen hundred prisoners live in pigpens, cowsheds, stables, bathhouses, laundry rooms, and other ancillary buildings.

Up to 40 percent of prisoners sleep on bare bunks without mattresses.

Drinking, gambling, hooliganism, and sexual relations with prisoner women are widespread in the camp. In just the first quarter of 1941, thirty-four babies were born in the Middle Belsk camp.

Head of the operations department of the GULAG of the NKVD USSR, Captain of State Security, Yorsh.

---

* On the first page of the document is scribbled: "Com. Nasedkin. Let's discuss. 19 May. Kruglov." Also, a stamp: "Taken under control by the Secretariat of the NKVD USSR."

As always, dismal living conditions prompted prisoners to escape. In 1939, as a result of the curbing of mass punitive operations and Beria's harsh measures to strengthen the regimen, the number of escapes was significantly lower than in 1937 and 1938 (see Document 97). In 1940, however, NKVD escape reports were not as rosy. Whereas, according to official statistics, there were 18,342 escapes from camps and colonies in 1939 (5,067 of them never apprehended), in 1940 the number was not significantly less, 18,075 (with 5,249 not apprehended).[60] In some cases the escapes were by groups, and guards were murdered, which was embarrassing to the NKVD leadership. On 5 July 1940, to cite one example, four prisoners from the Kargopol camp, headed by the convicted spy N. A. Zhdanov, managed an "armed escape" as they were being transported in a truck; in the course of their escape they disarmed and killed one guard and injured another. To capture them, a small army was pulled together: 130 guards plus local NKVD officers and groups of local residents. Three prisoners were soon apprehended, but it took eleven days to find Zhdanov, seventy kilometers away, and his capture was accidental: V. V. Godovikov, railway coupler at the Vandysh station of the Northern railway, discovered Zhdanov and reported him to the authorities. Godovikov was praised and received a 300-ruble bonus. The people's commissar of internal affairs issued a special order in connection with this escape, which had to be read to the armed guards of all camps and colonies.[61] A few months later, on 6 November 1940, another, more general order had to be issued: "On strengthening the effort to prevent escapes in the camps and colonies of the NKVD." The order strictly commanded authorities "to maintain the readiness of the guards and escorts to open fire on escapees if other measures cannot prevent the escape," and warned the heads of camp sections and guard commanders that in case of escapes, they "bear criminal responsibility under the military tribunal for weakening the regimen and the guard, which leads to escapes."[62]

The camp guards, angry, facing punishment for escapes, and encouraged to open fire on the escapees, henceforth used deadly force more often. According to operational reports, clashes between guards and prisoners were commonplace in the camps. Often these confrontations ended tragically. In most cases, the use of deadly force was ruled to be justified. Below is a characteristic excerpt from the March–early April report for one camp.

· 79 ·

Report no. 15, "On accidents in the camps and colonies
of the NKVD as of 18 April 1941"
18 April 1941[63]

Report no. 15

On the accidents in the camps and colonies of the NKVD USSR as of 18
April 1941.

Deliver to: Com. Nasedkin.

[. . .] Volga camp.

On 9 March of this year, prisoner P. K. Lukhanin attacked and hit guard
F. A. Potseluikin. Guard Potseluikin slightly bayoneted prisoner Lukhanin. The investigation proved that the cold weapon was used appropriately. Prisoner Lukhanin was put in a high-security cell.

On 12 March of this year, guard Panchenko shot a rifle and lightly injured prisoner Belakon, who had assaulted him with a sledgehammer. The operational representative of the operative chekist department ruled that the use of the firearm was justified.

On 15 March of this year, sentinel guard P. K. Dovbnia shot from a Nagan revolver and fatally injured prisoner S. V. Shaposhnikov, who had assaulted him with a knife in order to disarm him and to escape through the camp gates. Investigation is under way.

On 18 March of this year, thirty-three of the thirty-seven prisoners escorted by guard Makhaev attempted a "rush" escape. Guard Makhaev shot off his rifle and seriously injured prisoner Tkachenko in the back. An internal investigation established that the firearm was used appropriately.

On 24 March of this year, guard A. I. Khlebnikov shot from his rifle and injured prisoner M. K. Simonian, who had escaped from the restricted-regimen team. An internal investigation established that the firearm was used appropriately.

On 30 March of this year, guard I. I. Maideburga shot from a Nagan revolver and injured prisoner Krivitsky, who had attacked him with a knife during the evening roll call. An internal investigation established that the firearm was used appropriately.

On 4 April of this year, sentinel guard G. A. Timonenko shot from a Nagan revolver and injured prisoner N. L. Manuilenko, who had cut through the barbed wire and started running. The firearm was used appropriately.

[. . .]

Head of the Guard and Regimen Department,
Major of State Security Dobrynin.

In 1941 the NKVD issued new instructions to prevent escapes, which was a sign that the situation was not getting any better. On 25 April, Beria signed an order in connection with a group escape in the Aktiubinsk camp, where three prisoners killed the construction engineer and a guard, "took a rifle, live ammunition, the guard's clothes, and escaped from the camp. At the time of their capture they offered armed resistance." The order listed similar cases that took place in that camp in early 1941.[64]

The NKVD leaders believed that relatively mild punishment for escapes encouraged prisoners to flee. Apparently, the incident at the Aktiubinsk camp prompted calls for harsh penalties for escapees. On 28 April 1941, Beria, People's Commissar of Justice Rychkov, and Procurator of the USSR Bochkov issued a directive that called prisoner escapes "one of the most malicious forms of sabotage and disorganization of the camp life." The directive stipulated the most severe punishment for escapees, including shooting. It ordered that investigations of escapes be given high priority and that verdicts be announced to the prisoners of the camps where the escapes took place.[65]

Prewar mobilization was thus characterized by high mortality and disease rates, a hungry existence in filthy, cold barracks, severe exploitation and hard labor in adverse climatic conditions, escapes, arbitrariness on the part of guards and excesses by the camp administration, and shootings of "disrupters" and escapees. Most prisoners were crippled and starved. A similar situation, though not so extreme, existed in another part of the Gulag, where sentences of exile were carried out.

The Erosion of "Kulak Exile"

In the late 1930s–early 1940s the gradual erosion of kulak exile (officially called labor exile) accelerated (see Chapter 3). The adoption of a new constitution in December 1936 had a profound impact on the mood of those in labor exile. The Constitution proclaimed an automatic restoration of civil rights for all categories of the population previously disenfranchised, including former kulaks. The 25 January 1935 law that had prohibited special settlers who were former kulaks to leave exile, despite their restoration of civil rights, contravened the Constitution. But the authorities had no intention of adjusting the law to accord with the Constitution, which was essentially an exercise in pure propaganda.

The fate of a proposal by A. Ya. Vyshinsky and N. I. Yezhov to reorganize labor exile, which they presented to Stalin and Molotov in January–February 1937, is a good case in point.[66] The proposal was a compromise and offered half-measures in connection with the adoption of the new constitution. While supporting the ban on leaving exile, Vyshinsky and Yezhov suggested that "in 1939 relocation would be allowed within the same territory or province, and in 1940 [it would be allowed to anywhere within] the entire Union." To encourage former kulaks to stay in exile, the authors suggested the introduction of material incentives and the granting of certain privileges. At the same time, they recommended purging the labor settlements and sentencing to three–five years in camp those settlers "who are known to the NKVD to be hostile to the Soviet regime." Yezhov's "liberalism" can be explained by the intention of the NKVD to slough off the management of kulak exile and transfer it to local authorities.

We do not have information on who reviewed such initiatives. Subsequent events show, however, that the situation of the labor settlers was left virtually unchanged. The Great Terror effectively froze any solutions to labor settlement problems. In 1937 alone, according to NKVD reports, 17,385 special settlers were sentenced.[67]

Nevertheless, the authorities could not totally ignore the state of affairs in the labor settlements. Uncertainty brewed discontent among the settlers and confused local authorities.

· 80 ·

Report on the labor settlements of Ordzhonikidzevsk territory
29 April 1937[68]

Top secret.

To the Deputy People's Commissar of Internal Affairs of the USSR, Commissar of State Security, Third Degree, Com. Berman.

[. . .] Since the adoption of the Stalin constitution, certain settlers have started thinking that they will be allowed to leave freely. They have become convinced that in the near future, commandant offices will be removed and soviets will be set up. The majority of labor settlers have adopted a wait-and-see attitude.

At this time the following kinds of conversations have been registered: "They read the Constitution to us and explain that we already have civil rights, but for some reason [they] do not remove the commandant's offices and sentries. They no longer have the right to keep us under such strict watch. It's the local authorities that keep us here, and the center doesn't know about it. If we leave the Livensky settlement, they won't arrest us elsewhere" (labor settler Rogoza; Kista settlement).

"Soon there will be soviets, and everybody will be allowed to live where they want to, and we won't stay in Kievka for even one more day" (labor settler Gavriil Medvedev; Kievka settlement).

"We shouldn't be staying here anymore; we should leave for our homes. Still, they keep us here for some reason."

The difficult situation regarding food in the labor settlements and the uncertain legal situation of the settlers after the adoption of the Stalin constitution have contributed to the growing number of escapes from labor settlements.

Starting from January 1937, escapes have been systematically on the rise.

In addition to the enumerated causes, the following circumstances also significantly contribute to the increase in escapes:

The weak punitive policy of the people's courts and even the territorial court (on 16 January of this year, the appellate collegium of the Ordzhonikidzevsk territorial court reversed the decision of the people's court and freed from custody labor settler S. Lupar on the grounds that he was having [his civil rights] restored).

The failure to conduct a fight against escapes by local Soviet organs beyond the territory of the settlements.

Local Soviet organs and social organizations have interpreted article 135 of the Constitution as removing all limitations on the labor settlers and, in particular, invalidating the 24 January 1935 TsIK USSR resolution, which prohibits leaving the labor settlements [see Chapter 3].

We possess many documents showing that the kolkhozes, sovkhozes, and Soviet institutions accept the escapees, return to them their houses, and register them for permanent residency.

The Voroshilov kolkhoz in the village of Ispravnoe, Otradnensky region, Azov–Black Sea territory, admitted the escaped labor settler Sarchenko as a member and returned his house to him.

The board of the Kaganovich kolkhoz, Khristichev hamlet, Azov–Black Sea territory, admitted the escaped labor settler K. G. Martynenko as a kolkhoz member. The court ruled that the house he previously owned be returned to him.

The board of the Stalin kolkhoz, Sochi district, Azov–Black Sea territory, reported to us on 25 March that they had admitted the labor settler S. M. Yeremian as a member of the kolkhoz, and demanded that he be sent there.

About 300 escapees from the settlements of our territory work at the sovkhoz at the Baiaut station, Tajik SSR, etc.

Several organizations have asked us to clarify the legal situation in connection with the adoption of the Constitution.

Settlers themselves send numerous complaints to the central and territorial newspapers stating that the Constitution has not given them anything so far and asking they be informed when and how the Soviet Constitution will apply to them. [. . .]

The head of the NKVD USSR Administration for the Ordzhonikidzevsk territory, Captain of State Security, Bulakh.

This report reveals a rather common tendency in kulak exile. The number of escapes of special settlers remained high. In many cases, local authorities liberalized the regimen by referring to the Constitution: they discontinued the 5 percent deduction from labor settlers' salaries (deducted to support the NKVD apparatus that managed the settlements), issued passports to them, and sometimes even sent them to sanatoriums.[69] Still, government offices in Moscow were flooded with complaints from disgruntled labor settlers.

· 81 ·

Statement from labor settler Poroshkov
[Before 19 February 1938][70]

To the Chairman of the Supreme Soviet,
Com. Andreev.

All the Soviet people are jubilant about the Stalin constitution. The Constitution is the greatest creation by the leader of the people. It misses nothing, and all people's interests are addressed. But how are those in power implementing this law?

Article 135 of the Constitution gives everybody the right to elect and be elected. If so, then article 127 gives individual freedom, and nobody can be arrested except by order of the court or a resolution of the procurator. But what is happening to the settlers and labor settlers (I am referring to those who were not sentenced)? They do not give them residence permits, do not allow them to travel, and take 5 percent of their salary. Even children are not allowed to leave the area. An innocent young man can leave to study only with great difficulty, and even then he cannot go where he wants—even though Stalin openly said that children are not responsible for their parents. Article 1 of the classless constitution says: The republic is of workers and peasants. If so, there are no more settlers or labor [settlers]. There are no laws to keep them under arrest forever.

[. . .] We literally could not wait for the Constitution to be adopted, and what does the NKVD give us? I have to say that the low-ranking NKVD officials always calmed us down, but now [they] are saying nothing at all. We expect you to resolve this problem. It is not right to treat the workers who give all their work and talent to the Motherland in this fashion.

Poroshkov.

5 Ilyicha St., Pakhta-Aral Sovkhoz, Syrdaria Station

In early 1938 the government reviewed this and several other letters as evidence of the need to resolve the issue of labor settlers. The regime was particularly sensitive to the fact that the labor settlements had a large number of children and adolescents (358,000 out of 880,000 labor settlers as of 1 January 1938).[71] While refusing to resolve the problem as a whole, the authorities undertook a series of measures in 1938 that created certain possibilities for the settlers, or at least an illusion of possibilities. On 9 September 1938 the government legally equated regular and labor settlers' agricultural and artisan-industrial artels. On 18 September 1938 a Gulag circular letter allowed labor settlers to work as drivers and to drive cars within the permissible territory, among other things. Finally, on 22 October 1938, the government adopted the most significant resolution of all the resolutions issued under Stalin about kulak exile. According to this decree, labor settlers' children were released from exile upon reaching the age of sixteen, provided they were not "marred." However, they were issued passports in which it was noted that they were not allowed to live in "regimen" communities (the capital and other large industrial centers, border regions, etc.). This resolution was of pivotal importance. It terminated the institution of hereditary exile and permanently divided the old kulaks, who faced lifetime exile, from their children, who received their freedom, even though as second-class citizens.

As was usual with such decisions, implementation ran into numerous problems. In the first place, NKVD bosses proved reluctant to free labor settlers en masse. In 1940, according to the 22 October resolution, 165,000 young settlers were to be released. Only about 78,000 actually received their freedom.[72]

Commandants and their staff, in charge of the labor settlers, used all possible excuses to delay issuing passports. The law facilitated their reluctant response by requiring the release only of those who had not been "marred."

The chekists' open sabotage of this law was consistent with the tendency to strengthen the regimen in NKVD units after Beria was appointed people's commissar. Numerous facts attest to the notion that

NKVD bosses (clearly supported by the supreme leaders) were against any meaningful changes in kulak exile, preferred to maintain the status quo, and relied on a strengthening of the regimen in labor settlements and repression of escapees. The NKVD succeeded in weakening the draft resolution by the government on the legal status of labor settlers that was in preparation in 1939 and later in having the issue completely dropped as "nonessential."[73] At the same time, in 1940–41, the NKVD issued orders to make the punishment for escaping from exile more severe and specified measures to take in searching for escapees and preventing escapes. The orders also complicated the procedure for freeing labor settlers who married free citizens.[74]

In general, kulak exile served its traditional role. It confined about a million people who, while formally regaining their civil rights, were still suspected of being disloyal and even hostile to the regime. Reports about labor exile sent to Moscow by local NKVD departments upheld this notion.

· 82 ·

Excerpts from the report on the labor settlements in Chita province
in the second half of 1940[75]

---

8. Moral and political situation
Overall, [prisoners,] especially the old ones, are politically unreliable. It is revealed in their attitude toward actions by the Soviet regime.

During the subscription to the [state] loan of the Third Five-Year Plan, year 3,* some labor settlers expressed their dissatisfaction and said: "Since the Soviet regime took away all our property, we won't subscribe to the loan. . ." "I won't subscribe to the loan because I don't want to be down-and-out. . . ."

The government resolution on paid education in middle schools and colleges[†] caused dissatisfaction among labor settlers. They avoid doing [volunteer] social work. Labor settlers do not attend general meetings at which various social events are discussed.

---

* The SNK USSR resolution of 1 July 1940 ordered issuing the state loan of the Third Five-Year Plan (year 3) in the amount of 8 billion rubles (SZ, 1940, no. 16, art. 384).
† On 2 October 1940 the SNK USSR introduced paid education in middle schools and colleges in the amount of 200 rubles a year for Moscow and Leningrad and in the amount of 150 rubles for other cities (SZ, 1940, no. 27, art. 637).

Anti-Soviet elements are still plentiful among labor settlers and openly conduct anti-Soviet agitation. For example, labor settler Anna Blazhevich said: ". . . I am enslaved and probably will continue living like this, with no justice in sight. I don't have much time left and will spend the rest of my life in drudgery. . . ."

Labor settler Boyarchuk said at a board meeting: ". . . Who invented these laws to arrest innocent people for absenteeism? . . ."

Labor settler Romas said: "During the war between the USSR and Finland, Soviet newspapers lessened the casualties. We had more [casualties] than Finland, so if the Japanese come, the Soviet regime will be squashed, and we will start living then."

All these anti-Soviet conversations and agitation have been reported to the RO [district department] NKVD. All labor settlers, without exception, are discontented about not enjoying the full rights of citizens of the Soviet Union, for having no passports, and for not having the right to leave the special settlement.

Despite the fact that 50 percent of labor settlers have houses and some property, they are ready to leave the special settlement at any time. This means that the labor settlers refuse to accommodate themselves to exile and stay in the labor settlements only because they are not allowed to leave.

· 83 ·

Excerpts from a report on labor exile in Irkutsk province as of 1 January 1941
1 February 1941[76]

Top secret.

[. . .] Political-moral situation.

In the reported period, the mood of the labor settlers can be characterized as follows: The absolute majority of labor settlers are concerned with how to obtain passports and leave the labor settlements. Labor settlers continue to engage in various schemes to get out of the labor settlements, such as escaping, concealing their social origin, obtaining birth certificates without authorization, and marrying citizens who are not labor settlers in order to obtain passports and escape from the supervision of the local commandant's office.

The majority of labor settlers are dissatisfied with the regimen in labor settlements and even more so with the actions of the party and the Soviet regime. There have been no open anti-Soviet actions among labor settlers in the reported period. There were cases where labor settlers failed to stay permanently in their communities. Many labor settlers do not establish households, and many do not even have household goods. At the same time, there are labor settlers who, judging by how they have established their private households, have settled permanently in their communities.

The labor settlers reveal among themselves their dissatisfaction with the existing regimen and the Soviet system. The following facts are typical: On 15 December 1940, during a discussion of the international situation by a group of labor settlers, labor settler N. K. Zoliuk stated, in the presence of labor settler A. Babushkin: "There is no justice in the Soviet Union whatsoever, for it made agreements with foreign states and sends all the bread there. In exchange for bread, [it] receives cars and children's toys, and our workers go hungry as a result."

Labor settler Ya. A. Apin (Chermekhovskaya commandant's office) thinks that all decrees by the Supreme Soviet are unjust. Ya. A. Apin says: "The workers are now squeezed tighter than [they were] under landlords before."

Labor settler A. Simonov stated during his conversation with Romanov: "Under [Tsar] Nicholas [they] worked for twelve hours, and now in the Soviet Union they work for twelve hours." He added that "in the capitalist countries, although there is unemployment, the workers live well, while in the Soviet Union one can croak from working."

Labor settler P. Kotova said that "the Soviet regime is based on labor settlers. Had it been not for labor settlers, who would work for them[?]"

Labor settler A. Rtischev, May the First sovkhoz, said that "they starve us, the labor settlers, while sending bread abroad." The labor settlers have been arrested for anti-Soviet agitation.

Labor settler M. V. Antonenok said that "nobody is going to free us. One has to commit something to be convicted, serve the term, and then become a free citizen." Labor settler Antonenok has been arrested.

On 29 June 1940, during a discussion of the 26 June 1940 decree by the Presidium of the Supreme Soviet of the USSR, labor settler A. A. Kropotov said that "this decree does not affect us. It was written for free laborers, and they will not prosecute us. Therefore we, the labor settlers, don't have to know about it." Two days later, labor settler Kropotov was absent from work, for which he has been convicted.

Very many similar conversations by labor settlers have been registered during the reported period. All materials on the anti-Soviet and counter-revolutionary moods of the labor settlers are being forwarded to the heads of local RO NKVD [district departments].

It is important to mention that during the reported period, in the Cheremkhovskaya district commandant's office, four labor settlers were arrested and sentenced to seven to ten years in prison for anti-Soviet counterrevolutionary agitation. In the Tayshetskaya commandant's office, three labor settlers were arrested and sentenced, and in the Irkutsk commandant's office two people were arrested and sentenced.

In addition to that, in the reported period, cases of various other crimes committed by labor settlers have been registered, such as:

escapes—23

assisting the escapes—5

unauthorized absences—34

violations of the regimen—47

absenteeism from work—273

thefts—10

hooliganism—23

Among the labor settlers who were prosecuted, sixty-eight people have been sentenced to prison terms of one to ten years.

Such reports on the "political-moral situation," though processed by the chekist bureaucratic machine, nevertheless reflected the actual mood among the majority of former kulaks, who had lost all hope for regaining their freedom. There was nothing that they would be thankful to the Soviet regime for, and the authorities, knowing this full well, kept the powerful repressive machine at the ready. But the lives of hundreds of thousands of labor settlers were more than just a matter of direct conflict with the state. The kulak exiles lived by the same laws of survival and accommodation as did the rest of the country under the Stalinist regime.

Living conditions varied greatly for different groups of labor settlers. In general, the famine and mass deaths of the early period of special exile were gone, but the majority of labor settlers, as well as free citizens, still faced enormous hardships. The NKVD reports on labor exile often referred to unfavorable living conditions, especially of the settlers occupied in industry (that is, most of the settlers): they lived in inadequate barracks and dugouts, and there were no schools or hospitals.[77] At the same time, the endurance and tenacity of the former kulaks allowed them to not only survive but live fairly well and, in some cases, achieve a high level of comfort by Soviet standards. Among the agricultural cooperatives there were several "millionaire kolkhozes"—well-off farms that irritated the local authorities.

· 84 ·

Memorandum on the labor settlement in Irbit region, Sverdlovsk province
29 October 1939[78]

Top secret.

To the People's Commissar of Internal Affairs of the USSR, Com. Beria, Moscow.

To the Head of the UNKVD for Sverdlovsk province, Major of State Security, Com. Ivanov, Sverdlovsk.

Near the town of Irbit, right next to the L. M. Kaganovich Railroad, there is a kulak exile settlement of 496 families, about 1,948 people. Some employable settlers work at the diatomite plant (producing building bricks), some work in their New Life kolkhoz, and some do not work on a permanent basis, but own horses, fifty-nine total. This is considered inappropriate, but the OITK UNKVD for some reason allowed it (according to the settlement commander, Chaschin).

Some regional administrators believe that the [place of] kulak exile should be moved out of the town of Irbit to a different location. [. . .]

To satisfy the needs of the population, the Irbit town council is planning to organize a vegetable production sovkhoz on the land currently occupied by the New Life kolkhoz. This is quite feasible, and people could work at the plant and in the sovkhoz at the same time. However, I believe that it would be politically more appropriate to move the kulak exile away from the town and closer to timber farms or peat bogs.

The reason I believe it politically appropriate to move the kulak exile is because the former kulaks currently enjoy privileged conditions compared to the kolkhoz members, which negatively affects the local population. Why negatively? To answer this question, it is necessary to review the situation and economy of the kolkhoz.

In 1932 exiled former kulaks organized an informal agricultural cooperative team, later named the New Life agricultural cooperative. On 20 February a general meeting of the collective farm adopted and properly registered the statutes of an agricultural cooperative, just the way other collective farms do. However, the regional executive committee did not give the agricultural cooperative the entitlement to use the land forever.

At this time, the collective farm possesses property worth 600,000 rubles, including:

STZ tractors—2
ZIS truck—1
horses—180
cows in a collective herd—290

sows—18, increase—50

sheep—216

breeding does—100, increase—1,500

farm for raising animals for fur (foxes)—18

chicken farm—500

All this is high yield. For example, in 1938 the average yield of milk per fodder cow was 1,849 liters, and this year it will be 2,100 liters.* Only 1.5 percent of the cattle, pigs, etc., die.

The collective farm sows about 700 hectares, including 20 hectares with vegetables. The yield has reached eighteen centners [1,800 kilograms] per hectare.† The collective farm has a one-hectare fruit garden and a one-hectare hop field. The collective farm employs advanced agricultural techniques to manage the vegetable fields and uses by-products of the city and the plant. In particular, the used water from the diatomite plant is collected in a natural depression in the settlement, where it is pumped, via the Chigir water main, to the fields. As a result of using [such] agricultural techniques, the collective farm has high yields. The question is, Did the kulaks invent them all on their own? Not at all: In 1932, the regional department sent a free agronomist, Schupov, there. The collective farm pays him a salary in the amount of 750 rubles. Schupov is a former VKP(b) member, married to a kulak daughter, and is very arrogant. District authorities complain that he supposedly does not abide by Soviet laws.

Even though the district did not nominate him to attend the All-Union Agricultural Exhibition, Schupov went there. The exhibition committee named him a candidate for a governmental award.

Back to the issue of the privileged position of the kolkhoz compared to other kolkhozes of the district: the New Life kolkhoz, aside from hiring free specialists (which is not true for the district kolkhozes), such as an agronomist, an accountant, and a bookkeeper, has the advantage of being located near the town. This makes it easy to transport grain and other agricultural produce, both required supplies and [goods for] the market—an advantage that other local kolkhozes do not possess. Also, the kolkhoz has two tractors, for which it does not pay tax in kind—another advantage. There is no army recruitment nor work at the timber farms. Each year twenty–thirty people graduate from schools.

On this basis, the kulaks from the New Life kolkhoz promote the idea that only they, and not former fieldhands and the poor, can live well. They mock their former fieldhands and demoralize certain other collective farm-

---

* In the USSR in 1938 the average yield of milk per cow was 1,100 kilograms; in 1940 it was 1,017 kilograms (RGAE, f. 1562, op. 33, d. 805, l. 24).

† The average yield in 1939 in the USSR was 7.4 centners per hectare (1 centner equals 100 kilograms). See R. W. Davies et al., *The Economic Transformation of the Soviet Union, 1913–1945* (Cambridge, 1994), p. 291.

ers. Here is a typical example: Special settler Iakov Ivanovich Rechkalov, born in Rechkalov village council, Irbitsk region, invited his former field-hand (currently a collective farmer), Shorikov, into his house and started to persuade him in an anti-Soviet spirit: "The Soviet regime and the collective farms won't last long. We lived well in the past, and now we live better than you, and will live as we used to, see?" etc. As a result, Shorikov started to neglect his work and the kolkhoz property.

At this time, Rechkalov has been arrested and indicted under article 58-10, part 1 of the Criminal Code of the RSFSR. He had three accomplices.

The kulaks negatively influence the mindset of the collective farmers when they visit the nearby villages, i.e., in their residence areas, where they maintain certain connections with the population. [. . .]

That is why, as I said earlier, I believe that the kulak exile negatively affects the surrounding kolkhoz population. Therefore, I consider it politically beneficial to move the kulak exile away from the town and to organize a state vegetable farm on its land in order to cater to the needs of workers and employees of the enterprises of several regions.

Provisional head of the Irbitsk NKVD regional department, Sublieutenant of State Security, Patrakov.

The fate of the New Life cooperative was apparently rather grim, mostly because the case became public and drew attention in Moscow. In December 1939 the head of the UNKVD for Sverdlovsk province, Ivanov, reported to Beria's deputy, Mamulov: "I forwarded Com. Patrakov's memorandum to the secretary of the Sverdlovsk provincial VKP(b) committee so that the bureau of the VKP(b) provincial committee would resolve the issue of organizing the state vegetable farm to supply the population of Irbit. I believe that it is necessary to remove the special exile from the town because it demoralizes the population and the surrounding collective farms, since the majority of the special exiles are local kulaks."[79]

Still, the authorities were unable to completely inhibit the "enrichment" of able and entrepreneurial "kulaks." Many labor settlers tried, by fair means or foul, to expand and develop "private support plots," which often grew larger than allowed by the authorities. A memorandum prepared for Yezhov's report about the situation in the labor settlements as of 1 July 1938 noted that "A certain number of labor settlers took the road of kulak economic expansion. For example, in the Oborsk region of Khabarovsk province, sixty-four settler households have three–five cows, one horse, two–three pigs, and two–three young animals. They possess firearms and engage in hunting. In Irkutsk province, the growth [in the number] of cattle in private ownership exceeds the growth of the public herd."[80] In spite of the control of employment by the commandant's offices, many settlers engaged in private entrepreneurial activity. "Among the able-bodied men (Chita province, Primorsky territory) there are those who avoid working in production. The labor settlers with horses work as private carriers and speculate from their private plots,"* stated the review of labor exile in the first half of 1940.[81]

This avoidance is well illustrated by the number of able-bodied settlers who failed to report to work as ordered by administration. According to internal reports in 1938–40, they accounted for 15–20 percent of the settlers.[82] While the majority were women with children, students, and the sick, there were also various "inveterate refusers to work."

The majority of labor settlers (750,000 of the total 990,000 labor settlers in 1940) were used in production, as agreed between the NKVD and the industrial commissariats.[83] In many cases, the demands of industry made it impossible for settlers to stay in their prescribed locations. Local NKVD organs turned a blind eye to the labor settlers abandoning their hamlets. Thus, a review of labor exile in Arkhangelsk province conducted by the central NKVD apparatus in early 1941 revealed that, of the total 36,600 registered labor settlers, about 20,000 had "left their hamlets and resettled in the towns and villages of the province. [. . .] While living outside their settlements, the settlers are still assigned to the settlement's commandant office."[84]

Often industrial commissariats used labor settlers on important jobs requiring highly qualified workers, including defense factories as well as electric power stations. In January 1939 the Gulag apparatus prepared a memorandum on this issue for the deputy people's commissar of internal affairs, Merkulov. Reporting on the employment of labor settlers by defense enterprises, the authors of the document were rather pessimistic about the feasibility of resolving the problem: "Returning these labor settlers to the labor settlements meets with great difficulties because many labor settlers have been working at those enterprises for a number of years, received their education there, and obtained passports. Some of them started families with the workers of those enterprises."[85]

Thus, the reality of kulak exile, the objective needs of the economy,

---

* The original is vague, but this probably means that they were engaged in private entrepreneurial activity, selling produce at market prices, not fixed prices.

and the vagueness of the legal status of labor settlers limited NKVD control over the movement of the settlers. Some Gulag documents provide straightforward evidence of this.

· 85 ·

Excerpt from the report about the work of the commandant's offices
in the labor settlements of the Kolsky camp and Construction no. 33
of the NKVD in the second half of 1940[86]

The fight against escapes is insufficient and is particularly flawed at labor settlement number 2 in Kirovsk. This can be explained by the lack of a regimen in labor settlements, i.e., the commandant of the labor settlement has no administrative rights except to order a search, while the investigative organs and the procuracy offer no help at all. For example, the procurator of Kirovsk district, Com. Aksenov, regarding the return of the labor settlers whose [civil rights] were restored before the [adoption of the] Constitution and who have passports, said: "I have no right to sanction the escorted transfer, and I won't, except for those who have obtained passports illegally." Therefore, after we take measures to identify the escapee and his location, they request a resolution to transfer him, rendering further implementation, i.e., his return, impossible to accomplish.

Besides that, there are many unauthorized absences, especially during the period of summer vacations. Labor settlers leave on their own for resorts and sanatoriums, and upon their voluntary return to the settlement, the commandant's office cannot take any steps, lacking administrative rights. Thus, it does not prevent unauthorized absences, but encourages other labor settlers to violate the regimen. There even are cases where labor settlers come to the commandant's office and announce their unauthorized departure.

Commandant's offices take measures to exercise their rights, i.e., prosecuting at least those violators who illegally obtained passports. [. . .] A majority of public courts have been passing suspended sentences and ordering fines.

In labor settlement no. 4 in Kandalaksha, the public court of the second precinct reviewed two cases involving escape, that of labor settler Tatiana Mikhailovna Kudriavtseva (born in 1900) and that of labor settler Efim Andreyevich Repin (born in 1917), who had fraudulently and illegally obtained passports and were returned under escort. The court passed a suspended sentence, but the Murmansk provincial court acquitted them and closed the case.

Public courts currently reject such cases, claiming that since the labor settlers were exiled administratively and not by a court, they should be punished administratively. After the trial, the labor settler Repin escaped for the second time and was again returned to the labor settlement and remains unpunished.

It is particularly difficult to conduct a struggle against escapes and unauthorized absences among those labor settlers who had their civil rights restored before the Constitution [was adopted] and have passports, because they do not feel [that] any regimen [is in place], and cannot be effectively controlled, because they live among free laborers, i.e., not labor settlers.

Some organizations often do not want to observe the limitations imposed on labor settlers and issue them vouchers for resorts and sanatoriums without the approval of the commandant's office. There are cases where they were sent on business to other districts, including the regimen zones. For example, according to the People's Commissariat of Fisheries, labor settler Fyodor Yakovlevich Bespalov (his civil rights were restored before the Constitution; he had a passport and was a specialist in fishing) was sent, without the consent of the commandant's office, to the city of Kerch on the Black Sea.

Working in such conditions, where it is impossible to prevent violations [and] escapes, we were forced to ask the GULAG for instructions on how to conduct the fight against escapes. [. . .] Not until on 4 January 1941 did we receive a dispatch [. . .] saying that the escapees should be prosecuted, i.e., considered by the Special Council. This obviously is not enough for the leadership, because we do not know how to process the cases, who should process them and how, and who should arrest the escapees (the Procuracy does not authorize arrests).

In addition to that, an explanation is needed on how to process the resolutions to return the captured escapees to the settlement, both those with and those without passports, and finally, what administrative rights do the commandants' offices have to secure the regimen in the labor settlements?

Various sources suggest that the picture drawn by the Murmansk chekists was rather typical. These circumstances have to be taken into account when evaluating the situation in kulak exile on the eve of war.

According to NKVD reports, as of 1 January 1941 there were 930,000 labor settlers (compared to 998,000 in 1940 and 988,000 in 1939). The stagnation in number, and even reduction despite the increase in birth rate in the labor settlements and the arrival of new exiles, can be explained by the liberation of young people and by escapes, among other reasons.[87] A large portion of labor settlers (about 400,000 as of 1 January 1940) were children under sixteen who had to be freed from exile eventually.[88] It is difficult to determine the actual status of the 500,000–600,000 adult labor settlers. At the very least, many of them did not stay put in their settlements. As already noted, many former kulaks were merely registered in labor settlements while they lived in the cities or in the villages close to their workplace. Relatively free movement of labor settlers across the country was commonplace, including by those who had no intention of abandoning their settlement. In part, this is reflected by Gulag statistics on the many labor settlers who "voluntarily returned after escape" (2,480 in 1940).[89] The administrators of the settlements obviously preferred not to report temporary absences as escapes.

The settlers who had their civil rights restored before the adoption of the new constitution in December 1936 had more freedom of movement. Many managed to obtain passports, which gave them freedom to leave. The Gulag review showed that as of 1 July 1940, only 40,500 such labor settlers remained (compared to 131,000 as of 1 July 1939).[90]

The Gulag reports did not register the true scale of movement by labor settlers, including escapes and temporary absences. There were several reasons. On the one hand, registration was difficult given the dilution of exile by the loose regimen and given the wide utilization of settlers at workplaces outside the settlements. On the other hand, administrators were not interested in presenting objective reports. In 1940 the Gulag labor settlements department reported only 4,430 people as missing and 13,644 in the "other reasons for reduction" column.[91] A 1938 memorandum on the labor settlements openly admitted that that formula "disguises a certain number of escapes."[92]

Despite the efforts by the government, the kulak exile was shrinking, and the living conditions and legal status of settlers was becoming increasingly indistinguishable from that of the local population, especially peasants. Nevertheless, the system of special exile was not on the way out. On the contrary, it received a powerful boost in 1939–40, when new contingents of exiles started replacing the kulaks: the victims of the new world war and the territorial expansion of the Stalinist regime into Poland, the Ukraine, Belorussia, the Baltic states, and Moldavia.

The Fate of the New Special Settlers

Mass deportations of the population from western Ukraine, western Belorussia, the Baltic states, and Moldavia were conducted in several stages in 1940–41. Many things had changed since the similar deportations of kulaks a decade earlier. In some ways, the new settlers were in better circumstances: the country had overcome widespread famine, the territories for settlements had by then been developed, and the deportations themselves took longer and involved a smaller number of people, which helped to avoid extremes such as the Nazino Island horror of 1933. But for hundreds of thousands of new exiles the improvement was only marginal.

The first group of new settlers were the 140,000 Polish *osadniks*— Polish colonists, typically veterans of the 1919–20 Soviet-Polish war, who had received land in western Ukraine and western Belorussia. They were deported in February 1940.[93] The original plan was to accommodate these special exiles in settlements of 100 to 500 families. Their labor was to be used by the People's Commissariat of Forestry, and they were to be supplied according to the norms established for workers in the timber industry.[94] As had become usual, the plan was not backed up with sufficient material resources and was thwarted by Soviet inefficiency.[95] Regular inspections of the settlements revealed terrible living conditions, generating a long bureaucratic exchange of memorandums, but barely improved the situation.

· 86 ·

Memorandum from the People's Commissariat
of Health on the special settlements
3 September 1940[96]

Secret.
To the Deputy Chairman of the SNK USSR, Com. Vyshinsky.
[. . .]
1. General sanitary conditions of special settlements
Most places of accommodation for the special settlers are in the forest zones. Territories around special settlements are usually swampy. The majority of roads to the settlements are dirt roads, difficult to use during the rainy season. The accommodation of special settlers has not been secured.
Barracks made of planks, tents, and even two-level barges (in Komi

ASSR) are used as residence facilities. Settlers in the "Sosnovka" settlement, Asinovky district, Novosibirsk province, live in the open.

Barracks are highly crowded, with the living space not exceeding 1.5 square meters per person and, in some cases, no more than 0.5 square meters per person (Gorky, Molotovsk, Irkutsk provinces). Special settlers' families with children stay in the same ill-equipped facilities.

Individual beds in the barracks are a rare sight, and instead there are two-tier bunks. Settlers have only those bedsheets that belong to them. A large number of special settlers, including children, sleep on bare bunks.

The inspection conducted by the People's Commissariat of Health of the RSFSR has revealed totally unacceptable facts. In the Zelenoborsk special settlement, Vologda province, there are twelve people living in a barracks of ten square meters. There was a woman who had recently given birth, sitting on a dirty floor surrounded by her six children. Because of the cramped space, the children could not walk or sit. At the same time, 1,000 iron beds, mattresses, blankets, bedsheets, and other common articles intended for special settlers were discovered in the same settlement.

In Zharovsky special settlement, Vologda province, twenty-one people live in a room designed for eight. The windows of the barracks are broken, and the ceiling has collapsed. In the same Zarovsky special settlement, despite the cramped conditions, they stopped the construction of two barracks.

In the "Poldnevitsy" special settlement, Gorky province, special settlers are put in unacceptable conditions. The People's Commissariat of Forestry of the RSFSR and the administration of the Shartiug state timber industry enterprise have in effect derailed new construction in that settlement. The existing barracks are not winterized. Their capital repair has not been undertaken.

Water basins are rare in the barracks. Water boilers are absent (Molotov province). In most special settlements, the source of water is forest rivers. In old settlements, they take water from the mineshafts. There are no baths in [most] special settlements. The rare existing baths are in primitively equipped buildings, and their capacity is totally inadequate. Supplies of laundry soap to special settlements are poor. The settlement territory is filthy. Toilets are primitive, and refuse pits are nonexistent.

2. Food supply

Public food supply is not organized in all settlements and is available only to a limited number of special settlers, mainly families, with higher salaries. The majority of the population eat at home. In almost all settlements, the supply of products to the retail network is inadequate.

No food products have been supplied to Zelenoborsky special settlement, Vologda province, in the past two months. All food provided for the special settlers was used improperly.

In Maksakov Boom, Komi ASSR, eighteen people got mushroom poisoning (nine of them died). The only [available] product for adults and children in that section is bread.

In functioning dining halls, the food is monotonous and unwholesome: salted fish (Molotov province), noodles (Gorky province), cooked barley (Vologda province), with no fats or sugar. In some special settlements, even salt is lacking (Molotov province).

In some special settlements, they provide bread only to those able to work. When an employable family member is transferred to a work zone outside the settlement, the nonworking family is denied the opportunity to purchase products in the store.

Among special settlers, there are many invalids and elderly people.

3. Child services

Child facilities (nurseries, kindergartens) are not operating everywhere, and those that exist need to be expanded and supplied with household items and furniture. The main obstacle in the organization of nurseries is the lack of furniture and soft items.

In the nursery of Zelenoborsk special settlement, Vologda province, there are no beds for children, nor bedsheets, stools, or tables. Children sleep on the bare floor under a common sheet. At the same time, managers keep a full set of nursery equipment in the warehouse. After the People's Commissariat of Health inspection, the nursery was equipped in two days.

Food supply to the children is not functioning, and this matter requires urgent and thorough improvement, since children under fourteen form 40–70 percent of the entire special settler population. Children do not receive milk, sugar, or fats. Most children in the special settlements under review are extremely undernourished and emaciated. The nearly total absence of vitamin-rich products threatens the outbreak of scurvy.

As a result of this situation regarding the children's food supply, the death rate among the special settler children is high (in Gorky province, out of 119 special settlers who died, 40 were less than two years old).

4. Organization of labor and safety

A lack of skill in timber harvesting results in injuries and traumas to special settlers: concussions of the rib cage, traumas of extremities, etc. At the same time, special cadres are not trained in the specifics of the forestry business. As a rule, no special clothes or footwear is provided.

5. Illness and death rate

Soon after their arrival at their destination, the special settlers, lacking warm clothes and footwear, had a high rate of illness and an outbreak of spotted fever (carried from the place of their origin): sixty-six cases in Arkhangelsk province (three died), seventy-two cases in Komi ASSR (two died), four in Krasnoiarsk territory.

Owing to the unsanitary conditions in the settlements and the use of bad water, in June–July of last year there was an outbreak of enteric typhoid, in Krasnoiarsk territory—263 cases, in Gorky province—127, in Irkutsk province—24, and [there were] a large number of cases of intestinal disease in other regions where special settlers are placed.

In each case of diagnosed illness, people were hospitalized. Also, the population was given shots against enteric typhoid and dysentery, as well as smallpox shots for children (the majority of children under five were not vaccinated).

The realization of medical-sanitary procedures and their effectiveness is hampered by conditions that are out of the control of the health administration organs and require special attention. [. . .]

People's Commissar of Health of the RSFSR, Tretiakov.

The situation of Polish special settlers became particularly difficult with the advent of cold weather. In mid-October the NKVD and the People's Commissariat of Forestry prepared a memorandum for the government that stated: "Nearly 60 percent of the employable [osadniks] do not report to work as a result of lack of clothes and shoes, they cannot earn money, and their families are doomed to a hungry existence."[97] The harsh winter became a difficult trial for the osadniks. The inspections of selected special settlements in early 1941 found that they were on the verge of death.

· 87 ·

Excerpt from a report about the inspection of the Maramitsa
special settlement, Oparino district, Kirov province
[February 1941][98]

———————

[. . .]

1. The Maramitsa special settlement, Oparino district, is located in the woods, 19 kilometers away from the district center. The closest railway station is a halt on the Latvian Gorky railway (to the northeast), from which there is a connecting line going to the settlement.

2. In total, the special settlement houses 97 families; Polish families—70, Ukrainian families—27; total 550 people, including 119 men, 127 women, 50 teenagers, 129 schoolchildren, 94 preschool children, and 37 babies.

3. Special settlers work at the timber farms of the Oparino timber enterprise on contract with the department of corrective labor colonies of Arkhangelsk province.

4. The living quarters are wooden barracks with rooms that each ac-

commodate three families, with fifteen–sixteen people in two rooms, with two families in each from five people—sixty-four families, i.e., with an insufficient amount of air. On average, there are 2 square meters of space per person, with common bunks and overcrowding in most cases. The rooms are dim, the walls have darkened with time (they were whitewashed before), there are no vent sashes, and there are a lot of bedbugs. [. . .]

6. There is a simple wooden bathhouse in the settlement, capable of accommodating fifteen people an hour. The number of tubs and basins is insufficient. The bathhouse is primitive and urgently needs repairs. It is filthy, and in addition to that, moss makes its already miserable condition worse. [. . .]

Food supply.

9. Food supply, one of the most vital factors, is at a very low level. The Timber Trade Administration dining hall provides special settlers with lunches that are limited in assortment and low in calories:

Sauerkraut soup without meat—60 kopecks.

Millet or barley porridge without oil—38 kopecks.

Cabbage patties—50 kopecks. Meat dishes are very infrequent, animal or vegetable fats are insufficient, potatoes, carrots, onions and other vegetables are completely missing.

The salaries of special settlers are small, and they do not fulfill their work norms. The dining hall provides one serving of porridge for a family of eight people.

Special settlers have collected three tons of red bilberries, but the Timber Trade Administration management still cannot secure delivery (the distance is only twenty-five kilometers).

Working special settlers received only 550 grams of bread, and their dependents, 300 grams of bread, which has led to an emaciation of adults and, especially, children of all ages because of the lack of vitamins.

Children are too weak to walk across the room, to say nothing about attending school. Lack of vitamins resulted in rapid growth of hemorrhagic skin diseases—rashes, furunculosis. Children also suffer from open and latent forms of gland and pulmonary tuberculosis. There have been cases of night blindness among teenagers, rendering them unable to work.

The spirits of adults and children are depressed. To the question addressed to children of school age "Do you go to school?" they respond: "One can die illiterate."

10. On 17 February 1941 a medical exam was organized. [. . .] They examined 130 children, all of whom suffered from beriberi. Children are emaciated, all have bronchitis, and many get toxication from tuberculosis.

In early January 1941, there were cases of measles. Despite the early warning sent by the medical workers and the commandant of the settlement to the Oparino district department of health and the district NKVD administration, no timely measures were taken, and the vaccines arrived several days after children had contracted measles.

The measles were compounded by pneumonia and resulted in deaths. [. . .] Between 1 January and 15 February, there were seven deaths among babies, ten among schoolchildren, total—seventeen people. Between 25 April 1940 and 1 January 1941 thirty-eight people died of various diseases: fifty-five people total.

In the sixteen months between relocation and 1 July 1941, according to internal NKVD reports, 10,864 osadniks died: nearly 8 percent of the entire number of special settlers.[99]

Another wave of special settlers from Poland suffered a like fate. These were the refugees fleeing German troops on USSR-occupied territory who later decided to return home but were refused by German authorities. There were about 78,000–79,000 such special settlers.[100] They were sent to work primarily in the forest industry of the north and Siberia. Most of them were city dwellers—artisans, shopkeepers, specialists with higher education—and were not accustomed to hard physical labor, especially in the extreme conditions of Soviet exile. The majority of refugees were Jewish, and they were also subjected to anti-Semitic insults and discrimination by the local authorities and populations. According to the NKVD, during the eleven months of exile, 1,855 of these refugees died: 2.4 percent.[101]

· 88 ·

Excerpt from a report on the refugees in special settlements
in Novosibirsk province
7 February 1941[102]

Top secret

The movement of special-settler refugees and the location of settlements

Special-settler refugees arrived in Novosibirsk province in July 1940 for accommodation and employment at the timber industries of the People's Commissariat of Forestry USSR. [. . .]

Thus, we received, instead of 1,400 refugee families, 1,240 families with 3,800 people, and Tomasinlag, independently of us, also received 5,826 families with 18,090 people (including 1,476 individuals [who were not members of families]). Altogether, the province received 6,948 families with 21,759 people. [. . .]

The newly arriving refugees were accommodated in seventeen districts in the province, primarily in old settlements being vacated by labor settlers and local residents and in the facilities for seasonal Kuzbass workers. Tomasinlag put new arrivals in its former camp sections as prisoners were vacating them.

Because of this mass onetime arrival of a large contingent and the inadequate preparations for it, the accommodation [of the settlers] was carried out improperly, without taking into consideration the employment opportunities at the settlement sites. The accommodation at Tomasinlag was particularly poor, which resulted in mass discontent in some labor settlements and riots in individual special settlements. In particular, on 16 August 1940 about 1,500 refugees from "Taiga" special settlement (115 apartments) started a riot in reaction to the poor living conditions and food supply. They abandoned the settlement and moved, with children and belongings, to the Chulym River (twelve kilometers away from the settlement), demanding their return to the western UkSSR and BSSR [Belorussia] or to a warmer climatic zone. After arriving at the riverbank, they stuck together and for five days refused to submit to the demands of the authorities to return to the special settlement and insisted on being sent to the Ukraine. Special settlers from nearby settlements, Beregai, Kitsa, and Sibiriakov, supported the strikers, and also refused to work and demanded their [own] return to the Ukraine. The UNKVD and UITL [Administration of Corrective Labor Camps] terminated the strikes with the use of firearms and reestablished order in all settlements. Forty-five ringleaders and organizers of the riot have been arrested and prosecuted.

Considering that the living conditions at the Tomasinlag settlements remain extremely harsh, and in order to avoid similar excesses in the future, we had to ask that the GULAG unload the Tomasinlag via partial relocation of the refugees to other regions.

Following a GULAG instruction, we sent 5,001 people to Sverdlovsk province and conducted a relocation of 2,393 people within the local province. As a result, the living conditions, after appropriate renovations, have become almost normal.

Owing to a lack of free living space in other organizations, the relocation was conducted [by sending] small groups to different settlements, fifteen–fifty families to each. [. . .]

Morale and political situation.

At the time of special settlers' arrival at their places of accommodation in special settlements, they sometimes offered organized resistance, refused to stay in the provided housing, and demanded that they be returned to western Ukraine and Belorussia.

Some of them plainly demanded to be sent to Germany. Others, who were placed in particularly remote settlements in the depths of the taiga, refused to move there and demanded that they be placed in cities.

This organized resistance affected mainly Asinovsky, Teguldetsky, and

Zyriansky districts, where [settlers were] accommodated in the former camp section of the Tomasinlag NKVD. It is obvious that the special settlers fell under the counterrevolutionary influence of the prisoners who remained in the camp section at the time of the refugees' arrival.

After the NKVD conducted an investigation and arrested forty-five ringleaders and organizers of resistance, order in the special settlements was restored. Labor discipline, however, remained very low. Consequently, a series of show trials of those refusing to work were conducted, which for the most part improved labor discipline.

However, the situation regarding the fulfilling of norms is extremely bad. On average, production norms are fulfilled by no more than 60 percent, and, as a result, salaries are very low.

The morale of the overwhelming majority of special settlers is extremely low. Many of them openly declare that they will not live here and that if, by spring, the question of their transfer to cities with a more moderate climate is not resolved, and if they are not offered a job in their specialty, they (they claim) will leave the special settlements on their own, despite all the prohibitions.

The overwhelming majority of special settlers list the following as reasons for their inability to live in Siberia: a cold climate, which they supposedly cannot stand, intolerably hard work at the timber farms, not being used to physical labor, and the impossibility of finding work in their specialty, etc.

The following incident shows the mood of the special settlers. Students at the Asinsk middle school, special-settler-children Breskin and Shtulman (seventh grade), while making a "wall newspaper," substituted the portraits of Lenin and Stalin in the heading with a drawing of a passenger train. When asked why they did it, Shtulman replied: "It's a symbol of our going from the USSR to Germany, where we will have a better life." At school they call the pioneer ties [neckwear] "dog tongues."

An insignificant part of the refugees, mainly the Ukrainians and Belorussians, are in the mood to settle and obtain tools, cows, and private houses. They also perform well in production, but only a few belong to this category. [. . .]

The second deportation in 1940 was the transfer from the western parts of the Ukraine and Belorussia of the families of Polish prisoner-of-war officers, repressed Polish officials, and landowners and industrialists, as well as a small number of prostitutes. Sixty-one thousand of these people were brought to Kazakhstan in April 1940 and placed in "administrative exile," not in special settlements but in collective farms and near industrial enterprises. A detailed report from the Kazakhstan NKVD to Beria tells about the fate of these people.

· 89 ·

Memorandum on the accommodation of special settlers
from the western parts of the Ukrainian and Belorussian republics
and on operative work with them as of 15 October 1940
22 October 1940[103]

Top secret.
To the People's Commissar of Internal Affairs of the USSR,
Commissar of State Security, First Degree,
Com. L. P. Beria.
[. . .] 1. The quantity of special settlers and their accommodation
In May–April 1940, in compliance with SNK USSR Resolution no.
497-177-cc of 10 April 1940,* NKVD organs exiled to Kazakhstan
61,092 special settlers, most of whom were family members and relatives
of the former people and prostitutes repressed by the NKVD. The above
contingents have been placed in six regions of northern Kazakhstan. [. . .]
    2. Employment of special settlers
    [. . .] The majority of special settlers are placed, for the most part, in
kolkhozes and sovkhozes, and only a small part in industrial enterprises
and public organizations.
    A review of the employment situation of the special settlers showed that
the majority of them still have not been employed. As a result, most of
them have no means to support themselves.
    Specialists among the special settlers—engineers, doctors, agronomists,
metal workers, technicians, etc.—are not used in their areas of qualifica-
tion, despite the urgent need in the aforementioned specialties.
    Thus, in Kustanaisk region, there are 123 specialists among the exiles,
and only 3 of them (a metal turner and 2 electricians) are used according
to their specialty. They [currently] work rather well at the MTS [machine
tractor station].
    Some workers of the sovkhoz and the MTS made attempts to employ
the exiles in their specialty, but the chairman of the Kustanaisk regional
council, Dakhno, categorically prohibited it, saying: "We have plenty of
specialists of our own."
    A number of enterprises and the MTS of the Bulaevsk region initially
hired specialists from among the special settlers, but in August 1940 the
North Kazakhstan provincial Kazakh CP(b) [Communist Party (Bolshevik)] committee ordered that all settlers be immediately fired wherever
they worked according to their specialty. [. . .]

---

    * The resolution approving the NKVD instruction on deportations from western
Ukraine and Belorussia (GARF, f. R-5446, f. 5446, op. 1, d. 513, ll. 123–127).

Special settlers accommodated in the kolkhozes of the province have not worked for the entire summer. Those who work have not been paid for three–four months. As a result, there are cases of intumescence due to malnutrition. [. . .]

Without precise instructions on how to calculate workdays or pay for special settlers for their work, kolkhozes in different regions do it as they will. Some kolkhozes provide bread according to the number of workdays, just as to the kolkhoz members; others, only 50 percent or less; and some [kolkhozes] refrain from any payment at all until the issue is clarified. [. . .]

At a meeting of kolkhoz and rural executive committee chairmen, the secretary of the Fyodorovsky regional Kazakh CP(b), Antonov, issued a directive: "To discontinue all selling or advancing of products to Poles for their work, to give them the most difficult work, to demand the fulfillment of norms two times higher than those of the collective farmers, and to pay for the work thus accounted for two times less than to the collective farmers."

As a result of this directive, kolkhozes almost completely ceased to provide special settlers with any products, gave them the most difficult work, and rejected any (even justifiable) complaints over these issues. [. . .]

In the opinion of the directors of the sovkhozes, kolkhozes, and industrial enterprises, settlers for the most part show a good attitude toward work. Thus, in some kolkhozes of the Aktiubinsk province, in six months special settlers put out up to 500 and more workdays, while the average norm for the collective farmers is 300–350 workdays. However, lately, the majority of special settlers, not being remunerated for their labor, have been abandoning their work and conducting damaging anti-Soviet agitation. [. . .]

3. The living conditions of special settlers

No special buildings to house special settlers were built. Therefore, provincial and regional organizations were charged with accommodating them in the existing sovkhoz and kolkhoz buildings. An inspection of the settlers' accommodations revealed that the living conditions of the exiles do not meet the minimum requirements to secure a normal life. The majority of them stay in buildings unsuitable for living (cattle farms, sheds, bathhouses, etc.), without windows, doors, or even ovens.

For example, at the central farmstead of the Kustanaisk grain-producing sovkhoz, Karabalyk region, 120 exiled Poles stay in the bathhouse and other buildings unsuitable for living. About 50 people live in the aforementioned bathhouse. Highly congested [living quarters] resulted in epidemic diseases and seven deaths. [. . .]

In Golochshekin kolkhoz, the family of Anna Motyl, which consists of thirteen little children, stays in the street. Nobody lets her in. Neither she nor her children have clothes or shoes, and [there is] no food for the children. Motyl cannot work (she is sick and has a baby); her children go begging.

In Irtysh region, on 8 September, Polish settler Varvara Paniuk came to the NKVD regional department with small children and left four sons and two daughters, aged three to ten, at the RO NKVD, saying: "Take my children. They are starving, and I cannot feed them. If you refuse to take them, I will have to drown myself." After leaving the children at the RO NKVD, Paniuk left with a baby and vanished. (Her body was never found.) [. . .]

In the Charsky region, Semipalatinsk province, ten special settlers asked the NKVD regional department to take their children from them because they were unable to feed them during the winter. These special settlers have between six and nine underage children in their care. [. . .]

The situation of the special settlers who were accommodated in the kolkhoz living quarters in the *auls** is no better. There are occasions when collective farmers make settlers work in their vegetable gardens and attend to their cattle as payment for rent and food.

They charge special settlers extremely high rent—from 50 to 100 rubles per month—and require payment in clothes, luxury items, or merchandise. As soon as the landlords see that the settlers run out of items with which to pay the rent, they evict them with the help of the authorities. [. . .]

In view of the hard living conditions of the special settlers, the local population is greedy in petty ways and coerces them to sell various items for nothing in some areas. Thus, in Semipalatinsk one special-settler woman had to sell a gold watch for three poods† of potatoes, and another sold a gold watch for sixty rubles. [. . .]

There are cases where individual workers, capitalizing on the difficult situation of the special settlers, coerce women to sleep with them. [. . .]

In some locations, special settlers want to buy or build a hut, but the local soviets do not allow it. [. . .]

4. The attitude of the local party, soviet, and economic organizations toward the accommodation of the special settlers

Owing to the lack of clarity about the status of the special settlers transferred to the regions, the local economic and even party and soviet organs perceive them as "guests," who soon will either move to other locations or will all be arrested by the NKVD. This position determined the attitude of the local authorities. [. . .]

The chairman of the Mamliutinsk regional executive committee, Orlov, and the secretary of the regional party committee, Mashkov, instructed chairmen of the village soviets to use special settlers for road construction

* *Aul*—village in Central Asia (Trans.)
† Forty-eight kilograms.

without paying them for their work. This led to using some special settlers in other jobs without pay.

In Mamliutinsk and Presnovsk regions a number of landlords make the special settlers work for rent in their kolkhozes, in their homes, or in the vegetable garden, digging potatoes, providing fuel, and milking cows. Often collective-farmer housewives stay idle at home, do nothing in the household, and do not even report for the kolkhoz work. [. . .]

In the "Krasnoe Utro" kolkhoz, women special settlers were ordered to winnow grain, and accomplished three–four times the daily norm. Having seen the settlers' work, collective farmers protested, and [they] reproached the chairman for giving them easy work. Then the kolkhoz chairman made the Poles clean the threshing floor and made the collective farmers winnow the grain. It turned out that on the threshing floor the Poles yielded two times more [grain] than the collective farmers, who, at winnowing, could not fulfill a single daily norm. [. . .]

5. The situation regarding agent and operative work among special settlers

A review of agent and operative work among special settlers showed that a number of local departments have not paid serious attention to this work, as seen from the following table:*

Number of transferred special settlers—61,092
Number of informants among special settlers—579
Number of arrested special settlers—218
Number of escapees:
   Total escaped—182
   Number apprehended—134
   Number at large—48
Number of active operative cases of special settlers—17
Number of active logged cases—338

The recruitment of agents is conducted in a very primitive fashion. In some regions where special settlers are located, regional NKVD departments conduct hardly any agent and operative work among them. [. . .]

A large number of special settlers conduct broad anti-Soviet work by spreading various provocative rumors and attempt to knit together an anti-Soviet underground.

Thus, the special settler under surveillance, Vitkovsky, talking to the source "Bolislav," stated: "We have to be ready [to work] against the Soviet regime. We have to create an organization and conduct work so that, in case of a war against the Soviet Union, we will be ready to act against [the Soviet Union]. For that purpose it is essential to have a list of all Polish men."

---

* The table is simplified. Data on provinces are omitted.

The exiled former policeman, Khuba, conducts agitation among the settlers: "If we work well, the Soviet Union will get stronger, which is not in our interest. People here are dissatisfied and have a grudge against the Soviet regime. They have nothing and have seen nothing; the Soviet regime lies to the people."

Khuba hardly works himself and makes, just for necessities, 20–30 kopecks a day. When they ask him why he works so poorly, Khuba responds: "That's enough for me. I'm not going to stay here long anyway, and I will need my health in the future."

On 5 August of this year, special settlers disseminated anti-Soviet leaflets in Tavolzhan village, Lozovsky region.

Lately a connection between special settlers and the anti-Soviet elements under NKVD surveillance has been revealed. Thus, an exiled Trotskyist under NKVD surveillance, Khmelnitsky, in the very first days after the arrival of the Poles, established daily connections with them, and [now he] makes anti-Soviet statements: "Relocation of the Poles is barbaric. They ruined hundreds of families and deprived them of everything. Our Russia was and remains a barbaric country."

A freight forwarder at the Magadzhanovsk sovkhoz, Kalmynkin, came to the Poles' residence and said: "I wish I could help you to find work and apartments, but unfortunately I cannot do so in my position. All of us here live poorly." Then Kalmynkin invited the special settlers to his apartment for a heart-to-heart talk. [. . .]

People's Commissar of Internal Affairs of KSSR [Kazakhstan SSR],
Major of State Security, Babkin.
Deputy People's Commissar of Internal Affairs of KSSR,
Lieutenant of State Security, Kharitonov.

The last mass deportation from the occupied western territories was in May–June 1941 and affected approximately 87,000 people.[104]

By the standards of the Stalinist period, those deported in 1940–41 did relatively well. After the beginning of war with Germany, the Soviet and Polish governments signed a mutual assistance treaty against Germany. On 12 August 1941, Polish citizens were amnestied.[105] The majority of Polish prisoners of war, special settlers, and administrative exiles in 1940–41 were released and were granted the right to live in the USSR, except in the regimen areas, closed zones, and territories under martial law. Other victims of the prewar deportations (citizens of the Baltic states and Moldavia) remained in Soviet internal exile.

M. D. Berman

L. M. Zakovsky

V. G. Lomonosov

I. I. Pliner

Ya. D. Rapoport

N. A. Frenkel

M. P. Frinovsky

G. G. Yagoda

A. I. Uspensky

S. A. Goglidze

N. I. Yezhov

L. P. Beria

V. I. Mikhailov

Ya. M. Moroz

S. G. Firin

The Dmitlag newspaper, *Perekovka* ("Reforging"), of 20 August 1933

The newspaper *Vyshka* ("Oil Rig" or "Watchtower") of 11 August 1934, published by Oil Field no. 1, at Ukhta-Pechora camp

A camp in the Far East, late 1930s–early 1940s

The kulak exile settlement "Otrazhatel" on the Tom River, Kuznetsk, Siberia

S. Reikhenberg, *Emaciated Prisoner,* Magadan province, late 1930s–early 1940s

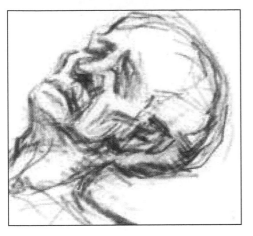

S. Reikhenberg, *Dying Prisoner*

S. Reikhenberg,
Prisoner in a Hat

S. Reikhenberg, *Two Prisoners*

I. Sukhanov, *A Barrack*, Temirtau, 1935–36

I. Sukhanov, *Camp Kitchen*,
Temirtau, 1935–36

S. Lukashov, *A Barrack on Medvezhia Mountain*, Karelia, 1936

From the album on the construction of the Soroka–Obozerskaya railway, 1940,
prepared by the construction site administration to accompany a report on work
completed

ПАРТИЯ ВЕДЕТ

From the album by the commission that inspected the Kolyma gold-mining enterprises of the Dalstroi trust, 1938

CHAPTER 7

The Victims

Contrary to expectations, Soviet archives do not contain systematic, complete, ready-to-use information on the number of those convicted and imprisoned. Now that the archives are partially open, historians can review many important documents, but elements of the new historical picture being created on the basis of these documents are still lacking. Some documents were lost (the prewar Gulag archives), while access to others is still restricted (the FSB archives). Many events were never registered and remain known only to their participants.

Documents from the archives do allow us to trace the dynamics of repression and the growth of the Gulag before World War II. These and similar materials have been reviewed by historians before, and they generated heated discussions.[1] Still, historians recognize that new archival statistics are useful for studying the development of the Stalinist Terror and the punitive organs, although answers cannot yet be provided for a number of important questions.

The Character and Scale of the Stalinist Repression

The following memorandums about repressions by the OGPU-NKVD organs, prepared after Stalin's death for the new leaders of the country, are the main source of our knowledge about the scale of repression.

Secret documents of the Khrushchev period frequently refer back to data in these reports.

· 90 ·

Memorandum on the number of those arrested and convicted
by OGPU-NKVD organs in 1930–36
11 December 1953[2]

Number Arrested

Year	Total	For counterrevolutionary crimes		For other crimes
		Total	For anti-Soviet agitation	
1930	331,544	266,679	No data	64,865
1931	479,065	343,734	100,963	135,331
1932	410,433	195,540	23,484	214,893
1933	505,256	283,029	32,370	222,227
1934	205,173	90,417	16,788	114,756
1935	193,083	108,935	43,686	84,148
1936	131,168	91,127	32,110	40,041
Total	2,255,722	1,379,461	249,401	876,261

Number Sentenced

Year	Total	To the ultimate penalty	To camps or prisons	To exile or deportation	To other punishment
1930	208,069	20,201	114,443	58,816	14,609
1931	180,696	10,651	105,683	63,269	1,093
1932	141,919	2,728	73,946	36,017	29,228
1933	239,664	2,154	138,903	54,262	44,345
1934	78,999	2,056	59,451	5,994	11,498
1935	267,076	1,229	185,846	33,601	46,400
1936	274,670	1,118	219,418	23,719	30,415
Total	1,391,093	40,137	897,690	275,678	177,588

Number Convicted By:

Year	Tribunals or courts	OGPU Collegium	Special Council	Troikas
1930	—	9,072	19,377	179,620
1931	—	13,357	14,592	152,747
1932	49,106	6,604	26,052	60,157
1933	214,334	—	25,330	—
1934	32,577	12,588	1,003	32,831
1935	118,465	—	29,452	119,159
1936	114,383	—	18,969	141,318
Total	528,865	41,621	134,775	685,832

Provisional head of the First Special Department of the MVD [Ministry of Internal Affairs] USSR,
Colonel Pavlov
11 December 1953.

· 91 ·

Memorandum on the number of those convicted by NKVD organs in 1937–38
11 December 1953[3]

Number Arrested

Year	Total	For counterrevolutionary crimes		For other crimes
		Total	For anti-Soviet agitation	
1937	936,750	779,056	234,301	157,694
1938	638,509	593,326	57,366	45,183
Total	1,575,259	1,372,382	291,667	202,877
Total in 1921–38	4,835,937	3,341,989	597,786	1,493,948

Number Sentenced

Year	Total	To the ultimate penalty	To prison terms				To exile, deportation	To other punishment
			25 years	20 years	15 years	Under 10 years		
1937	790,665	353,074	386	337	1,825	426,763	1,366	6,914
1938	554,258	328,618	1,342	1,178	3,218	199,771	16,842	3,289
Total	1,344,923	681,692	1,728	1,515	5,043	626,534	18,208	10,203
Total in 1921–38	2,944,879	745,220		1,632,106			369,874	197,679

Number Sentenced By:

Year	Military Collegium, military tribunals, or courts	Special collegium	Special Council	Troikas of the NKVD or UNKVD
1937	39,694	45,060	17,911	688,000
1938	95,057	—	45,768	413,433
Total	134,751	45,060	63,679	1,101,433
Total in 1921–38	713,301	108,740	309,131	1,813,707

Note: The "other punishment" category includes those with suspended sentences, those sentenced to corrective labor, those undergoing involuntary medical treatment, and those expelled from the country, among others.

Provisional head of the First Special Department of the MVD USSR, Colonel Pavlov.

11 December 1953.

· 92 ·

Memorandum on the number of those arrested and convicted
by NKVD organs in 1939–41
11 December 1953[4]

	Number Convicted for Counterrevolutionary Crimes	
Year	Total	Number convicted under Article 58-10
1939	63,889	24,720
1940	71,806	18,371
1941	75,411	35,116

	Punishment						
Year	The ultimate penalty	25 years	11 to 15 years	6 to 10 years	3 to 5 years	Exile, deportation	Other punishment
1939	2,552	526	883	23,723	29,534	3,783	2,888
1940	1,649	—	529	21,514	43,684	2,142	2,288
1941	8,001	—	507	40,678	23,815	1,200	1,210

	Number Sentenced By:	
Year	Military Collegium, tribunals, or courts	Special Council
1939	50,868	13,021
1940	28,894	42,912
1941	48,877	26,534

Provisional head of the First Special Department of the MVD USSR,
Colonel Pavlov.
11 December 1953.

When consulting these documents, it is important to remember the following. First, they reflect a significant part, but not the entire scope, of the Stalinist repressions. Second, we do not know the logic behind the compilation of these reports nor the nature of the sources. Even a perfunctory review shows the incompleteness of some of these figures.

The most reliable numbers are of those arrested by OGPU-NKVD organs. Such statistics refer only to those arrested by state security organs, excluding the police. Police arrests surpassed state security arrests several times over. But the police dealt primarily with less important criminal cases. Apparently, the OGPU-NKVD carefully counted those arrested, but not those convicted, in the cases it initiated and investigated. This explains the huge difference between the number of arrests and the number of convictions in Colonel Pavlov's memorandums. The authors of the 1953 report used only the materials available in a corresponding Ministry of Internal Affairs department. For 1930 and 1931, the ministry evidently had no information on those that it arrested who were convicted by the courts and tribunals, which is why only the data about the OGPU nonjudicial organs were included in the table. A similar situation existed with respect to the year 1932. For 1933, the number of those convicted by the troikas is missing, although we know that the troikas worked actively then.[5] It is also possible that the difference between the number of arrests and the number of convictions for 1933 came as a result of the 8 May 1933 directive to review cases and empty prisons (see Chapter 3).

The main obstacle to a deeper inquiry into these subjects is the lack of sources on the dynamics of repression by various punitive organs, which limits our ability to juxtapose different data. The following documents characterizing the repression in 1935 underscore the importance of such materials.

· 93 ·

Note from Vyshinsky on repressions by NKVD organs
4 February 1936[6]

Top secret.
Personal.*
To Com. V. M. Molotov.
Dear Viacheslav Mikhailovich,

One and a half year's work of the Special Council of the People's Commissariat of Internal Affairs of the USSR has shown that the majority of cases going through the Special Council can be divided into three categories: (1) cases on counterrevolutionary agitation, anti-Soviet gossip, talk, etc.; (2) cases involving speaking about terrorist plans and propositions and, in some instances, related to the initial preparation of terrorist acts; and, finally, (3) cases involving the so-called socially harmful and socially dangerous elements (repeat criminals, individuals connected to the criminal world, those with a parasitic lifestyle, etc.).

Since the Special Council reviews all cases in absentia, without summoning either the accused or the witnesses, the review of the cases (especially in the first two categories) and the passing of resolutions on them by the Special Council pose significant difficulties and are prone to mistakes.

The danger of mistakes is exacerbated by the fact that, in some instances, there are no witnesses in the cases and the cases are based on agent reports. Sometimes there is one witness, whose testimony often contradicts the testimony of the accused, who categorically deny their guilt.

However, it is in such cases that a particularly thorough and scrupulous review of the preliminary investigation is required.

In my opinion, this situation brings up the need to reduce to a minimum the review by the Special Council of the cases of counterrevolutionary agitation, counterrevolutionary terrorist conversations, etc., and to review most of these cases in the courts, where the presence and interrogation of the accused and the review of the witnesses' testimony, including confrontation, are obligatory.

The other question is the following. The Procuracy has the right, when protesting court verdicts, to free those wrongfully sentenced (article 440 of the Criminal Code of the RSFSR and similar articles of the Criminal Codes of the union republics). However, the Procuracy had no such right in the cases of those sentenced by the NKVD Special Council.

Likewise, the Procuracy is not empowered to free those under investiga-

---

* On the document, the secretary scribbled: "Com. Leplevsky took the original to give to Com. Molotov."

tion by the NKVD. When the Procuracy finds it necessary to do so, it can come up with proposals for NKVD organs, but the NKVD organs are not compelled to act on these proposals.

I think that the Procuracy should have the right to free [those arrested] when protesting the resolutions by the Special Council, as well as during the preliminary investigation.

At the same time, I would like to draw your attention to the fact that, in the past three years, the population of corrective labor camps, colonies, and prisons has grown substantially and reached 1,251,501 people as of 1 October 1935. In particular, whereas there were 268,730 prisoners in the NKVD corrective labor camps on 1 January 1932, on 1 January 1935 there were 816,800, and on 20 October 1935 [there were] 851,142.

My report does not account for prisoners in the internal prisons of the Administration of State Security of the NKVD USSR, nor those detained by police departments. The number of those detained by the police in the USSR is, on the average, 23,000 people.

Such an increase in the number of prisoners requires a series of measures to be taken that would force the investigative and procuratorial organs to review more carefully all the materials at their disposal, to prosecute citizens, and to send cases to the courts and the Special Council with more compelling evidence. At the same time, higher procuratorial organs and the courts should foster control over the quality of investigation and the justification for prosecution.

To that end, in my opinion, it is necessary to take the following judicial and administrative measures:

a. judicial: increase the role of the courts' administrative sessions, reorienting their work so as to fully guarantee the most scrupulous review of the investigative materials before approving indictments and sending cases to court (I have included concrete proposals in the draft Criminal Code of the USSR, currently reviewed by Com. Akulov's commission);

b. administrative: as a rule, send to courts the cases involving counterrevolutionary agitation and various sorts of anti-Soviet gossip and statements, which are currently reviewed by the NKVD Special Council; and

c. give the Procuracy the right to free those under NKVD investigation when the Procuracy finds no reason to keep them under arrest, and give the Procuracy the right to free those arrested by the NKVD Special Council where it protests the Special Council decisions.

In my opinion, accepting these proposals would improve the work of the NKVD and Procuracy organs in prosecuting citizens in administrative or legal form.

A. Vyshinsky.

Apparently, Vyshinsky also sent a copy of this letter to Stalin. Yagoda promptly responded with the following letter.

· 94 ·

Letter from Yagoda to Stalin and Molotov
11 February 1936[7]

Top secret.

To the Secretary of the CC VKP(b), Com. Stalin.

To the Chairman of the SNK USSR, Com. Molotov.

Regarding the 4 February memorandum from Vyshinsky:

1. Com. Vyshinsky raises the question of "the need to reduce to a minimum the review by the Special Council of the cases of counterrevolutionary agitation, counterrevolutionary terrorist conversations, etc., and to review most of these cases in the courts."

A review of the numbers of those prosecuted by GUGB organs in 1935 makes it evident that the majority of the cases investigated by GUGB organs are sent to the courts.

Thus, in 1935, throughout the entire [Soviet] Union, GUGB organs charged 293,681 people (193,083 of them were arrested).

Of all those charged:

—228,352 cases were sent to the Procuracy and the courts.

—only 33,823 cases were processed by the Special Council.

It is quite obvious that, by offering to concentrate the majority of cases in the courts, Com. Vyshinsky is trying to force open an already open door, because the vast majority of cases, as seen from the figures, are sent to the courts.

The number of cases processed by the Special Council is reflected in the convictions:

a. counterrevolutionary Trotskyites-Zinovievites—3,262 people

b. for counterrevolutionary agitation and slander, mostly in connection with Com. Kirov's murder—9,993 people

c. for terrorist intentions and counterrevolutionary slander of the party and government leaders—3,376 people

d. "former people" removed from Leningrad—5,130

e. for membership in anti-Soviet political parties, groups, etc.—3,623 people

f. currency speculators, adventurers, etc.—7,728 people

Besides the GUGB cases, local NKVD troikas and the troika of the chief police department reviewed, with the approval of the Special Council, 122,726 criminal cases of thieves, swindlers, hooligans, and repeat criminals (as part of the urban cleansing).[8]

As is evident from the above data, the Special Council, so emphasized by Com. Vyshinsky, processed only 12,000–15,000 cases of counterrevolutionary agitation, counterrevolutionary slander, and terrorist conversation—only a small part of all those charged by the GUGB.

The remaining cases fall into the categories that undoubtedly should be reviewed in administrative form ("former people" exiled from Leningrad; Trotskyists and members of other anti-Soviet parties; currency speculators, etc.).

Therefore, it is quite obvious that the Special Council cannot affect punitive policy either by the number or by the relative proportion of cases that it reviews, contrary, apparently, to what Com. Vyshinsky implies.

As to the aforementioned 15,000 cases of counterrevolutionary propaganda, slander, etc., it would be absolutely wrong to review such cases even at closed court sessions because we cannot let the courts become a podium for spreading counterrevolutionary slander against party policy or party and government leaders, which the Trotskyists would very much like, by the way.

Com. Vyshinsky justifies the need to "review most of these cases" in the courts because of the poor quality of the investigation and because of failures to confirm the accusations (lack of witnesses, etc.), but mainly because the procedure for reviewing cases by the Special Council when passing resolutions "poses significant difficulties and is prone to mistakes."

Such an approach is fundamentally wrong.

At the beginning of a case, and even during the investigation, we do not predetermine whether it goes to the court or to the Special Council. Therefore, it is impossible that the quality of the investigation is different for the cases sent to the court as opposed to those reviewed by the Special Council. In each case, the investigation is conducted according to procedural rules. In the course of investigation, the procurator fully oversees all stages of the case, from the time of arrest to the termination of the investigation. Therefore, if the procurator concludes that the case is insufficiently or poorly investigated, he issues appropriate orders in the course of the investigation, which are complied with.

Only after the investigation do we raise the question with the Procuracy about whether to send the case to the court or to the Special Council. The Procuracy sends us its written resolution.

Meanwhile, in his memorandum Com. Vyshinsky is trying to make it seem that in the cases reviewed by the Special Council the investigation is conducted in some special way. If that were the case, why did Com. Vyshinsky never protest a single resolution by the Special Council for one and a half years (a rather long period)? This is all the more surprising because the Procuracy directly participates in decision making for the cases and because Special Council resolutions cannot be implemented without the approval of the procurator of the [Soviet] Union.

Com. Vyshinsky, by bringing unsubstantiated complaints about Special

Council's review procedure, sets it apart from the review procedure in the courts. However, the Special Council was especially created to review cases in administrative form, which is different from regular court procedure.

Com. Vyshinsky formulates the question in such a form in order to question the appropriateness of the Special Council's existence, which is a wrong approach. The one and a half years of work by the Special Council has demonstrated the necessity of this organ, and the cases it has reviewed fully correspond to the idea behind its creation. As figures in this memorandum show, the NKVD consistently implements the party and government decision to transfer most cases to judicial organs. Further support is offered by the fact that some cases (711) that were given to the Special Council with approval by the Procuracy were nevertheless sent by the former to the judicial organs.

2. Com. Vyshinsky in his memorandum raises the question about the Procuracy having no right to free those under GUGB investigation or those convicted by the Special Council. This point is totally confusing.

As I have indicated, each individual under investigation is supervised by the Procuracy, from the time of arrest to the conclusion of the investigation. If the procurator considers it inappropriate to keep that person under arrest, he can come up with a proposal to free him. It is important to mention that in most cases, we have been releasing the arrested if the investigation determined their lack of association with the case.

As to those convicted by the Special Council, Com. Vyshinsky is oblivious to the fact that the role of the procurator in passing the resolution in [such] cases is different than in the courts. The procurator is not a party [to the case], as in court, but participates in the decisions in all cases reviewed by the Special Council. What prevents the Procuracy from rectifying or protesting the resolutions by the Special Council?

Apparently, either Com. Vyshinsky's proposals to grant the Procuracy the right to free someone is a pure misunderstanding, or he wants the right to free those under GUGB investigation and those convicted by the Special Council without NKVD knowledge and approval. This demand is unclear because until now, the Procuracy has never protested the existing order. Moreover, there has never been a case when the Procuracy's demand to free an individual under investigation or to reconsider a past resolution by the former OGPU or the Special Council was not complied with.

3. Judging by the total number of prisoners as of 1 January 1935 (1,251,501), Com. Vyshinsky draws the conclusion that there has been a significant growth in the number of prisoners in the camps, colonies, and prisons. The figure is correct and, by the way, was supplied by us. However, by not disclosing which organs accounted for the growth in the number of prisoners, Com. Vyshinsky failed to indicate the most important

point: of the total number of 1,251,501 prisoners, only 291,761 were convicted by the former OGPU and the Special Council over a number of years. These are the most dangerous political criminals, as well as subversives, spies, and gangsters. All the rest were sentenced by the courts.

Without comparing this figure to [the figures for] other years and without distinguishing between the arresting agencies, Com. Vyshinsky provides the following statistics to prove the increase in the number of prisoners in NKVD camps and prisons: as of 1 January 1932—268,730 people; as of 1 October 1935—816,800 people; as of 20 October 1935—851,142 people.

In 1932, however, only those convicted by the former OGPU organs were in the camps. In later years, the camps received employable prisoners convicted by the organs of NKIu. This, naturally, led to a significant growth. This is obvious from the following data:

—As of 1 January 1934, there were 215,503 prisoners convicted by the NKVD (42.2 percent of all prisoners) and 294,804 convicted by the NKIu (57.8 percent).

—As of 1 January 1935, NKVD—299,437 (41.3 percent), and NKIu—426,046 (58.7 percent).

—As of 1 October 1935, NKVD—291,761 (35.7 percent), and NKIu—525,039 (64.3 percent of all those convicted).

These figures clearly show who is accountable for the growth in the number of prisoners.

Apparently to support his conclusion about the growth in the number of prisoners, Com. Vyshinsky rather vaguely referred to the internal prisons of GUGB organs. He does not provide any figures, as if he has no access there and the internal prisons are closed to the Procuracy.

In total, as of 1 October 1935, throughout the [Soviet] Union, the GUGB organs accounted for 24,275 arrested people. Considering that 19,952 people were kept in common, pretrial jails, only 4,323 were kept in the internal prisons. It is quite obvious that the judicial organs serve as the main suppliers of prisoners.

Regarding Com. Vyshinsky's note as a whole, it is important to stress that the problem is not with the Special Council but with the judicial organs and the Procuracy. Therefore, the main task of the Procuracy today is stepping up supervision of the work of the judicial apparatus and its punitive practices, as outlined in our 14 June 1935 memorandum no. 56257 to the CC VKP(b).*

Suffice it to say that as of 1 October 1935, there were 50,992 inmates who had been in prisons and colonies for months waiting for a resolution of their appeals.

---

* This memorandum has not been found.

The number of cases under investigation that have not been reviewed by the courts grows from month to month. For example, the number of investigations in cases transferred from NKVD organs to the Procuracy and the courts alone are as follows:

as of 1 January 1935—62,149 people
as of 1 April 1935—68,885 people
as of 1 August 1935—79,860 people
as of 1 October 1935—84,190 people
and as of 1 January 1936—92,741 people.

These figures clearly demonstrate that the work of the courts is unsatisfactory. At the same time, in his memorandum Com. Vyshinsky does not offer an answer to this core question: how to improve the work of the courts.

It is certain that the main task of the Procuracy is to regularize the work of the courts and not the Special Council, which, being limited in its rights, does not play the role ascribed to it by Com. Vyshinsky.

People's Commissar of Internal Affairs, G. Yagoda.

Still, Vyshinsky continued to insist and several days later sent another letter to the supreme Soviet leaders.

· 95 ·

Letter from Vyshinsky to Stalin and Molotov
16 February 1936[9]

Top secret.
To the CC VKP(b), Com. I. V. Stalin.
To the SNK USSR, Com. V. M. Molotov.*

In connection to Com. Yagoda's 11 February letter, I have to report the following:

1. Com. Yagoda does not deny the growth in the number of prisoners in the camps, colonies, and prisons.

As I have already reported in my 4 February letter, there were 1,251,501 inmates in the prisons, camps, and colonies as of 1 October 1935, as opposed to 519,501 inmates on 1 January 1932, i.e., constituting an increase of 210.9 percent. This fact by itself is worthy of attention prior to considering who is responsible for this increase.

However, Com. Yagoda is trying to prove that this growth is due exclu-

* At the bottom of the letter, a secretary scribbled: "Com. Leplevsky personally picked up the envelope for delivery to Com. Molotov."

sively to the unsatisfactory work of the courts. He provides data on the number of cases that went through the courts and the Special Council and stresses the low number of cases that went through the Special Council.

But Com. Yagoda completely disregards the fact that the number of cases in the courts, under all conditions, directly depends on the number of cases initiated by the investigative organs, including NKVD organs. This is all the more important because the overwhelming majority of cases under investigation (90–95 percent) belong to NKVD organs (the Administration for State Security and the police), and only 5–10 percent of the cases are initiated by the organs of the Procuracy.

In reality, according to the Chief Administration for the Workers' and Peasants' Police, in 1935, throughout the entire [Soviet] Union, the Workers' and Peasants' Police initiated 2,401,412 criminal cases, and indicted 2,430,585 people, of which the police arrested 589,519.

It is particularly important that in 1935 the police on their own initiative closed 431,276 cases. About the same number of cases were closed by the Procuracy and the courts. Thus, police alone indicted over 800,000 people without probable cause in 1935. Com. Yagoda did not consider these important questions worthy of attention.

2. Com. Yagoda is against my suggestion to reduce the number of cases reviewed in administrative form by the Special Council and to refer them mainly to the courts. He justifies his opposition by the small number of cases reviewed by the Special Council (33,823).

It is hard not to notice that Com. Yagoda artificially splits those convicted by the Special Council into two categories—those convicted by the UGB (33,000) and those convicted by NKVD troikas and the Chief Directorate of police (122,000)—and consequently refers only to the cases processed by the UGB.

To characterize the role of the Special Council as an administrative court, it is essential to consider all those convicted in this form, i.e., more than 150,000 people, and not just 33,823 people. Considering also that a conviction by the Special Council usually ushers in repressions of the dependent family members of those repressed (exile from regimen regions, confiscation of passports, etc.), the role of the Special Council is undoubtedly more significant than it is portrayed by Com. Yagoda to be.

The lessening in the number of individuals [convicted by] the Special Council is evident from the statistics presented by Com. Yagoda about the "former" people removed from Leningrad. Com. Yagoda determines this figure to be 5,130. At the same time, Com. Yagoda completely ignores the family members and dependents of these "former" people, who were exiled from Leningrad together with the heads of families. In reality, the number of people exiled from Leningrad is two–three times more than the number given by Com. Yagoda. (According to the 27 March 1935 report by the Leningrad province procurator, Com. Palgov, 11,072 "former" people were removed from Leningrad, among them 4,833 heads of families and 6,239 family members.)

3. Com. Yagoda in his letter stresses that NKVD organs account for only 35.7 percent of camp prisoners. This is correct. Still, this percentage is not high enough, especially taking into consideration the fact that only a small number of cases fall under NKVD jurisdiction, compared to the broad authority and the amount of work of the courts.

The reduction in the number of those convicted by NKVD organs from 42.2 percent in 1934 to 35.7 percent as of 1 October 1935 is completely unnatural and is a result of the transfer of cases from the former OGPU Collegium to the courts (law of 10 July 1934).[10]

4. Com. Yagoda's statement that I have never protested resolutions of the Special Council over the one and a half years of its work is absolutely wrong. During this time, the Procuracy of the [Soviet] Union registered 1,344 protests with the Special Council against resolutions by the former OGPU Collegium and the Special Council itself (SPO [Secret Political Department]—369 protests, ECO [Economic Department]—644 protests, the main transport procuracy—115 protests, and 216 protests in connection with the cleansing of socially alien elements from Leningrad).

If Com. Yagoda refers to the lack of protests by the Procuracy of the [Soviet] Union with the Presidium of the TsIK USSR, that is also wrong, because the Procuracy of the [Soviet] Union filed a number of protests with the Presidium of the TsIK USSR. Most of them were terminated following petitions by the NKVD and redirected to the Special Council, where they were completely satisfied. [. . .]

5. It is also unclear why Com. Yagoda states that transferring some cases from the Special Council to the courts would convert the courts into a "tribune for disseminating counterrevolutionary slander against party policy, which the Trotskyists would very much like." Com. Yagoda is well aware that, according to the resolution of 10 July 1934, the most serious counterrevolutionary cases, including those on counterrevolutionary agitation, slander, etc., are as a rule transferred to the courts (special collegiums), which review these cases behind closed doors. If this current procedure of reviewing the most serious counterrevolutionary cases, requiring the ultimate penalty or incarceration for over five years (including the cases of Trotskyists) have not converted our courts into a tribune for disseminating counterrevolutionary slander (and he could not convert our courts into such a tribune because those are our courts), then this monstrous statement by Com. Yagoda is completely ungrounded and is dictated by considerations quite unrelated to our work.

6. Com. Yagoda believes that the issues that I raise in my 4 February note are related to my desire to eliminate the Special Council. This is an emotional reading [of it]. My note does not raise the question of liquidating the NKVD Special Council but of limiting the jurisdiction of the Spe-

cial Council as an administrative court that conducts its hearings in absentia, without witnesses, and, in some cases, only on the basis of agent reports or on the testimony of only one witness.

7. Com. Yagoda's statement that the essence of Procuracy work consists
of control over judicial organs and their punitive practice is completely erroneous. One of the most important tasks of the Procuracy, besides control over the courts, is control over NKVD organs.

As to the work of the courts, I reported about its deficiencies in a special
letter to the CC VKP(b) and the SNK USSR of 28 June 1935. The Procuracy of the USSR also reported to Com. Molotov about shortcomings in
the appeal process of the courts. At Com. Molotov's suggestion, the SNK
USSR discussed this question.

Questions of judicial control are among the most important aspects of
work for the Procuracy of the USSR. However, this by no means can jus-
tify weakening the Procuracy's control over administrative organs, including the work of the Special Council, which plays a role far greater in our
punitive policy than Com. Yagoda is trying to present.

8. Com. Yagoda apparently does not argue against my proposal to give
the Procuracy of the [Soviet] Union the right to change restraint measures
in cases investigated by NKVD organs. Com. Yagoda simply affirms that
the Procuracy actually enjoys this right. This is incorrect. The Procuracy
currently does not enjoy this right legally or in practical work. One could
mention several instances when the NKVD did not even comply with the
demands by the procurator [general] of the [Soviet] Union to free certain
individuals.

9. Com. Yagoda's remark that the Procuracy currently should concentrate mostly on improving the work of the courts is nothing more than an
attempt to remove or weaken the Procuracy's control over the cases investigated by NKVD organs, and goes against party and government directives, in particular such important directives as the ones of 8 May 1933,
10 July 1934, and 17 June 1935.[11]

A. Vyshinsky.

Comparing these two documents renders many interesting observations. Most important, Yagoda's information (Document 94) proves
that the memorandums by Colonel Pavlov (Documents 90–92) include only the cases investigated by the organs of the Main Directorate
of State Security of the NKVD. The memorandums leave out several
categories of those repressed in 1935. First are the many cases opened
by police. Vyshinsky's letter (Document 95) mentions 2,430,000 people charged with crimes by the police, of which 590,000 were arrested.
Second, Vyshinsky mentioned 5–10 percent of the total number of
cases (which was 2,700,000, if the numbers of those indicted by the

GUGB and the police are added together) as being initiated and investigated by the Procuracy. Thus, in 1935 there were about 3,000,000 active criminal cases. Of the people involved in those, at least 783,000 were under arrest at different times (590,000 by the police and 193,000 by the GUGB NKVD).

Approximately half of those indicted in 1935 were probably convicted. The 1935 report of the Supreme Court of the USSR specifies that 1,200,000 people had been convicted by the judicial organs of the union republics (excluding Uzbekistan and Tajikistan and excluding counterrevolutionary cases).[12] Considering that the statistics for the cases investigated by the NKVD included practically all those convicted for counterrevolutionary crimes, as well as those convicted by various tribunals, we arrive at 1,500,000 for the total number of convictions in the USSR for 1935. This figure matches the data provided by Vyshinsky and Yagoda. Certain factors lead us to believe that in 1936 the total number of convictions was slightly less: about 1,300,000.[13]

The aforementioned Supreme Court report and Colonel Pavlov's memorandums also outline the number of convictions in 1933 and 1934. For 1933, judicial organs of the USSR (excluding Uzbekistan and Tajikistan and excluding counterrevolutionary cases) convicted somewhat more than 2,000,000 people. Taken together with the approximately 240,000 convictions in OGPU cases (Document 90), the 1933 figure approximates 2,300,000. The similarly calculated number of convictions in 1934 would be about 1,600,000.

For 1930–32, in addition to the memorandum by Colonel Pavlov, there are data about convictions by the common courts of the RSFSR—a total of 3,400,000. According to the authors of the memorandum, this record is incomplete.[14] According to the 1937 census, the population of the RSFSR was 104,000,000 (there were 160,000,000 in the USSR as a whole). In 1933–35 the number of convictions in the USSR as a whole was about 50 percent higher than in the RSFSR.[15] If this proportion was consistent, the number for 1930–32 would be 5,000,000. The OGPU accounted for more than 530,000 people that were convicted mostly by nonjudicial organs (see Document 90). Thus, in 1930–32 at least 5,500,000 people were convicted. Considering the incomplete data, the actual number was most likely greater.

Even considering repeat convictions, it is safe to say that Soviet courts, tribunals, and nonjudicial organs convicted about 12,000,000 people altogether in 1930–36. Most of them were sentenced to corrective labor (but not imprisoned) or received suspended sentences.[16] In addition, about 2,500,000 "kulaks" and "socially harmful elements" were exiled to special settlements and labor outposts (only a small portion of them were considered part of the 12,000,000).

The number of victims of the regime who were not formally convicted but who were actually repressed is completely unknown. For example, during the famine years in the Ukraine, the so-called vagrant elements (starving peasants who roamed the country in search of food) were rounded up to form labor brigades that performed hard labor under the supervision of special commandants.[17]

In general, the number of indictments and arrests, as seen from the 1935 example, was significantly larger than the number of convictions. Likewise, not all of the kulaks ended up in special settlements: historians estimate that 2–3 million peasants sold their property and escaped from their villages before the dekulakization campaign or, as part of the "third category," were resettled within their native regions. The majority of them went to cities and to work at construction sites.[18]

The fate of the relatives of those repressed deserves special attention. According to the Yagoda and Vyshinsky letters (Documents 93–95), the reports did not include the family members of "socially alien elements" who were exiled or deported in 1935 as part of the campaign to cleanse the major cities and industrial centers.[19] The mechanism of "passportization" in large cities and regimen areas, which forced thousands of people to abandon their homes, has not been sufficiently studied. It is impossible to establish the number of relatives of "enemies of the people" who lost their jobs or were otherwise discriminated against. Also, in 1929–36 more than 1,100,000 people were expelled from the party.[20] Only a few of those who lost their party cards were actually prosecuted, but their fate was hard and often tragic.

If, according to the January 1937 census, the population of the USSR over sixteen years of age amounted to slightly over 100,000,000, then, in the early 1930s, about one-sixth of the adults in the population were subject to various repressions and persecutions. The regime considered these political and criminal convicts, exiles, "socially alien elements," expelled party members, and the rest to be potential members or supporters of a fifth column in case of war. This fear led logically to the Great Terror of 1937–38 (see Chapter 4).

For more than four decades, information about the scale of the mass punitive actions in 1937–38 has been based on NKVD data (Document 91): about 1,600,000 were arrested by state security organs (mostly on political charges) and over 680,000 were sentenced to be shot. Unlike in other periods, the origin of these figures is clear. They come from the local NKVD reports on the activities of the troikas. Researchers from the Memorial Society have studied these reports, preserved in the Federal Security Service (FSB) archive. In general, they confirmed the combined figure of 1,600,000.[21] This, however, does not prove the correctness of the reports sent to Moscow. To resolve this problem, a significant effort by many researchers would be needed, as well as full access to the statistics of the NKVD central apparatus and the primary sources on repressions in local NKVD archives. Until these data are obtainable, historians will have to regard the MVD figures on the 1937–38 terror as the minimal starting point.

Another part of the Great Terror was mass deportations. The largest was the deportation of 170,000 Koreans from the Far East in 1937.

As for the previous periods, the memorandum by Colonel Pavlov (Document 92) lists only a portion of the convictions. According to 1958 calculations by the Ministry of Justice of the USSR, in 1937–40 the courts convicted a total of 7,100,000 people, and in 1941, a total of 3,100,000 people.[22] Thus, in 1937–40 Soviet courts and nonjudicial organs convicted about 8,600,000 people. The huge increase in convictions resulted from the mass operations of 1937–38 and the 26 August 1940 decree on the violations of labor discipline and unauthorized absenteeism from work (more than 2,000,000 convictions in 1940).

Altogether, the number of convictions in 1930–40 probably approaches 20,000,000 (some of these were repeat convictions). The majority were sentenced to corrective labor (but not imprisoned) or received suspended sentences.[23] However, mild sentences were no guarantee against harsher punishment. In late 1937, for example, the Procuracy discovered in Bamlag "a large number of those sentenced by the courts to exile and corrective labor; these individuals have been kept in the camp for three and more years."[24] On the eve of the war, those sentenced to corrective labor were sent to construct projects of strategic importance along with camp prisoners (see Chapter 6). A certain number of underage prisoners stayed in the camps instead of being sent to juvenile colonies, which had a milder regimen. Further studies will undoubtedly help to expand this list and determine the number of prisoners overstaying their term in the camps.

Traditionally, historians have divided prisoners into political and

criminal categories, but this division is difficult to apply to Stalinist Soviet Union. Experienced scholars of the Soviet state and judicial system
include those convicted under the 7 August 1932 law on the theft of
public property in the category of political prisoners.[25] The Stalinist
state, aiming for a forceful solution of all social and economic problems, created—in addition to clearly political and criminal categories
of prisoners—a huge sector of convicts who are difficult to classify.
They were the victims of the regime's brutality and its terrorist nature
rather than ordinary criminals. They included millions of people—for
instance, the starving peasants who were sentenced to death or ten
years in prison for taking ears of grain from the kolkhoz fields under
the 7 August 1932 law. It is difficult to consider criminal all those millions convicted under the prewar decrees for being late to work or absent from work without leave. The same can be said for the victims of
the economic campaigns who were sentenced for a failure to fulfill the
plan. We still do not know the identities of those hundreds of thousands convicted by the troikas during the "cleansing of the cities" in
1935–36 (see Chapter 3; Documents 94–95) and during similar actions in other periods. A local official, only by taking a spontaneous
initiative, discovered that most of the victims of the Nazino tragedy
were not criminal "pauperized elements" but ordinary Soviet citizens
who happened to be apprehended during street searches or who forgot
their identification cards at home (see Chapter 2). In Russia in the
1990s, in the course of rehabilitating victims of political repression,
some of those convicted under criminal charges (for example, for
abuse of power) were recognized by the Procuracy as de facto political
prisoners.[26]

The distinctive feature of the Stalinist punitive system was the large
number of people sentenced to death. In 1930–40 at least 726,000
people were shot, most of them in 1937–38 (see Documents 90–92).
Executions, along with the high mortality rate during investigation
and en route to and within prisons and camps, reduced the ultimate
number of inmates.

As the list of victims of repression in the 1930s shows, the camp
population could expand very rapidly, but its growth was hindered by
the lack of infrastructure, the shortage of guards, and other deficits.
The inability to handle an expanded population explains the mass
shootings, the large number of people sentenced to corrective labor
and those given suspended sentences, and the attempts to create and
enlarge the network of labor settlements and explains why the camps,

colonies, and prisons did not grow as fast as the scale of the repression might suggest.

Camps, Colonies, Prisons, and Special Settlements and Their Population

Historians now have more reliable data about the size and composition of the camp population than about the general number of those repressed. Special departments within each camp were charged with keeping track of their "contingents" (the departments of accounting and distribution of prisoners and later the second departments). They sent their reports to the appropriate central department in Moscow (the department of accounting and distribution and, later, the Gulag second department). These departments provided raw data, which were aggregated into summary tables. These tables became available to researchers and have been widely used in historical literature. Unfortunately, more detailed data have been available only for the years from 1934, when the NKVD was created.

· 96 ·

Report on the number of prisoners in NKVD camps[27]

Top secret.

Year	As of 1 January	Average per Year
1930	179,000	190,000
1931	212,000	245,000
1932	268,700	271,000
1933	334,300	456,000
1934	510,307	620,000
1935	725,483	794,000
1936	839,406	836,000
1937	820,881	994,000
1938	996,367	1,313,000
1939	1,317,195	1,340,000
1940	1,344,408	1,400,000
1941	1,500,524	1,560,000

· 97 ·

Report on the movement of prisoners in NKVD camps[28]

	1934	1935	1936	1937
I. Present as of 1 January	510,307	725,483	839,406	820,881
II. Total arrived	593,702	524,328	626,069	884,811
From NKVD camps	100,389	67,265	157,355	211,486
From penitentiaries	445,187	409,663	431,442	636,749
[Captured] escapees	46,752	45,988	35,891	35,460
Other	1,347	1,412	1,381	1,116
III. Total reduction	378,526	410,405	644,594	709,325
To NKVD camps	103,002	72,190	170,484	214,607
To other penitentiaries	17,169	28,976	23,826	43,916
Freed	147,272	211,035	369,544	364,437
Died	26,295	28,328	20,595	25,376
Escaped	83,490	67,493	58,313	58,264
Other reduction	1,298	2,383	1,832	2,725
IV. Present as of 31 December	725,483	839,406	820,881	996,367

	1938	1939	1940	1941
I. Present as of 1 January	996,367	1,317,195	1,344,408	1,500,524
II. Total arrived	1,036,165	749,647	1,158,402	1,343,663
From NKVD camps	202,721	348,417	498,399	488,964
From penitentiaries	803,007	383,994	644,927	840,712
[Captured] escapees	22,679	9,838	8,839	6,528
Other	7,758	7,398	6,237	7,459
III. Total reduction	715,337	722,434	1,002,286	1,428,591
To NKVD camps	240,466	347,444	563,338	540,205
To other penitentiaries	55,790	74,882	57,213	135,537
Freed	279,966	223,622	316,825	624,276
Died	90,546	50,502	46,665	100,997
Escaped	32,033	12,333	11,813	10,592
Other reduction	16,536	13,651	6,432	16,984
IV. Present as of 31 December	1,317,195	1,344,408	1,500,524	1,415,596

These figures require explanation. Prisoners were sent from prisons and colonies to the camps according to warrants issued by the NKVD central office in Moscow, as reflected in the "from penitentiaries" row. This row generally reflects the arrival of new prisoners in the camps. The "to other penitentiaries" row indicates the prisoners sent to colonies and prisons for various reasons. It may also include the prisoners who were sentenced to death.[29] The "total arrived" and "total reduction" rows indicate the internal movements of prisoners between camps, which were also carried out on orders from Moscow.

According to this table, in 1934–40 more than 3,750,000 people went through the camps (some were the same people convicted more than once). The composition of the prisoner pool reflected the scale and the nature of the repressions.

Report on the composition of prisoners in NKVD camps by type of crime[30]

Type of Crime	As of 1 January							
	1934	1935	1936	1937	1938	1939	1940	1941
Counterrevolutionary crimes	135,190	118,256	105,849	104,826	185,324	454,432	444,999	420,293
% of entire list	26.5	16.3	12.6	12.8	18.6	34.5	33.1	28.7
Participation in a rightist-Trotskyite organization					12,260	25,026	18,822	18,749
% of entire list					1.2	1.9	1.4	1.3
High treason				433	449	1317	1344	1314
% of entire list				—	—	0.1	0.1	0.1
Terror				5746	6004	11,854	13,600	6941
% of entire list				0.7	0.6	0.9	1	0.5
Subversion				821	1642	6585	6722	3035
% of entire list				0.1	0.1	0.5	0.5	0.2
Espionage	5044	6949	7135	6567	6974	15,806	16,133	10,389
% of entire list	1.0	1.0	0.9	0.8	0.7	1.2	1.2	0.7
Wrecking							28,232	16,774
% of entire list							2.1	1.1
Leader of a counterrevolutionary organization							5377	
% of entire list							0.4	
Anti-Soviet agitation							185,528	188,427
% of entire list							13.8	12.9
Other counterrevolutionary crimes							149,229	135,732
% of entire list							11.1	9.3

Traitors' family members						13,172	13,044	12,128
% of entire list						1.0	1.0	0.8
Particularly dangerous crimes	77,546	98,068	148,323	171,236	154,437	194,945	48,398	60,676
% of entire list	15.2	13.5	17.7	20.9	15.5	14.8	3.6	4.1
Including:								
Gangsterism and brigandage	20,038	24,109	26,609	25,529	24,909	18,440	32,266	31,841
% of entire list	3.9	3.3	3.2	3.1	2.5	1.4	2.4	2.2
Other crimes violating the order	6655	23,811					186,873	257,320
% of entire list	1.3	3.3					13.9	17.6
Including:								
Hooliganism							98,142	147,393
% of entire list							7.3	10.1
Including:								
Those convicted under the 10 August 1940 decree by the Presidium of the Supreme Council of the USSR								28,180
Profiteering	6,655	8,873	8,982	9,276			32,265	36,347
% of the entire list	1.3	1.2	1.1	1.1			2.4	2.5
Violation of the law on passportization		14,938	19,642	18,798	22,916	21,075	17,477	22,522
% of the entire list		2.1	2.3	2.3	2.3	1.6	1.3	1.5
Theft of socialist property	93,284	123,913	118,860	44,409	33,876	27,661	25,544	22,441
% of the entire list	18.3	17.1	14.2	5.4	3.4	2.1	1.9	1.5
Abuse of power, economic and military crimes (Art. 193-17)	68,296	62,202	88,809	94,976	79,710	80,349	98,142	112,195

continued

As of 1 January

Type of Crime	1934	1935	1936	1937	1938	1939	1940	1941
% of the entire list	7.5	8.6	10.6	11.6	8	6.1	7.3	7.6
Personal offenses	24,124	32,404	46,419	53,603	60,778	63,225	69,902	75,517
% of the entire list	4.7	4.7	5.5	6.5	6.1	4.8	5.2	5.2
Crimes involving property	81,372	159,286	186,932	200,131	178,349	159,380	162,674	197,841
% of the entire list	15.9	21.9	22.3	24.4	17.9	12.1	12.1	13.5
Socially harmful and socially dangerous elements	40,629	79,464	96,196	103,513	160,415	285,831	254,093	171,173
% of the entire list	8	10.9	11.5	12.6	16.1	21.7	18.9	11.6
Military crimes	3,037	4,959	6,631	6,238	5,978	5,268	9,411	28,639
% of the entire list	0.6	0.7	0.8	0.7	0.6	0.4	0.7	1.9
Those arrested under Article 193-17								5,316
Those arrested under the 26 June 1940 decree by the Presidium of the Supreme Soviet of the USSR for unauthorized absenteesm from work								28,995
Other criminal offenses	10,174	23,124	21,741	23,151	114,584	25,029	44,372	49,800
% of the entire list	2	3	2.6	2.8	11.5	1.9	3.3	3.4
Without category	38,487							38,487

Report on the composition of prisoners in NKVD camps by prison term[31]

Prison Terms	As of 1 January							
	1934	1935	1936	1937	1938	1939	1940	1941
Under 1 year								
Total	121	7,656	5,120	12,888	13,949	2,897	5,377	37,761
% of the entire list		1.1	0.6	1.6	1.4	0.2	0.4	2.6
1 to under 3 years								
Total	15,627	47,289	90,991	116,975	115,578	110,644	241,993	386,851
% of the entire list	3.1	6.5	10.8	4.3	11.6	8.4	18	25.8
3 to 5 years								
Total	273,966	390,394	452,020	470,283	446,372	608,542	516,252	429,879
% of the entire list	53.7	53.9	53.8	57.3	44.5	46.2	38.4	28.6
Over 5 years to 10 years								
Total	216,744	274,473	283,972	214,496	358,691	590,112	567,340	563,814
% of the entire list	42.5	37.8	33.9	26	36	44.8	42.2	37.6
Over 10 years								
Total	3,849	5,671	7,303	6,239	5,981	5,000	13,446	6,452
% of the entire list	0.7	0.7	0.9	0.8	0.6	0.4	1	0.4
Total	510,307	725,483	839,406	820,881	996,367	1,317,195	1,344,408	1,500,524
Those sentenced to the ultimate penalty, substituted for a prison term	3,849	5,671	7,303	6,239	5,926	3,425	4,037	
% of the entire list	0.7	0.7	0.9	0.8	0.6	0.3	0.3	
Without category (those arrested without personal files)				55,796				75,767

Report on the composition of prisoners in NKVD camps by convicting organ[32]

[Number Convicted] as of 1 January

Convicting Organ	1934	1935	1936	1937	1938	1939	1940	1941
NKVD organs								
Total	215,489	299,337	282,712	253,652	496,191	782,414	732,702	566,309
% of the entire list	42.2	41.3	33.7	30.9	49.8	59.4	54.5	38.7
NKVD Special Council								
Total					36,865	109,327	126,374	120,148
% of the entire list					3.7	8.3	9.4	8.2
UNKVD special troikas								
Total						306,906	341,479	252,678
% of the entire list						23.3	25.4	17.2
Courts and tribunals								
Total	294,818	426,146	556,694	567,300	500,176	534,781	611,706	858,448
% of the entire list	57.8	58.7	66.3	69.1	50.2	40.6	45.5	58.6
Without category								38,620

Report on the composition of prisoners in NKVD camps by sex, age, and education[33]

Number as of 1 January	1934	1935	1936	1937	1938	1939	1940	1941
Total	510,307	725,483	839,406	820,881	996,367	1,317,195	1,344,408	1,500,524
Men								
Number	480,199	680,503	788,286	770,561	927,618	1,207,209	1,235,510	1,352,542
% of the entire list	94.1	93.8	93.9	93.9	93.1	91.6	91.9	92.4
Women								
Number	30,108	44,980	51,120	50,320	68,749	109,986	108,898	110,835
% of the entire list	5.9	6.2	6.1	6.1	6.9	8.4	8.1	7.6
Age group								
Under 18								
Number	6,124	9,402	6,547	5,672	12,531	15,279	7,124	66,603
% of the entire list	1.2	1.3	0.8	0.7	1.2	1.1	0.5	4.5
19 to 24								
Number	121,453	121,563	120,455	98,752	106,611	128,031	129,063	
25 to 30								
Number	133,700	174,212	377,900	385,567	441,390	486,044	467,585	563,760
% of the entire list	26.2	24	45	47	44.3	36.9	34.8	38.5
31 to 40								
Number	143,396	190,180	217,826	215,645	248,095	375,400	402,919	446,572
% of the entire list	28.1	26.2	25.9	26.3	24.9	28.5	30	30.5

continued

continued

Number as of 1 January

	1934	1935	1936	1937	1938	1939	1940	1941
41 to 50								
41 to 55								
Number	81,649	86,607	90,656	88,080	129,527	208,116	224,381	272,428
% of the entire list	16	11.9	10.8	10.7	13	15.8	16.7	18.6
51 to 60								
Over 55 to 70								
Number	22,964	21,943	24,427	24,791	46,829	82,325	93,839	74,227
% of the entire list	4.5	3.1	2.9	3	4.7	6.3	7	5.1
Over 60								
Over 70								
Number	1021	1576	1595	2374	11,384	22,000	19,497	4627
% of the entire list	0.2	0.2	0.2	0.3	1.2	1.7	1.4	
Age unknown								72,307

Education								
Higher								
Number	3572	4936	6799	8619	10,960	22,395	24,199	30,721
% of the entire list	0 7	0.7	0.8	1	1.1	1.7	1.8	2.1
Secondary								
Number	28,577	47,025	62,284	72,648	82,698	119,864	133,096	156,585
% of the entire list	5 6	6.5	7.4	8.9	8.3	9.1	9.9	10.7
Primary								
Number	199,530	316,779	388,813	404,776	500,176	661,232	666,826	758,077
% of the entire list	39 1	43.7	46.3	49.3	50.2	50.2	49.6	51.8
Semi-literate								
Number	217,390	271,830	300,675	266,704	316,844	400,744	407,355	413,122
% of the entire list	42 6	37.5	35.8	32.4	31.8	30.5	30.3	28.3
Illiterate								
Number	61,238	84,913	80,835	68,134	85,689	112,960	112,932	104,872
% of the entire list	12	11.6	9.7	8.4	8.6	8.5	8.4	7.1

Report on the composition of prisoners in NKVD camps by national minority and citizenship[34]

As of 1 January

	1934	1935	1936	1937	1938	1939	1940	1941
Russians	305,163	437,099	513,465	494,827	621,733	830,491	820,089	884,574
Ukrainians	97,468	124,737	151,261	138,318	151,447	181,905	196,283	189,146
Belorussians	23,984	39,072	40,375	39,238	49,818	44,785	49,743	52,064
Georgians			4,701	4,351	6,974	11,723	12,099	11,109
Armenians			4,365	5,089	6,975	11,064	10,755	11,302
Azerbaijanis							10,800	9,996
Kazakhs					11,956	17,123	20,166	19,185
Turkmen					4,982	9,352	9,411	9,689
Uzbeks	14,288	25,879	27,113	29,141	19,927	24,499	26,888	23,154
Tajiks					2,989	4,347	5,377	4,805
Kirgiz					2,980	2,503	2,688	2,726
Tatars					22,916	24,894	28,232	28,542
Bashkirs	2,041	3,656	3,526	3,694	3,985	4,874	5,380	5,560
Buriats						1,581	2,700	1,937
Jews	5,613	8,071	10,325	11,903	12,953	19,758	21,510	31,132
Germans					998	18,572	18,822	19,120
Poles					6,975	16,860	16,133	29,457
Finns					997	2371	2750	2614
Latvians					1,991	4,742	5,400	4,870
Lithuanians					998	1,050	1,344	1,245
Estonians					995	2,371	2,720	2,781

Romanians					160	395	270	329
Iranians							134	1107
Afghans						263	280	310
Mongols						35	70	58
Chinese					1,995	3,161	4,033	3,025
Japanese					23	50	80	119
Koreans					996	2,371	2,800	2,108
Others	61,750	86,969	84,275	94,320	60,604	76,055	67,455	148,460
Foreign citizens of:								
Afghanistan					44	132	134	106
Belgium					8	2	15	1
Bulgaria							10	50
England							5	
Hungary					5	10	14	340
Germany		32	29	20	37	922	130	218
Greece					27	395	403	865
Iran		172	102		199	658	807	606
Italy					5	15	10	8
China		677	940		1400	1733	1210	2032
Romania					35	135	90	554
USA						3	5	3
Slovakia								54
Turkey						35		39
Finland		83	141	158	99	136	120	37
France					1	4	3	1
Switzerland					3	1		5
Yugoslavia						8	10	11
Japan					200	125	50	5
Other					702	831	575	918
Without citizenship		292	229	326				35,174

The NKVD internal statistics tabulated above, while providing only general information about the prisoners and not allowing correlations between various records, nevertheless clearly show the social strata in the camps. It is easy to see that the true turning point in the development of the Gulag came with the 1937–38 mass operations. These led to a big jump in the number of political prisoners, as well as the length of their sentences. The education level in the camps became higher once managers, members of the intelligentsia, and other highly educated people were hit by the Great Terror.

Similar statistics for the colonies and prisons are not yet available. It is clear only that throughout the 1930s the number of prisoners there remained large and continued to grow. As mentioned in Chapter 3, a relatively small number of prisoners were there (under 150,000) in 1934, when the colonies were transferred from the People's Commissariat of Justice to the newly created NKVD USSR. As the scale of repression grew, the number of colony inmates grew, reaching 516,500 by 1 June 1941.[35] The colonies provided a workforce for the camps, whose prisoners performed the most important economic tasks. However, on the eve of war, the colonies became more often involved in the construction of strategic projects. The extraordinary decrees of 1940 on unauthorized absenteeism from work, as well as on petty theft and hooliganism at the workplace, spurred the growth of colony and prison populations. The number in prison increased from 350,000 to 488,000 between January 1939 and January 1941.[36]

The number of labor settlers changed little between 1932 and 1941 (1,300,000 and 930,000 people, respectively).[37] According to Gulag reports, however, these figures did not include the victims of such large-scale deportations as the Koreans in 1937 and the Poles and Germans in 1935 and 1939–40.

Information on the number of prisoners was strictly secret, and access was tightened over time. On 15 November 1939 the Gulag issued the special order "On identifying workers bearing personal responsibility for the security of information obtained about the contingents of prisoners in NKVD camps and colonies." Gulag bosses insisted on limiting "the number of bulletins on the statistics of prisoners and corrective laborers" and "stringently" accounting for information released "in order to secure safety and protect strict secrecy." A limited number of workers in the Gulag apparatus were allowed access to information on the prisoner workforce, and that was on a "need to know" basis. All of them were subject to special monitoring.[38]

NKVD bosses and the supreme leaders of the country received information about the number of prisoners on a regular basis. The OGPU-NKVD often referred to these data in their petitions to the government about camp supplies and financing. In 1934, for example, there was an active exchange of letters regarding the supply of food and clothes to the NKVD camps. These letters provide detailed information about the prisoners and the prospects of camp growth.[39] For the most part, the figures correspond to official NKVD statistics, with some exceptions. For example, the 179,000 prisoners referred to in the 1 January 1930 combined MVD statistics (Document 96) are, in earlier documents, cited in the 1 July 1930 data (excluding those being transferred between camps), which is probably more accurate.[40] In a report to Stalin on the results of economic activity in the camps in 1932, Yagoda gave the following figures: 266,000 prisoners as of 1 January 1932, and 342,000 as of 1 January 1933,[41] which differed by several thousand from the figures used in later bulletins (Document 96). The differences were probably a result of inconsistent methods of reporting, such as including or excluding prisoners en route. Such differences require attention but do not alter the general picture.

To study OGPU-NKVD statistics, it is essential to learn the rules and practices of creating reports in these organizations. This challenging and time-consuming task awaits a meticulous researcher. Still, some prewar materials in the Gulag archive allow us to make some preliminary observations. As is evident from the many orders and instructions, camp accounting was far from ideal. The most frequent violations were irregular reporting (the camps had to send reports to Moscow once or twice a month by confidential mail or telegrams) and inefficient recordkeeping—specifically, prisoner files were not kept up to date (which often resulted in prisoners overstaying their sentences or getting out early).

Materials from camp inspections reveal some of the mistakes in keeping track of prisoners. The 1 January 1939 inspection of Yagrinlag found forty-three prisoners missing, and the inspection of Arkhangelsk camp the same day found fourteen prisoners with no records.[42] In Karaganda camp, in late 1938, "some escaped prisoners were listed as present, and, conversely, some prisoners in the camp were listed as escaped."[43]

Obviously, write-ups of prisoners were intended to conceal the high mortality rate. The 28 February 1941 Gulag order "On the results of inspection in the second section of the Dzhezkazgan camp of the

NKVD USSR" noted that "184 camp prisoners who died have not been accounted for as such and are listed as present. There is no accounting for those who escaped."[44]

Although we have no information about the scale of such falsifications, they were clearly intentional and reflected the interests of the camp bosses. High mortality and escape rates could lead to harsh penalties, which encouraged the camp administrations to tweak the statistics. The Dzhezkazgan camp inspection may have revealed one such manipulation: dead prisoners were used to account for escaped prisoners, leaving a neat bottom line. At the same time, it is clear that such adjustments could not be made on a large scale. While the camp administrators were interested in making the reports look good and reduce the number of deaths and escapes (which also secured the supply of food and clothes), they were also aware that camp economic plans were based on the availability of employable prisoners. Camps could be inspected at any time. Also, Moscow kept close track of the movement of prisoners. The Gulag central office assigned and reassigned prisoners to camps and monitored the arrivals and departures of all trains with new prisoners.

All these factors ultimately balanced Gulag reporting, making it sufficiently accurate by the standards of closed Soviet statistics (as opposed to open statistics, which were more prone to falsification). At the same time, the OGPU-NKVD system of reporting itself embodied mechanisms for misrepresenting some important indices, such as the mortality rate. There is at least one reason for questioning certain reports on deaths in the camps: The information was supplied by two agencies, the sanitary departments and the accounting and distribution departments. The data of the accounting and distribution departments form the basis of the general reports on the movement of prisoners and are available starting in 1934 (Document 97). The reports of the sanitary departments are stored in other collections in the Gulag archive and provide information about the mortality rate in the early 1930s (in particular, during the 1933 famine—see Chapter 2).[45] The Gulag sanitary department did not register deaths in Sevvostlag and mostly listed deaths that occurred in camp hospitals. The Gulag bosses constantly insisted on making these reports more objective by including deaths outside hospitals, such as those that occurred at work and in the barracks and that resulted from accidents, camp gangsterism, and murders by the guards. Sanitary departments did not always comply with those instructions, however; they feared accusations of negligence and late hospitalization. These factors should be considered when using the sanitary departments' statistics on deaths in the early 1930s.

Information on deaths in Sevvostlag (Kolyma) for 1930–33 is lacking. According to Gulag statistics, 7,980 prisoners died in all the camps (4.2 percent of the entire camp population) in 1930.[46] For 1931, there are reports, compiled by the Gulag sanitary department, on the work of camp hospitals. These list 7,283 prisoners as having died in some camps in a seven-month period both inside and outside the hospitals. The department extrapolated this incomplete figure to the full year, basing the calculations on the annual average number of prisoners (251,300), which rendered a 3.6 percent death rate for all the camps. Thus, the sanitary department assumed that in 1931 slightly more than 9,000 prisoners died (excluding Kolyma).[47]

The claim of the department that its 1931 report included those who had died inside and outside the hospitals was a reaction to the Gulag bosses' demands to provide full statistics. In reality, however, the sanitary department did not follow those instructions (the vague statement "with allowance for those who died outside the hospitals" is telling). The full picture was revealed in 1932, when Gulag bosses received different figures from the sanitary departments and the accounting and distribution departments.

· 103 ·

Excerpts from circular letter no. 640178 from the GULAG of the OGPU
19 February 1933[48]

[. . .] The sanitary department has not registered all cases of death, and its figures are not consistent with URO reports. Some camps explain that this is because URO includes some late-month mortality cases in the next month's reports, whereas the sanitary department reports them for the current month. However, this explanation is not tenable in view of data for the entire year, since these factors cannot affect the final figures. The difference between sanitary department and URO data is substantial: for the Svirlag, for twelve months in 1932—1,448 and 1,562; for the Temlag—1,027 and 1,081; for the Belbaltlag, for eleven months in 1932—1,667 and 1,766, and so on, for all camps.

Considering that the sanitary department can easily account for the deaths in the hospitals, the excess deaths should be attributed to the instances outside the hospitals. [. . .]

This means that the sanitary departments are not interested in, or do not receive information about, deaths outside the hospitals. This situation is absolutely impermissible.

The deaths outside the hospitals should be strictly accounted for. On the one hand, they represent tardy hospitalization and dereliction by the medical personnel, and on the other hand, they include grave and deadly accidents. According to our instructions, we have to increase our efforts against all these, which is impossible without accurate registration and reporting by the sanitary department.

2. We have repeatedly demanded that all work accidents be registered and that reports be sent to us. Camps do not provide them. We cannot even create a summary of fatal accidents.

We have sent a form that has a special section about accidents for listing deaths in the hospitals and outside medical facilities. The camps do not follow up with this form.

I propose to:

1. investigate the reasons for the aforementioned shortcomings in reporting mortality rates in general and deadly accidents in particular.

2. make sure that the mortality statistics in the URO and sanitary department reports match. For that purpose, all instances of death must be verified by name. In case of a lack of concurrence, the sanitary department should provide explanations in the death report form.

3. regularly send descriptions (accounts) of work and work-related accidents, both deadly and less severe (avoiding, of course, the obviously petty occurrences). [. . .]

Head of the Chief Administration of the Camps of the OGPU, Berman
Sanitary Inspector, Ginzburg.

The letter refers only to the cases for which the URO figures exceeded the sanitary department's figures. However, the tables containing information from both agencies about the 1932 mortality rate in the camps, broken down by month, contained other important data. In some camps, the URO monthly figures were sometimes lower, although the totals for the year contained few or no discrepancies (except for the Central Asian camp, where the sanitary department reported 4,664 prisoner deaths, and the URO reported 4,378). This means that, at least for 1932, the URO statistics were also incomplete—a fact that is important to remember when using the 1932 mortality reports (13,197 deaths, according to the sanitary departments, and 13,267, according to the URO). Adding the missing Central Asian camp figures for July would bring the URO figure to around 14,000. In total, the death rate was about 4.8 percent of the total prisoner population (excluding Kolyma).[49]

For 1933, we only have data compiled by the sanitary department (67,297 died, or 15.2 percent of all prisoners, excluding Kolyma).[50] Documents do not suggest that the sanitary departments' reports had improved in the course of one year and more accurately registered cases of death both within and outside camp medical facilities. Considering Sevvostlag statistics and the general tendency to underreport deaths, we can guess that the known death rates in the early 1930s should be augmented.

Starting in 1934, the reports from both the sanitary departments and URO are available in the archives. The URO figures exceed the sanitary departments' figures by 1,000–1,500 for 1934–36, by 18,000 for 1938, by 22,500 for 1939, and by 12,000 for 1940. The larger URO figures included those who died in the Kolyma camp (not counted by the Gulag sanitary department) and those who died outside medical facilities (killed while trying to escape, victimized by camp gangsters, etc.).[51]

Not just camp inmates but inmates of prisons and colonies also died. That information is fragmentary, however. For 1935–40, there are reports of about 79,214 deaths in colonies and prisons.[52]

Among the underreported figures and lacunae in the archival documents are the deaths of prisoners who died while being transported to or between camps. It is unlikely that the sanitary department registered these deaths. There are reasons to believe that the URO also failed to include these figures in its reports on the movement of prisoners. Transporting the prisoners was the responsibility of convoy troops, who filled out the transfer forms. The most important forms certified the departure and arrival of prisoners, as well as deaths en route. It is also the case that many of those who died were unloaded at intermediate stations (this was registered in travel documents).[53] It is doubtful that the camp administrations accepted dead prisoners to include on their balance sheets. At any rate, among the data that the camp administrations had to report to the center about the movement and composition of prisoners was the category "acts [papers] on prisoner trains arrived."[54] To fully understand the system of reporting deaths en route would require an examination of the NKVD convoy troops' papers collected in the State Military Archive, which is currently unavailable to researchers.

We still cannot even approximately estimate the mortality rate en route. Various documents in the NKVD and the Gulag archives suggest that it was rather high, especially in the years of famine and mass repression, when many sick and exhausted people were loaded on trains.

One of the best-known cases of mass prisoner deaths during transportation is the December 1939 sinking of the steamer *Indigirka,* en route from Magadan to Vladivostok. According to official reports, there were 50 prisoners and 865 "former prisoners" (probably freed prisoners or people being sent to the settlements) on board, plus officers and guards. Of the 1,134 passengers, 741 died. More than 100 were rescued by the Japanese (the disaster occurred in the territorial waters of Japan).[55] The investigation revealed that the cause of the tragedy was an order by the deputy head of the Dalstroi administration for transportation to send people during stormy weather on a ship "uncertified for passenger transportation, inadequately prepared for it, and lacking sufficient life-saving devices."[56] It also became known that nobody had counted the passengers of the *Indigirka* and that the actual number could be larger than the official estimate.[57]

The story of the Gulag's *Titanic* became widely known because of the involvement of the Japanese in the rescue effort. Nothing is yet known about other such accidents, which does not mean they did not happen.

Another approach to studying the deaths en route is to focus on the Gulag reports on the numbers of prisoners departing and arriving in the NKVD camps. The nature of intercamp transfers supposes correspondence between these numbers. The table in Document 97 shows that in 1934–37 the difference was indeed small. A noticeable disparity in the numbers in 1938 and 1940 can be explained by a high mortality rate during relocation. This coincided with the general deterioration of conditions in the Gulag.

According to Gulag reports, then, here are the final statistics on prisoner deaths:

—in 1930–33 about 98,000 prisoners died in the camps (excluding those who died outside medical facilities, en route, and in Kolyma)

—in 1934–40 about 288,300 prisoners died (excluding those who died en route)

—in 1941 about 101,000 prisoners died (most of them died after the war with Germany broke out)[58]

Adding in the 79,214 prisoners who died in the colonies and prisons in

1935–40 and the 6,796 people who died in the colonies in early 1941 (except those en route),[59] the total official number of prisoners who died in the camps, colonies, and prisons between 1930 and early 1941 is about 500,000. Considering all the excluded categories (to be expanded as research progresses), this figure should be augmented.

An even greater number of people died in exile, mostly in kulak labor settlements. For the first two years of the mass deportations of peasants, 1930–31, we have only fragmentary evidence of the deaths of about 200,000 special settlers.[60] According to OGPU-NKVD internal accounts, 389,521 people died in kulak exile in 1932–40. This excluded those who died en route, as well as the peasants who died trying to escape (the official number of attempted escapes was a massive 600,000).[61] As mentioned in Chapter 2, there are reasons to believe that the reporting on special settlements was flawed; for example, special settlers who died could be listed as escaped.

Besides the "kulaks," a high mortality rate occurred among those exiled and deported during the "borderland cleansing" of 1935–37 (Poles, Germans, Koreans, and others), among Polish osadniks, and among refugees (see Document 24; Chapters 4 and 6).

Factors that contributed to a lowering of the death rate in the Gulag should also be taken into consideration. First, there were almost no babies or old people in the camps, colonies, and special settlements. Second, the disabled, the chronically ill, and children were regularly removed from camps and colonies (including their dispatch to the care of relatives). The departure of the most vulnerable members of the population undoubtedly improved camp mortality statistics. Although many freed prisoners died of illnesses and injuries incurred in the camps, their deaths no longer affected camp reports. It is impossible to count all such victims of the Gulag.

Conclusion

The Price of Terror

A s of 1 January 1941, there were 1,500,000 prisoners in NKVD corrective labor camps, almost 429,000 prisoners in labor colonies, and about 488,000 in prisons. In June, on the eve of the German invasion, there were about 1,500,000 people in labor and special settlements. Considering the growth in the number of prisoners in early 1941, it is possible to state that when the war started, there were about 4,000,000 people in all Gulag divisions. Another large group of people—possibly 2,000,000—were engaged in corrective labor, with a major part of their salaries being withheld by the state, and were constantly under the threat of renewed repression (for example, those sentenced for absenteeism from work could face prison if they were late to work for the second time). Many millions of Soviet citizens who were not in the Gulag on the eve of war had already been in the Gulag. Millions more had been indicted; they had not been sent to prison but had received suspended sentences or court acquittals or had had their cases closed during investigation or as the result of a campaign to empty prisons.

Exact quantifications are impossible. Considering that about 20,000,000 were convicted in 1930–41 (including repeat convictions; see Chapter 7) and about 3,000,000 were exiled and deported, it is obvious that the Stalinist regime persecuted a significant portion of the country's population in the 1930s. Even more were directly affected, of course: the relatives and families of those charged with crimes were harassed and discriminated against. According to the 1939 census, the total number of families in the USSR was 37,500,000, plus 4,000,000 single adults.[1] Thus, arrests, shootings, detentions by police and chekists, suspended sentences, and various kinds of discrimination were everyday realities for most Soviet families. As a result, the country was divided between those families who directly or indirectly suffered from repression and those who did not. The division played an important psychological role in Soviet life.

Despite strict secrecy and the significant pressure of propaganda, which distorted Soviet citizens' perception of reality, information about the NKVD prisons and camps made its way into society.[2]

· 104 ·

Circular letter no. 163 from the third department of the GULAG
of the NKVD USSR, "On strict control over the correspondence
of the ITL [corrective labor camp] prisoners"
16 August 1939[3]

Top secret.

Recently there have been cases of prisoners sending letters and various statements to their families for submission to high party and judicial organs.

Such slanderous letters are used for anti-Soviet purposes and to spread provocative rumors about the methods of investigation and conditions in the camps.

Such letters make it outside, avoiding censorship, via unescorted prisoners and free camp workers.[4]

Please take measures to prevent the sending of letters without the knowledge of the camp censors.

Investigate, via agents, the channels by which these letters get out, and, as appropriate, recruit or transfer to another camp section the individuals who collect and transport the letters out of the camp.

Report on the results of your actions.

Deputy head of the Third Department of the GULAG of the NKVD, Senior Lieutenant of State Security, Trofimov.

Most Soviet citizens clearly realized the threat of repression and adjusted their behavior accordingly. Fear of harsh punishment for minor violations was an important foundation and principle of Stalinist socialism. This fear, along with appeals to conscience (usually more effective with the younger generation), substituted, in large degree, for other social and economic regulators that were not present in the system, given the strict centralization, total nationalization, lack of private initiative, and forced destruction of traditional social institutions.

The reliance on violence to resolve daily social, economic, and political problems was the reason for the Stalinist Terror. Many theories develop the Western thesis of a "permanent purge" and its Russian parallel, a "subsystem of fear."[5] According to this point of view, a constant level of repression was vital for the Soviet regime, and it filled a wide variety of functions. It was used to maintain a grip on society, suppress the smallest manifestations of dissent and opposition, and strengthen the personal power of the supreme leader. Repressive campaigns were an effective means of influencing the group psyche, when make-believe enemies could be blamed for the failures and crimes of the ruling elite. Repression was a necessary condition of economic development, a way to replace economic stimuli with forced labor. A huge sector of the Soviet economy depended on the direct exploitation of convict labor. These observations can be elaborated on indefinitely.

It is also true that at times the Stalinist state used terror in various forms and to different degrees as a method of resolving period-specific problems. For example, in the early 1930s mass punitive actions were connected to the collectivization, extermination, and isolation of the most active and well-off segment of the peasantry. In 1937–38 terror was used to replace the old political elite with a new generation of Stalinist careerists and also to purge the country of a potential fifth column in case of war—those suspected of disloyalty and treason (see Chapter 4). All these specific goals prompted surges of terror. In other words, while the terror was at a "normal" level during normal times to sustain the normal functioning of the system, during the mass special operations it acquired the character of, in A. Nove's words, "excessive excesses."[6]

The recently available Politburo Special Files and similar NKVD documents allow researchers to trace in detail the implementation of the state terror. Orders to initiate these actions came directly from Moscow. The supreme leaders of the USSR determined the timing and order of the operations and established the quotas for arrests and executions. All the important decisions were approved by the Politburo, which also orchestrated the major trials in Moscow and elsewhere. Stalin instructed on the use of torture during interrogations. Each deviation from the determined schedule or quotas had to be approved by the Politburo or the NKVD. Archival documents fully establish Stalin's active and decisive role in making these decisions.

The absoluteness of central control does not mean that there were no local excesses—a matter of exceeding the quotas established in Moscow, committing brutal murders during interrogations, and so forth. But these "deviations" from orders were determined by the central directives themselves. Excesses were an inevitable and necessary component of terrorist actions, just as with any other planned campaigns. Moscow was well aware of local abuses, and although NKVD influence grew noticeably during the Great Terror, the central government fully controlled the situation throughout the country. The chekists' initiatives played a role in the escalation of terror, of course, but the center determined the limits of these initiatives. In not a single case did the NKVD decide on important issues without Stalin's approval.

Mass repressions started and ended on orders from above, whenever Stalin considered an action appropriate. Mass arrests, shootings, and excesses would end overnight. Yezhov, who had never played an independent role, was removed from his post and shot. The following purges of the NKVD were implemented under strict central control and taken just to the point of guaranteeing the success of the new political line, a point short of undermining the punitive system as a whole (see Chapter 5).

Available documents show that mass repressions had specific political goals: the extermination and isolation of real or imaginary opponents of the regime; the suppression of dissent; and the social unification of major regions of the country. A view of the repressions as a means to solve economic problems has also been very popular. In particular, in the context of delayed industrialization, this "type of labor mobilization . . . fitted well into the stage of extensive industrialization which lasted into the 1950s."[7] At first glance, considering the scale on which convict labor was utilized in the Soviet economy, this view appears to be logical and substantiated. It does not appear to contradict the facts proving the centralized character of terror, and it does give an explanation for the terror: it provided a workforce for the planned economy. Still, there is evidence that allows us to question this conclusion.

After receiving, in 1930, several hundred thousand prisoners and special settlers, the OGPU managed to employ them only with great difficulty (see Chapter 1). But even after all the prisoners were employed, and the OGPU-NKVD economy became hungry for more workers, mass repressions remained clearly political in nature. The best evidence for the predominance of political over economic stimuli of the repressions are the 1937–38 purges. Political goals (extermination of anti-Soviet and counterrevolutionary elements) were proclaimed in all the documents regulating mass operations, whereas the economic component (creation of new forest camps, for example) was presented only as the means to achieve the political goals. In practice, the growth in the number of prisoners as a result of the Great Terror not only failed to expand the Gulag economy but led to its stagnation and even decline. The NKVD bosses, occupied with repressions, paid little attention to economic issues. NKVD enterprises were debilitated by the arrests of their leaders, as well as by the emaciation of and high mortality rate among workers (Chapter 4).

The 1937–38 mass shootings are the most obvious evidence for the political motivation of the terror. A large portion of the hundreds of thousands of those executed were able-bodied men, many of them qualified specialists. The stated chief goal of the Great Terror was the physical extermination of enemies and not their use as a cheap labor force. In the end, the 1937–38 shootings reflected an understanding by the country's leaders of the limited capacity of the camps, prisons, colonies, and special settlements. Exceeding camp capacity led to a high mortality rate and disorganization of the entire Gulag system. After facing these problems in the early 1930s (particularly during the famine and the mass repression of 1932–33), the Stalinist leadership, in devising the plans for the great purge in 1937, sharply increased the allocation for "first category" enemies, who were to be exterminated, compared to "second category" enemies, who were to be imprisoned (see Documents 90 and 91).

The NKVD economy experienced its fastest growth shortly before the war, in 1940–41, when the repressions were conducted on a much smaller scale than in previous years. This increase in productivity was achieved by using "internal resources"—exploiting prisoners even more than before, toughening punishments for failure to fulfill plans, and streamlining camp management (see Chapter 6).

In general, the facts do not reveal a direct connection between the Great Terror (measured in absolute numbers and indictments) and OGPU-NKVD economic needs—but only in general. In some areas and periods, a connection between repressions and economic necessities might exist. First of all, this applies to the "intellectual zone" of the

Gulag, which included engineers and specialists at construction sites and in the numerous design offices that operated under chekist supervision. While we do not possess sufficient materials to research this sector of the Gulag economy in detail, some fragmentary evidence supports the theory that arrests were made on economic grounds.

In November 1930, for example, Gulag leaders wrote to the OGPU deputy chairman, Yagoda, about the lack of skilled engineers at the White Sea–Baltic Sea canal construction site: "It is possible partly to resolve the IT workforce problem for the Camp Administration as follows: The OGPU transportation department could lend to the Camp Administration, from the pool of arrested wreckers, two prominent dredging engineers (to devise a plan, make calculations, etc.), eight to ten engineers and technicians who could be used in the spring to actually perform the work, and between ten and fifteen arrested mid-level managers (dredgers). In addition, several more suitable individuals could be arrested in the course of investigation."[8] From this, it sounds as though entire design bureaus could be arrested and reorganized as special OGPU design bureaus—and extra workers could be found through more arrests—all through planned actions (see Chapter 5).

NKVD economic participation was different in different industries. It was high in nonferrous metal production. In 1940, Dalstroi produced 80 tons of gold. In 1941 the plan called for 85 tons (compare the national goal in 1936, which was 120.8 tons of gold, including 24 tons by Dalstroi).[9] In the prewar years, the NKVD took over many new enterprises and accounted for a substantial part of the national production of nickel (at the Norilsk industrial complex and Northern Nickel), cobalt, copper (Dzhezkazgan complex), and tin, molybdenum, and wolfram concentrate. The NKVD also played an important role in chromite ore extraction.[10] The use of convict labor in timber harvesting was widely practiced. On the eve of the war the NKVD provided 12–13 percent of all timber.[11]

For industry in general, convict labor was hardly irreplaceable. Gulag tree farms, though vast, were still supplementary to the enterprises of the People's Commissariat of Forestry. New forest camps were created as extensions of the punitive, rather than the economic, system. They were designed to urgently accommodate the new victims of mass repression. Many of the camps did not perform well and were soon liquidated (see Chapter 4). The number of prisoners in nonferrous metallurgy and mining was not very large. In Dalstroi's Sevvostlag in the early 1930s, there were under 50,000 prisoners. Only on the eve of war (1 January 1941) did their number reach 180,000. In the divisions of the Gulag that provided the workforce for the nonferrous metallurgy enterprises, there were just 55,000 prisoners.[12] Nor did other NKVD industrial enterprises play an important role in the industrialization of the country. A large group of prisoners worked to satisfy the needs of the Gulag itself (making clothes, footwear, and other merchandise for use in camps, camp construction, agricultural enterprises, etc.).

What was truly unique and important was the use of forced labor in capital construction. According to an early 1940 report about Gulag activities, "The role of the GULAG of the NKVD as the largest construction system in the USSR" was determined by the fact that "the GULAG manages, on basis of several orders from the CC VKP(b) and the SNK USSR, the construction of projects of exceptional economic importance."[13] A year and a half later, this statement was made even truer when the NKVD received a huge number of new construction sites to supervise (see Chapter 6). In 1940 the NKVD completed about 4.8 billion rubles' worth of construction work, and for 1941 the plan was for more than 7.5 billion rubles' worth.[14] In monetary terms, this constituted about 13–14 percent of the total capital works for that period. Furthermore, NKVD construction projects were usually considered shock work and thus were usually finished in a short time despite the harsh climate.

Undoubtedly, camps in the Stalinist economic system were the most convenient means to rapidly mobilize labor for large and remote construction projects. In many cases, it was impossible to bring in sufficient free workers. On the other hand, it is not always clear how important these projects were, built by prisoners at great sacrifice. The White Sea–Baltic Sea canal, a symbol of OGPU-NKVD construction projects in the 1930s that determined the style of development for the Stalinist Gulag, is a good case in point.

The Belomorkanal became a reality as a result of the interplay of several factors. On the one hand, Stalin and other Soviet leaders were convinced that the canal was of high strategic and economic importance. Documents justifying its construction mentioned the defense of a substantial part of the seacoast and protection of fishing areas and internal trade routes by "transferring submarines, surface torpedo ships and cruisers from the Baltic to the White Sea." On the other hand, it was planned, if war were threatened, to transport northern fishing trawlers to other seas to use them as minesweepers. The new canal facilitated connections with the outer world: "Both the Baltic and the Black seas are easy to blockade; therefore, the possibility of open access to the ocean in the north becomes exceptionally important in a time of war." The canal was also seen as an obstacle to "potential enemies with powerful navies" and as a "real threat" to Finland, a country "directly threatening our north"—the canal would force it to "review its foreign policy." Economic hopes for the canal were high: besides access to cheap hydroelectric power, after the completion of the Volga–Don canal there would be a developed transport network between the Northern Sea and the Black Sea and the potential exploitation of the riches of the Northern territory, among other possibilities.[15]

Despite such impressive future benefits, the resolution to build the canal would not have been adopted had the OGPU not possessed a large number of prisoners as a result of mass operations against the kulaks. The planned utilization of 140,000 prisoners for canal construction resolved the problem of employing the growing number of camp inmates and offered the OGPU a dazzling opportunity to engage in economic activities (see Chapter 1).

Nevertheless, the end result was much humbler than the proclaimed goals, which allows us to question the economic and military necessity of this project. The shallow depth of the canal allowed transit for only small ships and submarines. It also provided a rather poor transport route for commerce. As a result, immediately after construction was completed, discussions began about the possibility of deepening and widening it, as well as building a second line of locks. These plans were never implemented. According to a contemporary scholar, the canal "remained an expensive monument to Soviet economic mismanagement. . . . The canal's low impact on the economic development of the region soon became clear. Its strategic importance also was negligible."[16] In 1937, of all shipments moving through the canal, 69 percent were to or from the White Sea–Baltic complex (enterprises in the canal zone).[17] Thus, the canal was primarily an artery of local importance. In 1940 it was used at 44 percent of its capacity, and in 1950, only 20 percent.[18]

A student of another large OGPU-NKVD project, the Baikal–Amur railroad (BAM), comes to similarly skeptical conclusions.[19] In the 1930s more prisoners worked on the railroad than on any other OGPU-NKVD project. In early 1938 Bamlag, where they lived, housed more than 200,000 prisoners, and a few months later, several new camps were created around it.[20] Despite enormous material and human resources, the actual results were insignificant: the railroad could not be finished by the mid-1930s as planned. The sections that were put into operation meant little to the economy.

BAM and the entire railway-construction industry typified the criminality and thriftlessness of the Stalinist system of mobilizing forced labor. The simultaneous construction of many railroads without sufficient materials or financial backing created a huge stock of dead capital in the form of unfinished or useless railway lines. By 1938 the total length of unfinished railways approached 5,000 kilometers (excluding the roads that were completed, but barely used or not used at all).[21] The total growth of the operational Soviet railway system from 1933 to 1939 was 4,500 kilometers. Many kilometers of these useless or unused roads were built on the bones of prisoners.

Remarkable though the uselessness of the railroad construction was, that is not the only example of worthless Gulag projects. There were many more. In September 1940 construction on the Kuibyshev hydroelectric complex, begun in 1937, was halted.[22] This decision was prompted by the "shortage of a free workforce" for a great new construction project: the Volga–Baltic and North Dvina waterway. By that time, 126,700,000 rubles had been spent on the Kuibyshev complex,[23] and the Samara camp, which supplied labor for its construction, had 30,000 to 40,000 prisoners.[24]

There are still no in-depth studies of the scale and value of Gulag projects, and the NKVD role in building the industrial might of the country is still unknown. The examples show that it is impossible to evaluate the economic contribution of the camps in terms of capital investment. The forced-labor sector of the economy was so substantial that it encouraged the thriftlessness and mismanagement so characteristic of the Soviet economy in general. Large contingents of cheap and mobile camp labor made it easy to adapt plans for accelerated construction of huge projects without sufficient economic and technical preparation; the projects would be abandoned later with the transfer of prisoners to new sites. Suffice it to say that a large number of NKVD shock projects were financed, without previous plans or estimates, by de facto expenditures.

Naturally, OGPU-NKVD bosses tried, in their reports to the government, to stress the efficiency and importance of the Gulag economy. In May 1933 the deputy head of Dalstroi, Z. A. Almazov (later he became deputy head of the Gulag), wrote to the Sovnarkom: "To support one person at the [Kolyma gold] mines for a year, one ton of gross supplies (including construction materials) is needed; one person renders one kilogram of metal [gold] per year."[25] In a November 1935 letter to Stalin, Yagoda promised that the NKVD would build highways 50,000 rubles per kilometer cheaper on average than a civilian department (the Central Administration of Highways and Dirt Roads, which became part of the NKVD in October 1935). Yagoda justified his rate by invoking the lower cost of his administrative apparatus, as well as the higher production norms in the NKVD.[26]

The cost for extraction of gold and tin at NKVD projects was also lower. For 1939, the government established for Dalstroi an estimated cost of 6.9 rubles (compared to 5.2 rubles in the previous years) for producing one gram of gold, while the cost of gold extraction in the enterprises of the People's Commissariat of Nonferrous Metallurgy was between 15.30 and 16.70 rubles per gram. Similarly, the costs for one ton of tin produced by Dalstroi and the People's Commissariat of Nonferrous Metallurgy were 40.80 and 60.20 rubles, respectively.[27]

For leaders not concerned with morality the advantages of forced labor were indisputable. Exploitation of prisoners was a natural element of an economic system aimed at extensive growth at any cost. The "free" sector of the economy, which was ineffective and based in large part on noneconomic stimuli itself, usually could not provide a viable alternative to the NKVD economy and thus underscore its deficiencies. Enterprises using free workers were plagued by low productivity, poor work, high employee turnover, and other problems. Against this background, the mobility of prison labor and the possibility of its unlimited exploitation, including working people to death, was highly valued by the top political leaders and economic managers.

Still, even without considering the damage to morale caused by repression and the system of forced labor, there is evidence that the Gulag economy was more of a financial burden than a generator of income.

The untimely deaths of hundreds of thousands of people in the Gulag, the senseless wasting of energy and talent that could have been much more useful employed elsewhere, and the need to employ a large number of capable young people to service the punitive system decreased the productive potential of society substantially. The most glaring example is the fate of the Soviet agrarian sector. Mass extermination of the most productive "kulak" households led to a crisis of the entire agricultural complex, which resulted in the terrible famine of the early 1930s and subsequent smaller famines and permanent food crises that plagued the USSR for decades to come.

The peculiar conditions of the forced-labor economy (secretiveness, extreme working conditions, etc.) led to the widely accepted practice of inflated results and bogus reports. Stories of clever ploys to fool the system by "feeding trash" to it abound in prisoner memoirs.[28] Falsifications and exaggerations were a foundation of the forced-labor economy. Both prisoners and their wardens depended on "trash [*tufta*]" for survival, no matter how brazen were the wardens' pronouncements against lies.

· 105 ·

Order no. 50 for the construction site of the Moscow–Volga canal
and the administration of the Dmitrovsky camp
15 April 1933[29]

Camps have been adopting the use of some words from criminal jargon. Such words as *tufta, blat,** and *filon*† have become commonplace even in official letters, reports, etc.

Littering the language with criminal jargon poses a great danger, which, unfortunately, even the leaders of the construction work and the camp itself have not realized. They do not understand that incorporating the use of such words as *tufta, blat,* etc., is a result of the corresponding phenomena becoming commonplace.

Not only the chekists but also all conscientious prisoners being reeducated have to wage an all-out war against these most disgusting types of wrecking. Nonetheless, because these types of wrecking are defined by the new words, which fail to attract adequate attention, they have not been targeted for immediate eradication.

Without any doubt, the correct definition of these phenomena ("deception," "providing deliberately false information" instead of *tufta,* etc.) would draw immediate attention to them and would result in the appropriate administrative and social measures.

Prioritizing the task of fighting against deception and deliberately false information (which disrupt construction) and against bribery and abuse of power (which lead to squandering public property), I suggest that the cultural and educational department, as a high priority, wage a campaign to eliminate from the camp lexicon such words as *tufta* and *blat.*

---

* *Blat*—pull, protection, connections, illegal way of obtaining certain privileges.
† *Filon*—idler, slacker.

The reasons for this must be explained to everyone in the camps. They have to realize that by using these words, they help harbor acts of wrecking, with all the attendant consequences. High-ranking officials have to keep in mind that if such is required of ordinary camp workers, it applies to them even more so. They have to realize that it is necessary to refrain from the use of the aforementioned words in order for the corresponding phenomena to be eliminated from the camps.

For example, in the future, the unjustified difference between the daily reports on excavation work and the results of controlled measurements should be labeled as deliberately false information.

Head of construction, Kogan.

Head of the Dmitlag Administration, Radetsky.

Many key achievements of the camp economy were tufta—in essence, if not formally—because they were caused by the depredation of resources and not well-planned, well-managed work. The heads of NKVD enterprises had at their disposal huge territories for uncontrolled economic development and a docile workforce. This prompted them to shy away from creating permanent, long-term, capital-extensive projects and to concentrate instead on rapid exploitation of the richest areas. This explains the Dalstroi economic miracle of the late 1930s and the low cost of Kolyma gold. The boom did not last long, however. In 1935–38 the average gold content of the richest deposits was 19.3 to 27.0 grams per square meter of washed sand, but it was only about 7 grams in 1946–47. The quantity of extracted gold diminished accordingly.[30]

The NKVD economy, based primarily on hard physical labor, rejected technological progress. In 1939 mechanized timber removal by the People's Commissariat of Forestry (the main timber supplier) was 90 percent of total timber removal, while in the Gulag it was only 67 percent. Often NKVD enterprises were better equipped than similar enterprises of other agencies but used that potential far less. NKVD enterprises chose to resolve chronic problems, typical of the Soviet economy—the lack of qualified personnel and the poor quality of service and repairs—by the increased use of convict labor. Even NKVD official documents contain admissions that the Gulag enterprises "emphasized hard labor" and that "anti-mechanization moods prevailed there."[31]

· 106 ·

Memorandum on the use of construction machines
and equipment at NKVD sites
29 May 1940[32]

Secret.

To the Deputy Chairman of the Council of People's Commissars of the USSR, Com. Mikoyan.

As of 1 January 1940 the GULAG and the Administration of Railroad Construction sites had at their disposal 660,000,000 rubles' worth of construction equipment, which, in monetary terms, constituted 35 percent of the cost of all construction and assembly works for a full year.* This shows the high level of equipment supply to GULAG sites compared to sites of the People's Commissariat of Construction, which received 23 percent of the output.

A review by the Industrial Bank conducted in the first quarter of this year revealed huge shortcomings in the use of construction machines and equipment. A large portion of the construction machines and equipment stand idle. The use of the most important equipment is as follows: power shovels—40.6 percent; stone breakers—16.5 percent; concrete mixers—21.3 percent; tractors—11 percent; and motorized transports—11.6 percent. Shift production norms are fulfilled by no more than 60 percent.

The main reason for such poor use of construction machines and equipment is the bad organization of work at the construction sites, leading to long stoppages due to the lack of work orders, waits for repairs, delays in fuel delivery, etc. The GULAG and the Administration of Railroad Construction sites have unused construction equipment worth 91,000,000 rubles. This is the result of supplying equipment without considering the need for it.

At Volgostroi, a powerful imported excavator, "Lubec," has remained unused for more than three years and only now has been marked for sale as unnecessary equipment. A new "Dietcher" excavator remained unused for two years and is not planned to be used in the future. One section of this construction project received seven stiff-leg derricks of which only two are being occasionally used; the remaining five have remained stacked for two years. At the construction of the Moscow–Minsk highway, 112 dump trucks work for no more than two months a year and remain idle for the rest of the time. At construction work no. 203, five steam locomo-

---

* The level of mechanization was measured by the ratio of the cost of equipment to the cost of the construction work performed.

tives were used for the entire winter as stationary boilers; 39 large railroad cars, leased from the NKPS, are used as living quarters, offices, and warehouses.

While a large quantity of fixed assets remain unused, 120,000,000 rubles were used to purchase new construction machines and equipment in 1939, and in 1940 the plan is to spend 165,000,000 rubles on such construction equipment as excavators, concrete mixers, cement mixers, etc., which are plentiful at construction sites. Such unsatisfactory, and often criminal, use of construction machines and vehicles at some sites led to overspending 42,000,000 rubles on their exploitation in 1939.

Many construction sites do not have planned preventive repair or service of fixed assets, which accelerates their breakdown. Many sites also lack scheduled repairs, and the quality of capital repairs is low. [. . .] In 1939 the GULAG and the Administration of Railroad Construction allocated 112,900,000 rubles for capital repairs but used only 46,700,000 rubles, or 41.4 percent. The remaining 66.2 percent, despite the requisition, was used inappropriately.

Such an inadmissible attitude toward the repair of fixed assets can in part be explained by the oversupply of construction equipment. At many sites, expensive equipment in short supply remains outside for months and even years, without lubrication, and thus deteriorates. At construction site no. 203, winches, pumps, carts, and other equipment remain outside. A lathe for drum turning and other machines have been in the open for two years there. At construction site no. 200, a fifteen-ton derrick has been rusting outside for over two years, and there is a mobile concrete mixer with completely decayed tires.

Stripping of the equipment at construction sites occurs on a regular basis. At the Moscow–Minsk highway construction project, a large number of machines and tools have been stripped of their most valuable parts. At the central warehouse, there is a ChTZ tractor missing seven track shoes, tracks, and a dynamo; the KhTZ tractor is missing gears and its steering mechanism, etc. At construction site no. 203, locomobile no. 38 was brought from the quarry to the fleet without boiler fittings. The six fixed motors from the derricks were sent to construction sections for other purposes, and the cranes were left without motors. [. . .]

For 1940, the GULAG and the Administration of Railroad Construction sites have an assignment to sell 60,000,000 rubles' worth of unused equipment and materials. Nevertheless, despite the obvious underestimation of this task, in the first quarter of this year only 5,000,000 rubles [worth of equipment] were sold. At the five construction sites that we inspected alone, the current plan of 31,600,000 rubles [for selling excess equipment] can be increased by 13,500,000 rubles.

It is worth mentioning that the NKVD does not take the necessary mea-

sures to assure that the sites fulfill the order to sell excess construction
equipment. [. . .]

Manager of the Industrial Bank, Grossman.

Several months later, another inspection showed that, in 1940, the
situation regarding the use of equipment at NKVD construction sites
had not changed.[33] Archival materials show that there was an alternative to the Gulag camps built around large construction and mining
centers. OGPU plans from the early 1930s to replace camps gradually
with special settlements, focusing on agricultural and timber harvesting, were not completely utopian (see Document 6; Chapters 1 and 2).
On the other hand, certain factors promoted the Gulag as the supplier
of a cheap workforce for the hard physical work of construction and
mining. One was the Stalinist policy of isolating the ever-growing
number of "dangerous criminals." Another was the extreme mobilization of the Soviet economy, which became more pronounced as war
loomed nearer.

Although it is possible to argue about the effectiveness of the Gulag
economy compared to the "free" sector, the destructive social and
moral consequences of the repressions are obvious. The widespread
denunciations of the Stalinist period became a symbol of the social
devastation wreaked upon the country. Still, recent studies show that
the denunciations did not cause the Great Terror, as some believe. In
1937–38 voluntary denunciations led to only a small number of arrests. The chekists usually identified their new victims by falsifying
cases of large counterrevolutionary organizations on the basis of confessions extracted under torture.[34] Moreover, according to Sheila Fitzpatrick, the archives contain a huge number of letters and statements
in defense of those arrested, which refutes the popular theory of the
"atomized" Russian family. Apparently, family ties became stronger,
not weaker, under repression. The reason is obvious: the conviction of
a family member led to the persecution of the entire family.[35]

Of course, this does not deny the existence of widespread denunciations in Stalin's USSR. The state encouraged denunciations and supported the unmaskers. As is typical in an atmosphere of mass repression and fear, provocateurs and criminals came to the fore benefiting
from the sufferings of others. They filled the NKVD apparatus and
other state offices and rapidly advanced to higher positions. It is also
true that a certain portion of the population remained indifferent to
the terror or even supported it. When high-ranking state and party of-

ficials were arrested and shot for abuse of power, some people met the news with joy and felt that justice was being served. Most of those who took advantage of the many vacant positions to build successful careers believed that their predecessors were true enemies of the people. In part, the instinct for self-preservation contributed to these beliefs: to survive, one had to identify oneself with the Stalinist regime and not question its integrity.

The hysteria generated by mass operations against the enemies of the people led to high aggressiveness, extreme intolerance, and a strong tendency to find easy explanations of real-life problems (wrecking, criminal intent, etc.). Terror made people fear initiative; it made them play it safe or endorse complete inaction. Lack of initiative was punished much more mildly than the inevitable mistakes committed by active and involved people. The mass operations, many of which were aimed at certain nationalities, fostered xenophobia, nationalism, and anti-Semitism in a population with a predominantly Russian ethnicity, and fostered a reciprocal hatred of Russia and the Russians among other peoples of the USSR. The repercussions of this ethnic exclusiveness became evident in the late 1980s–early 1990s when the historical memory of repressions proved to be one of the strongest arguments in favor of the independence of the republics from the Soviet Union.

In the long run, the punitive organs in the Stalinist state strongly affected the development of state institutions and the formation of civil society first in the USSR and now today's Russia. Russian citizens continue to perceive the state as a hostile force, the embodiment of arbitrariness and violence. The extreme harshness of the laws generated the habit of circumventing them. Most chekists and workers at other punitive organs who committed grave crimes against humanity not only avoided punishment but made successful careers and served as examples to their followers. This corrupted the state apparatus and put the punitive organs above the law.

Ironically, spite and even hatred for the punitive organs, which were designed to secure order and uphold the law, went hand in hand with sympathy for criminals and transgressors. This tendency is closely related to the brutality of the law enforcement agents, their disregard for the law, and the mass convictions of innocent people and acquittals of real criminals. A large number of Soviet families had firsthand experience with the camps and the arbitrariness of the regimen and could make their own judgments.

The internal OGPU-NKVD documents often referred to the prisoners as the "camp population." This bureaucratic term, though cynical, reflected the reality. Indeed, the camps can be seen as settlements, both geographically and socially. The "camp population" formed a specific social stratum; its members survived the extreme conditions by creating their own laws and customs. The camps produced a specific culture, mode of living, and even language. The culture, carried by the millions of former prisoners and guards, was disseminated throughout the country and affected the entire Soviet society. It is especially evident in the remote regions that were colonized almost exclusively by convicts. Thus the Gulag spread beyond the barbed wire. Society absorbed the criminal mindset, the reliance on violence, and the prison culture. This spread of the Gulag is a real problem—as real as the monstrous price paid by millions for the establishment and expansion of Stalinism.

Brief Biographies

For more information on the people listed here, see N. V. Petrov and K. V. Skorkin, *Kto rukovodil NKVD. 1934–1941. Spravochnik* (Moscow, 1999); A. I. Kokurin and N. V. Petrov, *GULAG (Glavnoe upravlenie lagerei). 1917–1960* (Moscow, 2000); Yu. Shapoval, V. Pristaiko, and V. Zolotorev, *ChK-GPU-NKVD v Ukraini* (Kiev, 1997).

Agranov, Ya. S. (1893–1938). A party member from 1915, he was the OGPU representative for Moscow province in 1931–33 and deputy OGPU chairman in 1933–34. In 1934–37 he was first deputy people's commissar of internal affairs of the USSR. Head of the UNKVD for Saratov province in May–July 1937, he was arrested in July 1937 and shot in August 1938.

Akulov, I. A. (1888–1937). A party member from 1907, he was first deputy chairman of the OGPU from 1931, secretary of the CC of the Ukrainian Communist Party for Donbasss (the Donets coal basin) from 1932–33, procurator of the USSR between 1933 and 1935, and secretary of the TsIK of the USSR from 1935. He was arrested in July 1937 and shot in October.

Alekseev, N. N. (1893–1937). A party member from 1919, he was the OGPU plenipotentiary representative for the Central Black Soil region from 1930 and for Western Siberia from 1932. He was assistant to the head of the Gulag in 1935 and deputy head of the Volga camp from 1935. He was arrested in June 1937 and shot in December.

Almazov, Z. A. (1898–1940). A party member from 1919, he was assistant to the head of construction of the Vishersky pulp and paper factory of the OGPU in 1931. From 1932 he was assistant to the director of the Dalstroi trust, and from 1933, assistant to the head of the Gulag. In 1935 he became head of the White Sea–Baltic Sea industrial complex, and in 1936, head of the White Sea–Baltic Sea camp. In 1938–39 he was head of the Usolsk and Ust-Borovsky camps. He was arrested in April 1939 and shot in January 1940.

Andreev, A. A. (1895–1971). A party member from 1914 and a Politburo member from 1932 to 1952, he was chairman of the CCC and people's commissar of the RKI from 1930 to 1931, people's commissar of communications from 1931 to 1935, and secretary of the CC VKP(b) and chairman of the CPC from 1935.

Antipov, N. K. (1894–1938). A party member from 1912, he was people's commissar of mail and telegraph from 1928, deputy people's commissar of the RKI in 1931, deputy chairman of the Soviet Control Commission of the SNK from 1934, and commission chairman from 1935. He was shot in 1938.

Austrin, R. I. (1891–1937). A party member from 1907, he was the OGPU plenipotentiary representative in the Northern territory (Arkhangelsk) from 1929; he became head of the UNKVD for this region in 1934. He was the UNKVD head for Kirov province in 1937 until he was shot in November.

Babkin, A. N. (1906–1950). A member of the VKP(b) from 1928, between 1939 and 1940 he was head of the UNKVD for Tula province, and from 1940 he was people's commissar of internal affairs and people's commissar of state security of the Kazakh SSR.

Belonogov, S. F. (1895–1942). A party member from 1919, he was assistant to the chairman and chairman of the administrative and inspections department of the Administration of Camps of the OGPU. From January 1932 he occupied various important positions in the police. He was arrested in November 1939 and sentenced to eight years in September 1941. He died in a camp in December 1942.

Beria, L. P. (1899–1953). A party member from 1917, he was a candidate Politburo member in 1939–46 and a member of the Politburo in 1946–53. Between 1931 and 1938 he was first secretary of the CC of the Georgian Bolshevik party and of the Trans-Caucasian territorial committee of the VKP(b). He was deputy people's commissar and people's commissar of internal affairs from 1938. He was arrested in July 1953 and shot in December.

Berman, M. D. (1898–1939). A party member from 1917, he became deputy head of the Gulag in 1931, then head in June 1932. From August 1937 he was people's commissar of communications. He was arrested in December 1938 and shot in March 1939.

Berzin, E. P. (1893–1938). A party member from 1918, he became head of construction of the Vishersky pulp and paper factory of the OGPU. He was director of the Dalstroi trust from November 1931. He was arrested in December 1937 and shot in August 1938.

Bochkov, V. M. (1900–1981). A party member from 1919, he served with the border troops in 1922–35. In 1938–40 he was head of the Chief Administration of Prisons and head of department of the GUGB NKVD. He was procurator of the USSR between 1940 and 1943.

Bokyi, G. I. (1879–1937). A party member from 1900, he was head of the special department of the VChK-GPU-OGPU in 1921–34 and head of the GUGB NKVD in 1934–37. He was arrested in May 1937 and shot in November.

Bukharin, N. I. (1888–1938). A party member from 1906, he was a member of the party Politburo in 1924–29 and one of the leaders of the so-called right deviation. In 1929 he was removed from the Politburo and made head of sector at the VSNKh. He was arrested in February 1937 and shot in March 1938.

Bulakh, P. F. (1898–1938). A member of the VKP(b) from 1931, he occupied various positions in OGPU special departments between 1923 and 1936. In 1937–38 he was head of the UNKVD for Ordzhonikidze territory. He was arrested in April 1938 and shot in July.

Chalov, A. A. (1898–?). A VKP(b) member from 1928, he was head of the Gulag sanitary department between February 1938 and May 1940.

Chernyshev, V. V. (1896–1952). A party member from 1917, he was deputy people's commissar of internal affairs and head of the GURKM from 1937; head of the Gulag from 1939; then deputy people's commissar of internal affairs until 1952.

Chugunikhin, F. R. (1891–?). A party member from 1917, he worked in NKVD organs from 1937. He was head of section of the Gulag planning department. In the 1940s he worked in the financial departments of MVD economic ventures.

Dibobas, A. S. (1896–?). Though not a party member, he came to work in the Cheka in 1919. In the 1930s he was deputy head of Gulag inspection. He was fired from the NKVD in 1939.

Eikhe, R. I. (1890–1940). A party member from 1905, he was first secretary of Siberian and Western Siberian territorial VKP(b) committees. Between 1937 and 1938 he was people's commissar of agriculture. He was arrested in April 1938 and shot in February 1940.

Eikhmans, F. I. (1897–1938). A party member from 1918, he worked in Cheka organs. He was head of administration of the Solovki camp from 1923; head of the ULAG OGPU in 1930; and deputy head of the

OGPU-GUGB-NKVD special department from 1931. He was arrested in July 1937 and shot in September 1938.

Firin, S. G. (1898–1937). A party member from 1918, he was, from 1932, assistant to and, from 1933, deputy head of the Gulag. He was head of the Dmitrovsky camp from September 1933. He was arrested in May 1937 and shot in August.

Frenkel, N. A. (1883–1960). Sentenced to ten years for embezzlement in 1923, he was released in 1927, and his conviction was canceled in 1932. He was head of the production department of the Solovetsky camp directorate, 1927–29; head of the Gulag production department, 1930–31; assistant head of the White Sea–Baltic Sea canal construction, 1931–33; head of construction of the BAM and the BAM camp, 1933–38; and head of the Chief Administration of Camps for Railway Construction of the NKVD-MVD, 1940–47.

Frinovsky, M. P. (1898–1940). A party member from 1918, he worked in Cheka organs from 1919. He was chairman of the GPU of Azerbaijan, 1930–33; head of the chief directorate of OGPU–NKVD border defense and internal troops, 1933–37; deputy people's commissar and first deputy people's commissar of internal affairs, 1936–38; and people's commissar of the navy, 1938–39. He was arrested in April 1939 and shot in February 1940.

Garanin, S. N. (1898–?). A party member from 1919, he was head of the Northeastern camp between December 1937 and September 1938. He was arrested in October 1938 and sentenced to eight years in prison in 1940.

Gertsovsky, A. Ya. (1904–?). A VKP(b) member from 1939, he worked in Cheka organs from 1920. In the late 1930s he was deputy head of the NKVD special department. He was arrested in 1953.

Goglidze, S. A. (1901–53). A party member from 1919, he was people's commissar of internal affairs of the Trans-Caucasian Federation, head of the UNKVD, and people's commissar of internal affairs of Georgia in 1934–38 and head of the UNKVD for the Leningrad province between 1938 and 1941. In the 1940s–50s he worked in the MGB-MVD. He was arrested in July and shot in December 1953.

Gorbach, G. F. (1898–1939). A party member from 1916, from the early 1920s until 1937 he worked in OGPU–NKVD organs in the Northern Caucasus. In April 1937 he became deputy head of the UNKVD for the Western Siberian territory. From July 1937 he was head of the UNKVD for Omsk province; from August 1937, head of the UNKVD of the Western Siberian territory; from October 1937, head of the UNKVD for Novosibirsk province; and from June 1938, head of the UNKVD for the Far Eastern territory and the Khabarovsk territory. He was arrested in November 1938 and shot in March 1939.

Gorianov, A. G. (1898–1937). Party member from 1920. From 1929 he worked in the economic department of the Gulag of the OGPU. In 1931 he became head of the central design office at Factory No. 39. From 1934 he was head of the forest guard department of the NKVD USSR, and from 1935 he was head of the Chief Administration of State Surveys and Cartography of the NKVD. He was arrested in July 1937 and shot in October.

Gorlinsky, N. D. (1907–64). He worked in Cheka organs from 1920. In the 1930s he was in GPU-NKVD organs in the Ukraine. In 1938 he worked in the central apparatus of the GUGB NKVD USSR. In 1939–40 he was deputy people's commissar of internal affairs of the Ukraine. In the 1940s–50s he headed various regional state security organs. From March 1953 he was head of directorate of the MVD USSR. He was fired in 1954.

Gorshkov, A. A. (1895–?). A party member from 1917, he worked in the economic directorate of the Gulag of the OGPU. He was head of the Kazakhstan camp in 1930–32 and head of the Siberian camp in 1932–34. From 1935 he was deputy head of the Dmitrovsky camp.

Granovsky, G. M. (1901–?). A member of the VKP(b) from 1938, he was representative and head of department of the Vinnitsa GPU administration of the Ukraine from 1933. In 1938 he became head of the accounting and distribution department of the Gulag.

Griadinsky, F. P. (1893–1938). A party member from 1912, in 1930–37 he was chairman of the Western Siberian territorial executive committee. He was arrested in September 1937 and shot in February 1938.

Grossman, V. Ya. (1895–?). A party member from 1917, he was general manager of the Industrial Bank of the USSR from 1937.

Ivanov, I. V. (1902–76). A member of the VKP(b) from 1926, he was a party worker in 1934–38 and head of the UNKVD for Sverdlovsk province in 1939–40.

Kaganovich, L. M. (1893–1991). A party member from 1911, he was a member of the Politburo in 1930–57. In 1928–39 he was secretary of the Central Committee, first secretary of the Moscow VKP(b) committee, chairman of the Party Control Commission, and people's commissar of communications.

Kalinin, M. I. (1875–1946). A party member from 1898, he was a member of the Politburo in 1926–46. He was chairman of the VTsIK and TsIK of the USSR from 1919 to 1938 and chairman of the Presidium of the Supreme Soviet of the USSR from 1938.

Kamenev, L. B. (1883–1936). A party member from 1901, he was a member of the Politburo in 1919–25. As one of the leaders of the opposition, he was often persecuted. He was sentenced to death at the August 1936 trial of the "anti-Soviet united Trotskyite-Zinovievite center."

Kharitonov, F. P. (1907–?). A party member from 1930, in 1937–40 he worked in the central apparatus of the GUGB NKVD USSR. He became deputy people's commissar of internal affairs of Kazakhstan in October 1940; people's commissar in February 1941; and deputy people's commissar again from August 1941. Between 1943 and 1960 he occupied important positions in the MVD and the KGB.

Khrushchev, N. S. (1894–1971). A party member from 1918, he was a candidate member of the Politburo from 1938 to 1939 and a full member from 1939 to 1964. He conducted party and executive work in the Ukraine from 1921, party work in Moscow from 1931. In 1935–38 he was first secretary of the Moscow city and provincial committees of the VKP(b); in 1938–47, first secretary of the CC of the Communist Party of the Ukraine.

Kirov, S. M. (1886–1934). A party member from 1904, he was a member of the Politburo from 1930. In 1926 he became first secretary of the Leningrad provincial and city VKP(b) committees. He was assassinated on 1 December 1934.

Kiselev, N. M. (1912–43). Member of the VKP(b) from 1931. Between 1932 and 1936 he conducted Komsomol work. In 1937–38 he worked at the central NKVD archive. From September 1938 he worked at the GUGB NKVD USSR. In 1939–40 he was head of the UNKVD for Saratov province.

Kobulov, A. Z. (1906–54). A member of the VKP(b) from 1932, he worked in the GPU-NKVD of Georgia in 1927–38. In 1938–39 he was first deputy people's commissar of internal affairs of the Ukraine. In the 1940s–50s he occupied important positions in the NKVD-MVD. He was arrested in June 1953 and shot in October 1954.

Kogan, L. I. (1889–1939). A party member from 1918, he was head of the Gulag and head of construction of the White Sea–Baltic Sea canal in 1930–32. In 1932–36 he headed construction of the Moscow–Volga canal. From August 1936 he was deputy people's commissar of forestry. In December 1938 he was arrested, and in May 1939, shot.

Kolesnichenko, V. A. Head of section of the Gulag political department from 1937, he was deputy head of the Southeastern camp from May 1938. He was fired in January 1939, probably after being arrested.

Konradov, M. V. (1898–?). A member of the VKP(b) from 1930, he worked in OGPU organs from 1924. In the 1930s he was head of the Gulag labor settlements department. In 1954 he retired from the MVD on account of poor health.

Krasikov, P. A. (1870–1939). A party member from 1892, he was deputy chairman of the Supreme Court of the USSR from 1933.

Kruglov, S. N. (1907–77). A member of the VKP(b) from 1928, he conducted party work between 1931 and 1938. In 1938–39 he was the

NKVD special representative; in 1939–41, deputy people's commissar of internal affairs for personnel and first deputy people's commissar; and in 1945–53, people's commissar and minister of internal affairs.

Krylenko, N. V. (1885–1938). A party member from 1904, he was people's commissar of justice of the RSFSR from 1931 and people's commissar of justice of the USSR from 1936. He was arrested in February 1938 and shot in July.

Kuibyshev, V. V. (1888–1935). A party member from 1904, he was member of the Politburo in 1927–35. He was chairman of the VSNKh from 1926, chairman of the State Planning Committee (Gosplan) and deputy SNK and STO chairman from 1930, and first deputy chairman of the SNK and STO and chairman of the Soviet Control Commission of the SNK USSR from 1934.

Lagunov, N. M. (1905–?). A VKP(b) member from 1927, he was deputy head and head of the UNKVD for Leningrad province in 1939–41. In the 1940s he occupied high positions in the MGB-MVD. He was dismissed in November 1951.

Levin, N. P. (1905–?). A non-party member, he was an economist with the Gulag planning group in 1932–35 and worked in the Gulag's accounting and distribution department in 1935–38. In 1938–40 he was deputy head, and in 1940–47 head, of the Gulag archival department. He was dismissed in 1950 on account of poor health.

Lomonosov, V. G. (1896–1939). A party member from 1919, he worked in the VChK from 1921. Between 1935 and 1938 he was head of the UNKVD and people's commissar of internal affairs of the Dagestan ASSR. He was arrested in December 1938 and shot in September 1939.

Mamulov, S. S. (1902–76). A party member from 1921, he conducted party work in Georgia between 1925 and 1938. He was deputy head of the NKVD secretariat, 1939–46, and deputy minister of internal affairs of the USSR, 1946–53. He was arrested in June 1953 and stayed in prison from 1954 to 1968.

Menzhinsky, V. R. (1874–1934). A party member from 1902, he headed the OGPU from 1926 to 1934.

Merkulov, V. N. (1895–1953). A party member from 1925, he worked in Cheka-OGPU organs in Georgia in 1931–38. He was deputy head of the GUGB NKVD USSR, 1938–41; people's commissar and minister of state security, 1943–46; and minister of state control, 1950–53. He was arrested in September 1953 and shot in December.

Messing, S. A. (1890–1937). A party member from 1908, he worked in the Cheka from 1918. He was head of the OGPU foreign department and deputy OGPU chairman in 1929–31. He was fired in 1931, arrested in 1937, and shot that September.

Mikhailov, V. I. (1901–40). A party member from 1919, he worked in the

GPU from 1922. In 1936–37 he was head of the NKVD department in Tula city. From September 1937 he was people's commissar of internal affairs of the Tatar ASSR. He was arrested in January 1939 and shot in February 1940.

Mikoyan, A. I. (1895–1978). A party member from 1915, he was a member of the Politburo in 1935–66. He was people's commissar of supplies, 1930–34, and people's commissar of the food industry, 1934–38.

Molotov, V. M. (1890–1986). A party member from 1906, he was member of the Politburo in 1925–57. He was secretary of the VKP(b) Central Committee, 1921–30, and chairman of the SNK USSR, 1930–41.

Monakov, S. F. (1897–1939). A party member from 1919, he worked in the Cheka from 1921. From January 1938 he was people's commissar of internal affairs of Turkmen SSR. He was arrested in September 1938 and shot in February 1939.

Moroz, Ya. M. (1898–1940). He worked in the GPU of Azerbaijan from 1927. In 1929 he was sentenced to prison for illegally executing a prisoner. A prisoner himself, he headed the OGPU expedition to Ukhta and Pechora. From 1931 he was head of the Ukhta-Pechora camp. In September 1931 he was reinstated as a party member. He was arrested in August 1938 and later shot.

Nasedkin, V.·G. (1905–50). A VKP(b) member from 1937, he worked in the Cheka from 1921. He occupied important positions in the NKVD apparatus from 1935 and was head of the Gulag in 1941–47.

Nodev, O. Ya. (1896–1938). A party member from 1914, he worked in the Cheka from 1921. From July 1937 he was people's commissar of internal affairs of Turkmen SSR. He was arrested in December 1937 and shot in August 1938.

Ordzhonikidze, G. K. (1886–1937). A member of the Bolshevik party from 1903 and of the Politburo from 1930 to 1937, he was VSNKh chairman from 1930 and people's commissar of heavy industry from 1932. He committed suicide as a result of a conflict with Stalin.

Pankratiev, M. I. (1901–74). A party member from 1920, he was a military procurator of the main military procuracy in 1933–38; procurator of the RSFSR from May 1938; and procurator of the USSR in 1939–40.

Panteleev, A. I. (1907–41). A member of the VKP(b) from 1932, he worked in the GPU-NKVD in the Ukraine, 1932–35, and was operative representative at the central apparatus of the GUGB NKVD USSR, 1937–38. From January 1939 he was people's commissar of internal affairs and people's commissar of state security of Dagestan ASSR; from July 1941, people's commissar of internal affairs of Yakut ASSR.

Piatakov, Yu. L. (1890–1937). A party member from 1910, he was a leader of the opposition. He was expelled from the party in 1927. After being readmitted in 1928, he worked as deputy VSNKh chairman and, from 1932, as deputy people's commissar of heavy industry. He was arrested in September 1936 and shot in January 1937.

Pliner, I. I. (1896–1939). A party member from 1922, he was assistant to the head of the Gulag, 1933–35; deputy head of the Gulag, 1935–37; and head of the Gulag, 1937–38. He was arrested in November 1938 and shot in February 1939.

Popov, S. P. (1904–40). A party member from 1928, he worked in OGPU-NKVD organs in Western Siberia in 1932–37. In 1937 he became head of the fourth department of the directorate of state security of the UNKVD of Western Siberian territory. From October 1937 he was head of the UNKVD of Altai territory. He was arrested in December 1938 and shot in January 1940.

Poskrebyshev, A. N. (1891–1965). A party member from 1917, he was head of the secret department of the Central Committee from 1930 and head of its special sector (Stalin's de facto office) from 1934.

Radek, K. B. (1885–1939). He joined the Social Democratic (later, Bolshevik) party in 1903 and was a leader of the opposition. He was expelled from the VKP(b) in 1927, then readmitted in 1930. Between 1932 and 1936 he headed the bureau of international information of the Central Committee. He was arrested in September 1936 and killed in prison in May 1939.

Radetsky, V. T. (1895–?). A party member from 1918, he worked in Cheka organs from 1918. From 1933 he was deputy head of the Dmitrovsky camp administration. In June 1937 he was discharged from the NKVD.

Rakovsky, K. G. (1873–1941). A party member from 1917, he was one of the leaders of the opposition. He was expelled from the VKP in 1927 and exiled. He returned from exile in 1934 and worked in various state offices. He was readmitted to the party in 1935 and worked, until his arrest in January 1937, as head of division in the People's Commissariat of Health of the RSFSR. He was shot in September 1941.

Ramzin, L. K. (1887–1948). Director of the All-Union Institute of Heating Engineering, he was arrested in 1930 and convicted in the Industrial Party case. In prison he worked in the OGPU technical bureau and earned an early release.

Rapoport, Ya. D. (1898–1962). A party member from 1918, he was deputy head of construction of the White Sea–Baltic Sea canal from 1931; deputy head of the Gulag and deputy head of construction of the Moscow–Volga canal from 1932; head of the Dmitrovsky camp from 1933; head of construction of the Rybinsk and Uglich hydrosystems and head of the Volga camp from 1935; and head of the Chief Administration of Camps for Hydrotechnical Construction of the NKVD from 1940. From 1941 to March 1953 he was in charge of several NKVD-MVD construction projects.

Rudzutak, Ya. E. (1887–1938). A Bolshevik party member from 1905, Politburo member in 1926–32, and a candidate Politburo member in 1934–37, he was deputy chairman of the SNK and STO USSR in 1926–37 and, at the same time, in 1931–34, chairman of the CCC and people's commissar of the RKI. He was shot in 1938.

Rychkov, N. M. (1897–1959). A party member from 1917, he was procurator of the RSFSR from August 1937 and people's commissar and minister of justice of the USSR in 1938–48.

Rykov, A. I. (1881–1938). A party member from 1898, a Politburo member in 1922–30, and chairman of the SNK USSR in 1924–30, he was a leader of the "right deviation." After being removed from the Politburo, he was people's commissar of communications in 1931–36. He was arrested in February 1937 and shot in March 1938.

Serebriakov, L. P. (1888–1937). A party member from 1905, he was secretary of its Central Committee in 1920–21. One of the opposition leaders, he was expelled from the party in 1927. After being readmitted, he worked in economic management. He was arrested in August 1936 and shot in January 1937.

Shanin, A. M. (1894–1937). A party member from 1918, he was secretary of the OGPU collegium, 1923–31; deputy head and head of the OGPU administrative directorate, 1930–31; and deputy OGPU representative for the Western Siberian territory from 1932. From 1933 he occupied high positions in the OGPU-NKVD central apparatus. He was arrested in April 1937 and shot in August.

Sheludchenko, M. I. (1898–1940). A party member from 1920, he worked in Cheka-GPU-NKVD organs of the Ukraine in 1920–37. From October 1937 he was deputy people's commissar of internal affairs of Tatar ASSR. He was arrested in May 1939 and shot in February 1940.

Smirnov, G. I. (1903–38). He was deputy chairman of Gosplan in 1934–36 and, from 1937, chairman. He was executed.

Sokolnikov, G. Ya. (1888–1939). A party member from 1905, he was deputy people's commissar and people's commissar of finances of the RSFSR and the USSR from 1921; Soviet ambassador to Great Britain, 1929–32; and deputy people's commissar of foreign affairs later. In 1935–36 he was deputy people's commissar of forestry. He was arrested in July 1936, sentenced to ten years in prison in January 1937, and killed there in May 1939.

Stetsky, A. I. (1896–1938). A party member from 1915, in 1930–38 he was head of the party propaganda and agitation department of the Central Committee. He was shot in August 1938.

Syrtsov, S. I. (1893–1937). A party member from 1913, he was secretary of the Siberian territorial committee of VKP(b) in 1926–29 and chairman of the SNK RSFSR in 1929–30. Accused of factionalism and fired, he worked as a economic manager. He was shot in 1937.

Tolmachev, V. N. (1886–1937). A party member from 1904, in 1928–30 he was people's commissar of internal affairs of the RSFSR, then, after 1931, an economic manager. He was accused of anti-party activity in late 1932, expelled from the party in January 1933, and sentenced to three years in camps. In September 1937 he was convicted again and shot.

Tomsky, M. P. (1880–1936). A party member from 1904 and a member of the Politburo in 1922–30, he was a leader of the "right deviation." After being expelled from the Politburo, he worked as an economic manager; in 1932–36 he was manager of the United State Publishing House. Facing arrest, he committed suicide in August 1936.

Tretiakov, A. F. (1905–66). A member of the VKP(b) from 1926, he was head of division in the People's Commissariat of Health of the USSR in 1939–40 and people's commissar of health of the RSFSR in 1940–46.

Trofimov, B. P. (1902–75). A party member from 1918, he worked in the Cheka from 1921. In 1927–37 he worked in the transport department of the OGPU-NKVD USSR. From March 1939 he was deputy head, and from September 1939 head, of the Gulag's third department. Between 1940 and 1953 he occupied important positions in local and central offices of the NKVD-MVD USSR.

Tukhachevsky, M. N. (1893–1937). A party member from 1918, he became deputy RVS chairman in 1931. In 1934 he was deputy people's commissar of defense and, from 1936, first deputy people's commissar of defense. He was arrested in May 1937 and shot in June.

Tupolev, A. N. (1888–1972). An aircraft designer and member of the Soviet Academy of Sciences, he was arrested in 1937 and worked in the special NKVD design bureau until his release in 1941.

Ulrikh, V. V. (1889–1951). He was chairman of the Military Collegium of the Supreme Court of the USSR in 1926–48.

Usievich, A. A. (1898–?). A non-party member, he worked in the Cheka, Chief Directorate of Customs, and People's Commissariat of Foreign Trade. From 1933 he was one of the managers of the Moscow–Volga canal construction. Between 1939 and 1954 he occupied various positions in economic departments of the NKVD-MVD USSR.

Uspensky, A. I. (1902–40). A party member from 1920, he worked in the Cheka from 1920. He was assistant to and deputy OGPU representative and deputy UNKVD head for Moscow province in 1932–35; deputy commandant of the Kremlin from 1935; UNKVD head for Orenburg province in 1937; and people's commissar of internal affairs of the Ukraine from 1938. He was arrested in April 1939 and shot in January 1940.

Vasiliev, I. V. (1899–?). A party member from 1920, he became head of the Gulag political department and deputy head of the Gulag in 1938. In 1940 he was head of the Elenovsky POW camp (Stalin province) and deputy head of the camp and construction administration of the Khimki district of the Gulag (Moscow province).

Voroshilov, K. Ye. (1881–1969). A member of the party from 1903 and a Politburo member from 1926 to 1960, he was chairman of the RVS USSR in 1925–34 and people's commissar of the army and the navy. In 1934–40 he was people's commissar of defense of the USSR.

Vul, L. D. He was head of the police department of Moscow and Moscow province. He was shot in 1937.

Vyshinsky, A. Ya. (1883–1954). A member of the RSDRP (Menshevik) from 1903, he joined the Bolsheviks in 1920. In 1931–33 he was deputy people's commissar of justice and procurator of the RSFSR. In 1933 he became deputy procurator of the USSR; from 1935 to 1939, he was procurator.

Yagoda, G. G. (1891–1938). A party member from 1907, he was deputy OGPU chairman from 1924; people's commissar of internal affairs of the USSR, 1934–36; and people's commissar of communications, 1936–37. He was arrested in March 1937 and shot in March 1938.

Yanson, N. M. (1882–1941). A party member from 1905, he was deputy people's commissar of the RKI USSR from 1925; people's commissar of justice of the RSFSR in 1928–31; people's commissar of water transport in 1931–33; and deputy people's commissar of water transport from 1934. He was arrested in December 1937 and shot in June 1938.

Yenukidze, A. S. (1877–1937). A party member from 1898, he was secretary of the Presidium of the TsIK of the USSR from 1922 to March 1935. In June 1935 he was removed from the CC and expelled from the party for "political and moral degradation," and made an economic manager. He was arrested in February 1937 and shot in October.

Yevdokimov, E. G. (1891–1940). A party member from 1918, between 1919 and 1933 he worked in Cheka-OGPU organs. In 1934–37 he was first secretary of the Northern Caucasus and Azov–Black Sea territorial committees and the Rostov provincial committee of the VKP(b). From May 1938 he was deputy people's commissar of water transport of the USSR. He was shot in February 1940.

Yezhov, N. I. (1895–1940). A party member from 1917, he worked on party assignments in various regions in the 1920s and in the Central

Committee apparatus in 1925–29. In 1930 he became deputy people's commissar of agriculture. From late 1930 he headed various departments of the Central Committee and was secretary of the CC and chairman of the CPC from February 1935. Between 1936 and 1938 he was people's commissar of internal affairs of the USSR. He was arrested in April 1939 and shot in February 1940.

Yorsh, Ya. A. (1906–?). A member of the VKP(b) from 1929, he worked in economic departments of the OGPU-NKVD from 1931. From March 1941 he was head of the operative department and deputy head of the Gulag.

Zakovsky, L. M. (1894–1938). A party member from 1913, he worked in the VChK from 1917. In the 1920s–30s he headed various regional GPU departments. In 1932–34 he was the OGPU representative and people's commissar of the NKVD of Belorussia. From December 1934 he was head of the UNKVD of Leningrad province, and from January 1938, the UNKVD of the Moscow province. In April 1938 he became head of construction of the Kuibyshev hydrosystem. He was arrested in April 1938 and shot in August.

Zhdanov, A. A. (1896–1948). A party member from 1915, he was a candidate Politburo member in 1935–39 and a full member from 1939. In 1922–34 he was head of the department and first secretary of the Nizhegorodsky (Gorky) VKP(b) territorial committee. From 1934 he was secretary of the CC. In 1934–44 he was first secretary of the Leningrad provincial and city party committees.

Zinoviev, G. Ye. (1883–1936). A member of the party from 1901 and of the Politburo in 1921–26, he was a leader of the opposition. He was repressed several times. At the August 1936 trial of the "anti-Soviet united Trotskyite-Zinovievite center" he was sentenced to death.

Selected Camps and Projects of the OGPU-NKVD

For more information on camps and projects, see M. B. Smirnov, *Sistema ispravitel'no-trudovykh lagerei v SSSR. 1923–1960. Spravochnik* (Moscow, 1998).

Aktiubinsk camp, Kazakh SSR (February 1940–April 1946). Number of prisoners: 4,500 (1 July 1940); 8,079 (1 January 1941). Activities: construction of the Aktiubinsk ferroalloy complex; extraction of chrome ore and pentlandite, other projects.

Arkhangelsk camp (July 1938–October 1940). Number of prisoners: 8,315 (1 October 1938); 8,813 (1 January 1940). Activities: construction of the Arkhangelsk pulp and paper mill.

Astrakhan camp. *See* Prorva Island camp

Baikal-Amur camp (Bamlag), Svobodny, Far Eastern territory (November 1932–May 1938). Number of prisoners: 3,800 (12 December 1932); 200,907 (1 January 1938). Activity: construction of the Baikal–Amur railway. Broken into several railway camps in 1938.

Balakhninsky camp, Nizhegorodsky territory (April 1932–early 1934). Number of prisoners: 4,100 (December 1932); 4,655 (1 January 1934). Activities: peat cutting.

Bamlag. *See* Baikal-Amur camp

Belbaltlag. *See* White Sea–Baltic Sea camp

Bira camp, Far Eastern railway (April 1939–January 1942). Number of prisoners: 12,866 (1 January 1940); 12,007 (1 January 1941). Activities: timber cutting.

Central Asian camp (Sazlag), Tashkent (1930–43). Number of prisoners: 2,660 (1 June 1930); 34,240 (1 January 1939); 12,034 (1 January 1941). Activities: working on farms specializing in cotton and working in cotton-manufacturing plants.

Construction no. 200. *See* Luzhsky camp

Construction no. 211. Construction of the strategic highway Emilchino to Mogilev to Podolsky, Ukraine.

Dallag. *See* Far Eastern camp

Dalstroi trust. Created in November 1931 to explore and exploit gold deposits along the Kolyma River. From the late 1930s, also specialized in tin production. Workforce provided by the Northeastern camp. In March 1953 the trust was transferred from the Ministry of Internal Affairs to the Ministry of Metallurgy.

Dmitrovsky camp (Dmitlag), Moscow province (September 1932–January 1938). Number of prisoners: 88,534 (1 January 1934); 192,034 (1 January 1936). Activities: construction of the Moscow–Volga canal and other facilities in and around Moscow.

Dzhezkazgan camp, Karaganda province (April 1940). In April 1943, reorganized as a division of the Karaganda camp. Number of prisoners: 6,444 (1 July 1940); 13,706 (1 January 1941). Activities: construction of the Dzheskazgan copper-smelting complex.

Far Eastern camp (Dallag), Khabarovsk (1929–April 1939). Number of prisoners: 9,200 (1 January 1930); 64,249 (1 January 1939). Activities: timber cutting, gold and coal mining, railway construction, fishing and fish processing, etc.

Ivdel camp, Sverdlovsk province (organized in August 1937; still in operation on 1 January 1960). Number of prisoners: 16,230 (1 January 1938); 22,255 (1 January 1941). Activities: timber cutting.

Karaganda camp (Karlag), Karaganda (September 1931–July 1959). Number of prisoners: 10,400 (December 1932); 33,747 (1 January 1941). Activities: agriculture.

Kargopol camp, Arkhangelsk province (August 1937; still in operation on 1 January 1960). Number of prisoners: 15,217 (1 January 1938); 25,218 (1 January 1941). Activities: timber cutting.

Karlag. *See* Karaganda camp

Kazakhstan camp, Alma-Ata (organized in 1930; reorganized as Karaganda camp in September 1931). Number of prisoners: about 5,000 (1 July 1930); 15,500 (15 April 1931). Activities: timber cutting, agriculture.

Krasnoiarsk camp, Kansk (February 1938; still in operation on 1 January 1960). Number of prisoners: 9,924 (1 April 1938); 17,829 (1 January 1941). Activities: timber cutting.

Lokchimsky camp, Pezmog, Komi ASSR (organized in August 1937; integrated into the Ustvymsky camp in August 1940). Number of prisoners: 18,937 (1 January 1938); 22,585 (1 January 1940). Activities: timber cutting.

Luzhsky camp, Luzhskaya Bay, Leningrad province (August 1937–July 1941). Number of prisoners: 6,645 (1 January 1938); 7,821 (16 June 1941). Activities: construction of hydrosystems in Luzhskaya Bay for the navy base (Construction no. 200).

Middle Belsk camp, Sredne-Belaya station, Khabarovsk territory (April 1939–February 1949; separated from the Far Eastern camp). Number of prisoners: 3,783 (1 January 1940); 4,892 (1 January 1941). Activities: agriculture.

Nizhne-Amursky camp, Komsomolsk na Amure, Khabarovsk territory (May 1939–September 1947). Number of prisoners: 27,166 (1 January 1940); 50,535 (1 January 1941). Activities: construction of the western part of the Baikal–Amur railway, from Komsomolsk to Sovetskaya Bay.

Northeastern camp (Sevvostlag), Nagaevo Bay, Far Eastern territory; Magadan, Khabarovsk territory (organized in April 1932; reorganized in the early 1950s). Number of prisoners: 11,100 (December 1932); 179,041 (1 January 1941). Activities: serving the Dalstroi trust.

Northern Camps of Special Designation, Ust-Sysolsk, Komi ASSR; Solvychegodsk (Syktyvkar), Arkhangelsk province (organized in June 1929; in June 1931 reorganized into Ukhta-Pechora, Ustvymsky, and Temnikovsky camps and the Vaigach OGPU expedition). Number of prisoners: 9,250 (1 October 1929); 49,716 (1 January 1931). Activities: oil exploration, timber cutting, and highway construction.

Northern Pechora camp, Komi ASSR (May 1940–July 1950). Number of prisoners: 3,851 (1 July 1940); 91,664 (15 June 1941). Activities: construction of the Kotlas–Vorkuta railroad.

Northern railway camp, Kniazhpogost, Komi ASSR (organized in May 1938; in July 1950 it was merged with the Northern Pechora camp to form the Pechora camp). Number of prisoners: 25,199 (1 October 1938); 84,893 (1 January 1941). Activities: construction of the Kotlas–Vorkuta railroad.

Northern Urals camp, Irbit, Sverdlovsk province (February 1938; still in operation on 1 January 1960). Number of prisoners: 18,571 (1 April 1938); 27,327 (1 January 1941). Activities: timber cutting.

Onega camp, Plesetskaya station, Arkhangelsk province (February 1938–May 1942). Number of prisoners: 13,352 (1 April 1938); 18,367 (15 June 1941). Activities: timber cutting.

Pechora camp (Pechorlag). *See* Northern Pechora camp; Northern railway camp

Prorva Island camp (Prorvlag), Caspian Sea, Kazakhstan (September 1932; renamed Astrakhan camp in April 1940). Number of prisoners: 2,000 (December 1932); 5,044 (1 January 1940). Activities: fishing.

Sarovsky camp, Sarovsky monastery, Gorky territory (separated from the Temnikovsky camp in August 1934; reorganized as the Sarov juvenile colony in December 1935). Number of prisoners: 3,349 (1 January 1935); 2,310 (1 January 1936). Activities: timber cutting.

Sazlag. *See* Central Asian camp

Second railways. Construction of second (parallel) railways for one-line railroads in the Far East: Karymskaya–Khabarovsk in 1933–37, and Khabarovsk–Voroshilov from 1936.

Segezh camp, Karel SSR (October 1939–June 1941; separated from the White Sea–Baltic Sea camp). Number of prisoners: 7,951 (1 January 1940); 6,785 (1 January 1941). Activities: construction of the Segezh pulp and paper chemical complex, the Segezh hydrolysis plant, and Kondopozhsky sulfite liquor plant.

Sevvostlag. *See* Northeastern camp

Siberian camp (Siblag), Novosibirsk, Mariinsk (organized in the fall of 1929; still in operation on 1 January 1960). Number of prisoners: 4,592 (1 January 1930); 43,857 (1 January 1941). Activities: agriculture, timber cutting, road construction, etc.

Solovetsky camp, Arkhangelsk province and Kem, Karel ASSR (organized in October 1923; reorganized in December 1931 as the White Sea–Baltic Sea camp; separated and re-created in January 1932; merged finally with the White Sea–Baltic Sea camp in December 1933). Number of prisoners: 3,049 (September 1923); 53,123 (1 January 1930); 71,800 (1 January 1931). Activities: timber cutting, fishing, consumer goods manufacturing.

Soroka camp, Belomorsk, Karel ASSR (May 1938–April 1942). Number of prisoners: 476 (1 July 1938); 52,379 (1 January 1941). Activities: constructing railways, including the Soroka–Obozerskaya (Northern) railway.

South camp, Ulan Ude, Mongol-Buriat ASSR; Taishet, Irkutsk province (May 1938; reorganized into the Taishet camp in April 1943). Number of prisoners: 39,772 (1 November 1938); 7,430 (1 January 1941). Activities: construction of the Ulan–Ude–Naushki railway (Construction no. 202), the Taishet–Bratsk section of the Baikal–Amur railway.

Svirsky camp (Svirlag), Lodeinoe Pole station, Leningrad province (September 1931–no later than July 1937). Number of prisoners: 47,400 (December 1932); 22,774 (1 January 1937). Activities: supplying lumber to Leningrad, producing consumer goods.

Taishet camp, Irkutsk province (August 1937–October 1939). Number of prisoners: 13,333 (1 January 1938); 14,365 (1 January 1939). Activities: timber cutting.

Temnikovsky camp (Temlag; June 1931–November 1948). Number of prisoners: 25,541 (1 January 1934); 17,865 (1 January 1941). Activities: supplying lumber to Moscow, manufacturing consumer goods.

Tomsk-Asino camp (Tomasinlag), Novosibirsk province (August 1938–November 1940). Number of prisoners: 11,912 (1 January 1938); 13,073 (1 January 1940). Activities: timber cutting.

Ukhta-Izhemsky camp, Chibiu (Ukhta), Komi ASSR (separated from the Ukhta-Pechora camp in May 1938; merged with the Pechora camp in May 1955). Number of prisoners: 30,453 (1 July 1938); 23,214 (1 January 1941). Activities: exploration for and extraction of oil.

Ukhta-Pechora camp (Ukhtpechlag), Chibiu (Ukhta), Komi ASSR (6 June 1931–May 1938). Number of prisoners: 13,400 (December 1932); 54,792 (1 January 1938). Activities: exploration for and extraction of oil and coal, serving the Ukhta-Pechora trust.

Ukhta-Pechora trust of the OGPU-NKVD. Created in November 1932 to explore and exploit mineral deposits in the Pechora basin (mostly oil and coal), and to perform related work (road and house construction, agriculture, etc.).

Ushosdorlag (Shosdorlag), Khabarovsk (separated from the Far Eastern camp in November 1937; closed in February 1940). Number of prisoners: 42,853 (1 January 1938). Activities: road construction in the Far East.

Usolsk camp, Solikamsk, Sverdlovsk province (organized in February 1938; still in operation on 1 January 1960). Number of prisoners: 10,746 (1 April 1938); 27,150 (1 January 1941). Activities: timber cutting.

Ustvymsky camp, Vozhael, Komi ASSR (organized in August 1937; still in operation on 1 January 1960). Number of prisoners: 5,222 (1 January 1938); 14,056 (1 January 1941). Activities: timber cutting.

Viatka camp, Kirov province (February 1938; still in operation on 1 January 1960). Number of prisoners: 11,855 (1 April 1938); 15,878 (1 January 1941). Activities: timber cutting, timber processing.

Vishersky camp (Vishlag), Malaya Vizhaikha, Ural province (1928–July 1934). Number of prisoners: 7,873 (1 January 1930); 3,525 (1 April 1934). Activities: cutting timber, constructing the Vishersky pulp and paper mill, providing workers to chemical factories, etc.

Vladivostok camp (April 1939–1943). Number of prisoners: 56,033 (1 January 1940); 34,192 (1 January 1941). Activities: fishing and fish processing, highway construction.

Volga camp (Volgolag), Rybinsk, Yaroslavl province (December 1935–March 1942). Number of prisoners: 19,420 (1 January 1936); 87,791 (1 January 1941). Activities: construction of the Rybinsk and Uglish hydrosystems and other projects.

Vorkuta camp, Komi ASSR (separated from Ukhta-Pechora camp in May 1938; still in operation on 1 January 1960). Number of prisoners: 15,009 (1 July 1938); 19,080 (1 January 1941). Activities: coal mining.

White Sea–Baltic Sea camp (Belbaltlag), Medvezhegorsk, Karelo-Finn ASSR (December 1931–September 1941). Number of prisoners: 107,900 (December 1932); 67,928 (15 June 1941). Activities: construction of the White Sea–Baltic Sea canal; from 1933, supporting the White Sea–Baltic Sea OGPU-NKVD industrial complex (servicing the waterway, cutting timber, constructing the Segezh pulp and paper chemical complex, Tulomsk hydroelectric power station, Monchegorsk nickel complex, etc.)

Yagrinsky camp (Yagrinlag), Molotov (Severodvisk), Arkhangelsk province (April 1938–January 1953). Number of prisoners: 8,289 (1 July 1938); 31,116 (1 January 1941). Activities: building the city and the shipbuilding yard.

Excerpts from the Criminal Codes of the RSFSR and the Constitution of the USSR

Criminal Code of the RSFSR

Article 35

Expulsion beyond the boundaries of the RSFSR or beyond the boundaries of any area with obligatory settlement or prohibition to reside in other areas, or without these limitations, in combination with corrective labor or without corrective labor, can be imposed by a court on the convicted individuals if the court considers their continued residence in that area to be socially dangerous.

Expulsion beyond the boundaries of the RSFSR or beyond the boundaries of any area, with obligatory settlement in other areas, shall be ordered for a term from three to nine years; as an additional measure, this can be applied only for a term of up to five years. Expulsion beyond the boundaries of the RSFSR or the boundaries of any area with obligatory settlement in other areas, in combination with corrective labor, can be applied only as a main measure of social defense. Expulsion beyond the boundaries of the RSFSR or the boundaries of any area, in combination with the prohibition to reside in certain areas or without this limitation, shall be ordered for a term of from one to five years.

If one of these measures is ordered by a court in addition to the deprivation of liberty, the term of this additional measure begins from the day marking the end of incarceration.

Those sentenced to expulsion beyond the boundaries of any area with obligatory settlement in other areas who serve their prison term in the corrective labor camps, upon serving their term, are settled in the area for the period during which they are deprived of the right to freely choose the place of their residence. They shall be given land and offered paid work.

Expulsion beyond the boundaries of the RSFSR, as well as expulsion beyond the boundaries of any area in any form, cannot be applied to individuals under sixteen years of age.

Article 58-1a

Treason against the motherland, i.e., acts done by citizens of the USSR to damage the military power of the USSR, its national sovereignty, or the inviolability of its territory, such as espionage, betrayal of military or state secrets, crossing over to the enemy, and flight abroad (by surface or air), shall be punishable by the ultimate measure of criminal punishment—shooting with confiscation of all property—or, under mitigating circumstances—deprivation of liberty for a term of ten years with confiscation of all property.

Article 58 2

Armed uprising or incursion with counterrevolutionary purposes on Soviet territory by armed gangs, seizure of power in the center or provinces with the same purposes and, in particular, with the aim of forcibly severing any territory from the USSR or an individual union republic, or of breaking agreements between the USSR and foreign states shall be punishable by—the ultimate measure of social defense—shooting, or by proclamation as an enemy of the workers, with confiscation of property and with deprivation of citizenship of the union republic and thus of citizenship of the Soviet Union and expulsion beyond the borders of the USSR, with the allowance under mitigating circumstances of reduction to deprivation of liberty for a term of no less than three years, with confiscation of all or part of [the offender's] property.

Article 58-6

Espionage, i.e., the transmittal, seizure, or collection, with the purpose of transmittal, of information that is a specially kept state secret, due to its content, to foreign governments, counterrevolutionary organizations, or private individuals, shall be punishable by deprivation of liberty for a term not less than three years, with confiscation of all or part of one's property, or in those cases where the espionage brought or could bring especially severe consequences for the interests of the USSR, by the ultimate measure of social defense, shooting or proclamation as an enemy of the workers, with deprivation of citizenship of the union republic and thus of citizenship of the USSR and perpetual expulsion beyond the borders of the USSR with confiscation of property.

Transmittal, seizure, or collection for the purpose of transmittal of economic information, not constituting by its content specially kept state secrets, but not subject to publication either owing to direct legal prohibition or owing to the decision of the management of the department, institution, or enterprise, whether for a reward or for free, to organizations and persons listed above, shall be punishable by deprivation of liberty for a term of up to three years.

Article 58-7

The undermining of state industry, transport, trade, currency, or the credit system; likewise, cooperation, done with counterrevolutionary purposes, by means of a corresponding use of state institutions and enterprises or impedance of their normal activity, and, likewise, the use of state institutions and enterprises or impedance of their activity, done in the interests of former owners or interested capitalist organizations, shall be punishable by measures of social defense, indicated in Article 58-2 of this Code.

Article 58-8

The perpetration of terrorist acts, directed against representatives of Soviet authority or activists of revolutionary workers' and peasants' organizations, and participation in the performance of such acts, even by persons not belonging to counterrevolutionary organizations, shall be punishable by measures of social defense, indicated in Article 58-2 of this Code.

Article 58-10

Propaganda or agitation containing a call for the overthrow, subversion, or weakening of Soviet authority or for the carrying out of other counterrevolutionary crimes (Articles 58-2 to 58-9 of this Code), and likewise the distribution or preparation or keeping of literature of this nature shall be punishable by deprivation of liberty for a term of not less than six months.

The same actions during mass disturbances, or with the use of religious or nationalist prejudices of the masses, or in a war situation, or in areas proclaimed to be in a war situation, shall be punishable by measures of social defense, indicated in Article 58-2 of this Code.

Article 58-11

Any type of organizational activity, directed toward the preparation or carrying out of crimes indicated in this chapter, and likewise participation in an organization formed for the preparation or carrying out of one of the crimes indicated in this chapter, shall be punishable by measures of social defense, indicated in the corresponding articles of this Code.

Article 82

The escape by the arrested individual from custody or from imprisonment: deprivation of liberty for a term of up to three years.

Escape from the place of obligatory settlement (exile) or while en route there, and likewise the evasion of corrective labor by those sentenced to exile: substitution of exile for deprivation of liberty for the same term.

Unauthorized return by the deportee to the locations forbidden for settlement: substitution of deportation for deprivation of liberty or exile for the same term; exile can be used to substitute only for deportation ordered for a term of no less than three years.

Article 193-17

a) The abuse of power, use of excessive power, inaction by the authority, and likewise neglect of duty by the command staff of the Workers' and Peasants' Red Army, if these actions were done systematically or from mercenary motives or out of other personal interest, and likewise if they resulted in disorganization of the forces or activity entrusted to [the authority], or betrayal of military secrets, or other grave consequences, or likewise without the said consequences but they could obviously have led to them, or likewise perpetrated at the time of war or during military operations, shall be punishable by deprivation of liberty for a term of no less than six months.

b) The same actions under especially aggravating circumstances shall result in the ultimate measure of social defense.

Code of Criminal Procedure of the RSFSR
Article 440

The People's Commissar of Justice, the Procurator of the Republic, and the Chairman of the Supreme Court have the right to request a case for review at any stage of the procedure from all judicial organs of the RSFSR.

Territorial and provincial procurators, procurators of the autonomous republics and provinces, and chairmen of the territorial (provincial) courts, main courts of the autonomous republics, and provincial courts of the autonomous republics have the right to request cases from the judicial organs of their territory (province) and republic for review. The district procurator has the right to request cases from the judicial organs of his district.

Organs requesting a case for review, excluding the district procurator, have the power to halt the implementation of a sentence.

If the implementation of a sentence is halted, the return of the case or its submission for review shall take place within 10 days of its receipt.

Article 458

Liberation on parole can be authorized by the allocation commission only after the individual sentenced to deprivation of liberty or forced labor serves no less than half the length of the sentence, except in cases of grave incurable disease or mental illness, when liberation on parole can be ordered by the court before the expiration of half the length of the sentence. [. . .]

Corrective Labor Code of the RSFSR

Article 124

Liberation on parole can be authorized by supervisory commissions for those deprived of liberty, and likewise those in exile with corrective labor without deprivation of liberty, who have served no less than half of the length of the measure of social defense ordered by the court, counting workdays.

Constitution of the USSR

Article 127

Citizens of the USSR are guaranteed personal inviolability. No person may be placed under arrest except by decision of a court or with the sanction of a procurator.

Article 135

Elections of deputies are universal: all citizens of the USSR who have reached the age of 18, irrespective of race or nationality, religion, education and residential qualifications, social origin, property status or past activities, have the right to vote in the election of deputies and to be elected, with the exception of insane persons and persons who have been convicted by a court of law and whose sentences include deprivation of electoral rights.

Notes

INTRODUCTION

1. For more information about archival sources of the Soviet period see Andrea Graziosi, "The New Soviet Archival Sources: Hypothesis for a Critical Assessment," in *Cahiers du Monde Russe,* 40, nos. 1–2 (1999), pp. 13–64.

2. GARF, fond R-9479, opis' 1, delo 64, listy 9–10.

3. GARF, f. R-9479, op. 1, d. 12, l. 342.

4. GARF, f. R-9414, op. 1, d. 3322, l. 9.

5. GARF, f. R-8131, op. 32, d. 3286, l. 363.

6. There are also regional OGPU-NKVD archives, which are not well studied. Only a few works refer to these collections. See, e.g., R. Podkur, *Za povidomlenniam radians'kykh spetssluzhb* (Kiev, 2000).

7. In the documents reproduced in this *History of the Gulag* numbers may not add up because of mistakes in the original, whether in the sum or in particular figures. Sometimes, too, numbers were omitted.

8. For a review of these publications see R. W. Davies, *Soviet History in the Yeltsin Era* (Basingstoke, England, 1997). For a detailed bibliography and discussion of some results of studying the problems of terror and the Soviet punitive system of the last ten years see *Cahiers du Monde Russe,* 42, nos. 2–4 (2001) (special issue dedicated to the history of the Soviet political police in 1918–53).

9. M. Smirnov (comp.), *Sistema ispravitelno-trudovykh lagerei v SSSR. 1923–1960* (Moscow, 1998); A. Kokurin and N. Petrov (comps.), *Lubianka. 1917–1960* (Moscow, 1997); N. Petrov and K. Skorkin (comps.), *Kto rukovodil NKVD. 1934–1941* (Moscow, 1999); A. Kokurin and N. Petrov (comps.), *GULAG (Glavnoe upravlenie lagerei). 1917–1960* (Moscow, 2000); Yu. Shapoval et al., *Cheka-GPU-NKVD v Ukraini* (Kiev, 1997); *Repressii protiv poliakov i polskikh grazhdan* (Moscow, 1997); *Repressii protiv rossiiskikh nemtsev. Nakazannyi narod* (Moscow, 1999); Peter Solomon, *Soviet Criminal Justice Under Stalin* (Cambridge, 1996), pp. 153–95; N. Vert, *Gosudarstvo protiv svoego naroda.*

Chiornaia kniga kommunizma (Moscow, 1999), pp. 66–260; J. Arch Getty and Oleg V. Naumov, *The Road to Terror* (New Haven, 1999); S. S. Vilenskii et al. (comps), *Deti GULAGa. 1918–1956* (Moscow, 2002); M. Jansen and N. Petrow, *Stalin's Loyal Executioner: People's Commissar Nikolai Ezhov, 1895–1940* (Stanford, Calif.: Hoover Institution Press, 2002); M. Jacobson, *Origins of the GULAG: The Soviet Camp System, 1917–1934* (Lexington, Ky., 1993); A. Applebaum, *Gulag: A History of the Soviet Camps* (London, 2003). GARF, in cooperation with the Hoover Institution on War, Revolution and Peace and the ROSSPEN publishing house, will soon publish a six-volume collection of Gulag documents, *Stalinskii Gulag [Stalinist Gulag]*. Another book published in connection with this collaboration is P. R. Gregory and V. Lazarev (eds.), *The Economics of Forced Labor: The Soviet Gulag* (Stanford, Calif., 2003).

10. V. P. Danilov and S. A. Krasil'nikov (eds.), *Spetspereselentsy v Zapadnoi Sibiri. 1930–1945* (Novosibirsk, 1992–96), vols. 1–4; V. P. Danilov, R. Manning, and L. Viola (eds.), *Tragediia sovetskoi derevni. Kollektivizatsiia i raskulachivaniie. Dokumenty i materialy* (Moscow, 1999–2004), vols. 1–5.; V. Shashkov, *Spetspereselentsy na Murmane. Rol spetspereselentsev v razvitii proizvodstvennykh sil na Kolskov poluostrove. 1930–1936* (Murmansk, 1993); T. Slavko, *Kulatskaia ssylka na Urale. 1930–1936* (Moscow, 1995).

11. *Gulag v Karelii. Sbornik dokumentov i materialov. 1930–1941* (Petrozavodsk, 1992); O. Elantseva, *Obrechennaia doroga. BAM: 1932–1941* (Vladivostok, 1994); V. Berdinskikh, *Viatlag* (Kirov, 1998); A. Shirokov, *Dalstroi: Predystoriia i pervoe desiatiletie* (Magadan, 2000).

CHAPTER 1. ORIGINS OF THE STALINIST GULAG

1. RGASPI, f. 17, op. 3, d. 746, ll. 2, 11.

2. In contrast to the terror in the countryside, the 1920–30s repression in the cities is not well studied. In recent years, several documentary studies of the most prominent cases have been published. See, e.g., V. Prystaiko and Iu. Shapoval, *Sprava "Spilku vyzvolennia Ukrainy": Nevidomi dokumenty i fakty* (Kiev, 1995); Prystaiko and Shapoval, *Mykhailo Grushevsky: Sprava "UNTs" i ostanni roky (1931–1934)* (Kiev, 2000); Lars Lih, O. Naumov, and O. Khlevniuk (eds.), *Stalin's Letters to Molotov: 1925–1936* (New Haven, 1995), pp. 187–223; A. L. Litvin (comp.) *Men'shevistskii protsess 1931 goda: Sbornik dokumentov v 2-kh knigakh* (Moscow 1999).

3. Documents show that in those years the government was waging a real war with the peasantry. See Lynne Viola, *Peasant Rebels Under Stalin: Collectivization and the Culture of Peasant Resistance* (New York, 1996); V. Vasiliev and L. Viola, *Kollektivizatsiia i krestianskoe soprotivleniie na Ukraine (noiabr' 1929–mart 1930)* (Vinnitsa, 1997); N. Ivnitsky et al. (eds.) *Tragediia sovetskoi derevni*, vol. 2, *Noiabr' 1929–dekabr' 1930* (Moscow, 2000).

4. For discussion of the preparation and implementation of the policy of dekulakization see L. Viola, "The Role of OGPU in Dekulakization, Mass Deportation, and Special Resettlement in 1930," *Carl Beck Papers in Russian and East European Studies*, no. 1406 (2000).

5. RGASPI, f. 17, op. 162, d. 8, ll. 60, 64–69; *Istoricheskii arkhiv*, no. 4 (1994), pp. 147–52.

6. First published in *Neizvestnaia Rossiia. XX vek*, 1 (1992), pp. 237–45.

7. GARF, f. R-9401, op. 1, d. 4157, l. 202.

8. Ivnitsky et al., *Tragediia sovetskoi derevni*, vol. 2, p. 704.

9. GARF, f. R-8409, op. 1, d. 547.

10. GARF, f. R-8409, op. 1, d. 547. The document is marked as sent to the OGPU Presidium on 8 August 1930.

11. For the OGPU data see RGASPI, f. 17, op. 120, d. 52, ll. 20, 59; I. E. Plotnikov', "Kak likvidorovali kulachestvo na Urale," *Otechestvennaia istoriia*, no. 4 (1993), p. 162. This information is confirmed by other sources: N. A. Ivnitsky, *Kollektivizatsiia i raskulachivaniie (nachalo 30-kh godov)* (Moscow, 1994), p. 218.

12. I. E. Plotnikov', in *Otechestvennaia istoriia*, no. 1 (1995), pp. 161–64.

13. V. P. Danilov and S. A. Krasil'nikov (eds.), *Spetspereselentsy v Zapadnoi Sibiri. 1930–1945*, vol. 1: *1930–vesna 1931* (Novosibirsk, 1992), p. 227. A similar situation in the Northern territory is described in Lynne Viola, "The Other Archipelago: Kulak Deportations to the North in 1930," *Slavic Review*, 60, no. 4 (2001), pp. 739–52.

14. Ivnitsky et al., *Tragediia sovetskoi derevni*, vol. 2, p. 27.

15. GARF, f. R-9479, op. 1, d. 89, l. 205; V. N. Zemskov's chapter in Yu. A. Poliakov (ed.), *Naselenie Rossii v XX veke*, vol. 1 (Moscow, 2000), p. 277.

16. RGASPI, f. 17, op. 162, d. 10, l. 51; *Istoricheskii arkhiv*, no. 4 (1994), p. 155.

17. RGASPI, f. 17, op. 120, d. 26, ll. 203–207. See also *Otechestvennaia istoriia*, no. 1 (1995), pp. 172–74.

18. *Spetspereselentsy v Khibinakh* (Apatity, 1997), p. 79.

19. GARF, f. R-9479, op. 1, d. 89, ll. 205–206; Poliakov, *Naselenie Rossii v XX veke*, vol. 1, pp. 277, 279.

20. RGASPI, f. 17, op. 162, d. 11, l. 167; *Istoricheskii arkhiv*, no. 4 (1994), p. 176.

21. GARF, f. R-3316, op. 1, d. 448, ll. 66–70; *Neizvestnaia Rossiia. XX vek*, 1: 207–8, 222–23, 227.

22. *Otechestvennaia istoriia*, no. 1 (1995), pp. 167–71.

23. RGASPI, f. 17, op. 120, d. 6, l. 239; *Istoricheskii arkhiv*, no. 3 (1994), pp. 128–38; L. I. Gintsberg, "Massovye deportatsii krestian v 1930–1931 godakh i usloviia ikh sushchestvovaniia v severnykh kraiiakh," *Otechestvennaia istoriia*, no. 2 (1998), pp. 194–95.

24. See the Gulag circular letter of 17 August 1931, "On organizing the struggle against escapes of the special settlers" (GARF, f. R-9479, op. 1, d. 5, ll. 41–42; V. P. Danilov and S. A. Krasil'nikov (eds.), *Spetspereselentsy v Zapadnoi Sibiri. 1930–1945*, vol. 2: *Vesna 1931–nachalo 1933* (Novosibirsk, 1993), pp. 58–60; the 13 September 1931 Gulag memorandum "On the Cheka servicing of special settlers" (GARF, f. R-9479, op. 1, d. 5, ll. 64–65).

25. RGASPI, f. 17, op. 126, d. 10, l. 126.

26. GARF, f. R-9479, op. 1, d. 89, l. 206; Poliakov, *Naselenie Rossii v XX veke*, p. 279.

27. RGASPI, f. 17, op. 162, d. 10, l. 53; *Istoricheskii arkhiv*, no. 4 (1994), p. 158; Code of Laws [SZ] SSSR, 1931, no. 44, art. 298.

28. GARF, f. R-9479, op. 1, d. 3, l. 84; Danilov and Krasil'nikov, *Spetspereselentsy v Zapadnoi Sibiri*, vol. 2, p. 55.

29. GARF, f. R-8131, op. 37, d. 20, l. 51.

30. RGASPI, f. 17, op. 162, d. 10, ll. 154–159; *Istoricheskii arkhiv*, no. 4 (1994), pp. 165–69. This resolution by the Politburo was presented as the 16 August 1931 SNK resolution (see RGASPI, f. R-5446, op. 1, d. 459, ll. 165–174).

31. RGASPI, f. 17, op. 162, d. 10, l. 148; *Istoricheskii arkhiv*, no. 4 (1994), p. 164.

32. R. W. Davies et al. (eds.), *The Stalin-Kaganovich Correspondence, 1931– 36* (New Haven, 2003), pp. 69–70.

33. GARF, f. R-9479, op. 1, d. 10, l. 1.

34. GARF, f. R-9479, op. 1, d. 11, ll. 51–54; Danilov and Krasil'nikov, *Spetspereselentsy v Zapadnoi Sibiri*, vol. 2, pp. 89–93.

35. GARF, f. R-9479, op. 1, d. 3, ll. 127–128; Danilov and Krasil'nikov, *Spetspereselentsy v Zapadnoi Sibiri*, vol. 2, pp. 62–63.

36. First published in *Iz istorii raskulachivaniia v Karelii, 1930–1931: Dokumenty i materialy* (Petrozavodsk, 1991), pp. 227–34. See also GARF, f. R-9479, op. 1, d. 3, ll. 132–141; Danilov and Krasil'nikov, *Spetspereselentsy v Zapadnoi Sibiri*, vol. 2, pp. 68–76.

37. TsA FSB [Central Archive of the Federal Security Service], 2 April 1932 circular letter no. 338 from the OGPU, "On the termination of penal teams in special settlements."

38. GARF, f. R-9479, op. 1, d. 11, l. 34.

39. GARF, f. R-9414, op. 1, d. 89, l. 206; Poliakov, *Naselenie Rossii v XX veke*, p. 279.

40. TsA FSB, f. 2, op. 8, d. 116, l. 61.

41. GARF, f. R-9414, op. 1, d. 2919, l. 55.

42. GARF, f. R-9479, op. 1, d. 3, ll. 23–24.

43. TsA FSB, f. 2, op. 8, d. 117, ll. 123–126.

44. RGASPI, f. 17, op. 3, d. 784, l. 2.

45. GARF, f. R-9414, op. 1, d. 2919, ll. 63–63 rev. The first draft of this memorandum mentioned 50,000 weak, sick, invalid, and elderly prisoners. Ibid., p. 61 rev.

46. GARF, f. R-5446, op. 11a, d. 725, l. 3.

47. GARF, f. R-5446, op. 11a, d. 725, l. 7.

48. GARF, f. R-5446, op. 11a, d. 725, ll. 5–6.

49. GARF, f. R-5446, op. 11a, d. 725, ll. 1–3.

50. GARF, f. R-5446, op. 11a, d. 725, ll. 12–13.

51. GARF, f. R-5446, op. 11a, d. 725, l. 14.

52. *Istoricheskii arkhiv*, no. 4 (1997), pp. 153–54.

53. Lih, Naumov, and Khlevniuk, *Stalin's Letters to Molotov*, p. 212.

54. RGASPI, f. 17, op. 3, d. 799, l. 5.

55. *Sistema ispravitelno-trudovykh lagerei v SSSR, 1923–1960: Spravochnik* (Moscow, 1998), p. 103.

56. GARF, f. R-5446, op. 11a, d. 60, l. 4. On the evacuation of prisoners from lumberyards see M. Jacobson, *Origins of the GULAG: The Soviet Prison Camp System, 1917–1934* (Lexington, Ky., 1993), pp. 126–27.

57. *Dokumenty vneshnei politiki SSSR*, vol. 13 (Moscow, 1967), pp. 566–68, 584–85.

58. RGASPI, f. 17, op. 3, d. 813, l. 15.

59. Lih, Naumov, and Khlevniuk, *Stalin's Letters to Molotov,* p. 228.

60. GARF, f. R-5446, op. 1, d. 462, l. 35.

61. TsA FSB, f. 2, op. 11, d. 537, ll. 284–285.

62. RGASPI, f. 17, op. 162, d. 11, ll. 57–63. There have been many studies of Dalstroi based on new archival documents. See D. Nordlander, "Origins of a Gulag Capital: Magadan and Stalinist Control in the Early 1930s," *Slavic Review* 57, no. 4 (1998), pp. 791–812. A. I. Shirokov in his book *Dalstroi: predystoriia i pervoe desiatiletiie* (Magadan, 2000) provides an extensive bibliography of relevant titles in Russian.

63. RGASPI, f. 17, op. 162, d. 12, l. 8; GARF, f. R-5446, op. 1, d. 462, ll. 138–139 (the 20 March 1932 SNK resolution "On Kolyma").

64. GARF, f. R-5446, op. 17, d. 278, l. 75; GARF, f. R-5446, op. 14a, d. 48, l. 37.

65. GARF, f. 9414, op. 1, d. 2920, l. 179.

66. A. N. Kaneva, "Ukhtpechlag, 1929–1938," *Zven'ia. Istoricheskii almanakh,* vol. 1 (Moscow, 1991), pp. 331–56.

67. GARF, f. R-9414, op. 1, d. 2920, l. 179.

68. RGASPI, f. 17, op. 3, d. 904, l. 10; M. I. Khlusov (comp.), *Ekonomika GULAGa i ee rol' v razvitii strany v 30-e gody* (Moscow, 1998), p. 27.

69. GARF, f. 5674, op. 3, d. 24, ll. 211–218 (STO [Labor and Defense Council] resolution of 16 November 1932).

70. The coalmining data are from TsA FSB, f. 2, op. 11, d. 537, l. 286.

71. RGASPI, f. 85, op. 1, d. 181, ll. 18–19.

72. G. K. Ordzhonikidze, *Rechi i stat'i,* vol. 2 (Moscow, 1957), pp. 308–10.

73. RGASPI, f. 17, op. 162, d. 11, l. 97.

74. About this and other design bureaus see R. W. Davies, *Crisis and Progress in the Soviet Economy, 1931–1933* (Basingstoke, England, 1996), pp. 36–37; R. Medvedev, *O Staline i stalinizme* (Moscow, 1990), pp. 255–56.

75. GARF, f. R-3316, op. 64, d. 1130, ll. 1–4.

76. GARF, f. R-3316, op. 64, d. 1130, ll. 8–9.

77. Davies, *Crisis and Progress in the Soviet Economy,* pp. 82–85; H. Kuromiya, *Stalin's Industrial Revolution: Politics and Workers, 1928–1932* (Cambridge, England, 1988), pp. 272–76.

78. GARF, f. R-9414, op. 1, d. 2920, l. 163.

79. TsA FSB, f. 2, op. 11, d. 537, l. 282.

80. RGASPI, f. 17, op. 3, d. 926, l. 24.

81. RGASPI, f. 17, op. 3, d. 926, l. 23.

82. *Belomoro-Baltiiskii kanal imeni Stalina: Istoriia stroitel'stva* (Moscow, 1934); M. Gorky, L. Averbach, and S. G. Firin (eds.), *The White Sea Canal* (London, 1935). I am grateful to R. W. Davies for pointing out this fact to me.

83. RGASPI, f. 17, op. 3, d. 885, l. 6; GARF, f. R-5446, d. 902, l. 8. The SNK USSR issued the corresponding decision on 28 October 1932 (GARF, f. R-5446, op. 1, d. 466, l. 58).

84. RGASPI, f. 17, op. 3, d. 904, l. 6.

85. O. P. Yelantseva, "BAM: pervoe desiatiletie," *Otechestvennaia istoriia,* no. 6 (1994), pp. 90–95.

86. GARF, f. R-5446, op. 1, d. 456, l. 23; Khlusov, *Ekonomika GULAGa,* p. 28.

87. GARF, f. R-9414, op. 1, d. 2920, ll. 39–40.

88. GARF, f. R-5446, op. 89, d. 20, l. 262.

89. GARF, f. R-5446, op. 89, d. 20, ll. 257–258.

90. GARF, f. R-5446, op. 89, d. 20, ll. 262–264.

91. "Otchet komissii po obsledovaniiu Solovetskikh lagerei, 15–30 aprelia 1930 goda" (TsA FSB, f. 2, op. 8, d. 116).

92. *Zvenia,* vol. 1 (1991), p. 383.

93. Memorial Society Archive, f. 2, op. 2, d. 84, ll. 72–73.

94. GARF, f. R-8131, op. 37, d. 20, l. 48.

95. GARF, f. R-8131, op. 37, d. 20, l. 45.

96. GARF, f. R-9414, op. 1, d. 3, ll. 51–52.

97. GARF, f. R-9414, op. 1, d. 2920, l. 88.

98. GARF, f. R-9414, op. 1, d. 2736, l. 4.

99. GARF, f. R-9414, op. 1, d. 2920, l. 140.

100. GARF, f. R-9414, op. 1, d. 1132, l. 3.

101. GARF, f. R-9414, op. 1, d. 1133, ll. 59–60.

102. GARF, f. R-9401, op. 12, d. 98, ll. 15–18. This instruction was announced in the 22 November 1931 letter, no. 412, by the Main Camp Administration.

103. GARF, f. R-9401, op. 12, d. 94, part 2, ll. 120–121.

104. TsA FSB, f. 2, op. 11, d. 537, l. 291.

105. SZ, 1930, no. 22, art. 248.

106. GARF, f. R-9401, op. 12, d. 102, Part 2, ll. 4–6.

107. SZ, 1930, no. 22, art. 248.

108. GARF, f. R-9414, op. 1, d. 1132, l. 2; d. 3, l. 71.

109. GARF, f. R-1235, op. 66a, d. 72, ll. 70–71. The circular letter appeared after the 3 August 1931 appeal by the secretary of the All-Russian Central Executive Committee (VtsIK) Presidium to the Gulag head, Kogan: "Following up on our conversations regarding the Dukhobortsy vegetarians, I am asking you [. . .] once again to remind and instruct those responsible about discontinuing the practice of forcing meat on the Dukhobortsy and other sectarians and to replace it with meatless food." GARF, f. R-1235, op. 66a, d. 72, l. 72. The Dukhobory was a sect of spiritual Christianity that emerged in Russia in the late eighteenth century. The members rejected Orthodox rites and sacraments, as well as the priesthood and monasticism. In the nineteenth century many Dukhobory moved to Canada.

110. GARF, f. R-3316, op. 65, d. 71, l. 1. The document is marked as presented to A. S. Yenukidze.

111. See Documents 14 and 15.

112. GARF, f. R-3316, op. 65, d. 71, ll. 2–5.

113. GARF, f. R-3316, op. 65, d. 71, ll. 6–7.

CHAPTER 2. FAMINE

1. Yu. A. Poliakov (ed.), *Naselenie Rossii v XX veke,* vol. 1 (Moscow, 2000), pp. 265–76; V. P. Danilov et al. (eds.), *Tragediia sovetskoi derevni: Kollektivizatsiia i raskulachivanie,* vol. 3 (Moscow, 2001), pp. 866–87.

2. See I. E. Zelenin, "Zakon o piati koloskakh: Razrabotka i osushchestvleniie," *Voprosy istorii*, no. 1 (1998), pp. 114–23; R. W. Davies et al. (eds.), *The Stalin-Kaganovich Correspondence, 1931–36* (New Haven, 2003), pp. 168–70.

3. V. P. Danilov and S. A. Krasil'nikov (eds.), *Spetspereselentsy v Zapadnoi Sibiri. 1930–1945,* vol. 3: *1933–1938* (Novosibirsk, 1994), p. 264.

4. Ibid., p. 42.

5. Ibid., p. 78.

6. RGASPI, f. 17, op. 162, d. 14, l. 96.

7. RGASPI, f. 17, op. 162, d. 14, l. 96.

8. GARF, f. R-3316, op. 64, d. 1266, l. 42.

9. TsA FSB, f. 2, op. 11, d. 546, ll. 92–94.

10. TsA FSB, f. 2, op. 11, d. 548, l. 102.

11. GARF, f. R-3316, op. 64, d. 1423, ll. 3–9. On 22 February 1933, Deputy Chairman of the GULAG of the OGPU Prokofiev sent this memorandum to the secretary of TsIK USSR, A. S. Yenukidze. The document bears a mark indicating that Yenukidze had read it. Ibid., l. 1.

12. GARF, f. R-3316, op. 64, d. 1826, ll. 4–10.

13. GARF, f. R-5446, op. 1, d. 468, ll. 141–147; RGASPI, f. 17, op. 162, d. 14, ll. 76, 89–92 (the 8 March 1933 Politburo resolution).

14. TsA FSB, f. 2, op. 11, d. 546, l. 79.

15. TsA FSB, f. 2, op. 11, d. 546, l. 79.

16. GARF, f. R-5446, op. 15a, d. 1073, l. 32.

17. First cited in M. Fainsod, *Smolensk Under Soviet Rule* (Cambridge, Mass., 1958), pp. 185–88; published in J. Arch Getty and Oleg V. Naumov, *The Road to Terror* (New Haven, 1999), pp. 114–18.

18. TsA FSB, f. 2, op. 11, d. 537, l. 244.

19. GARF, f. R-5446, op. 15a, d. 1073, l. 35.

20. The Velichko letter can be found among the materials of the Politburo sessions (RGASPI, f. 17, op. 163, d. 992, ll. 20–30; published in *Istochnik*, no. 2 [1998], pp. 59–67) and in the Novosibirsk archive (Danilov and Krasil'nikov, *Spetspereselentsy v. Zapadnoi Sibiri*, vol. 3: *1933–1938*, pp. 89–110).

21. GARF, f. R-5446, op. 14 a, d. 245, l. 79.

22. GARF, f. R-5446, op. 14 a, d. 245, ll. 56, 66.

23. GARF, f. R-9479, op. 1, d. 19, l. 9.

24. GARF, f. R-9479, op. 1, d. 24, l. 3; GARF, f. R-5446, op. 1, d. 469, l. 161.

25. *Istochnik*, no. 2 (1998), p. 64–66.

26. RGASPI, f. 17, op. 163, d. 992, l. 20; *Istochnik*, no. 2 (1998), p. 67.

27. RGASPI, f. 17, op. 162, d. 16, ll. 14–15.

28. Poliakov, *Naselenie Rossii v XX veke*, pp. 279, 300.

29. GARF, f. R-9414, op. 1, d. 2920, l. 187.

30. TsA FSB, f. 2, op. 11, d. 537, ll. 278–279.

31. GARF, f. R-9479, op. 1, d. 19, l. 1. Berman sent Yagoda a similar report a month later, in early June (GARF, f. R-9479, op. 1, d. 19, ll. 5–6).

32. GARF, f. R-9414, op. 1, d. 1913, ll. 4–6.

33. The 13 December 1933 Gulag report to Yagoda gave a detailed analysis of the situation regarding the funds for cloth, blankets, and footwear in the first

quarter of 1934. Owing to general shortages, the initial requests by the camps were drastically cut: three and a half times less cloth was provided, not a single pair of knee-high boots was provided out of the requested 80,000 pairs, and only 70,000 pairs of lace-up boots were provided out of 120,000 requested. Gulag leaders reported that, as a result of such supplies, some of the prisoners "would inevitably be undressed." (GARF, f. R-9414, op. 1, d. 1913, ll. 9–10).

34. GARF, f. R-9414, op. 1, d. 1913, l. 2.
35. GARF, f. R-9414, op. 1, d. 1913, l. 2.
36. GARF, f. R-9414, op. 1, d. 2741, l. 11.
37. GARF, f. R-9414, op. 1, d. 2741, l. 58.
38. GARF, f. R-9414, op. 1, d. 2741, l. 21.
39. TsA FSB, f. 2, op. 11, d. 537, l. 279.
40. GARF, f. R-9489, op. 1, d. 1, ll. 1–4.
41. TsA FSB, f. 2, op. 11, d. 546, l. 79; TsA FSB, f. 2, op. 11, d. 537, l. 240.
42. GARF, f. R-9414, op. 1, d. 2741, l. 47.
43. GARF, f. R-9414, op. 1, d. 2741, l. 57.
44. TsA FSB, f. 2, op. 11, d. 534, l. 176; V. N. Zemskov, "Zakliuchennye v 1930-e gody," *Otechestvennaia istoriia,* no. 4 (1997), p. 58.
45. TsA FSB, f. 3, op. 1, d. 314, ll. 137–138. On the sharp increase in the number of prisoners transported see the memorandum on convoy troops, GARF, f. R-5446, op. 22, d. 82, l. 3.
46. GARF, f. R-5446, op. 14a, d. 745, l. 8.
47. The 17 March 1933 group complaint from "old disabled men" sent to Kalinin stated: "Since December 1932, because of famine, old men have been dying such that not a day passes without one or sometimes two or three dead." GARF, f. R-1235, op. 66a, d. 111, ll. 9–10. On 15 April this letter was sent to local authorities for investigation. Similar complaints were received from other prisoners, including political ones; see GARF, f. R-3316, op. 64, d. 1496, ll. 1–6.
48. GARF, f. R-1235, op. 66a, d. 111, l. 8.
49. GARF, f. R-9479, op. 1, d. 16, l. 12. Document title.
50. Danilov and Krasil'nikov, *Spetspereselentsy v Zapadnoi Sibiri,* vol. 3, pp. 119, 287–88.
51. Poliakov, *Naselenie Rossii v XX veke,* p. 279.
52. Ibid., p. 300.

CHAPTER 3. STABILIZATION OF THE SYSTEM

1. GARF, f. R-5446, op. 1, d. 469, l. 114 (the 8 August 1933 SNK USSR resolution).
2. GARF, f. R-5446, op. 1, d. 469, ll. 142–143 (the 17 August 1933 SNK resolution).
3. GARF, f. R-5446, op. 1, d. 469, l. 225.
4. GARF, f. R-5446, op. 1, d. 474, ll. 20–22.
5. GARF, f. R-5446, op. 15a, d. 1172, l. 12.
6. GARF, f. R-5446, op. 15a, d. 1172, l. 4.

7. GARF, f. R-5446, op. 15a, d. 1172, l. 2.

8. F. Benvenuti, "The 'Reform' of the NKVD, 1934," *Europe-Asia Studies,* 49, no. 6 (1997), pp. 1037–56.

9. GARF, f. R-5446, op. 16a, d. 1359, ll. 155, 164, 165, 203–215.

10. GARF, f. R-5446, op. 16a, d. 1310, ll. 13–14.

11. RGASPI, f. 17, op. 3, d. 948, ll. 95–100. See also P. Solomon, *Soviet Criminal Justice Under Stalin* (Cambridge, 1996), pp. 153–95.

12. Eugine Huskey, "Vyshinskii, Krylenko, and the Shaping of the Soviet Legal Order," *Slavic Review,* 46, no. 3 (1987), pp. 420–21.

13. O. Khlevniuk, *Politburo. Mekhanizmy politicheskoi vlasti v 30-e gody* (Moscow, 1996), pp. 127–34.

14. RGASPI, f. 17, op. 162, d. 17, l. 87.

15. *Reabilitatsiia. Politicheskiie protsessy 30–50-kh godov* (Moscow, 1990), p. 170; RGASPI, f. 17, op. 162, d. 17, l. 124.

16. V. K. Vinogradov et al. (comps.), *Genrikh Yagoda. Narodny komissar vnutrennikh del SSSR. General'ny komissar bezopasnosti* (Kazan', 1997), pp. 465–76; see also Documents 94, 95.

17. RGASPI, f. 588, op. 2, d. 155, ll. 66–67; *Istochnik,* no. 6 (1997), pp. 109–10.

18. *Izvestiia TsK KPSS,* no. 10 (1989), p. 81.

19. For more on purges in the cities see D. R. Shearer, "Social Disorder, Mass Repression, and the NKVD During the 1930s," *Cahiers du Monde Russe,* 42, nos. 2–4 (2001), pp. 505–34; P. M. Hagenloh, "'Socially Harmful Elements' and the Great Terror," in Sheila Fitzpatrick (ed.), *Stalinism: New Directions* (London, 2000), pp. 286–308.

20. For more on the border zone purges see T. Martin, "The Origins of Soviet Ethnic Cleansing," *Journal of Modern History,* 70, no. 4 (1998), pp. 848–50.

21. GARF, f. R-9479, op. 1, d. 36, l. 23.

22. GARF, f. R-9479, op. 1, d. 30, l. 13.

23. Martin, "Origins of Soviet Ethnic Cleansing," pp. 849–50.

24. GARF, f. R-9479, op. 1, d. 30, l. 11.

25. RGASPI, f. 17, op. 120, d. 177, l. 22.

26. RGASPI, f. 17, op. 120, d. 240, ll. 21–22.

27. RGASPI, f. 17, op. 117, d. 873, l. 23.

28. GARF, f. R-8131, op. 37, d. 73, ll. 234–235. The full text of the letter was published in *Sovetskoe rukovodstvo. Perepiska. 1928–1941 gg.* (Moscow, 1999), pp. 322–30.

29. GARF, f. R-8131, op. 37, d. 71, ll. 127–133.

30. GARF, f. R-8131, op. 37, d. 73, ll. 217–226.

31. O. Khlevniuk, *1937: Stalin, NKVD i sovetskoe obshchestvo* (Moscow, 1992), pp. 63–66.

32. RGASPI, f. 17, op. 163, d. 1052, l. 152.

33. RGASPI, f. 17, op. 3, d. 969, l. 21. Passed as a 29 July 1935 resolution of the SNK and TsIK USSR.

34. RGASPI, f. 17, op. 163, d. 1106, ll. 135–137.

35. RGASPI, f. 17, op. 3, d. 970, ll. 144–145.

36. GARF, f. R-5446, op 18a, d. 896, l. 52.

37. GARF, f. R-9401, op. 1, d. 466, ll. 150–157.

38. GARF, f. R-8131, op. 37, d. 28, ll. 29–32.

39. GARF, f. R-9401, op. 12, d. 100, l. 74.

40. GARF, f. R-9401, op. 12, d. 100, ll. 91–92.

41. Memorial Society Archive, f. 2, op. 1, d. 4, l. 80.

42. GARF, f. R-9479, op. 1, d. 26, ll. 37–38.

43. GARF, f. R-9479, op. 1, d. 26, l. 37.

44. GARF, f. R-9401, op. 12, d. 94, part 1, l. 18.

45. GARF, f. R-9401, op. 12, d. 94, part 1, l. 18 rev. (the 2 April 1936 order by the people's commissar of the interior of the USSR, no. 100, "On measures to improve the work of corrective labor camps").

46. GARF, f. R-5446, op. 1, d. 480, l. 194.

47. SZ, 1935, no. 36, p. 452; GARF, f. R-5446, op. 16a, d. 656, ll. 21–33.

48. RGASPI, f. 17, op. 3, d. 971, ll. 33, 37.

49. GARF, f. R-5446, op. 1, d. 484, ll. 125–126.

50. Ibid., l. 17.

51. GARF, f. R-5446, op. 20a, d. 461, l. 40; op. 20, d. 62, l. 170.

52. GARF, f. R-5446, op. 20a, d. 249b, l. 2; op. 17, d. 278, l. 75; M. I. Khlusov (comp.), *Ekonomika GULAGa i ee rol' v razvitii strany v 30-e gody* (Moscow, 1998), p. 74; A. I. Shirokov, *Dal'stroi: Predystoria i pervoe desiatiletie* (Magadan, 2000), p. 103.

53. Sources put this number between 32.5 and 33.4 tons. See Khlusov, *Ekonomika GULAGa*, p. 76; Shirokov, *Dalstroi*, p. 103.

54. GARF, f. R-5446, op. 20a, d. 249b, l. 2; op. 17, d. 313, l. 140 (3 April SNK resolution); Shirokov, *Dalstroi*, p. 103.

55. GARF, f. R-9414, op. 1, d. 1155, ll. 20–22.

56. GARF, f. R-9414, op. 1, d. 1155, ll. 20–22.

57. GARF, f. R-9414, op. 1, d. 2926, ll. 73–74.

58. GARF, f. R-9401, op. 12, d. 99, ll. 40, 43, 49.

59. Memorial Society Archive, f. 2, op. 1, d. 4, ll. 32–33.

60. GARF, f. R-9414, op. 1, d. 8, ll. 46–48 (the 10 September 1934 Gulag order "On verifying the NKVD camp prisoners' bonus workday count").

61. GARF, f. R-9401, op. 12, d. 98, ll. 32–37.

62. GARF, f. R-9479, op. 1, d. 21, l. 66.

63. GARF, f. R-9489, op. 2, d. 35, l. 47.

64. GARF, f. R-9489, op. 2, d. 76, l. 88.

65. Ibid., l. 3.

66. Ibid., l. 6.

67. Ibid., l. 58.

68. Ibid., l. 80.

69. GARF, f. R-1235, op. 66a, d. 165, l. 130.

70. GARF, f. R-9484, op. 2, d. 85, l. 245.

71. See Document 30.

72. GARF, f. R-9484, op. 2, d. 85, l. 412.

73. On 21 September 1936, an order was issued to indict prisoner foremen guilty of beating their supervisors (see GARF, f. R-9489, op. 2, d. 85, ll. 409–410).

74. GARF, f. R-9489, op. 2, d. 85, l. 390.

75. GARF, f. R-9414, op. 4, d. 11, ll. 133–149.

76. GARF, f. R-8131, op. 37, d. 111, l. 8 (report to Yezhov).

77. Similar phenomena in the Belbaltlag (free movement of prisoners; prisoners living outside camp zones in private apartments) are described in N. Baron, "Production and Terror: The Operation of the Karelian GULAG, 1933–1939," *Cahiers du Monde Russe*, 43, no. 1 (2002), pp. 161–62.

78. GARF, f. R-9414, op. 1, d. 2921, l. 209.

79. M. B. Smirnov (comp.), *Sistema ispravitelno-trudovykh lagerei v SSSR. 1923–1960. Spravochnik* (Moscow, 1998), pp. 373–74.

80. GARF, f. R-5446, op. 71, d. 176, l. 13.

81. GARF, f. R-5446, op. 26, d. 24, l. 20.

82. *Stalinskoe Politburo v 30-e gody. Sbornik dokumentov* (Moscow, 1995), p. 144.

83. RGASPI, f. 17, op. 163, d. 1059, ll. 23–24; Peter Solomon, *Soviet Criminal Justice Under Stalin* (Cambridge University Press, 1996), pp. 197–211.

84. Later, the list of crimes included in the 7 April resolution was expanded. The 10 December 1940 decree by the Presidium of the Supreme Soviet of the USSR amended it by adding actions that could lead to train crashes. The 31 May 1941 decree stipulated that juveniles aged fourteen and older would be prosecuted for all other crimes as well. GARF, f. R-8131, op. 32, d. 4573, l. 188.

85. *Stalinskoe Politburo v 30-e gody,* pp. 144–145. The resolution about juvenile criminal responsibility caused a stir in the West. French writer Romain Rolland raised this issue during his 28 June 1935 meeting with Stalin. Stalin insisted that the law had been passed "with pedagogical aims in mind" to prevent hooliganism among children (*Istochnik,* 1996, no. 1, pp. 144, 146).

86. GARF, f. R-8131, op. 37, d. 71, l. 222.

87. GARF, f. R-3316, op. 64, d. 1619, l. 88.

88. GARF, f. R-8131, op. 37, d. 71, ll. 222–223.

89. GARF, f. R-8131, op. 37, d. 137, l. 4.

90. GARF, f. R-8131, op. 37, d. 137, l. 4.

91. SZ, 1935, no. 16, p. 155.

92. GARF, f. R-9401, op. 12, d. 103, ll. 6–8; S. S. Vilenskii et al. (eds.), *Deti GULAGa. 1918–1956* (Moscow, 2002), pp. 187–91.

93. GARF, f. R-9401, op. 12, d. 103; *Sbornik rukovodiashchikh postanovlenii,* vol. 1, l. 19 (NKVD circulation only).

94. Vilenskii et al., *Deti GULAGa,* pp. 195–97.

95. GARF, f. R-9401, op. 12, d. 103, ll. 22–23, 29–30, 32–33; *Sbornik rukovosiashchikh postanovlenii,* vol. 3, ll. 33–34; v. 4, ll. 9–14, 47–53.

96. GARF, f. R-9401, op. 12, d. 103; *Sbornik rukovosiashchikh postanovlenii,* vol. 2, l. 33.

97. GARF, f. R-9401, op. 12, d. 103; *Sbornik rukovosiashchikh postanovlenii,* vol. 4, ll. 5–6.

98. GARF, f. R-9401, op. 12, d. 100, l. 94; d. 103, l. 30.

99. GARF, f. R-5446, op. 20a, d. 944, l. 100.

100. GARF, f. R-5446, op. 20a, d. 948a, l. 12.

101. *Pravda,* 2 December 1935.

102. SZ, 1934, no. 33, p. 257.
103. GARF, f. R-9479, op. 1, d. 29, ll. 12–13.
104. GARF, f. R-9479, op. 1, d. 29, l. 15.
105. GARF, f. R-9479, op. 1, d. 29, l. 17.
106. GARF, f. R-3316, op. 64, d. 1668, l. 1.
107. SZ, 1935, no. 7, article 57.
108. GARF, f. R-9401, op. 12, d. 94, l. 166.
109. GARF, f. R-5446, op. 1, d. 109, ll. 274–275.
110. GARF, f. R-9401, op. 12, d. 94, l. 182.
111. GARF, f. R-8131, op. 37, d. 58, ll. 177–178.
112. GARF, f. R-8131, op. 37, d. 58, ll. 167–168.
113. RGASPI, f. 17, op. 163, d. 1089, ll. 63–65.
114. GARF, f. R-5446, op. 18a, d. 620, ll. 16–19.
115. GARF, f. R-5446, op. 1, d. 110, ll. 372–375.
116. GARF, f. R-5446, op. 20a, d. 926, ll. 24–32.
117. RGASPI, f. 17, op. 3, d. 978, ll. 58, 176.
118. GARF, f. R-5446, op. 18a, d. 617, ll. 11–12.
119. GARF, f. R-9401, op. 12, d. 106, l. 42.
120. *Naselenie Rossii v XX veke. Istoricheskie ocherki*, vol. 1: *1900–1939* (Moscow, 2000), p. 279 (section by V. N. Zemskov); GARF, f. R-9479, op. 1, d. 36, l. 40.
121. GARF, f. R-9479, op. 1, d. 36, l. 40.

CHAPTER 4. THE GREAT TERROR

1. M. Jansen and N. Petrow, *Stalin's Loyal Executioner: People's Commissar Nikolai Ezhov, 1895–1940* (Stanford, 2002), pp. 359–60.
2. Excerpts from this telegram were made public for the first time by Khrushchev at the 20th CPSU Congress. See *Reabilitatsiia. Politicheskie protsessy 30–50-kh godov* (Moscow, 1990), p. 32. The original telegram preserved in Stalin's personal archive was published in English in R. W. Davies et al. (eds.), *The Stalin-Kaganovich Correspondence, 1931–36* (New Haven, 2003).
3. RGASPI, f. 17, op. 3, d. 981, l. 50.
4. L. P. Rasskazov, *Karatel'nye organy v protsesse formirovaniia i funktsionirovaniia administrativno-komandnoi sistemy v sovetskom gosudarstve. 1917–1941* (Ufa, 1994), p. 311.
5. RGASPI, f. 17, op. 163, l. 1140, l. 55.
6. *Istochnik*, no. 0 (1993), p. 23, translated in J. Arch Getty and Oleg V. Naumov (eds.), *The Road to Terror* (New Haven, 1999), p. 557.
7. Khlevniuk, "Objectives of the Great Terror," in E. A. Rees (ed.), *Soviet History, 1917–53: Essays in Honour of R. W. Davies* (London, 1995), pp. 158–76; Khlevniuk, "Reasons for the 'Great Terror': The Foreign-Political Aspect," in S. Pons and A. Romano (eds.), *Russia in the Age of Wars, 1914–1945* (Milan, 2000), pp. 159–70.
8. First published in *Trud*, 4 June 1992, p. 1, and published in English in Getty and Naumov, *Road to Terror*, pp. 470–71.
9. Rasskazov, *Karatel'nye organy*, p. 235.

10. *Leningradskii martirolog. 1937–1938*, vol. 2 (St. Petersburg, 1996), pp. 452–53. For a detailed history of this operation, see N. Okhotin and A. Roginskii, "Iz istorii 'nemetskoi operatsii' NKVD, 1937–1938," in *Repressii protiv sovetskikh nemtsev. Nakazanyi narod* (Moscow, 1999), pp. 35–75.

11. Getty and Naumov, *Road to Terror*, pp. 473–80. For a thorough analysis of this document and the operation against anti-Soviet elements see R. Binner and M. Junge, "Wie der Terror 'Gross' wurde: Massenmord und Lagerhaft nach Befehl 00447," *Cahiers du Monde Russe*, 42, nos. 2–3–4 (2001), pp. 557–614.

12. *Moskovskiie novosti*, 21 June 1992. The full text of operative order no. 00485 of the people's commissar of internal affairs, passed on 11 August 1937, appears in *Leningradskii martirolog. 1937–1938*, vol. 2, pp. 454–56. For more on this operation see N. V. Petrov and A. B. Roginskii, "'Pol'skaia operatsiia' NKVD, 1937–1938," in *Repressii protiv poliakov i pol'skikh grazhdan* (Moscow, 1997), pp. 22–43.

13. NKVD Order no. 00593 on the Kharbinians was published several times. See, for example, *Leningradskii martirolog. 1937–1938*, vol. 3 (St. Petersburg, 1998), pp. 583–85.

14. For more on the "national operations" see T. Martin, "The Origins of Soviet Ethnic Cleansing," *Journal of Modern History* 70, no. 4 (1998), pp. 852–58.

15. A. I. Kokurin and N. V. Petrov (comps.), *GULAG (Glavnoe upravleniie lagerei) 1917–1960* (Moscow, 2000), pp. 106–10.

16. For an analysis of the provincial show trials in 1937 see Sheila Fitzpatrick, *Stalin's Peasants* (Oxford, 1994), pp. 296–312.

17. It is impossible to determine the exact number of trials sanctioned by the Politburo because the resolutions did not always give exact figures. For example, on 14 November 1937 the Politburo allowed the Arkhangelsk provincial committee to conduct two to three trials of wreckers in the timber industry. It is not always clear whether the Politburo sanctioned these open trials. Thus, on 15 November, it instructed the Novosibirsk provincial party committee to "charge and shoot those accused of the explosion in Prokopievsk and to publish the notice of execution in the Novosibirsk press."

18. *Belaia kniga o deportatsii koreiskogo naseleniia Rossii v 30–40-kh godakh*, vol. 1 (Moscow, 1994); N. F. Bugai, "Vyselenie koreitsev s Dal'nego Vostoka," *Voprosy istorii*, no. 5 (1994), pp. 141–48.

19. GARF, f. R-5446, op. 22a, d. 48, ll. 16–17. On the first page of the document Molotov wrote: "With C[omrade] Chubar."

20. V. N. Uimanov, *Repressii. Kak eto bylo. Zapadnaia Sibir' v kontse 20-kh— nachale 50-kh godov* (Tomsk, 1995), p. 129. Jansen and Petrow discovered new information about the July 1937 meeting of the regional NKVD bosses in Moscow, where the bosses discussed details of the operation that had yet to be ordered (Jansen and Petrow, *Stalin's Loyal Executioner*, pp. 83–86).

21. I. N. Kuznetsov, *Repressii 30–40-kh godov v Tomskom krae* (Tomsk, 1991), pp. 224–25.

22. *Sovetskoe rukovodstvo. Perepiska. 1928–1941* (Moscow, 1999), pp. 398–99 (the 1 February 1939 memorandum from the procurator of the USSR, Vyshinsky, to Stalin and Molotov).

23. RGASPI, f. 17, op. 127, d. 51, ll. 25–29 (materials of the inquiry into the vi-

olations of socialist legality in Sverdlovsk province in 1937–38); *Vozvrashchenie k pravde (Iz istorii politicheskikh repressii v Tverskom krae v 20–40-kh i nachale 50-kh godov). Dokumenty i materialy* (Tver, 1995), pp. 69–70 (excerpts from a memorandum by the head of the party organizational work department of the Kalinin provincial VKP(b) committee on the review of the NKVD leaders in the province); *Rasplata. Prokurorskiie sud'by* (Moscow, 1990), p. 17.

24. I. Nikolaev and I. Ushnitsky, *Tsentral'noe delo. Khronika stalinskikh repressii v Yakutii* (Yakutsk, 1990), pp. 43–47.

25. A. I. Solzhenitsyn, *Arkhipelag GULAG,* vol. 1 (Moscow, 1989), pp. 99–145; R. Medvedev, *O Staline i Stalinizme* (Moscow, 1990), pp. 432–41; Robert Conquest, *The Great Terror: A Reassessment* (London, 1990), pp. 109–34; Kuznetsov, *Repressii 30–40-kh godov v Tomskom krae,* pp. 221–23; V. Iu. Vasiliev et al., *Politicheskiie repressii na Podol'e (20–30 gg. XX v.)* (Vinnitsa, 1990), pp. 199–210.

26. GARF, f. R-8131, op. 37, d. 118, ll. 53–55.

27. GARF, f. R-8131, op 37, d. 140, ll. 24–25.

28. B. F. Sultanbekov, *Pervaia zhertva genseka. Mirsaid Sultan-Galiev: Sud'ba, liudi, vremia* (Kazan', 1991), pp. 204–5.

29. GARF, f. R-8131, op. 32, d. 6329, ll. 12–16.

30. GARF, f. R-8131, op. 37, d. 145, ll. 49–84.

31. Petrov and Roginskii, "'Pol'skaia operatsiia' NKVD," p. 30.

32. According to Order no. 00447 of the people's commissar of internal affairs, Omsk province received the first category limit of 1,000 people. The limit was surpassed five and a half times in the course of ten days, apparently with Moscow's agreement and as a result of the appropriate NKVD order. In August 1937–November 1938, the troika in Omsk province convicted 25,400 people altogether; 16,000 of them were shot (V. M. Samosudov, *Bol'shoi terror v Omskom Priirtyshie* [Omsk, 1998], pp. 160–61, 241).

33. *Izvestiia,* 3 April 1996.

34. *Moskovskiie novosti,* 21 June 1992, p. 19.

35. Ibid.; Getty and Naumov, *Road to Terror,* , pp. 518–19.

36. *Izvestiia,* 3 April 1996; Getty and Naumov, *Road to Terror,* pp. 520–21.

37. Archive of the President of the Russian Federation [APRF], f. 45, op. 1, d. 729, ll. 94–95.

38. GARF, f. R-5446, op. 22a, d. 79, ll. 7–8.

39. In the 24 December 1937 letter, Ezhov informed Molotov that 75 million rubles were provided from the SNK USSR reserve fund to conduct operations under Order no. 00447. Owing to the sharp increase in the number of those repressed, however, another 28 million rubles had to be spent. Ezhov asked the government to provide 8 million to cover this cost (another 20 million had to be taken from the NKVD budget) and to provide an additional 22 million rubles for the operation in the first quarter of 1938. The Sovnarkom approved this request (GARF, f. R-5446, op. 22a, d. 79, ll. 2–3).

40. GARF, f. R-5446, op. 22a, d. 79, l. 9.

41. *Izvestiia,* 3 April 1996; Petrov and Roginskii, "'Pol'skaya operatsiia' NKVD."

42. Okhotin and Roginskii, "Iz istorii 'nemetskoi operatsii' NKVD," p. 62; Petrov and Roginskii, "'Pol'skaia operatsiia' NKVD," p. 33.

43. *Moskovskie movosti,* 21 June 1992; Getty and Naumov, *Road to Terror,* pp. 531–32.

44. *Istoricheskii arkhiv,* no. 1 (1992), pp. 125–28; Getty and Naumov, *Road to Terror,* pp. 532–37.

45. Petrov and Roginskii, "'Pol'skaia operatsiia' NKVD," p. 38.

46. *Kniga pamiati zhertv politicheskikh repressii Novgorodskoi oblasti,* vol. 3 (Novgorod, 1994), pp. 59–60.

47. GARF, f. R-8131, op. 32, d. 4287, ll. 36–37.

48. GARF, f. R-9492, op. 6, d. 14, ll. 12, 29; S. G. Wheatcroft, "Victims of Stalinism and the Soviet Secret Police," *Europe-Asia Studies,* 51, no. 2 (1999), p. 337.

49. I. Chukhin, without quoting his source (which was probably a document from the TsA FSB), writes that Beria wrote in a statement on receiving the NKVD files, sent to Stalin, that a police troika sentenced about 200,000 people for up to five years in prison (I. Chukhin, *Karelia-37: Ideologiia i praktika terrora* [Petrozavodsk, 1999], p. 81).

50. TsA FSB (compilation of orders to conduct mass repressions).

51. *Leningradskii martirolog. 1937–1938,* vol. 1 (St. Petersburg, 1995), p. 61. Similar editions include *Belaia kniga o zhertvakh politicheskikh repressii: Samarskaia oblast',* vols. 1–11 (Samara, 1997–99) and *Kniga Pamiati zhertv politicheskikh repressii respubliki Bashkortastan,* vols. 1–2 (Ufa, 1997–99). M. Ilic's estimates based on the two volumes of the *Leningradskii martirolog* show that the majority of the victims of the Great Terror were industrial workers, peasants, artisans, and other workers: M. Ilic, "The Great Terror: Leningrad—A Quantitative Analysis," in S. G. Wheatcroft (ed.), *Challenging Traditional Views of Russian History* (Basingstoke, England, 2002), pp. 154–57.

52. C. Kuhr, "Children of 'Enemies of the People' as Victims of the Great Purges," *Cahiers du Monde Russe,* 39, nos. 1–2 (1998), pp. 209–20.

53. GARF, f. R-5446, op. 22a, d. 95, l. 8.

54. Ezhov's note was sent to the governments of the Ukraine and Russia. Chairman of the SNK of the Ukraine D. Korotchenko responded that it would be possible to accommodate 2,000 children of repressed parents only if additional orphanages were built, because the existing orphanages were overcrowded, and asked for 2.65 million rubles for this purpose (GARF, f. R-5446, op. 22a, d. 95, l. 5). The SNK RSFSR chairman, N. A. Bulganin, agreed to accommodate 3,000 children without additional allocations (l. 11). The matter was not addressed for two more months. On 4 August, Yezhov's deputy, Zhukovsky, again asked the SNK to provide means for the transfer of the children (l. 10). On 9 August the SNK satisfied this request (l. 13).

55. GARF, f. R-8131, op. 37, d. 137, l. 4 (the February 1940 memorandum from the procurator of the USSR, M. I. Pankratiev, and the people's commissar of internal affairs, Beria, to Stalin and Molotov).

56. *Leningradskii martirolog. 1937–1938,* vol. 2, illustration 78–79.

57. *Memorial'noe kladbishche Sandromakh. 1937: 27 oktiabria-4 noiabria (Solovetskii etap)* (St. Petersburg, 1997), p. 160.

58. Memorial Society Archive, f. 2, op. 1, d. 50, l. 27.

59. Memorial Society Archive, f. 2, op. 1, d. 84, l. 32.

60. GARF, f. R-8131, op. 37, d. 145, l. 27.

61. GARF, f. R-5446, op. 20a, d. 178, ll. 67–68, 77–78.

62. GARF, f. R-9401, op. 12, d. 95, l. 50.

63. GARF, f. R-9401, op. 12, d. 316, l. 393.

64. GARF, f. R-9414, op. 1, d. 1138, ll. 87–88.

65. GARF, f. R-9414, op. 1, d. 1138, l. 40.

66. GARF, f. R-8131, op. 37, d. 111, l. 34.

67. GARF, f. R-8131, op. 37, d. 111, l. 7–9.

68. GARF, f. R-9414, op. 4, d. 11, ll. 141–143. For the first part of the report see Document 39.

69. GARF, f. R-5446, op. 20a, d. 376, ll. 105–106; d. 377, l. 200.

70. GARF, f. R-5446, op. 22a, d. 139, l. 21.

71. The history of these camps still has to be studied. So far, there has been only one attempt to give a general description of one of them: V. Berdinskikh, *Viatlag* (Kirov, 1998).

72. All data about the forest camps are from GARF, f. R-9114, op. 1, d. 1138, ll. 59, 63.

73. GARF, f. R-9414, op. 1, d. 2740, l. 53.

74. *Sistema ispravitel'no-trudovykh lagerei v SSSR. 1933–1960* (Moscow, 1998), p. 69.

75. GARF, f. R-9414, op. 1, d. 1138, ll. 30, 37.

76. GARF, f. R-5446, op. 22a, d. 134, l. 17.

77. GARF, f. R-5446, op. 22a, d. 134, l. 41.

78. GARF, f. R-9414, op. 1, d. 1138, ll. 37, 38.

79. V. N. Zemskov, "Zakliuchennye v 1930-e gody: Sotsial'no-demografi-cheskiie problemy," *Otechestvennaia istoriia*, no. 4 (1997), p. 77.

80. On camps see Document 97; on prisons and colonies see GARF, f. R-9414, op. 1, d. 2740, l. 52.

81. GARF, f. R-9414, op. 1, d. 1140, l. 83.

82. GARF, f. R-9414, op. 1, d. 19, ll. 412–414; d. 17, ll. 20–21.

83. GARF, f. R-9414, op. 1, d. 1140, l. 83.

84. GARF, f. R-9414, op. 1, d. 19, ll. 199, 284.

85. GARF, f. R-5446, op. 1, d. 493, ll. 152–154 (the 10 August 1937 resolution by the SNK USSR and the CC VKP[b]).

86. GARF, f. R-5446, op. 1, d. 493, ll. 192–194 (the 17 August 1937 SNK and CC VKP(b) resolution).

87. GARF, f. R-5446, op. 1, d. 494, ll. 48–49.

88. GARF, f. R-5446, op. 22a, d. 89, l. 255 (the 27 April 1938 resolution by the Economic Council of the SNK USSR).

89. GARF, f. R-5446, op. 1, d. 497, l. 56 (the 11 February 1938 resolution by the SNK USSR and the CC VKP[b]).

90. GARF, f. R-5446, op. 1, d. 498, ll. 76–78 (the 16 May 1938 resolution by the SNK USSR and the CC VKP[b]).

91. GARF, f. R-5446, op. 1, d. 498, l. 80 (the 17 May 1938 SNK USSR resolution).

92. GARF, f. R-5446, op. 22a, d. 40, ll. 56–57.

93. GARF, f. R-9414, op. 4, d. 3, ll. 18–29.

CHAPTER 5. BERIA'S "REFORMS"

1. *Istoricheskii arkhiv,* no. 1 (1992), pp. 125–28; J. Arch Getty and Oleg V. Naumov, *The Road to Terror* (New Haven, 1999), pp. 532–37.

2. For more on Beria's career see A. Knight, *Beria: Stalin's First Lieutenant* (Princeton, 1993).

3. N. V. Petrov and K. V. Skorkin, *Kto rukovodil NKVD. 1934–1941. Spravochnik* (Moscow, 1999), p. 501.

4. GARF, f. R-9401, op. 2, d. 1, ll. 6–7.

5. GARF, f. R-8131, op. 37, d. 136, ll. 2, 12–13.

6. GARF, f. R-5446, op. 23a, d. 318, l. 14.

7. GARF, f. R-8131, op. 37, d. 118, ll. 65–67.

8. GARF, f. R-8131, op. 37, d. 139, ll. 86–87.

9. *Reabilitatsiia: Politichskiie protsessy 30–50-kh godov* (Moscow, 1990), pp. 40–41. A revealing aspect of Stalin's power was the profound impact that his cryptic memorandums, telegrams, and letters had on the evolution of state policy. Such occasional communications proved decisive in resolving a variety of inner-party and bureaucratic struggles.

10. GARF, f. R-9492, op. 1a, d. 7, ll. 137–139. A similar letter to Vyshinsky is in GARF, f. R-8131, op. 37, d. 141, ll. 14–16.

11. GARF, f. R-8131, op. 37, d. 145, l. 240.

12. GARF, f. R-8131, op. 37, d. 210, l. 3.

13. GARF, f. R-5446, op. 24a, d. 234, l. 2.

14. GARF, f. R-5446, op. 24a, d. 234, l. 4.

15. GARF, f. R-8131, op. 37, d. 148, ll. 208–209.

16. GARF, f. R-8131, op. 37, d. 145, ll. 232–234.

17. GARF, f. R-8131, op. 37, d. 183, l. 44.

18. GARF, f. R-8131, op. 37, d. 138, l. 295.

19. GARF, f. R-8131, op. 37, d. 136, l. 6.

20. For cynical explanations by Molotov justifying the reasons for the Great Terror, see F. Chuev, *Sto sorok besed s Molotovym* (Moscow, 1990), pp. 390, 391, 416.

21. Note from the representative of the Party Control Commission of the CC VKP(b) for Chita province "On the distortions in the work of the Chita provincial procuracy and the provincial NKVD board."

22. GARF, f. R-8131, op. 37, d. 148, l. 2 (the 3 January 1940 memorandum from the provisional procurator of the Navy of the USSR to the Procuracy of the USSR).

23. GARF, f. R-9401, op. 1a, d. 32, ll. 12–13.

24. The establishment of the *sharashki* (special design and technical bureaus under NKVD control) in fact rescued some talented scientists from a worse fate. S. P. Korolev, who in later years designed the rockets that carried *Sputnik* and Iurii Gagarin into space, was transferred to a sharashka from Magadan after serving a short term as a common laborer in the gold mines of Dalstroi.

25. For more about Central Construction Bureau no. 29 see G. Ozerov, *Tupolevskaia sharaga* (Posev, 1971); A. I. Kokurin, "Otchet o rabotakh Osobogo

tekhnicheskogo buro s 1939 po 1944," *Istoricheskii arkhiv,* no. 1 (1999), pp. 87–93.

26. GARF, f. R-8131, op. 32, d. 4002, ll. 32–34.

27. GARF, f. R-9414, op. 1, d. 1140, l. 118.

28. GARF, f. R-9414, op. 1, d. 1140, ll. 38–41.

29. Order no. 00173 by the people's commissar of internal affairs of the USSR, of 25 February 1939, provided 75,000 prisoners for railway construction in the Far East (GARF, f. R-9401, op. 1a, d. 32, ll. 121–122).

30. Order no. 016 by the people's commissar of internal affairs of the USSR, of 25 January 1939, required the dispatch to Sevvostlag of only those prisoners "capable of performing hard physical labor" (GARF, f. R-9401, op. 1a, d. 38, ll. 113–114).

31. GARF, f. R-5446, op. 1, d. 503, ll. 73–78. See also O. P. Yelantseva, *Stroital'stvo no. 500 NKVD SSSR: zheleznaia doroga Komsomol'sk-Sovetskaia gavan' (1930–40-e gody)* (Vladivostok, 1995).

32. GARF, f. R-5446, op. 23a, d. 121, ll. 6–9.

33. For more on the system of release on parole and on counting workdays see Chapters 1 and 3.

34. GARF, f. R-5446, op. 23a, d. 76, ll. 6–9.

35. GARF, f. R-5446, op. 23a, d. 70, ll. 29–30.

36. GARF, f. R-5446, op. 23a, d. 121, ll. 2–5.

37. GARF, f. R-5446, op. 23a, d. 121, l. 1.

38. GARF, f. R-7523, op. 67, d. 1, l. 5.

39. Getty and Naumov, *Road to Terror,* pp. 549–50.

40. GARF, f. R-5446, op. 23a, d. 70, ll. 31–41, 64–65. On the 14 August 1939 NKVD order to introduce new food and clothing allowances for prisoners see A. I. Kokurin and N. V. Petrov, *GULAG. 1917–1960* (Moscow, 2000), pp. 476–89.

41. GARF, f. R-5446, op. 1, d. 504, ll. 4–6.

42. GARF, f. R-5446, op. 24a, d. 18, l. 73.

43. RGASPI, f. 17, op. 3, d. 1018, l. 20. For more on the new main administrations within the NKVD see Chapter 6.

44. GARF, f. R-9414, op. 1, d. 2989, ll. 101–104.

45. TsA FSB, f. 3, op. 7, d. 798, ll. 32–33.

46. GARF, f. R-9414, op. 1, d. 24, l. 195.

47. GARF, f. R-9414, op. 1, d. 25, ll. 78–82.

48. GARF, f. R-9414, op. 1, d. 2989, ll. 84–92.

49. The Chief Administration of Prisons of the NKVD USSR was created on 29 September 1938. See A. I. Kokurin and N. V. Petrov, *Lubianka. VChK-KGB. 1917–1960. Spravochnik* (Moscow, 1997), pp. 21, 131.

50. GARF, f. R-5446, op. 23a, d. 70, l. 77.

51. GARF, f. R-5446, op. 23a, d. 76, l. 36.

52. GARF, f. R-8131, op. 37, d. 118, l. 81.

53. GARF, f. R-9414, op. 1, d. 12, ll. 333–335.

54. GARF, f. R-9401, op. 1a, d. 32, ll. 209–210.

55. GARF, f. R-9401, op. 12, d. 316, t. 1, ll. 377–378 rev.

56. GARF, f. R-9401, op. 1a, d. 50, l. 204.

57. Order no. 00762 by the people's commissar of internal affairs of the USSR,

of 26 November 1938, outlined the new procedures of arrest and prosecution in accordance with the SNK USSR and the CC VKP(b) resolution to stop mass operations and the activities of troikas (GARF, f. R-9401, op. 2, d. 1, ll. 1–9).

58. GARF, f. R-9401, op. 1a, d. 50, ll. 200–201.

59. GARF, f. R-9414, op. 1, d. 1143, l. 408.

60. GARF, f. R-9414, op. 1, d. 1152, ll. 2–4.

61. GARF, f. R-9401, op. 12, d. 316, t. 1, l. 337; f. R-9414, op. 1, d. 24, ll. 80–82; d. 25, l. 57.

62. GARF, f. R-9401, op. 12, d. 316, t. 1, l. 348.

63. GARF, f. R-9414, op. 1, d. 2756, ll. 66–69. This was an attachment to the 21 February 1939 Gulag circular letter no. 781450.

64. GARF, f. R-9414, op. 1, d. 2989, ll. 66–67.

65. GARF, f. R-9414, op. 1, d. 20, l. 101.

66. GARF, f. R-9401, op. 12, d. 319, t. 1, l. 476.

67. GARF, f. R-9414, op. 1, d. 2989, ll. 66–68.

68. GARF, f. R-9414, op. 1, d. 2989, ll. 48–49.

69. GARF, f. R-9401, op. 1a, d. 50, ll. 149–152.

70. GARF, f. R-9401, op. 1a, d. 51, ll. 86–88.

71. GARF, f. R-9401, op. 1a, d. 51, l. 142.

72. GARF, f. R-9414, op. 1, d. 12, l. 342.

73. For more on the timber camps and their status in 1938 see Chapter 4.

74. M. B. Smirnov, *Sistema ispravitel'no-trudovykh lagerei v SSSR. 1923–1960. Spravochnik* (Moscow, 1998), pp. 303–4.

75. GARF, f. R-9414, op. 4, d. 12, ll. 24–38.

76. "Provisional instruction on the management of prisoners in the corrective labor camps of the NKVD USSR" was issued by the people's commissar of internal affairs on 2 August 1939. The instruction ordered the creation of central detention facilities and detention cells in the camp sections and regulated the application of detention. See Kokurin and Petrov, *GULAG. 1917–1960,* pp. 456–76.

77. As of 1 October 1938, there were 258 juveniles in the Krasnoiarsk camp between sixteen and eighteen years old (GARF, f. R-9414, op. 1, d. 1140, l. 10).

CHAPTER 6. MOBILIZATION AND REPRESSION

1. O. A. Gorlanov and A. B. Roginskii, "Ob arestakh v zapadnykh oblastiakh Belorussii i Ukrainy v 1939–1941 gg.," *Repressii protiv poliakov i pol'skikh grazhdan* (Moscow, 1997), p. 86.

2. For example, see V. I. Passat, *Trudnye stranitsy istorii Moldovy. 1940–1950* (Moscow, 1994), p. 165.

3. A. E. Gurianov, "Pol'skie pereselentsy v SSSR v 1940–1941gg.," in *Repressii protiv poliakov I pol'skikh grazhdan* (Moscow, 1997), pp. 116–120; Gurianov, "Masshtaby deportatsii naseleniia vglub' SSSR v mae-iune 1941," in ibid., p. 159.

4. N. S. Lebedeva et al., *Katyn. Plenniki neobiavlennoi voiny. Dokumenty i materialy* (Moscow, 1997), pp. 390–92, 521. Until the time of Mikhail Gorbachev, when Soviet complicity was officially acknowledged, the USSR repeatedly blamed the Katyn tragedy on the Nazis.

5. *Voenno-istoricheskii zhurnal*, no. 1 (1991), p. 17.

6. For more about these campaigns see Peter Solomon, *Soviet Criminal Justice Under Stalin* (Cambridge, 1996), pp. 299–336.

7. GARF, f. R-5446, op. 24a, d. 18, ll. 68–74, 133.

8. GARF, f. R-5446, op. 24a, d. 49, l. 52.

9. GARF, f. R-5446, op. 24a d. 18, ll. 118–119.

10. GARF, f. R-5446, op. 25a, d. 18, ll. 90–93, 134.

11. RGASPI, f. 17, op. 3, d. 1018, l. 5; GARF, f. R-5446, op. 1, d. 509, l. 184 (the 26 December 1939 SNK resolution).

12. GARF, f. R-5446, op. 24a, d. 15, ll. 20–22.

13. RGASPI, f. 17, op. 3, d. 1023, l. 8; GARF, f. R-5446, op. 1, d. 513, ll. 37–59 (the 10 May 1940 SNK resolution).

14. GARF, f. R-5446, op. 1, d. 517, ll. 20–21.

15. RGASPI, f. 17, op. 3, d. 1027, ll. 75, 153–168; GARF, f. R-5446 , op. 1, d. 517, l. 212.

16. GARF, f. R-5446, op. 24a, d. 49, ll. 51–52.

17. GARF, f. R-5446, op. 24a, d. 1343, ll. 45–46.

18. GARF, f. R-5446, op. 1, d. 510, ll. 164–168.

19. GARF, f. R-5446, op. 1, d. 512, ll. 1–3.

20. RGASPI, f. 17, op. 3, d. 1028, l. 36; GARF, f. R-5446, op. 1, d. 518, l. 193.

21. RGASPI, f. 17, op. 3, d. 1028, ll. 153–164; GARF, f. R-5446, op. 1, d. 525, ll. 1–39.

22. This was a 24 October 1940 Politburo resolution (RGASPI, f. 17, op. 3, d. 1028, ll. 82, 245–248), adopted as a 25 October SNK resolution (GARF, f. R-5446, op. 1, d. 519, l. 105).

23. RGASPI, f. 17, op. 3, d. 1025, ll. 38, 140–143.

24. GARF, f. R-5446, op. 24a, d. 4, l. 59.

25. GARF, f. R-5446, op. 25a, d. 7228, ll. 12–13.

26. GARF, f. R-5446, op. 25a, d. 7228, ll. 18–26; d. 2, ll. 16–17; d. 3, l. 18.

27. GARF, f. R-5446, op. 25a, d. 3, l. 18.

28. GARF, f. R-5446, op. 25a, d. 7181, l. 60.

29. On 25 April the NKVD was additionally charged with construction of five military airfields for the People's Commissariat of the Navy in 1941. For that purpose, the government ordered the people's commissar of the navy, N. G. Kuznetsov, to assemble, by 15 May 1941, six construction battalions, each consisting of 1,000 people.

30. A. I. Kokurin and N. V. Petrov, *Lubianka. VChK-KGB. 1917–1960. Spravochnik* (Moscow, 1997), pp. 25–28.

31. GARF, f. R-5446, op. 25a, d. 7225, ll. 2–3.

32. GARF, f. R-5446, op. 1, d. 514, l. 59.

33. RGASPI, f. 71, op. 10, d. 130, ll. 173, 179.

34. GARF, f. R-5446, op. 1, d. 514, l. 56.

35. GARF, f. R-8131, op. 32, d. 4001, l. 179; op. 37, d. 336, l. 50.

36. GARF, f. R-5446, op. 1, d. 524, l. 107.

37. GARF, f. R-9414, op. 1, d. 1148, ll. 268–269.

38. GARF, f. R-9401, op. 12, d. 316, t. 1, ll. 179–180.

39. J. A. Getty, G. T. Rittersporn, and V. N. Zemskov, "Victims of the Soviet Penal System in the Prewar Years: A First Approach on the Basis of Archival Evidence," *American Historical Review* (October 1993), p. 1048.

40. GARF, f. R-9401, op. 12, d. 316, t. 1, ll. 139–141.
41. GARF, f. R-9401, op. 1, d. 1155, l. 34; d. 1154, l. 98.
42. GARF, f. R-9414, op. 1, d. 1164, l. 117.
43. GARF, f. R-5446, op. 1, d. 514, l. 56.
44. GARF, f. R-9401, op. 12, d. 316, t. 1, l. 178.
45. GARF, f. R-9414, op. 1, d. 32, ll. 21–23.
46. GARF, f. R-9414, op. 1, d. 45, ll. 40–41.
47. GARF, f. R-9414, op. 1, d. 1434, ll. 15–16.
48. GARF, f. R-9414, op. 1, d. 1151, ll. 1–129.
49. GARF, f. R-9414, op. 1, d. 2762, l. 158.
50. GARF, f. R-9401, op. 12, d. 316, t. 1, l. 308.
51. For the number of prisoners at the camp see GARF, f. R-9414, op. 1, d. 1151, l. 76.
52. *Pkaianie. Komi Respublikanskii martirolog zhertv massovykh politichekikh repressii,* vol. 2 (Syktyvkar, 1999), p. 178.
53. GARF, f. R-9414, op. 1, d. 1161, l. 64.
54. GARF, f. R-9414, op. 1, d. 1161, l. 64.
55. GARF, f. R-9414, op. 1, d. 42, ll. 40–41.
56. GARF, f. R-9414, op. 1, d. 2762, l. 158.
57. GARF, f. R-9414, op. 1, d. 31, ll. 126–127; d. 2762, ll. 25, 35, 114–115, 158.
58. GARF, f. R-9414, op. 1, d. 42, ll. 2–3.
59. GARF, f. R-9414, op. 1, d. 39, ll. 23–24.
60. GARF, f. R-9414, op. 1, d. 2519, l. 11.
61. GARF, f. R-9401, op. 12, d. 319, t. 1, l. 391.
62. GARF, f. R-9401, op. 12, d. 319, t. 1, ll. 386–387.
63. GARF, f. R-9414, op. 1, d. 39, ll. 7–11.
64. GARF, f. R-9401, op. 12, d. 319, t. 1, ll. 360–361.
65. GARF, f. R-9401, op. 12, d. 319, t. 1, l. 365.
66. The author has found an unsigned and undated copy of the note from Vyshinsky and Yezhov sent to Stalin and Molotov in the Archive of Special Settlements of the NKVD. The contents suggest that it was written around January–February 1937 (GARF, f. R-9479, op. 1, d. 54, ll. 1–2). Indirect proof of its delivery is in the 15 February 1937 memorandum from Vyshinsky to the TsIK USSR, which mentions his presentation to Stalin and Molotov on the situation of special settlers (GARF, f. R-3316, op. 64, d. 1833, l. 10).
67. GARF, f. R-9479, op. 1, d. 47, l. 13.
68. GARF, f. R-9479, op. 1, d. 40, ll. 26–28.
69. GARF, f. R-9479, op. 1, d. 41, ll. 7–8.
70. GARF, f. R-8137, op. 37, d. 111, l. 80.
71. GARF, f. R-9479, op. 1, d. 47, l. 12.
72. GARF, f. R-9479, op. 1, d. 62, ll. 1–2, 71.
73. GARF, f. R-5446, op. 25a, d. 25.
74. GARF, f. R-9479, op. 1, d. 56, ll. 5–6.
75. GARF, f. R-9479, op. 1, d. 60, l. 173.
76. GARF, f. R-9479, op. 1, d. 60, ll. 9–10.
77. GARF, f. R-9479, op. 1, d. 62, ll. 7–8.
78. GARF, f. R-9479, op. 1, d. 60, ll. 136–140.

79. GARF, f. R-9479, op. 1, d. 60, l. 135.

80. GARF, f. R-9479, op. 1, d. 48, l. 12.

81. GARF, f. R-9479, op. 1, d. 62, l. 7.

82. GARF, f. R-9479, op. 1, d. 47, l. 30; d. 62, l. 7.

83. GARF, f. R-9479, op. 1, d. 62, l. 6.

84. GARF, f. R-9479, op. 1, d. 77, l. 163.

85. GARF, f. R-9479, op. 1, d. 55, l. 5.

86. GARF, f. R-9479, op. 1, d. 60, ll. 71–72.

87. GARF, f. R-9479, op. 1, d. 62, ll. 63–64, 70–71.

88. GARF, f. R-9479, op. 1, d. 62, l. 4.

89. GARF, f. R-9479, op. 1, d. 62, l. 71.

90. GARF, f. R-9479, op. 1, d. 59, l. 1.

91. GARF, f. R-9479, op. 1, d. 62, l. 71.

92. GARF, f. R-9479, op. 1, d. 48, l. 12.

93. A. E. Gurianov, *Pol'skie pereselentsy v SSSR v 1940–1941*, p. 120; GARF, f. R-9479, op. 1, d. 62, l. 67.

94. GARF, f. R-5446, op. 1, d. 510, l. 170.

95. GARF, f. R-5446, op. 24a, d. 147, ll. 69–70.

96. GARF, f. R-5446, op. 24a, d. 3, ll. 118–122.

97. GARF, f. R-9479, op. 1, d. 66, l. 16.

98. GARF, f. R-9479, op. 1, d. 75, ll. 279–282. The review was conducted on 16–17 February 1941 by a sanitary inspector of the department of corrective labor colonies of UNKVD of Kirov province.

99. Gurianov, *Pol'skie spetspereselentsy v SSSR*, p. 124.

100. Ibid, p. 120; GARF, f. R-9479, op. 1, d. 61, l. 27.

101. Gurianov, *Pol'skie spetspereselentsy v SSSR*, p. 124.

102. GARF, f. R-9479, op. 1, d. 78, ll. 127–148.

103. GARF, f. R-9479, op. 1, d. 59, ll. 24–58.

104. Gurianov, "Masshtaby deportatsii naseleniia vglub' SSSR," p. 159.

105. N. S. Lebedeva, "Armiia Andersa v dokumentakh rossiiskikh arkhivov," in *Repressii protiv poliakov i pol'skikh grazhdan* (Moscow, 1997), pp. 178–83.

CHAPTER 7. THE VICTIMS

1. See J. A. Getty, G. T. Rittersporn, and V. N. Zemskov, "Victims of the Soviet Penal System in the Prewar Years: A First Approach on the Basis of Archival Evidence," *American Historical Review* (October 1993); S. G. Wheatcroft, "Victims of Stalinism and the Soviet Secret Police: The Comparability and Reliability of the Archival Data—Not the Last Word," *Europe-Asia Studies,* 51, no. 2 (1999), pp. 315–45; Robert Conquest, "Comment on Wheatcroft," *Europe-Asia Studies,* 51, no. 8 (1999), pp. 1479–83; E. Bacon, *The Gulag at War: Stalin's Forced Labour System in the Light of the Archives* (London, 1994); M. Ellman, "Soviet Repression Statistics: Some Comments," *Europe-Asia Studies,* 54, no. 7 (2002), pp. 1151–72.

2. GARF, f. R-9401, op. 1, d. 4157, l. 203.

3. GARF, f. R-9401, op. 1, d. 4157, l. 202.

4. GARF, f. R-9401, op. 1, d. 4157, l. 204.

5. *Stalinskoe Politburo v 30-e gody. Sbornik dokumentov* (Moscow, 1995), pp. 62–64.

6. GARF, f. R-8131, op. 37, d. 70, ll. 103–106.

7. GARF, f. R-8131, op. 37, d. 70, ll. 138–142.

8. On the operations of urban cleansing and the activities of the police troikas, see Chapter 3.

9. GARF, f. R-8131, op. 37, d. 70, ll. 134–136.

10. For more on the 1934 reorganization of the judicial and extrajudicial systems, see Chapter 3.

11. On the 8 May 1933 instruction, see Chapter 3. The 17 June 1935 directive was the SNK and CC VKP(b) resolution on the order for arrests, which required the approval of the Procuracy and the heads of departments and party committees dealing with NKVD actions (GARF, f. R-5446, op. 1, d. 481, ll. 178–179).

12. GARF, f. R-9474, op. 1, d. 97, l. 6.

13. Cf. GARF, f. R-9474, op. 1, d. 104, l. 4; f. R-7523, op. 6b, d. 242, l. 3; Document 90.

14. GARF, f. R-7523, op. 6b, d. 242, ll. 2–3.

15. GARF, f. R-9474, op. 1, d. 97, l. 59.

16. According to A. Kokurin and Yu. Morukov, in *Svobodnaia mysl'*, no. 12 (2001), p. 101, in 1930–36 judicial and nonjudicial organs sentenced 2,760,000 people to prison. The authors do not explain their method of calculation.

17. RGASPI, f. 17, op. 42, d. 80, l. 80.

18. V. P. Danilov and N. A. Ivnitsky (eds.), *Dokumenty svidetel'stvuiut* (Moscow, 1989), pp. 46–47.

19. See also GARF, f. R-8131, op. 37, d. 58, l. 138; V. K. Vinogradov et. al. (comps.), *Genrikh Yagoda. Sbornik dokumentov* (Kazan', 1997), pp. 465–76.

20. This number represents the difference between the number of those expelled and the number of those restored to membership in these years. See RGASPI, f. 17, op. 117, d. 873, l. 23.

21. *Repressii protiv poliakov i pol'skikh grazhdan* (Moscow, 1997), p. 38.

22. GARF, f. R-9492, op. 6, d. 14, ll. 6, 7.

23. According to Kokurin and Morukov, in *Svobodnaia mysl'*, in 1930–40 judicial and nonjudicial organs sentenced 5,580,000 people to prison.

24. GARF, f. R-9414, op. 1, d. 1135, l. 79.

25. V. M. Kuritsyn, *Istoriia gosudarstva i prava Rossii. 1929–1940* (Moscow, 1998), p. 112.

26. *Zhertvy i palachi* (newspaper), no. 2 (1994). Interview with the head of the rehabilitation department of the General Procuracy of the Russian Federation.

27. GARF, f. R-9414, op. 1, d. 1155, l. 1.

28. GARF, f. R-9414, op. 1, d. 1155, l. 2.

29. Yu. Morukov, "Smertnost' osuzhdennykh v GULAGe v 1930–1956 godakh" (manuscript).

30. GARF, f. R-9414, op. 1, d. 1155, ll. 3–6. Lacunae correspond to the periods when data on certain categories of prisoners were not collected.

31. GARF, f. R-9414, op. 1, d. 1155, l. 7.

32. GARF, f. R-9414, op. 1, d. 1155, l. 8. Lacunae correspond to the periods when data on certain categories of prisoners were not collected.

33. GARF, f. R-9414, op. 1, d. 1155, ll. 9–10. Lacunae correspond to the periods when data on certain categories of prisoners were not collected.

34. GARF, f. R-9414, op. 1, d. 1155, ll. 11–12. Lacunae correspond to the periods when data on certain categories of prisoners were not collected.

35. Getty et al., "Victims of the Soviet Penal System," p. 1048; GARF, f. R-9414, op. 1, d. 1155, l. 34.

36. Ibid.

37. GARF, f. R-9479, op. 1, d. 89, l. 216; *Naselenie Rossii v XX veke*, vol. 1 (Moscow, 2000), pp. 279–80.

38. GARF, f. R-9414, op. 1, d. 25, ll. 123–124.

39. GARF, f. R-5446, op. 16a, d. 1310, ll. 15–20, 32–33; f. R-9414, op. 1, d. 1913, ll. 21–23, 59–60, 82–85.

40. GARF, f. R-9414, op. 1, d. 1140, l. 108. Cf. data on individual camps from July–August 1930 in d. 2919, l. 55.

41. TsA FSB, f. 2, op. 11, d. 537, l. 278.

42. GARF, f. R-9114, op. 1, d. 21, l. 151.

43. GARF, f. R-9114, op. 1, d. 12, l. 354.

44. GARF, f. R-9414, op. 1, d. 32, l. 42.

45. The consolidated reports by the Gulag sanitary department are the most popular (GARF, f. R-9414, op. 1, d. 2740).

46. Yu. Morukov's statistical evaluation is in *Svobodnaia mysl'*, no. 10 (2000), p. 114.

47. GARF, f. R-9414, op. 1, d. 2740, ll. 1–2.

48. GARF, f. R-9414, op. 1, d. 2741, l. 7.

49. GARF, f. R-9414, op. 1, d. 2470, l. 5.

50. GARF, f. R-9414, op. 1, d. 2470, ll. 8, 9, 53. See also Chapter 1.

51. Morukov, in *Svobodnaia mysl'*, p. 114.

52. *Naselenie Rossii v XX veke*, vol. 1, p. 320.

53. Information about the reporting system of the convoy troops was kindly provided by A. E. Gurianov, who has studied the archives of the convoy troops in connection with the 1939–41 deportations.

54. GARF, f. R-9414, op. 1, d. 1156, ll. 64–65.

55. GARF, f. R-8131, op. 37, d. 145, l. 238; op. 32, d. 3286, l. 127; *Sovetskoe rukovodstvo. Perepiska, 1928–1941* (Moscow, 1999), p. 402 (the 15 December 1939 report by the procurator of the USSR, Pankratiev, to Stalin and Molotov).

56. GARF, f. R-8131, op. 32, d. 3286, l. 127.

57. *Izvestiia*, 11 November 1999, p. 8 (article by S. Maksimova based on the court materials from the Primorsky territorial archive).

58. GARF, f. R-9414, op. 1, d. 1155, l. 2.

59. GARF, f. R-9414, op. 1, d. 2765, ll. 1–6.

60. *Tragediia sovetskoi derevni. Kollektivizatsiia i raskulachivanie. Dokumenty i materially*, vol. 2 (Moscow, 2000), p. 27; *Naselenie Rossii v XX veke*, vol. 1, p. 287.

61. *Naselenie Rossii v XX veke*, vol. 1, p. 280.

CONCLUSION

1. *Vsesoiuznaia perepis' naseleniia 1939. Osnovye itogi* (Moscow, 1992), p. 90.

2. Freed prisoners had to sign a form that aimed at preserving secrecy: "I . . . give this affidavit to the Administration of State Security affirming that I will not relate to anybody anything I saw or heard while under arrest. I am aware that for violating this regulation, I will be charged with a crime, which I certify with my signature herein" (R. Podkur, *Za povidomlenniam radians'kych spetsslushb* [Kiev, 2000], p. 138).

3. GARF, f. R-9401, op. 1a, d. 50, l. 218.

4. Cases of sending letters via unescorted prisoners are described in various memoirs. See, for example, E. Ginzburg, *Krutoi marshrut* (Moscow, 2000), pp. 219–20.

5. The term was introduced by G. Popov, a popular economist and politician during the time of Gorbachev.

6. A. Nove (ed.), *The Stalin Phenomenon* (New York, 1993), p. 28.

7. T. Brass and M. van der Linden (eds.), *Free and Unfree Labour: The Debate Continues* (Bern, 1997), p. 362.

8. GARF, f. R-9414, op. 1, d. 1805, l. 66.

9. GARF, f. R-5446, op. 25a, d. 7184, l. 101, 102; op. 17, d. 313, l. 140.

10. GARF, f. R-5446, op. 25a, d. 7181, l. 6; op. 1, d. 176, l. 268; d. 177, l. 9.

11. GARF, f. R-5446, op. 1, d. 177, l. 25; M. I. Khlusov (comp.), *Ekonomika GULAGa i ee rol' v razvitii strany. 1930-e gody. Sbornik dokumentov* (Moscow, 1998), p. 141.

12. *Sistema ispravitel'no-trudovykh lagerei v SSSR. Spravochnik* (Moscow, 1998), p. 108.

13. A. I. Kokurin and N. V. Petrov (comps.), *GULAG (glavnoe upravlenie lagerei). 1917–1960* (Moscow, 2000), p. 766.

14. GARF, f. R-5446, op. 25a, d. 7181, ll. 17, 60.

15. GARF, f. R-9414, op. 1, d. 1806, l. 1 ("On the construction of the Baltic–White Sea route," a memorandum written to support the draft resolution by the government to build the canal).

16. Yu. Kilin, *Karelia v politike sovetskogo gosudarsva. 1920–1941* (Petrozavodsk, 1994), pp. 122–27.

17. V. G. Makurov, "Belomorsko-Baltiisky kombinat v Karelii," in *Novoe v izuchenii istorii Karelii* (Petrozavodsk, 1994), p. 157.

18. GARF, f. R-5446, op. 81b, d. 6645, l. 52.

19. O. P. Elantseva, "BAM: Pervoe desiatiletie," *Otechestvennaia istoriia*, no. 6 (1994), pp. 89–103.

20. *Sistema ispravitel'no-trudovykh lagerei v SSSR*, pp. 153–54.

21. Elantseva, "BAM," p. 102.

22. It was halted by the 24 September 1940 SNK and CC VKP(b) resolution (GARF, f. R-5446, op. 1, d. 73, l. 212), approved by the Politburo on 23 September 1940 (RGASPI, f. 17, op. 3, d. 1027, l. 75).

23. GARF, f. R-5446, op. 81, d. 6691, l. 69.

24. *Sistema ispravitel'no-trudovykh lagerei v SSSR*, pp. 370–71.

25. GARF, f. R-5446, op. 14a, d. 48, l. 18.

26. GARF, f. R-5446, op. 18a, d. 656, ll. 23, 26.

27. GARF, f. R-5446, op. 23a, d. 105, ll. 40, 42.

28. *Zariadit' tuftu*, literally, "feeding trash," meant providing fake reports, falsifying results. See Zh. Rossi, *Spravochnik po GULAGu*, vol. 1 (Moscow, 1991), p. 414.

29. GARF, f. R-9489, op. 2, d. 15, ll. 61–61 rev.

30. GARF, f. R-9401, op. 1, d. 2642, l. 211.

31. GARF, f. R-9401, op. 12, d. 94, part 1, l. 89 (the 20 October 1937 order by the people's commissar of internal affairs "On preparations for construction in 1938 and improvements in the organization of labor").

32. GARF, f. R-5446, op. 24a, d. 4, ll. 39–42. On the first page, Mikoyan scribbled: "To Com. Molotov."

33. GARF, f. R-5446, op. 24a, d. 4, ll. 43–46.

34. S. M. Popova, "Sistema donositel'stva v 30-e gody (K probleme soznadiia bazy dannykh na materialakh Urala)," *Klio,* no. 1 (1991), pp. 71–72.

35. Sheila Fitzpatrick, "Signals from Below: Soviet Letter of Denunciation of the 1930s," *Journal of Modern History,* 68, no. 4 (December 1996), pp. 849–50.

Index of Documents

Dates in brackets are extrapolated.

INTRODUCTION

CHAPTER I. ORIGINS OF THE STALINIST GULAG

CHAPTER 2. FAMINE

CHAPTER 3. STABILIZATION OF THE SYSTEM

CHAPTER 7. THE VICTIMS

CONCLUSION

General Index

Abanin, A. D., 168
Abbakumov, P. F., 168
Abramov, A. A., 168
Administration for Railroad Construction in the Far East, 199
Administration for Special Construction, 107
Administration for State Security (UGB), 99, 101, 294–98, 300
Administration of Corrective Labor Camps (UITL), 280
Administration of Corrective Labor Colonies (UITK), 215
Administration of Settlements, 21
administrative abuses: Baikal-Amur camp (Bamlag), 102; camp violations, 110; Dmitrovsky camp (Dmitlag), 102–3, 115–18; embezzlement, 214; exhausted workers, 75–76; falsification, 117; food rations, 37, 72–73; Krasnoiarsk camp (Kraslag), 229; Nazino Island, 65; penal system, 49, 51–52, 60–62, 189; Siberian camp (Siblag), 41, 103; Solovetsky Camp of Special Designation (SLON), 40–41; special settlements, 17–19, 22; torture, 101–4, 117–18; Ukhta-Pechora Camp (Ukhtpechlag), 103
agents provocateurs, 151
Agranov, Ya. S., 141, 345
agriculture: children, 124–25; corrective labor camps, 71; labor settlements, 55, 57; mass executions, 337–38; mortality rates, 212; New Life kolkhoz, 267–69;

People's Commissariat of Justice (NKIu), 85; workforce availability, 199
aircraft construction, 32–33, 196–98
Akhunsky camp, 86
Akimov, 161
Akopian, 94
Aksenov, 271
Aktiubinsk camp, 258, 358
Akulov, I. A., 84–85, 101–3, 294, 345
Aleksandrov, 102
Alekseenko, 159
Alekseev, N. N., 66, 345
Aleksian, 94
Almazov, Z. A., 336–37, 345–46
Altai territory, 154–55, 157
Andreev, A. A., 17, 32, 346
Anfilov, G. I., 105, 108–9
Anisimov, I. V., 152
Antipin, 230
Antipov, N. K., 68, 346
anti-Semitism, 279, 343
anti-Soviet agitation: *See* counterrevolutionaries
Antonenok, M. V., 265
apatite railroad, 26
Apin, Ya. A., 265
arbitrary shootings, 61–62, 101–2, 230
Archivasov, Ya. E., 230
Arkhangelsk camp, 129, 172, 358
Arkhangelsky (prisoner), 228–29
Armavir, 60
armed guards, 222–23, 256–57
Ashkhabad province, 159–61

BOOKS IN THE ANNALS OF COMMUNISM SERIES